CLAIRVOYANCE (FOR THOSE IN THE DESERT)

CLAIRVOYANCE

(FOR THOSE IN THE DESERT) **JOANNA FRUEH**

Performance Pieces, 1979–2004

Duke University Press   *Durham & London*   2008

Duke University Press gratefully acknowledges

the support of the University of Nevada, Reno, which

provided funds toward the production of this book.

Printed in China on acid-free paper ∞

Designed by C. H. Westmoreland

Typeset in Warnock Light and Gill Sans Light

by Keystone Typesetting, Inc.

Library of Congress Cataloging-in-Publication Data

appear on the last printed page of this book.

TO THE SONORAN DESERT

❧ CONTENTS

❧ ACKNOWLEDGMENTS

I thank the following people and places for one, some, or all of these gifts: generosity, creativity, friendship, love, faith, and welcome. Specifically:

People in my personal life

Thomas Kochheiser, for the fervor and beauty of your music: the kind that you composed and played on your guitar, and more profoundly, the kind that lives in your soul and appeared in the joy of our performances.

Russell Dudley, for the intense loveliness of photographs: the ones that more than simply document my performances and the ones on which we collaborated in our home and garden; for writing and performing our amorous and Sonoran passions in *Amazing Grace.*

Jill O'Bryan, for a fairy-light and highly erotic collaboration: photographs that see the light of the Sonoran Desert, of me; an introduction that is truly "fucking hot"—full of romantic passion, ardent intelligence, creative leaping, scholarly depth, sweet story-telling, humor that makes me laugh out loud, and a clarity of vision that helps me to recognize my own.

The men whose minds, hearts, and bodies have inspired my erotic life and intellect. Tom and Russ, you're paramount among those muses.

Renee Wood, a flagrantly talented and fabulously knowledgeable musician, whose saying, "You're a singer," to me, your sister, increases the innocence of my voice.

Tanya Augsburg, you ground me in the present by giving me perspective on my past and future.

Becky Bogard, your sane and loving vision helps me to see what's right in front of me.

People I met and worked with as a performer

Especially . . .

Every audience; your presence gives me mine. Audience members who spoke with me after I performed: you gave me insight into my work, into life, and into love; indeed, you gave me love.

David Goicachecca at Brock University, St. Catharine's, Ontario, your organization of the Alphonso Lingis Conference on a Postmodern Ethics of Joy and Coronation Glory provided a plethora of fascinating papers and conversations—including our own in the Buffalo airport—and a batch of eye-opening responses to my writing and acting.

David Lazar at Columbia College Chicago, the sensuous language with which you introduced me to the audience at Ohio University overjoyed me.

Betsy Lyon—the Betsy in Betsy's Bake Shop—your chocolate cake for my perfor-mance *The Aesthetics of Orgasm* at the Sheppard Fine Arts Gallery, University of Nevada, Reno, was spectacularly sumptuous: in scale—a minimalist sculpture about a foot high; in beauty—lustrous deep brown topped with a pyramid of large roses the color of blushing cheeks; and in chocolatey perfection—densely moist and richly flavored.

Marsha Meskimmon at Loughborough University, a not-too-long train ride from London, your warmth is with me still.

Nancy Moyle, the "mistress" of Dish, a welcoming and cozy breakfast and lunch place in Reno. The cookies that you provided for my studio shoot of *The Performance of Pink*—heart-shaped and pink sugar–sprinkled—sparkled for the camera and drew my exclamatory compliments as I ate them while performing. And I am longing now for the cake you baked for my performance of *Ambrosia* at the Nevada Museum of Art: its glamorously visual innocence—frosted white and decorated with white roses; the delicate luxuriousness of its white interior.

Robyn Warhol at the University of Vermont, your good cooking and girl talk, the Ben and Jerry's chocolate ice cream you provided for my performance *Erotic Faculties (Red)* were all delicious.

Marysia Zalewski at Queens University, Belfast (now at the University of Aberdeen), your enthusiasm for my presenting *The Aesthetics of Orgasm* in Belfast at the conference Beyond Sex and Gender: The Future of Women's Studies?, organized by the Women's Studies Network, UK, comforted me. For we knew the performance would arouse a variety of strong responses from a feminist audience.

People who helped with the preparation of the manuscript

Brian Porray, your typing several chapters during a busy fall 2005 semester made my life easier.

Ben Tedore, your kind nature colored every bit of working with you on the digital preparation of images.

Places that helped to fund the color reproductions

The Creative Activity Fund at the University of Nevada, Reno, School of the Arts. Larry Engstrom, director of the School of the Arts, thank you for helping in the first-time publication of most of the performance documentation in this book and of Jill O'Bryan's and my Sonoran photographs.

People at Duke University Press

Ken Wissoker, your suggestion to produce a volume that spans my career has become a thrilling reality, and your excitement throughout the coming into being of *Clairvoyance (For Those In The Desert)* continues to delight me.

Courtney Berger, your gracious, precise, and speedy responses to my questions and confusions brought smiles and calm to me.

Katharine Baker, your light touch enhances the smoothness and clarity of my sentences.

Cherie Westmoreland, the creativity and freshness of your design invite the reader into a space and spaciousness of elegant allure.

Publishers of my work

You welcomed its unconventional combination of autobiography, poetry, theory, sentimentality, fiction (on occasion), and art and cultural criticism.

Format: Art and the World, a short-lived journal coming out of the Chicago art world, offered a home to my literary experiment, "Confessional Criticism: The Concupiscent Critic," in the August 1979 issue.

Ann Holden, founder of Freshcut Press, gave me the opportunity to create an artist's book of enchanting and erotic beauty, BRUMAS: *A Rock Star's Passage to a Life Re-Vamped* (Oberlin, Ohio, and Ukiah, Calif.: Freshcut Press, 1982).

Peggy Doogan inspired me to research, imagine, and live the life of a saint in "Vermilion," *St. Lucy/Oedipus: A Collaboration* (Tucson, Ariz., 1989).

Caprice, a literary journal out of Wichita—and out of the blue—requested a writing, and I sent an excerpt from Russell's and my "Amazing Grace," which appeared in the July 1990 issue.

The following presses and journals have given permission to reprint previously published material:

University of California Press (Berkeley, Los Angeles, and London):

Erotic Faculties (1996): "A Few Erotic Faculties"; "Demento Beauty"; "Mouth Piece"; "Pythia"; "There Is a Myth." © 1996, The Regents of the University of California.

Monster/Beauty: Building the Body of Love (2001): "Border Cowgirl"; "Dressing Aphrodite"; "Endymion"; "Fire Hands"; "Scarlet Women"; "Sade, My Sweet, My Truffle; or, Giving a Fuck." © 2001, The Regents of the University of California.

❧ NOTA BENE

Dates given in the table of contents and at the beginning of each chapter indicate the year that I wrote a piece, which may or may not be the year in which the piece was first performed.

Material in several of the chapters is repeated in others. In truth to the development of my writing, I wish for the reader to see such repetitions.

In several of the chapters, I have made minor changes in the originally performed or published text.

Writings that were previously published with endnotes do not include them in this volume. Because *Clairvoyance (For Those In The Desert)* is a book of poetry and prose that I have performed, I wish for the reader to feel the performed flow of language. Sources that I name in the body of a piece remain as I originally referred to them. In cases where I did not name a source and credit is due, I include such credit as a stage direction in this book.

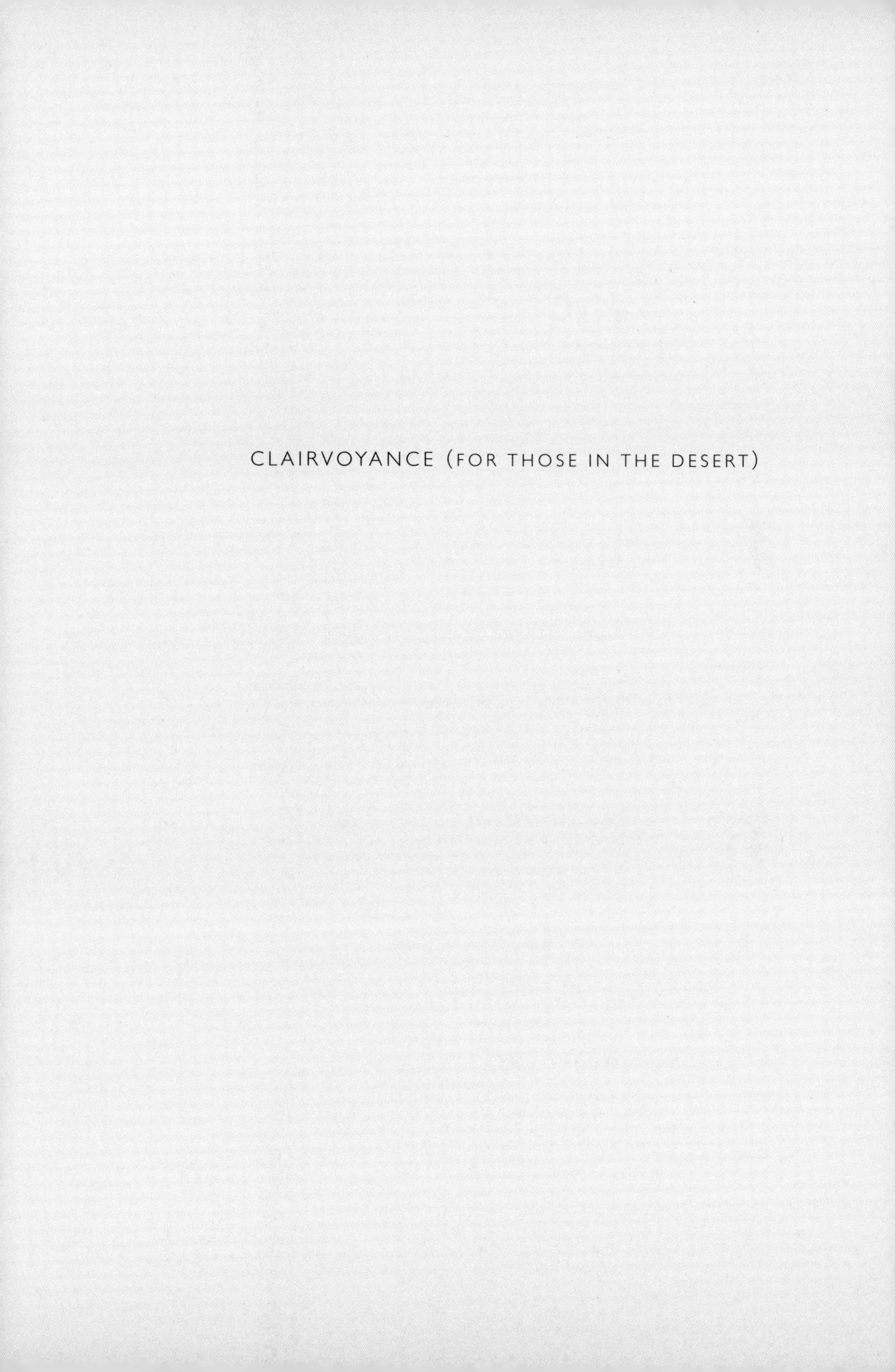

CLAIRVOYANCE (FOR THOSE IN THE DESERT)

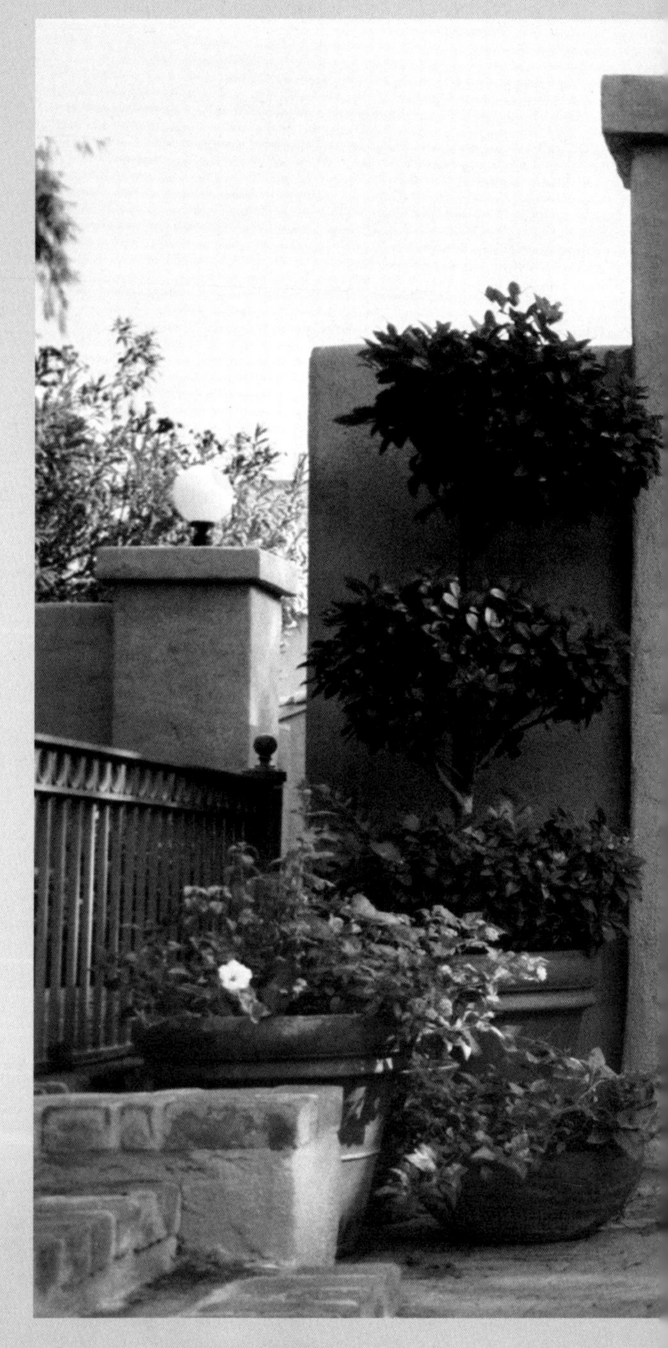

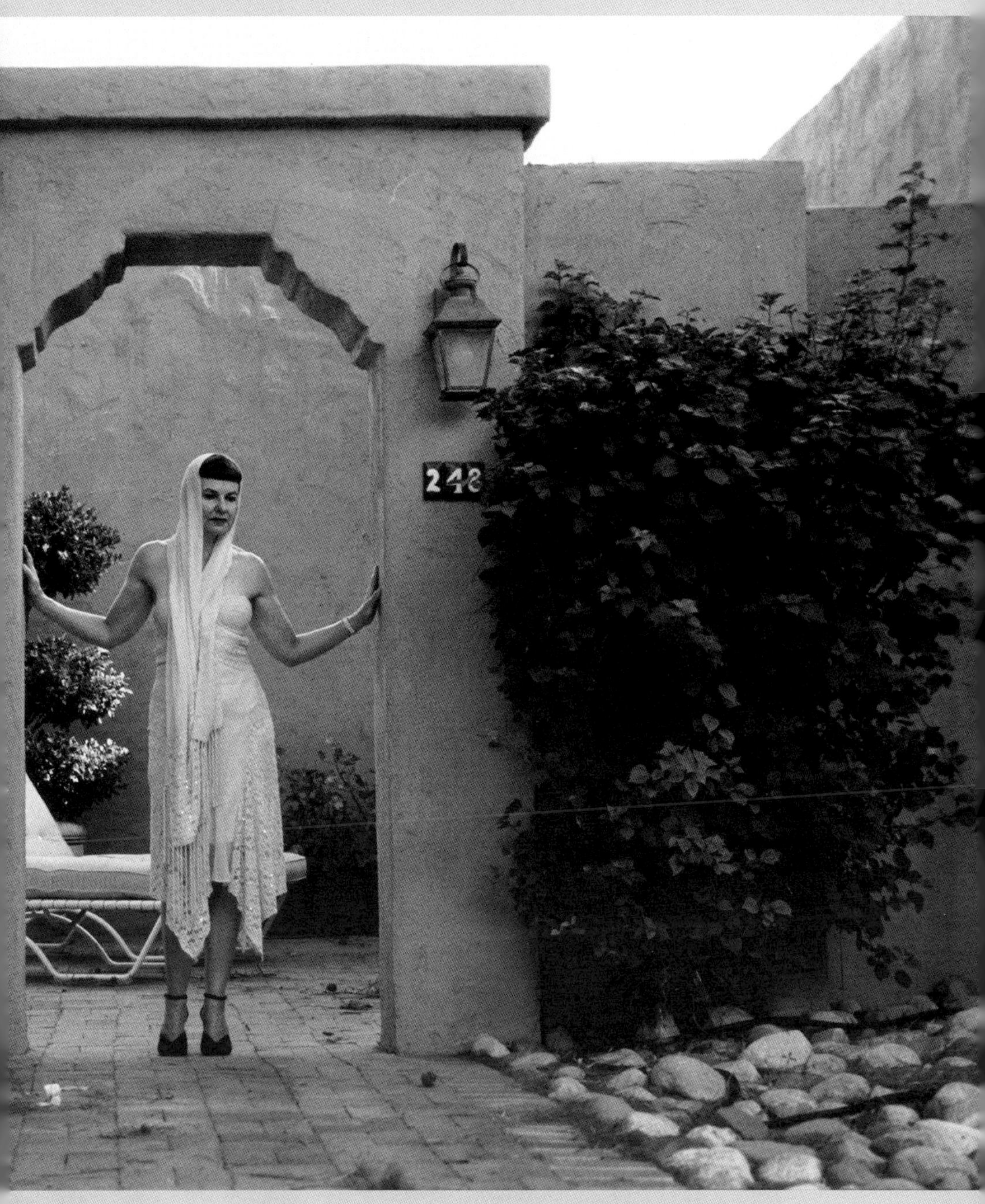

Jill O'Bryan and Joanna Frueh, *threshold*. From the series *Joanna in the Desert*, 2006.

An Introduction by Jill O'Bryan

Joanna's Pink Fairy Palace, her name for the Arizona Inn, is a glistening deep pink adobe, filled with green gardens of desert fauna and flora (also pink sometimes). The Tucson heat is ravishing outside the Pink Fairy Palace, but within its garden walls the heat is simply absorbing—it melts you into itself, you become one with its sexiness. The heat is overwhelming like this: no matter what you are thinking or doing, like the Furies it constantly interjects itself and demands the submission of your soul-and-mind-inseparable-from-body.

The heat is hot like this: they say that men think of sex every thirty seconds, so do women, so does the Tucson heat.

The heat is like this: you can see it. It performs for the camera. Perfect for Joanna.

Clairvoyance (For Those In The Desert) is a collection of Joanna Frueh's performance texts, prose, poetry and lyrics. It is arranged chronologically so the reader can experience both the development and transformation of her performative self into a mature actress with uniquely erotic language and stage presence. From the beginning, Frueh has performed scathingly honest investigations of being and presence—her presence, stage presence, the state of being present. She melds her desires to tell tale of being (whole, in-the-moment, sexually embodied) with her critical feminist thinking about eroticism as a way of life, and enacts them together as prosaic performances of self. As she does so, I experience her work as occupying a magical space of critical thinking in between performance and life and in between art and eros.

As an actress, Frueh shamelessly unveils her oral, sexual, emotional, and intellectual desires to present fully her soul-and-mind-inseparable-from-body, a term that she invented. Her performances are a proving ground for her theories of eroticism as a way of life and for her celebration of female embodiment and self-love. Through her tales of lush sexuality she exemplifies herself as one who lives her provocative poetry and prose without fear.

Joanna's feminist perspective, which is experiential, mystical, erotic, romantic, and innovatively intellectual, unbridles the asexual world of academia by giving permission to include personal experience in academic scholarship. Frueh's own sexual experiences unlock the implicit desires in feminist theory. Frueh believes that these desires include both the articulation and the *practice* of gender, pleasure, sexuality and femininity.

Frueh performs without fear. Her self-love is celebratory self-acceptance rooted in the early feminist cry, "The personal is political." Within the current political context, as the Bush regime murders civil rights, one response to the question "Where is the revolution?" may be to goad the politics of power by challenging individuals to take responsibility for themselves—for their own embodiment. The personal IS political, and so is the flesh.

Joanna's current performances resonate with the heat of love: of self, of others, of sex, of feeling life, of happiness, and, most of all, of transformation. She tells tale of a profound transformation in *Swooning Beauty,* and her performances in this volume enact that transformation.

In our conversations Joanna has fantasized about being on *The Oprah Winfrey Show*, thinking that by telling her own tale of transformation to a large female audience she may help others understand how to be with eros and blossom. She is most interested in serving humankind. Kindly. She has written that "without self-love we diminish our proximity to freedom."[1] But Joanna is also an actress. She recently called me up very excited to tell me that she had chosen her outfit for *Oprah.* She projects herself into the world successfully, and her projections yield results. This is the message of her erotic prose that she has been performing for years. Acting tickles her, makes her hot, and she loves it. She's an actress who performs because she has to. It's a fundamental part of her being and always has been.

Joanna the Actress

Joanna was always an actress. In *Swooning Beauty* she portrays herself as the Sugar Plum Fairy—eleven years old and still going: "So I liked pink underwear, wore a pink tutu, and became the Sugar Plum Fairy. . . . Dad loved the Sugar Plum Fairy and asked her to perform. . . . I pranced around and executed absurdly clumsy leaps and sloppy pirouettes. . . . Like Dad, Russell knew and loved the Sugar Plum Fairy" (*SB*, 109, 110). In the pink, Joanna starred in elementary and high school plays. A space traveler, the stepmother in Snow White, the actress. She was learning about presence—how to project it, live it, be it. She inherited one of her nicknames, Cleo (after Cleopatra) due to her dramatic Egyptian-style hairdo—straight bangs, shoulder-length brunette hair. Now this *do* is one of her trademarks. The others are pink fairy beings and chocolate, interests also cultivated as a child: "Chocolate, art, sex and beauty: my calling was pleasure. I did not become a hedonist, a sybarite, a slave to pleasure, but rather its faith-hound and philosopher" (*SB*, 109).

Joanna is a singer. When in high school, she formed a folk group with her three best friends. They were the Sugarhill Four. It later became a rock group. She was the lead singer. When they were juniors or seniors, they cut a single with Mercury, a big label in Chicago: "The A side stunk, though it became successful in Atlanta. . . .The B side . . . should have been the A side. I wrote it, lyrics and melody. 'My Lonely Life' was a perfect teenage ballad of misery" (*SB*, 70). The Sugarhill Four performed on Chicago's public television station when Joanna was sweet sixteen. Joanna took voice lessons, performed in clubs, and then became a rocker.

Joanna is a strip tease. She strips for me, for you, for all of us. She performs her secrets. In adolescence she fantasizes about being a stripper: "every once

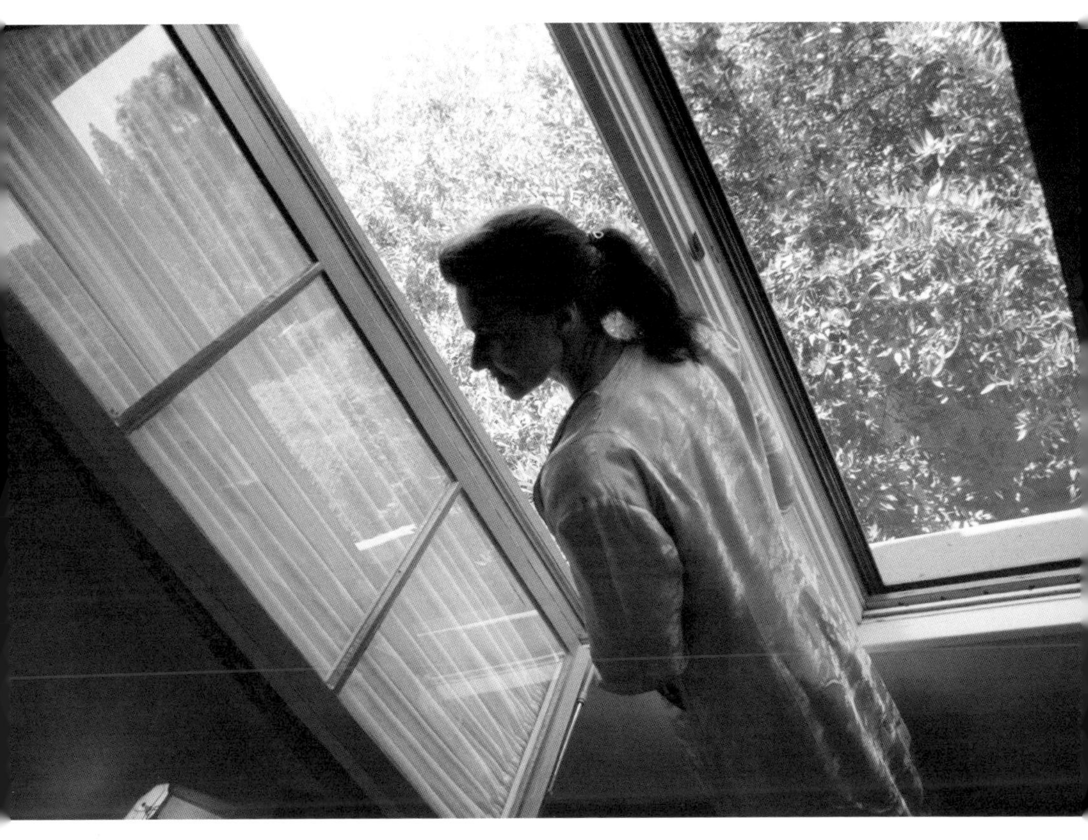

Jill O'Bryan and Joanna Frueh, *listening to sunlight.*

From the series *Joanna in the Desert,* 2006.

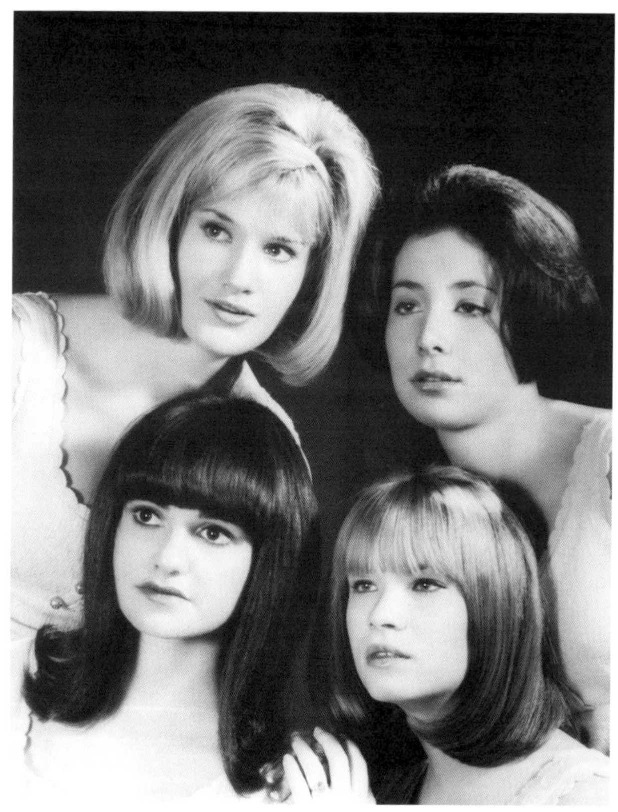

Portrait of the Sugarhill Four, c. 1964. Clockwise from bottom left: Joanna Frueh, Sharon O'Melia, Deborah Rubin, Suzanne Dienner.

in a while she still imagined herself as Rosy Dawn or Gloria Midnight, queen with the velvet cunt." But this quote is from the fiction piece *Dual Conception* (in this volume, 95), in which she goes through a pregnancy as Iris, with (her husband) Childe. She is of the Annunciation, and not a stripper at all.

Gold. This is the color that I see while watching Joanna perform. Even in her red lipstick and wearing pink or white, her presence is gold. Perhaps this is because she puts herself in the spotlight while performing and we are all in the dark watching her. Perhaps it's because she calls herself an actress and I equate gold with actresses—gold jewelry, golden goblets to drink from, riches, fairy tales. (Fairies are golden, aren't they?) So gold may be the color of her presence; and it's also the color of her language that fills the ears and eyes of us willingly receptive Chamberlings. That's who we are as audience members, as readers. Chamberlings. Those who linger in the chamber of stories, who desire nothing more than to be told a story. Nothing gives me more pleasure than being a Chamberling. " 'Golden' was the epithet used more than any other by the Greeks to describe Aphrodite, the most golden girl of ancient Greece," writes Joanna in *Swooning Beauty*. "As I feel my goldenness, more and more since my parents' deaths, I'm able to hear and hold, within my golden core, facts about myself that people tell me. I shied from such facts before, deflecting my recognition of them as congruencies with my soul-and-mind-inseparable-from-body, deflecting them as though they were spears rather than arrows of eros" (*SB*, 72).

Joanna's performances are autobiographical in nature and she presents her self, soul-and-mind-inseparable-from-body, while reading from her scripts, almost always placed on a music stand in front of her. This book is a collection of those scripts, which are also prose, poetry, songs, and stories. Some have been previously published along with her more scholarly texts (and *as* scholarly texts), but this book is the first celebration of Joanna, the performance artist, or, as she prefers to be called, the actress. As Joanna lovingly steps away from her roles as university teacher and academic, she ravenously pursues her roles as actress and writer of poetry and prose. She has already entered an extremely creative and prolific time in her life, so this may be the first volume of scripts, with other volumes to follow. As I write this in July 2006, she is leaving her professorship at the University of Nevada, Reno, leaving Reno, where she has lived for sixteen years, and moving to her beloved Tucson to focus on writing and performing. Place as a vehicle for transformation is a recurring theme in Joanna's life and work. It has been Greece, and it has been Tucson. This time it's Tucson once again, a place of clairvoyance for those in the desert.

Frueh's scholarship always informs her performance texts. So do erotic love affairs, songs, childhood memories, fairies, Tom, Russell, Mel (a fictional character in *Swooning Beauty*) and other men, sexy costumes, flowers, champagne, cakes and cookies. It is the shameless inclusion of the intimate details of her lifelong transformation that allows us to behold here her evolution from a woman with many roles—teacher, scholar, art critic, performer, lover—into a soul-and-mind-inseparable-from-body.

Joanna has been shamelessly unwilling to exclude her experiences of embodiment from her work. As a result, her discussions of sexual desire and embodiment inform and enrich her contributions to feminist theory—namely, her view of eroticism as a way of life—and she has emerged as a significant poet.

Desiring woman, embodied theorist, and poet: as such, Joanna has revolutionized academic language. She speaks with a tongue that is shockingly intimate and unnervingly revealing. She is assertive about freely unveiling her private self. By doing so she dismisses academic dogmas that discourage overt sexual behavior and a sexualized voice. Her unabashedly honest descriptions of embodiment are sexy, and her feminist thinking is derived from her experience of being as well as her vast knowledge: of art and art history, feminist theory, teaching, and performing.

The structure and aesthetics of Joanna's performances undermine the traditional stage and audience separation. She speaks to us—delivers a monologue of autobiographical prose and poetry that mingles with some really brilliant theoretical thinking. She demonstrates her soul-and-mind-inseparable-from-body with her presence and her presence of mind. How? She excitedly describes her orgasms, her delight of sex with men, and performs her voracious appetite for love, chocolate, red lipstick. She insists that her presence is made up of self-love and embraces eroticism as a way of life. She overcomes grief and transforms herself from Brumas into Ambrosia, and we know it's true because her presence permeates the audience, sometimes like an intoxicating perfume, and sometimes like a beast growling in ecstasy.

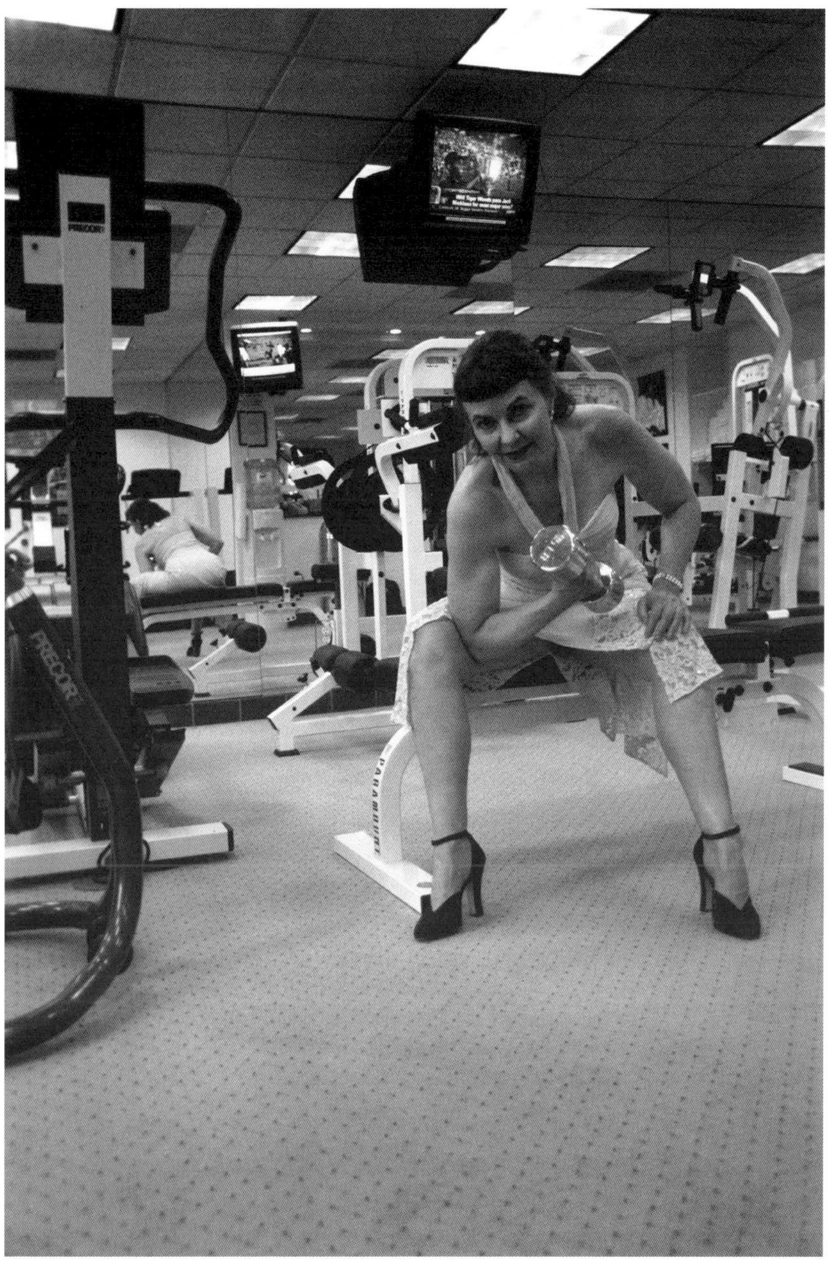

Jill O'Bryan and Joanna Frueh, *embodied theory*.

From the series *Joanna in the Desert*, 2006.

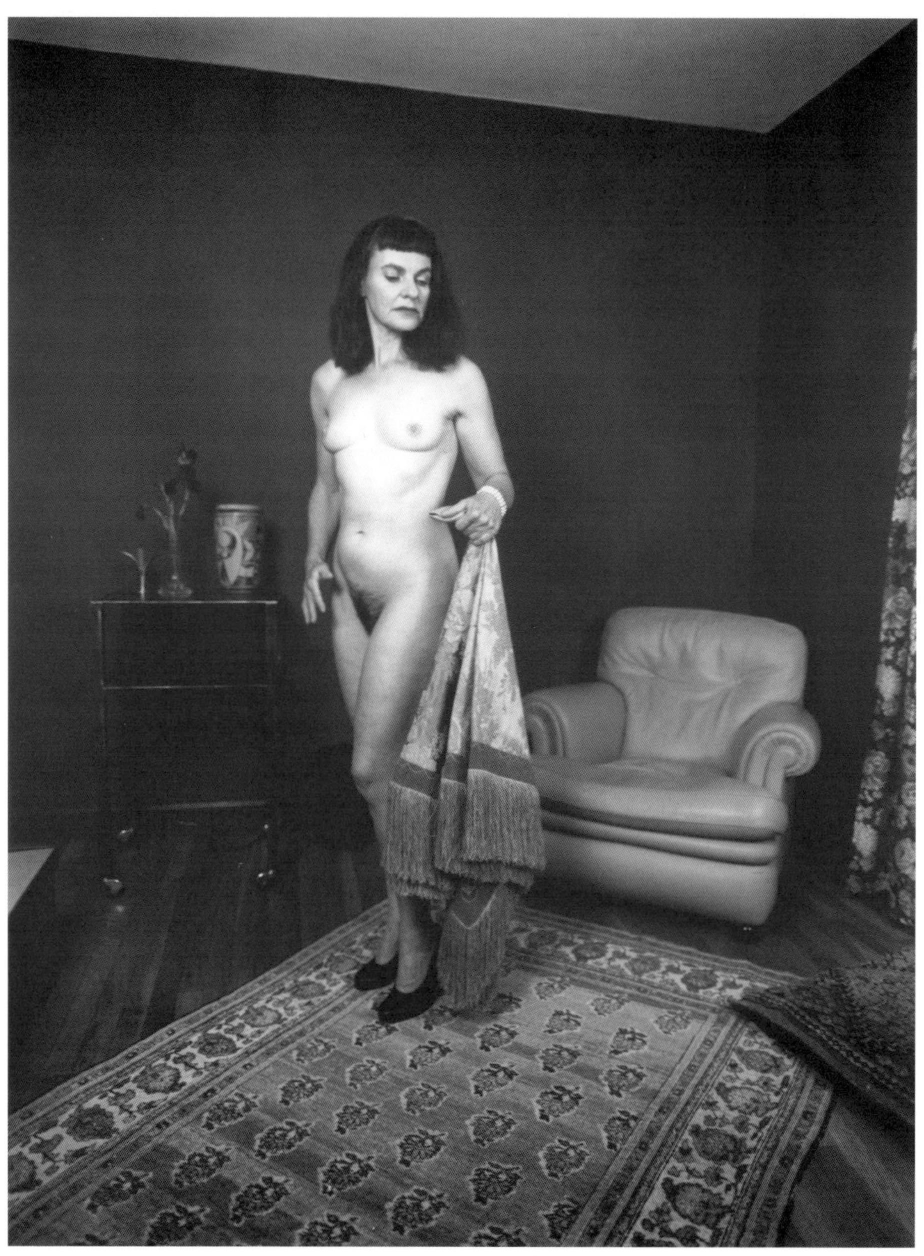

Joanna Frueh and Russell Dudley, *Aphrodite of Knidos in the Flesh*, 1999.

Photo courtesy of Frueh and Dudley.

In short, her performances are not only enjoyable to attend, they are also inspiring. They make me want to perform, not formally for an audience, but exceptionally for myself. Frueh's work is an antidote to the plethora of feminist theory that ridicules, constricts, politicizes our every move. I am personally drawn to it because it allows me to resolve some of the conflicting anomalies in my life with the theory that I so heartily believe in, write about, and read.

Narcissism and Mirrors

Joanna has always stood her ground as a scholar, teacher, and writer. Politically she is a rebel. A passage from *Swooning Beauty* addresses her relationship to both her students and feminist theory in general:

> Through the years, young feminist women students have occasionally asked me how I can bear to devour feminist scholarship, which, to them, concentrates on women's torments, belittlement, and self-berating—even when presenting women's achievements and victories. Those passionate and curious students have told me that such analyses and histories are torture to read, depressing. I've heard them thinking to themselves that feminist scholarship is a misanthropic literature, and I've always affirmed to those students the value of feminist scholarship and the joy it can give its reader; because knowing the truth is inspiring, and it spurs some of us to change what supposed truths have wrought. (*SB*, 279)

Her own work counters the feminist scholarship that focuses on "women's torments, belittlement, and self-berating." Joanna's scholarship is about self-recognition as self-love. Aphrodite has been portrayed throughout the history of art as a narcissist—a nude admiring herself in a mirror. Knowing this, Joanna writes, "Women look too much in mirrors, we're told by a culture that is telling us to scrutinize the hell out of ourselves because we're *not* goddesses. Woe are we in our ugliness, but we'll keep looking, just to check up on it. We'll conform to negative feminine narcissism. We come to believe it through the cultural abuse that's heaped upon women's physical appearance" (*SB*, 200).

Joanna, deferring to her *Webster's* dictionary, looks up *narcissism*. Self-love is the first definition, followed by a semicolon and then the judgment: "excessive interest in one's own appearance" (*SB*, 200). Excessive. This is the word to subvert. Self-love is excessive. But self-knowledge is the cohabitant of self-love. It is fundamental to the recognition of oneself as human. Eros, as a fundamental part of self-knowledge, is the sanctity of embodiment—a recognition and celebration of being embodied. Joanna's term *soul-and-mind-inseparable-from-body* describes being in the world—embodied, self-loving, and self-knowing. "Eros is fundamental to swooning beauty, eros being the rich and gorgeous complexity of soul-and-mind-inseparable-from-body" (*SB*, 250).

And vanity? Joanna's performances of eros and self-love celebrate women's beauty. Vanity is the affirmation of this self-love. The artwork intent on shifting the frame within which female beauty is depicted is always directly relational to the mirror. Artwork that addresses female beauty must contend with this stereotype of female beauty as narcissistic.

In *The Art of Reflection* (1996) Marsha Meskimmon writes about how Joan Semmel's painting *Me Without Mirrors* (1974) confronts stereotypical ideals of the female nude. There is no face in this image. Semmel is nude, reclining on a bed and drying herself off with a towel. She's a bather but paints only what she can see of herself without a mirror, her body from the chest down.[2] As a bather she references this stereotypical motif of the female nude while also subverting it. Hers is a headless self-portrait that is not seductive. Instead, the painting reveals her investigation of her particular body as a geometrical paradigm for the frame of the missing mirror. Thus her breasts loom in the foreground, framing the bottom of the image, her arms move up each side of the canvas, and one crossed-over leg completes the frame on the top of the image. Meskimmon points out that Semmel subverts the "iconography of 'vanity.'"[3] Vanity, as a motif, is twofold. For example, in Velázquez's *Venus with Her Mirror (Rokeby Venus)*, Venus seduces us with her body as she turns her back to us to admire her face in a mirror held by Cupid. She draws the viewer into her gaze upon her own face (only visible in the mirror) and her enjoyment of her own beauty, beautification, and sensuous self-desire. Within the context of seduction, her self-admiration enhances our admiration of her.

Joanna explains her dedication to eros and self-love as a revolutionary feminist strategy. She became a leader in the erotic revolution after she read

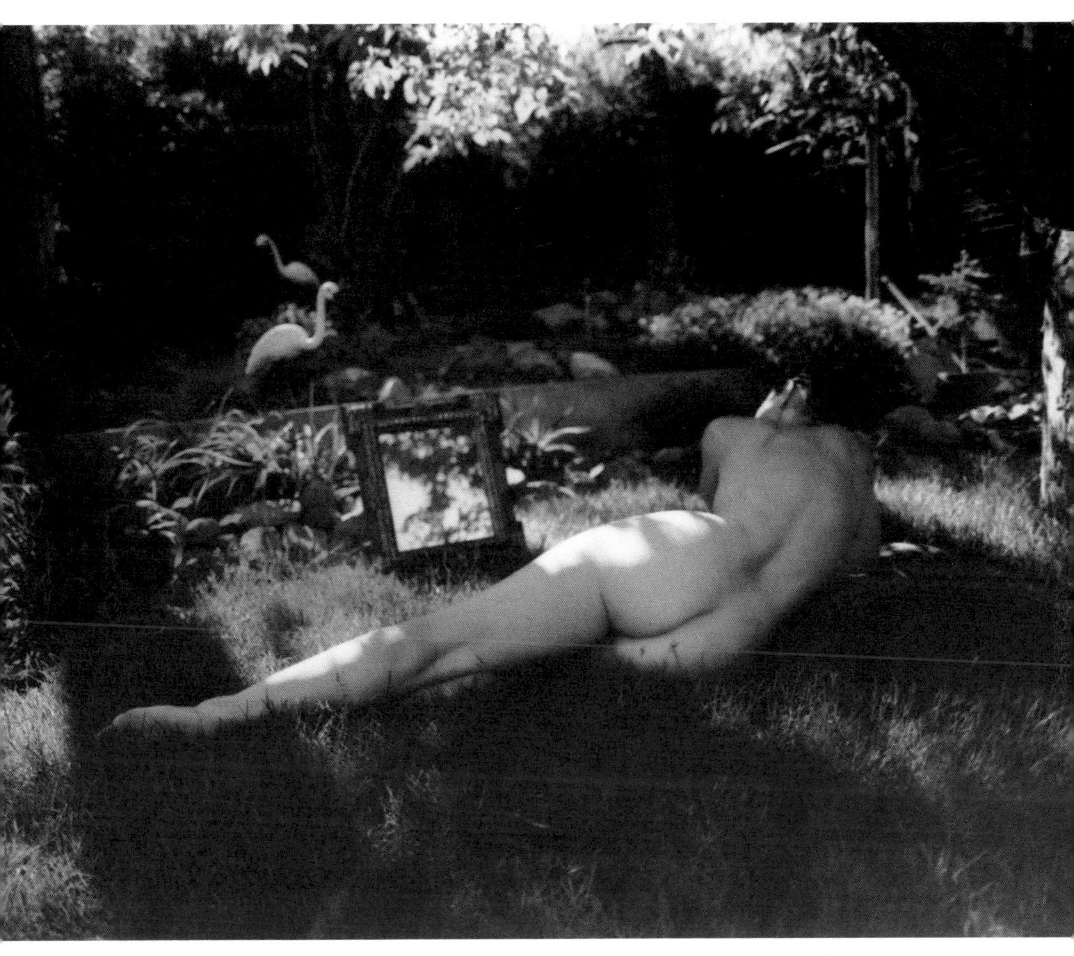

Joanna Frueh and Russell Dudley, *Seeing Clearly with the Companionship of Pink Flamingos (after Velázquez's Venus with a Mirror [Rokeby Venus]),* 1999. *Photo courtesy of Frueh and Dudley.*

Marcuse's *Eros and Civilization* in college. Marcuse argues that the pleasure principle be raised above the reality principle, and Joanna read this as revolution, in which women could "[focus] on their greatest pleasure—which is their beauty and its action—difficult as that may be" (*SB*, 211).

But eros is tricky business. Many feminist artists have performed the sensuous body as a political statement with regard to the male gaze. Carolee Schneemann experimented with the erotic body as material, and Frueh has pointed out Schneemann's "probing, exposing, and loving" touch, her "continu[ing] to divest the female body of iconicity," and her creation of a pleasure beyond the phallus.[4]

In her 1963 *Eye Body: 36 Transformative Actions*, Schneemann covered her naked body with paint, grease, ropes, chalk, plastic, and snakes. She was transgressing boundaries: as an erotic female nude she doubled as both artist and object of art.

Frueh has written extensively on the work of Hannah Wilke and other artists who probe the complexities of both being a woman artist and creating images of women: "We see women artists being the subjects and producers of culture. Using visual rhetoric invented by men, such as the female nude, to emancipate it. Diving deep into the masculine womb and surfacing: Carolee Schneemann the magic ground for snakes, the voice of fearless sex; Nancy Spero turning the dead into joyous athletes, launching battalions; Rachel Rosenthal baring age and nakedness; Joan Semmel staring without being a voyeur; Bailey Doogan depicting what she has named the angry aging bitch. We know the power of images and the importance of transforming them."[5]

But more important than the contextualization of Frueh's work within contemporary women's art is this: the texts in *Clairvoyance* should be contextualized both within the genre of erotic poetry and prose and within the nexus of the poet-performer.

As an erotic poet Joanna has many lovers, including Dante Gabriel Rossetti, Charles Baudelaire, Henry Miller, the Marquis de Sade, and Alphonso Lingis. The female lovers I think of with regard to her work are Anaïs Nin, Marguerite Duras, and Sappho.

Joanna wrote her doctoral dissertation on Rossetti, and as Tanya Augsburg points out in " 'The Siren Is Also a Mystic': An Introduction," a catalogue essay

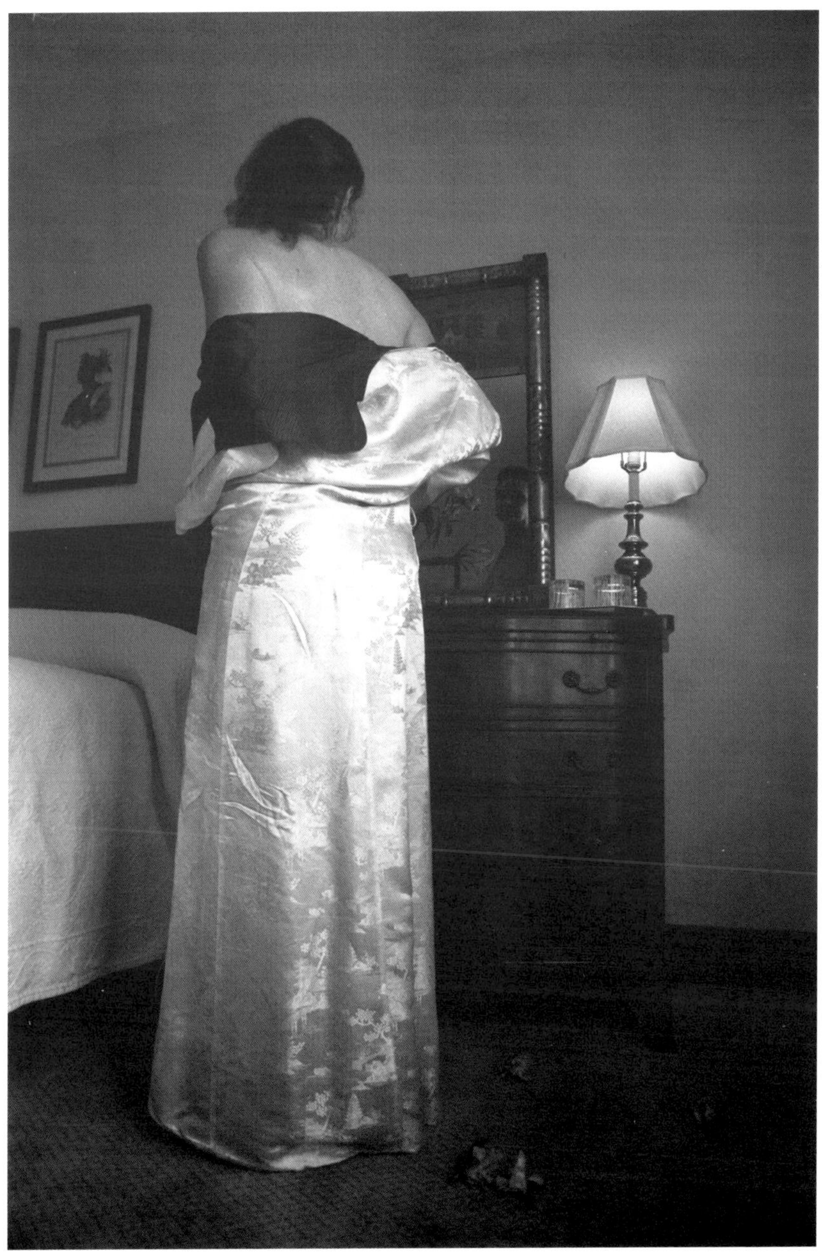

Jill O'Bryan and Joanna Frueh, *disrobing narcissism.*

From the series *Joanna in the Desert*, 2006.

for Frueh's 2005 retrospective exhibition, he has had a profound influence on her body of work ever since. Joanna is a Rossetti woman. As Venus Verticordia in the photograph *Venus Verticordia 2005* (2004), created by Frueh and Russell Dudley, she placed herself inside of Rossetti's painting *Venus Verticordia* and his sonnet of the same name.[6]

The doubling of poetry/prose and the visual—for example, Rossetti's double works, Blake's composite art, Ernst's collages—is an artform that Joanna utilizes as well. The photographs of Joanna that frequently accompany her texts are erotic (taken by artists with whom she collaborates, such as Russell Dudley, Frances Murray, and me). The photographs pay homage to her writing by capturing moments of her constantly erupting play with eros. But mostly Joanna's doubling occurs in performance, where she gives her texts presence. She presents them. The integrity of the writing as prose/poetry does not require that it be performed. The texts are complete as literature; when performed, they become something else completely—theater.

Joanna is afraid neither of performing, nor articulating, nor wearing her sensuality. She wears it as Cleopatra does: bright red lipstick, skin-tight dresses —pink ones. (The claim "Pink is a state of mind," which she says in *The Performance of Pink* [in this volume, 323; hereafter cited as *PP*], resonates throughout her work.) She performs her love of fucking. And in doing so she faces her fears of men and of the man, woman, child, and fairy that she has become. "Seductive though I was, I did not uncover my phallically flirting hips. That required a happiness that is relatively new to me. I attracted men, and they attracted me, but I feared them. What do you do with a man?" (*SB*, 118–119).

And then she became one.

In her deeply erotic *The Aesthetics of Orgasm* she pays deference to Mme Duclos, one of Sade's star collaborators. Like Duclos, Joanna takes a hard stand:

We both tell stories about our lives, our sex, our good looks, our manly aggressions on men's bodies. My midlife authority is precisely a vehicle for identifying with the midlife Duclos, with being, like her, a man in the guise of femininity. . . . Nevertheless, it's no wonder that I say, only half-jokingly, that at the age of fifty-two I realized I was a man. . . . Desire is limitless: deal with it." (*The Aesthetics of Orgasm*, in this volume, 297–98; hereafter cited as *AO*)

But when Joanna speaks of herself as a man I also hear Rossetti amusing himself with his masculine women:

> Yet, Jenny, looking long at you,
> The woman almost fades from view.
> A cipher of man's changeless sum
> Of lust, past, present, and to come,
> Is left. A riddle that one shrinks
> To challenge from the scornful sphinx.[7]

It is curious that Joanna has been so heavily influenced by the fantasies of Rossetti. She certainly has not fashioned herself after them, but, unlike most feminists, she has explored her own sexuality without eliminating—and, in fact, by exploring—the male gaze. Her insights into this have allowed her to see herself as a sexualized and primally sexed woman.

The most recently performed piece in *Clairvoyance* is *Ambrosia*, which Joanna debuted in 2004 at a conference dedicated to the philosopher Alphonso Lingis's work. The theme of the piece is innocence, and she specifically refers to Lingis's *Dangerous Emotions*, in which there is a chapter titled "Innocence." Most intriguing to me is Joanna's highlighting of an active rather than a passive innocence (represented by the idea of the "innocent victim").

Joanna is also an action hero. In *Swooning Beauty* she conjures an image of Mel Gibson in one of his roles as action hero. She speaks of the decisiveness, responsibility, and forcefulness the action hero takes on when he acts. She also speaks of her fondness for the command "Do it" (*AO*, 298). But her action hero is also a "fairy man." From Mel Gibson's roles she invents *Mel,* her fairy man—action hero that is also herself as a man. Joanna, as *Mel,* is able to both act as a man and enjoy the actions of men, a condition that she describes in this passage from *The Aesthetics of Orgasm*:

> Let me assert that all of us women don't need or want plying with foreplay, although I've read since I was a girl that we do. Some of us need and love, a lot of the time, decisiveness and force akin to the action hero's when he is at the pinnacle of knowing what he has to do, when he can't afford to make mistakes, when his focus is absolute. (*AO*, 298)

Joanna is a rebel, and with her exploration and appropriation of the action hero she lovingly stares into the face of feminism, takes a stand, and ecstatically gets fucked by a man.

> Here I stand. Here I am with another person. Here I am with another penis, another navel, another set of the same circumstances in a different body led by a different ego, defense mechanisms, and compensatory behaviors.
>
> Here I am in an inescapable way. Here I am, in all my blushes and whatever little pimples exist today on my high round ass.
>
> Orgasm puts you in your place. Here I *am*. Here *I* am. Or, with one or more partners, here we *are*, here *we* are. (*AO*, 299)

And again . . .

> Is your cock your center, like my cunt is mine, and if so, do you feel that when we fuck I am embracing the center of you?
>
> Yes. We know each other's center in the paradoxical dissolution or exchange of self into the lover, into the de-centering, into the loss of identity that is the clearest clarity. (*AO*, 300)

Lingis might reply:

> The caressing hands move aimlessly over the flesh in random, repetitious movements. The muscles tighten, harden, the limbs grope and grapple, pistons and rods of a machine that has no idea what it is trying to achieve. Then it collapses, gelatinizes, melts, runs. The trapped blood surges and pounds, the heat billows, the spirit vaporizes in gasps and sighs. In dissolute ecstasy the body that had become ligneous, ferric, coral, now curdles, dissolves, liquefies, vaporizes, becomes radioactive, solar, nocturnal."[8]

And Baudelaire might respond:

> Allowing love, she lies seductively
> And from the high divan smiled in her ease
> At my love-ocean's deep felicity
> Mounting to her as tides draw in the seas.[9]

Within their sequencing, Joanna's performances are as geographically informed as they are chronological, autobiographical, or even narrational. Place, sense of place, and geographical places resound with more than just sentiment. And due to Joanna's fearless indulgences in sentimentality, sense of place (from the garden to the desert) has become an undividable part of her soul-and-mind-inseparable-from-body. This phenomenon is there from the start.

First introduced in *The Concupiscent Critic* are two locations that inform Joanna's *self*, places she relates to foremost, and before any other character that appears in the narration. This overt characteristic of Frueh's performances, that her (sense of) self is dramatically informed by place, appears in *The Concupiscent Critic* as a duality. Her powerful identity with Chicago enhances but is also in conflict with her experience of tropical Mexico, where the story takes place.

In *BRUMAS,* the place is Greece. It overtakes her and appears again and again as a lover. In the performance *Clairvoyance (For Those In The Desert),* when pining for Tucson, Joanna and her husband Tom are "aliens." She returns to Tucson over and over in her work, and now—as I write this—she is preparing to move there again. Tucson is Joanna's muse.

The concupiscent critic is dressed in a mauve silk blouse and a mid-calf wool crepe skirt, and pinned into her hair are red gladioli. Her costume here, as always in Joanna's performances, is perfectly chosen either to drive home or to stand in contrast to the images that emerge throughout the performance. Here she is in Mexico discovering traces of Chicago that are entrenched in her being. The costume is one she wears in Chicago, with a trace of Mexico added in—the *glads.*

Even though extreme sensuality exists for the critic in both places, her first images are of darkness; as she walks on the beach taking in the smells and images and recognizing her responses to them, "the daylight ha[s] disappeared, and, as always she ha[s] missed the moment of darkness" (*The Concupiscent Critic*, in this volume, 52; hereafter cited as *CC*). And then, the darkness in the city: "In the city she rarely planned acute observations of nature. She sat at her desk and turned on the light when she could no longer read the words she was writing. Sometimes, alone in the apartment at night, she switched off all the lamps, stood by a window with her hands on the glass and tried to see the stars. In summer the leaves looked amber beneath the streetlamps' garish light. If a murder were to occur, the knife would glisten red before even entering a victim's body" (*CC*, 52).

I quote this astonishing beginning to *The Concupiscent Critic*, the beginning of the first performance, and also of this book, because Joanna's conjuring of darkness, missing moments, and murder are dumbfounding within the context of her current work, which is about eros, being light, with light, of light—fairy light. While this book offers the clarity of Joanna's thinking and the development of her oeuvre, it also discloses Joanna's transformation from angrily bearing the weight of life to relishing and loving her embodied self, partially discovered through her love affair with the Sonoran Desert, where her experiences of eros burn her soul into her body.

The Concupiscent Critic does not linger on its opening images, and it is the sensuality of the language and Joanna's presence in the moment that give the piece its meaning. The concupiscent critic is driven by art, city life, her relationships with artists, and—while enjoying Mexico—the breezes, the Pacific, the sun and sand. But the critic is surprised at how Chicago haunts her, and she understands its immersion into her being as a trace of her life there that she cannot leave behind.

Joanna lived in Chicago, writing her dissertation and creating a vibrant career as a cutting-edge art critic when she wrote and performed *The Concupiscent Critic*. At that time she also lived with "an amazon—a tall, strong, big-boned, blond artist." And the artist's paintings: "Prismacolor self-portraits, portraits of friends and lovers (including me), and fantasy environments housing lovemaking women couples" (*SB*, 135).

The critic returns to Chicago, having sensed the beginnings of a new relationship with a woman. The man she had an affair with in Mexico is left behind: "Pacific. She was hardly pacific. The city had disturbed her serenity. The artist who had drawn her haloed by bleeding hearts could not be forgotten. This time memory was not enough, and John, who sang to her at night about a sailor lost at sea, would never follow her home" (*CC*, 56). For the reader, the memories in *The Concupiscent Critic* appear as present and clear as the reality the critic is reporting. So the narrative conjures up for me a painting in which the subject is portrayed several times in different areas of the canvas, suggesting temporal abstraction, but emphasizing the probing of conflicts in her soul. Baring her body is not a problem. Baring her soul is. In my imagined painting the concupiscent critic and Joanna the actress appear next to one another in the center of the canvas. Hovering above them are the critic with the amazon artist and her portrait of Joanna. Next to them on the left, Piero's *The Resurrection of Christ* (which Joanna erotically describes in *The Concupiscent Critic*). And to the right, the critic and John on the Mexican beach. At the bottom, an image of the critic's honest sexual pleasures as aroused by touch— the touch of water, of a paintbrush, the touch of skin: "John's body, like that of Piero's deity, did not in and of itself arouse her. The tender maleness of a lean anatomy and smooth skin did. 'Come faster,' she cried, 'and kiss me'" (*CC*, 53).

While telling us about herself, the critic reveals herself to be the harbinger of many others' secrets. However, "She [does] not want her life publicly dismembered and assume[s] that neither [do] these touching raconteurs. Scars and liberations demanded the continuation of the privacy in which they had been conceived" (*CC*, 55). This is a striking admission, which, for me, is emphasized in the third verse of "The Dudes Have Danced the World to Death," the first song in *Justifiable Anger*, when Joanna haughtily judges soul-baring:

> The boys sport top hats when they twirl
> They think they're Fred Astaire
> They charm the pants off any girl
> Whose silliness lays her soul bare
> (*Justifiable Anger*, in this volume, 77)

Is baring herself Joanna's most secret fear? If so, she spends the rest of her performing life successfully confronting that fear. Joanna bares her body easily, perhaps as a masthead that announces her soul. "The body is itself a kind of plot, it is a ground of being. As such, it can be a cemetery, a graveyard of our unactivated wants, and it can be a garden, a sanctuary from which to act" (*SB*, 61). Joanna loves gardens.

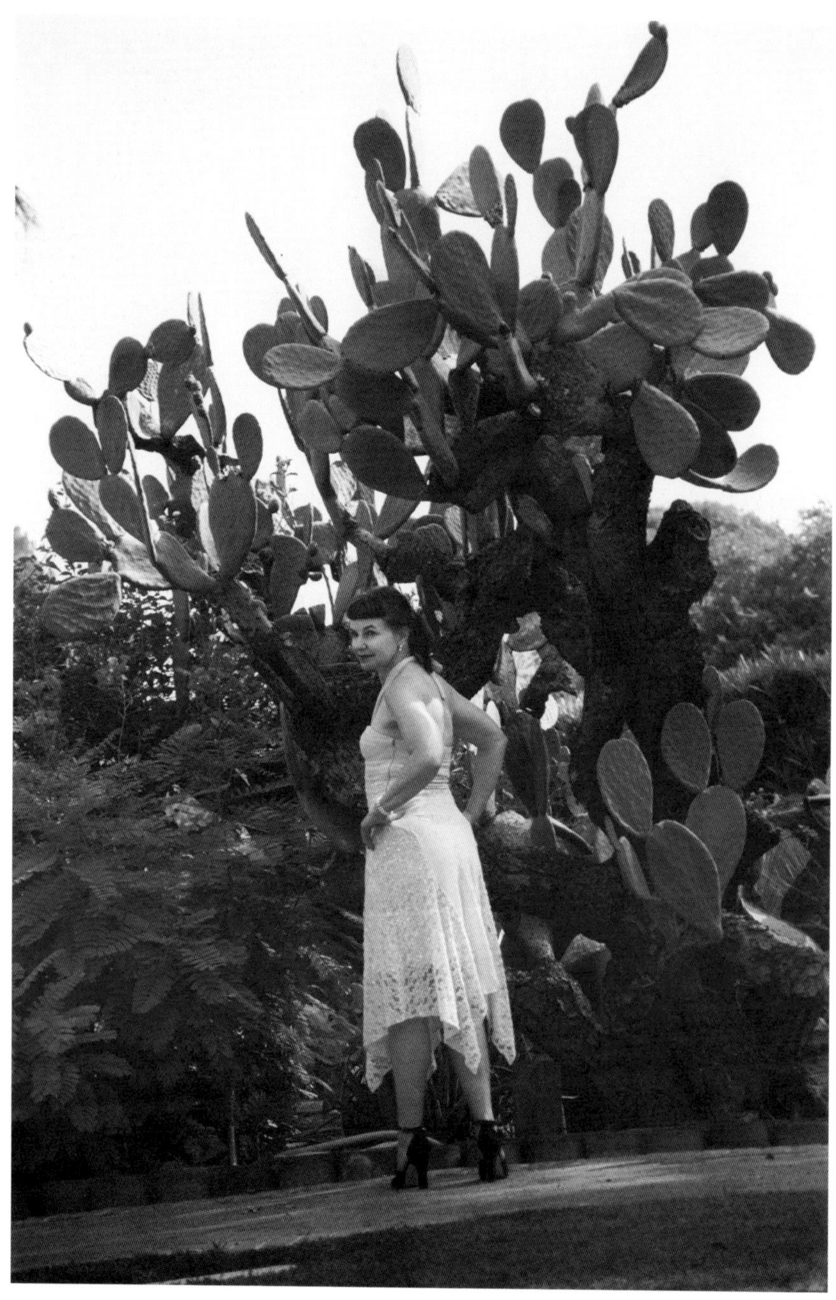

Jill O'Bryan and Joanna Frueh, *prickly pear*. From the series *Joanna in the Desert*, 2006.

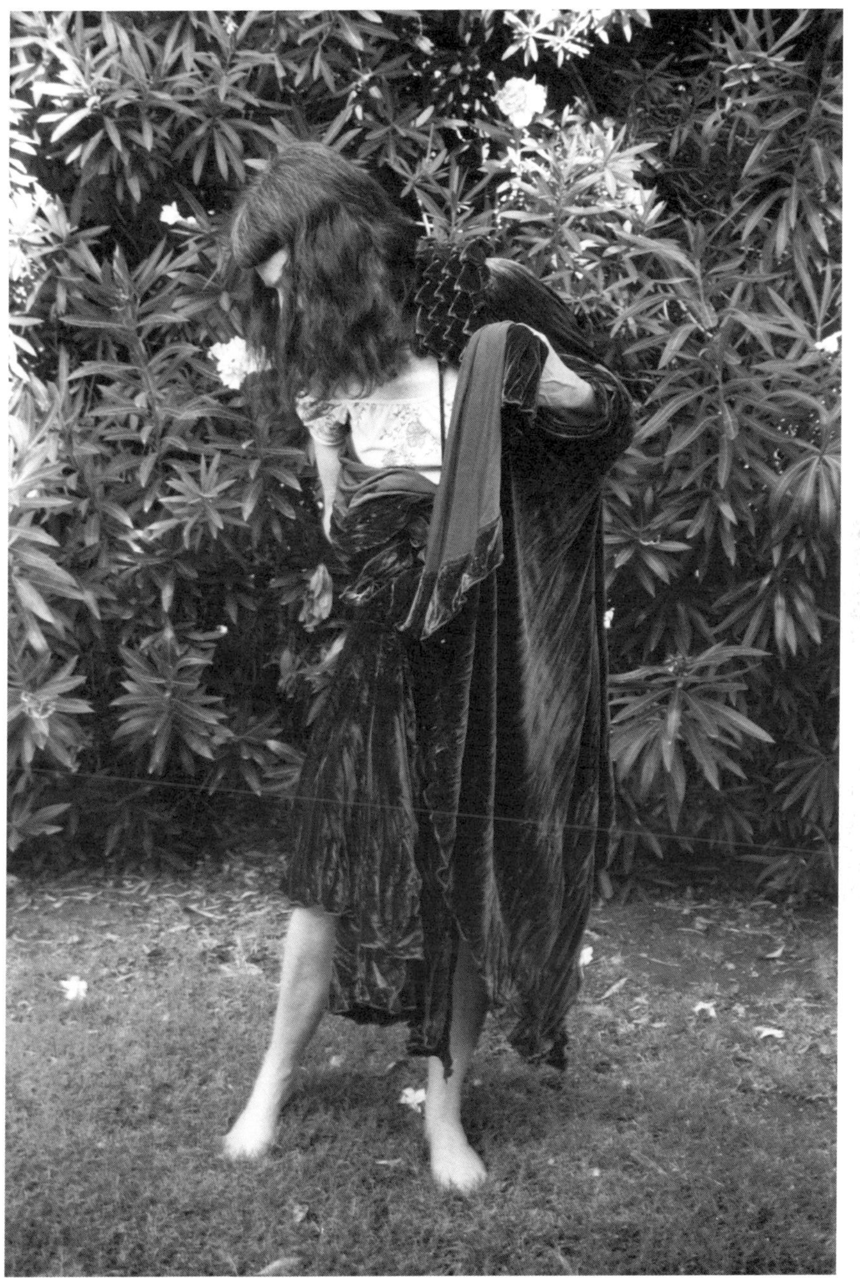

Jill O'Bryan and Joanna Frueh, *oleander*. From the series *Joanna in the Desert*, 2006.

BRUMAS and *Justifiable Anger* are sharp and angry but cannot be reduced to these qualities alone. The lyrics are clever, compelling, and insolent. Brumas is a rock star—a death rocker with a wicked tongue, a sexy punk. *BRUMAS* is a dark piece—one of Joanna's darkest. The prose is in the third person, the five rock songs in the first. She gives herself distance in order to describe her character as a section of herself—the rock star sliced off from herself—a sliced-off fantasy, and an alien.

> I am an alien,
> A race apart.
> We have no soul,
> We have no heart.
> We breathe no air,
> We eat no food,
> We feed each other's evil mood.
> I am an alien. (*BRUMAS*, in this volume, 63)

Brumas literally puts herself beside herself so we can see *how* she performs—what she does on stage when feeling sexy, and when feeling icy. (In *Swooning Beauty*, Joanna writes about being beside herself with grief.) *BRUMAS* is the story of the protagonist's relationship to her audience: "She would never have to perform again if just one audience would rise to her rage" (62). She does not belong, and does not yearn to belong to the human race, to the earth, but one night the audience moves her: "Tonight the final applause touched her deeply. She said no 'thank-yous' because she was afraid that her voice would crack. The thousands of hands clapping sounded like a hum, and she did not sense the agitated bodies that had prayed to her as she sang. She believed that a myriad of fingers was tugging at her viscera, that she grew a harp inside her taller than the mountainside she owned near the shore of an ocean she rarely saw, that the melody played was too sweet for tears, just right for tortured screams" (62). Brumas the rock star transforms herself from an alien (as a self-made monster) to a person who understands her own empowerment as embodiment. The transformation takes place when she decides serendipitously to leave New York and go to Greece. There, in a place of light, she strips off her makeup and her black clothes. There she wears white, becomes a siren, cuts her black hair off and waits for the blonde halo to grow in.

Theory

Joanna's prose and poetry constitute a theater of self with two wings: narration of self and presence of self. The two are intertwined within one another as necessary others (just as we, the readers and listeners, are also necessary others to the poet). The narration and being of self do not exist in a binary relationship. One is not external and the other internal. But the complexity of their relationship engages all of us, in the form of desire to know oneself, to be known, to be present, and to be heard. The poet has always had a higher calling: to perform presence as melodic language so that we can hear it and be present through it. Poet-performers seek knowledge of self, so that they can speak it. Antonin Artaud and Charles Bukowski come to mind as two who performed their poetry from the bottom of the abyss. Joanna can speak from the abyss, but she is always focused upward and outward, so that as the scarlet woman she takes delight in eros, as the rock star Brumas she travels to the light in Greece and transforms herself, and as Pythia she speaks from the temple at Delphi: "Gold flows from the graceful tongue, and silence is golden, too. Maybe you do not hear my words, for speech is the most easily misinterpreted of human behaviors" (*Pythia*, in this volume, 232).

The poet understands speech as behavior and (mis)interpretation as something both to overcome and to relish, because presence is the antithesis of interpretation. Interpretation is not required when presence is there. Norman O. Brown once wrote, "There is only poetry."[10] Hayden White writes of Brown, "I have a friend who works on presence, most particularly the difference between presence and meaning. He points out that we moderns have tended to overvalue meaning at the expense of presence. We are not content to be, we must also mean. But a poem does not mean. It is. It is presence."[11]

Joanna lives and performs her poetry. Instead of there being a disjuncture between living and performing, there is a melding that appears to dissolve any disjuncture between the two. And this melding is one of Joanna's most prized undertakings. She says that she wishes to serve her fellow humankind by presenting her own transformation, toward which she has been working most of her life. As a poet she has the ability to engagingly (re)enact her transformation for us. Honest and gutsy, Joanna lays out her thinking and feeling, her sex and body so that we are able to bear witness to past presences that are here and now, and not lacking; she appears to hide nothing.

Throughout her book *Relating Narratives: Storytelling and Selfhood*, Adriana Cavarero terms the unique individual the "narratable self." She speaks about the innate sense that we each have that our story is unique, belonging solely to each one of us, and that it is unrepeatable, by both ourselves and by others. Moreover we recognize this about each other individual, and whether we know them well or not, we recognize that all others have a unique story. What is important, therefore, is not the detail in each person's story, but that each person has one, just as we do. This knowledge imparts a sense of self that in turn implants the desire for the narration of our story, by ourselves or others.

My point here is not to go into the formation of the subject and its relationship to language, of which much has already been written, but rather to track the desire for narration, and indeed to discuss the manifestation of this desire in the narration itself. The revelation of the self is manifested more by the desire to narrate one's own tale than by the tale itself, which is why, through the language of the poet, one who is inspired by language, we are exposed to perfectly composed combinations of the desire to be and the narration of being.

Autobiography, or, in regard to Joanna's work, autobiographically inspired poetry and prose, is more than just the narration of the self; it is also the fruition of memory, which is inherently abstract, malleable, manipulable, and vulnerable to both our own language and that of others. But Joanna sheds her vulnerability through profound interactions with others, interactions that are political as well as poetic.

In the political (as well as ontological) sphere, Hannah Arendt and Emmanuel Levinas both argue that it is only by being with others that we know ourselves. Arendt writes that every interaction in which one tells a tale of oneself is a political interaction. She argues that the public realm is "a space of appearance," and that "without trusting in action and speech as a mode of being together, neither the reality of one's self, of one's own identity, nor the reality of the surrounding world can be established beyond doubt."[12] Levinas creates an ontological ethics based on the face-to-face relation in which being is experienced in relation to the other (in an unequal and infinite responsibility toward the other). In this face-to-face relation, ethics exists prior to being; it conditions being. The priority of being-for-the-other comes before being.[13]

So when Joanna speaks of serving humankind I interpret it as an enactment of presence. Joanna is present, and here and now taking and giving political and artistic space.

You = Joanna

Twisting turning
Now you're burning
"Joanna, sing!"
Tucson is waiting.

Joanna, when we meet in Tucson to shoot *Joanna In The Desert* I am there to participate in presence—not yours, not mine, but the artistic one that comes so easily to you as a performer, and to me as an artist. This is ours together.

DAY ONE, JULY 15, 2005
Noon, Pink Fairy Palace.

Joanna and I lunch by the pool. I'm just getting warmed up, so I shoot portraits of her as we speak. As I upload them now I remember our conversation . . . and many other conversations we have over the next four days.

3:00 PM

We drive out to the saguaros. I experience them for the second time in my life as magnificently present—a gift of our land and yet otherworldly. Joanna greets them again, reflecting their postures in her own, having fallen in love with them many years ago.

Joanna, in khakis, a loose white man's shirt, and a big floppy hat, stands on a ledge, and in the valley below, there are saguaros—miles and miles of them. Looking down into that valley I recognize the sublime—it hits me with recognition—and it makes me jump inside. This landscape courts immediacy. It's filled with an aging and vulnerable species of creature that stands and slowly grows for an eternity—the saguaros.

Saguaro buds begin to appear in mid-April around the top of the main trunk and arms. The buds open into large white flowers from late April through early June. Each flower opens in the middle of the night and closes the following day. Saguaro flowers are pollinated by nectar-feeding bats, birds, and insects. After a saguaro flower has been pollinated, it begins its transformation into a fruit. Near the end of the ripening period, the bright red fruits begin to split open. Saguaros first flower around age fifty.[14]

> Desert Sex
>
> . . .
>
> The desert says one woman is overripe
> In the Summer
> When the succulents flower
> And their bodies croon and flame with color
> The fruits of the prickly pear she says
> Look like cunts
> Oranges pomegranates
> Fall for you
> To pick up
> Skin parted pulp displayed juices
> Sticky on your hands
>
> . . .
>
> Saguaros raise their arms as clichés turn to love
> And point to the nooks
> Where drivers drunk on desert sex have parked their cars
> (A Few Erotic Faculties, in this volume, 128–29; hereafter cited as FEF)

We shoot until we cannot stand the sun any longer. The desert is not kind to humans. We burn and dehydrate quickly here. We drive down into the valley of the saguaros. You look for a turn-off from the road that you always miss, that you have tried to find with your friend Peggy many times, that you are now trying to find with me, but we are having the same problems that you had when with Peggy. It is because the land is so enchanting. It is here that we talk for the first time about the light and how gentle it is despite the harshness of the environment. I tell you about photons—particles of light that penetrate your skin and move into mine, then back again. I tell you that I am fascinated with quantum physics and that if I had it to do over again I would be a physicist instead of an artist—this is where it's happening now, I say, not in art, which has become drearily repetitive, but in physics, where the physical is slamming right into the metaphysical. You are fascinated with the idea of photons and together we name the light in Tucson—that feels more than light, that has its own presence mingling with ours—"photonic air." We click. We have named our departure point and now the collaboration can begin.

(Actually it had already begun. Our first photographs—those impromptu ones taken on the cliff overlooking the saguaros—turned out well. I just didn't know this yet.)

As an artist I am interested in being inside of this "photonic" energy, in seeing what is manifest in that experience. It is why being present at Joanna's performances inspired me to write about them. And in my studio, to deal with my mother's illness and death, I am making marks that last the duration of one breath. Putting these marks side by side results in large graphite drawings that are really meditations about counting breaths, about holding a pencil for the first time and writing one's name, practicing penmanship, being a motherless child, forming oneself—feeling one's presence, being. They are about the first drawing I made with a safety pin on the freshly painted walls of my bedroom while I was supposed to be napping. I was three. I reminisce about this because I remember my first experience of being. I remember it clearly and now it is coming back to me in the desert. This makes sense to me. I am here with the lady of presence herself and I understand instantly her being drawn to the desert. It is present.

So, having written about performance, I am now going to attempt to photograph it, and I have a few things going for me: a collaboration with Joanna, the actress (fiery fairy presence complete with red lips and costumes); the photonic air of Tucson; the gaiety of the Pink Fairy Palace; and the majesty of the saguaros. (Of course, the saguaros may work against me. They have been photographed so many times before. As I'm walking out the door to leave for Tucson, Charles, my husband, says to me, "Focus on your subject, not the saguaros. If you want photos of the saguaros just go to *National Geographic*." It is good advice. I'm not here to take them on.)

We return from the saguaros as the light is fading and a storm is rolling in. I am with the woman of words in the car—and we have no words. The distance, always deceptive in the desert, gleams at us in wildly colored brake lights. Were they always that wild? During the day, passing cars do not even enter my consciousness out here. But at night the headlights form a stupidly human trajectory that ignorantly cuts through the landscape. It is obvious that we humans do not belong in this strange beauty except to worship it as other. This desert belongs to the planet. Not to us.

We have a delightful dinner on a terrace within the Pink Fairy Palace. You announce that you are going to have steak—that you need red meat—you enjoy it immensely. Blood red. I get to see another part of your voracious appetite for life, body, presence, food. We laugh . . . we know we have good collaborative energy.

We are the only ones on the terrace. Everyone else is in the restaurant on the other side of sliding glass doors listening to a pianist play piano bar–type songs. Another evening we will go into the restaurant and you will request that he play "Some Enchanted Evening." You will stand by the grand piano and listen. Like a movie star. I wonder, did you remember your mother playing the piano then? She was a performing musician. Your sister is also a performing musician. You are a singer, a punk rock star, a swooner in the desert. A family of performers.

DAY TWO, JULY 16, 2005

7:00 AM

We meet at dawn for our first shoot at the Pink Fairy Palace. I get lost in the Fairy Palace passageways on my way to your room.

I get lost every time I go to your room. It's because of this peculiar discombobulation that we decide to shoot photos in the pink adobe passages.

We begin at the fairy fountain, a circular white marble fountain located where several paths converge. It's an ornament placed in the center of green grass with flower beds on the periphery. It's awkward and you are a bit tense. Me too. Together we make some stiff snapshots. Real failures. Your poses don't work and neither does my framing, but we establish a great director/ actor relationship, relax, and begin to move. This will not be the pattern for the rest of the shoot. When we relocate to a thicket in the garden and you drape yourself in a long, mushroom-brown velvet cloak, it's the lingering poses that work.

Our language finds a shorthand. Both art historians, we are able simply to name a painting, photograph, sculpture and you assume the pose, or the feeling, or the sentiment. You are not afraid of sentiment. I had always been afraid of it, but now I'm indulging myself in your love of it. In fact I court it.

Lingering in your cloak in the close gardens with flowers in the trees and white metal benches with flowered ironwork, you become the Rossetti woman, and Adele H.—of the nineteenth century—and I resign myself to making photos that will either be intolerably kitsch, or not. To give myself a better chance of succeeding, I shoot in both color and black and white.

> In Joanna's velvet cloak
> Joanna strokes herself
> "Joanna, burn!"
> Sade is yearning.

We lunch by the pool, then retire to our rooms for a siesta. I cannot sleep, even though I'm tired. I want to see the photos we've already shot. Are they hot? Fucking hot? Or not?

4:00 PM

Look at the photos! More than not, they work. They're hot. We're hot.

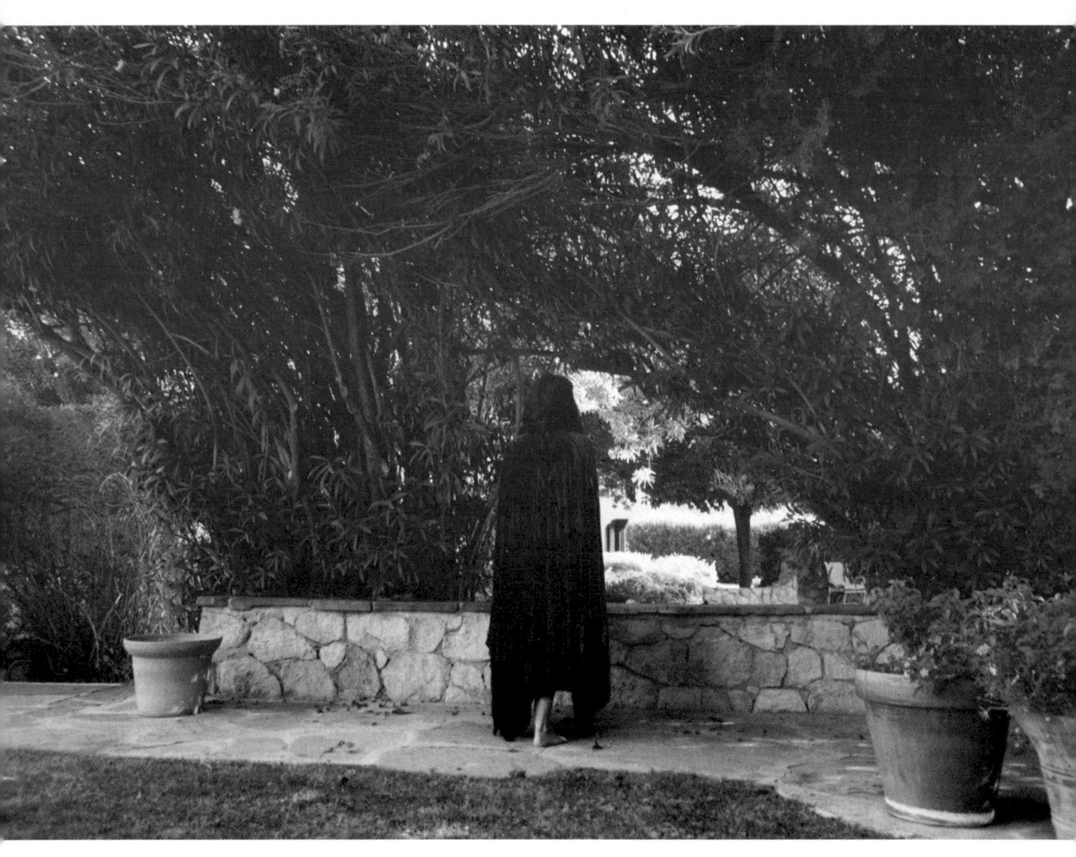

Jill O'Bryan and Joanna Frueh, *mistress of plants.*

From the series *Joanna in the Desert*, 2006.

We go to one of your old Tucson abodes, near the corner of Third Avenue and Fifth Street. While we're chronicling your past in Tucson you become child-like. I photograph you in front of your old house from several angles, but really, the truest is the snapshot taken first. These types of moments are best left as "family moments": the child in her Easter bonnet in front of the new house taking one impatient second out of her play to pose; the woman in her sun bonnet in front of her old house posing as play. These are snapshot moments, historical chronicles of posing.

We move on to a favorite bar, the Shanty, where you used to hang out. Another snapshot in your sun bonnet.

At How Sweet It Was we shop for costumes. We begin with a skirt hanging on a mannequin outside the door, and move immediately to the white vintage dresses hanging just inside the door. We each pick out a dress, then move on to the smoking jackets, the bathrobes, the crazy white bridal dresses, the hats, the bed jackets. You try things on, and I am reminded of Peggy's essay about shopping with you—"Shameless Pleasure"—in the catalogue for your recent retrospective exhibition. Here we are at the same store (located several blocks from its earlier location) re-enacting Peggy's memories, the shameless pleasure in which she witnesses you. We play . . . you play. I pick out costumes, you try them on, I shoot. You buy a pink satin bed jacket.

> Thinking pinking we are stinking
> With substances from our pink linking
> With Eros and with Aphrodite
> We are rooted we are flighty
> In the very best of ways
> Flying happy flying gay
> Flying in our pink array (*PP*, 325)

You also buy a full-length white muslin slip dress with lace and tiny buttons down the front. It resembles the undergarment that Katharine Ross is wearing when Robert Redford comes in to seduce her in *Butch Cassidy and the Sundance Kid*. You also buy a white satin bathrobe that resembles a formal fitted

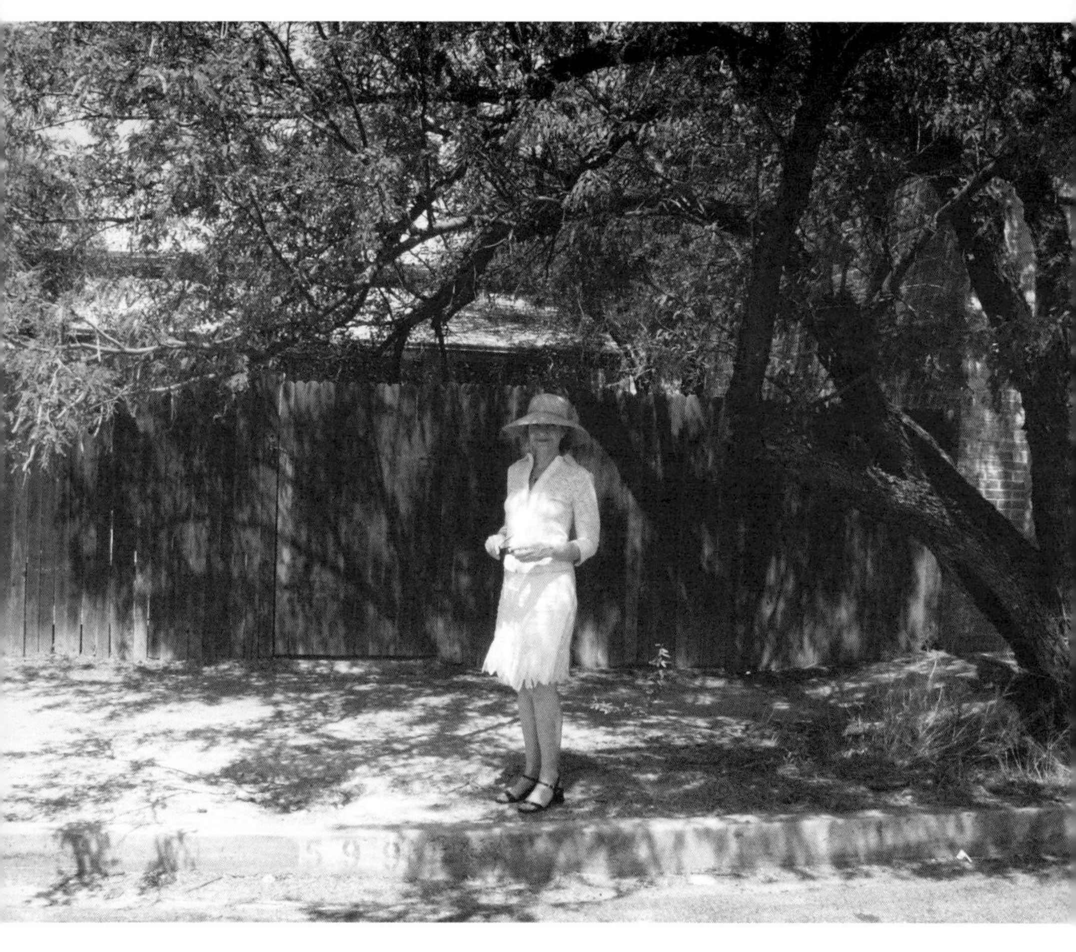

Jill O'Bryan and Joanna Frueh, Joanna in front of her first Tucson home, 2006.

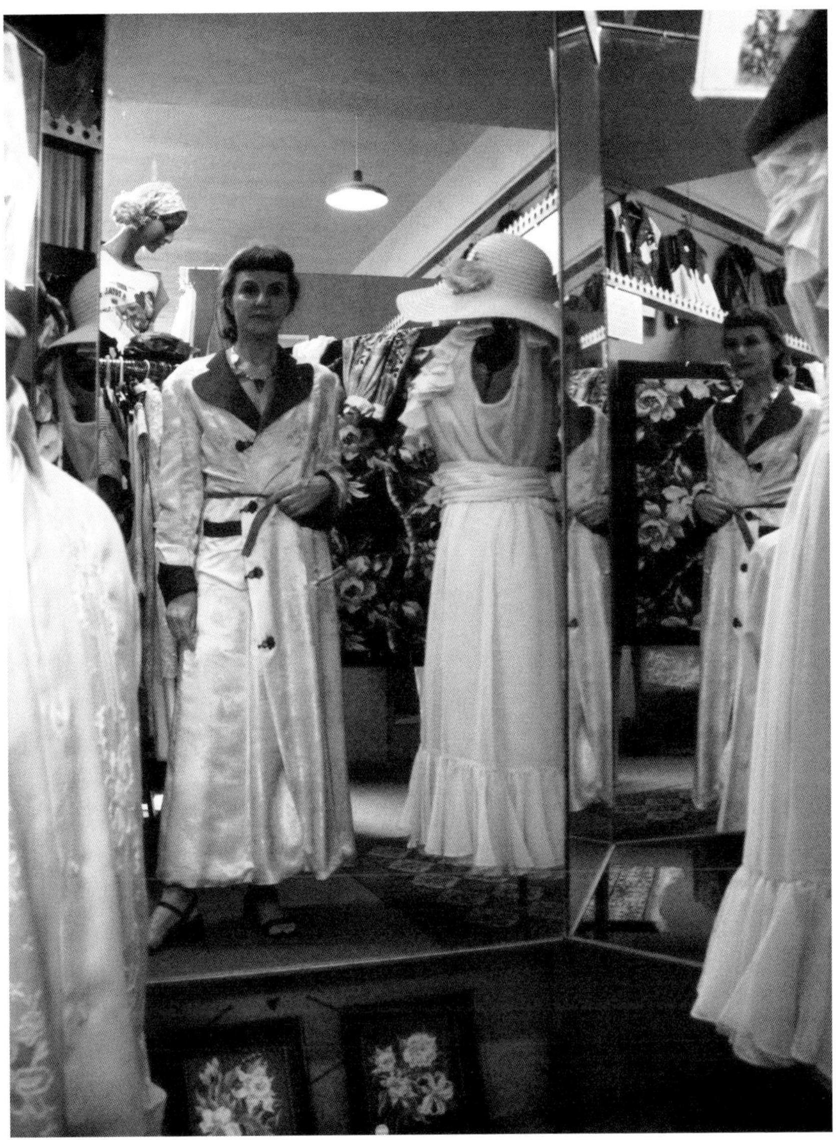

Jill O'Bryan and Joanna Frueh, Joanna shopping for vintage clothing in Tucson, 2006.

coat or gown. It has a royal purple satin lining that extends itself out as the collar, and purple satin buttons down the front. I buy a mauve smoking jacket. You don't buy the white, bridal-veil-like full-length skirt that reveals your bareness underneath, so of course I become obsessed with this garment—the only one you don't buy. I envision you wedding the saguaros and convince you that you should do so. Just before we head out to the desert that afternoon, you buy it. For me. For you. In it you become bride of the desert.

ORACULAR EROS

The Pythias were the oracles at Delphi, the brides of Apollo. Joanna is a Pythia. She worships the desert sun god and speaks for him. In her performance *Pythia*, Joanna wears a long skirt, this time deep red-brown velvet, with bare feet and a gold-beaded and sequined shawl that reveals her breasts.

Eros is the son of Aphrodite and Ares. He is the god of love, also known as Cupid. Joanna, you surround yourself with god-men. Are you happy?

Each Pythia at Delphi was divine, made of words that carried powerful erotic energy and that laid down the law. There is a debate as to whether Pythia spoke in coherent words or ululated fantastic hallucinations that were then interpreted and reiterated by the priests of Apollo. But Joanna as Pythia is a singer and a poet. She speaks of grace, melody, and Eros:

Ascetic thinking separates people from one another, as the law does, too, in contrast to love. Erotic thinking, which is dependent melody, alleviates the loneliness of words. Melodies are dragon lines, moving to center after center of meaning. The law of light and of risen and rising angels restricts what any of us can say. What we cannot say we can sing about. So song enhances living as grace notes enhance melody. Do not misunderstand enhancement as ornamentation, the way dictionaries misrepresent the grace note as embellishment. Enhancement is necessary, for it heightens awareness. (*Pythia*, 238)

The poet-performer is at her most powerful in *Pythia*. With a gavel, she pronounces the law that is as brutal and erotic as it is graceful and melodic. Once again, "gold flows from the graceful tongue, and silence is golden, too. Maybe you do not hear my words, for speech is the most easily misinterpreted of human behaviors" (232). Yes. It is. And since the first words spoken— "And the word was God"—we have struggled to be present, to utter the words that expose who we are: to project our "I" in the name of being and presence. The command "Know thyself" was carved on the temple at Delphi and later advocated by Socrates. And you, Joanna, say:

> The Word
> A woman at the window whispers to me
> As we leave
> The Word is Flesh (*FEF*, 135)

Performing *Dressing Aphrodite* Joanna, as usual, is the word as flesh. She wears a clingy, full-length ecru dress. *Dressing Aphrodite* is a critique of the pressure placed on women to force themselves into the molds of beauty held out to us, the current ideal we all know already. It is tall, skinny, and white. But Joanna steps into Aphrodite's shoes, and from there she proposes monster/beauty:[15]

> Ecru and whiter white cloth are always dirty. White is the sign of visible and potential dirt. Dirty as the ground, as sweat, as excrement, and the making of love. Dirtiness is one of monster/beauty's attractions. Because she perverts, subverts, and diverts the purity of white, wearing white for monster/beauty is a partially perverse strategy.

> Dressed or undressed, Aphrodite is always a nude.
> For the Greeks, nudity displayed liberty and power. Aphrodite's nudity manifested her divine authority and her authority in the arts of love. Nudity, the beautiful dress of skin and flesh, is aesthetic/erotic technology, and as such it provides human beings with the pleasure needed for vitality of the soul. Nudity suggests possibilities, potentials; we need not read it as a goad to be a particular body type. (Remember: the Knidia's successors varied from full to slim.) (*Dressing Aphrodite*, in this volume, 268)

Joanna, you are nude in the desert surrounded by saguaros, sand, insects, dirt. Put on the full-length muslin slip with buttons down the front. We have brought your colors to the desert: fresh white lilies to put in your hair, a white lace cloth for you to sit on, bright red high heels to pump you up, white pearls for your throat—they set off your bright red lipstick—a pink satin bed jacket, and the white wedding-veil skirt. You're barefoot. You meditate in muslin, in a cross-legged yogic pose. Then you strip.

As Pythia you pronounce to the men who come to seek your counsel: "Listen. Nobody likes you. Not even the one you call wife. You come to me for counsel, climb the mountain, slow, breathless, dazed by exertion. Were your feet bare like mine, they would be bleeding. Me, I wear my blood on my mouth. True red. It is not a simple color" (*Pythia*, 225). No. It is not. And you are clever enough to have created a work called *Mouth Piece* in which you tell us all about it. Your voice teacher dresses you in gowns to sing, and later he is murdered—stabbed to death by a disgruntled lover. Your voice teaches you to color your mouth bright red. Your words teach you to face your fears head on and to devour them, and they teach you how to speak.

"Joanna, put on your fire-engine-red high heels."

Nude except for the heels, you walk to a more perfect spot among the cactus. They tear at me, but I protect you. I shoot you from below. I am expecting the vulnerability of the nude within the cacti to grab me. We work at this together—getting grabbed by nudity . . .

You put on your pearls, the white bridal-veil skirt, and the red high heels. "Take the lilies . . . turn around . . . lean down . . . throw away the lilies . . . pick up the lilies . . . put on the pink bed jacket . . . take it off . . . lean forward, backward, sideways. Turn your back to me. Face me." As the sun moves, the light changes from exotic pink to purple. It evens out just for a moment—no more harsh shadows. The light is soft, mystical—the physical turning into the metaphysical . . . photonic light (to me), fairy light on you. Breathless. I like working this way. In the frenzy of shooting I have repeatedly backed into cactuses. I pull their needles out of my body for the rest of the time I am in Tucson. Shocked by the desert . . . desert shock.

Breathless. In *Breathing* you and Russell proposed to come closely face to face and breathe. It is the most erotic image that has ever been put into my head. That you wrote it for you and Russell and never performed it makes me sad. Perhaps you did perform it in private?

8:30 PM

Back at the Pink Fairy Palace we have a late dinner on the same terrace, the one that's adjacent to the piano man behind the sliding glass doors. We skillfully plan our next day. You will be the movie star at the pool, the Maxfield Parrish girl on the branches of trees, the Moroccan woman in pink, and the be-pearled woman in the yellow chair. The monsoons have started, so we are worried we'll be rained out. We are not.

DAY THREE, JULY 17, 2005

6:00 AM

When we meet at sunrise we again go to the fairy fountain, this time to shoot you in the pink wedge shoes and the white satin robe with purple satin lining as you walk toward the fairy fountain. With you wearing sunglasses we shoot a series of movements—gestures bred by assuredness, self-love, and inexorable self-confidence—the stuff that makes an actress. The stuff. We're after that star stuff.

7:00 AM

We move to the pool.

Here we have an audience. At the terrace by the pool people begin to arrive for breakfast. Three women watch—a teenager, a fortyish woman, and an elderly woman. Later the fortyish woman tells us how exciting and beautiful we are as we work together. Her teenage daughter leers at us, killing our reception of her mother's exuberance. The older woman looks simply stunned at the fortyish woman's response to us, possibly appalled that she has spoken to us. It is intriguing for me to confront an audience. I am confused by the differing responses. Joanna is not.

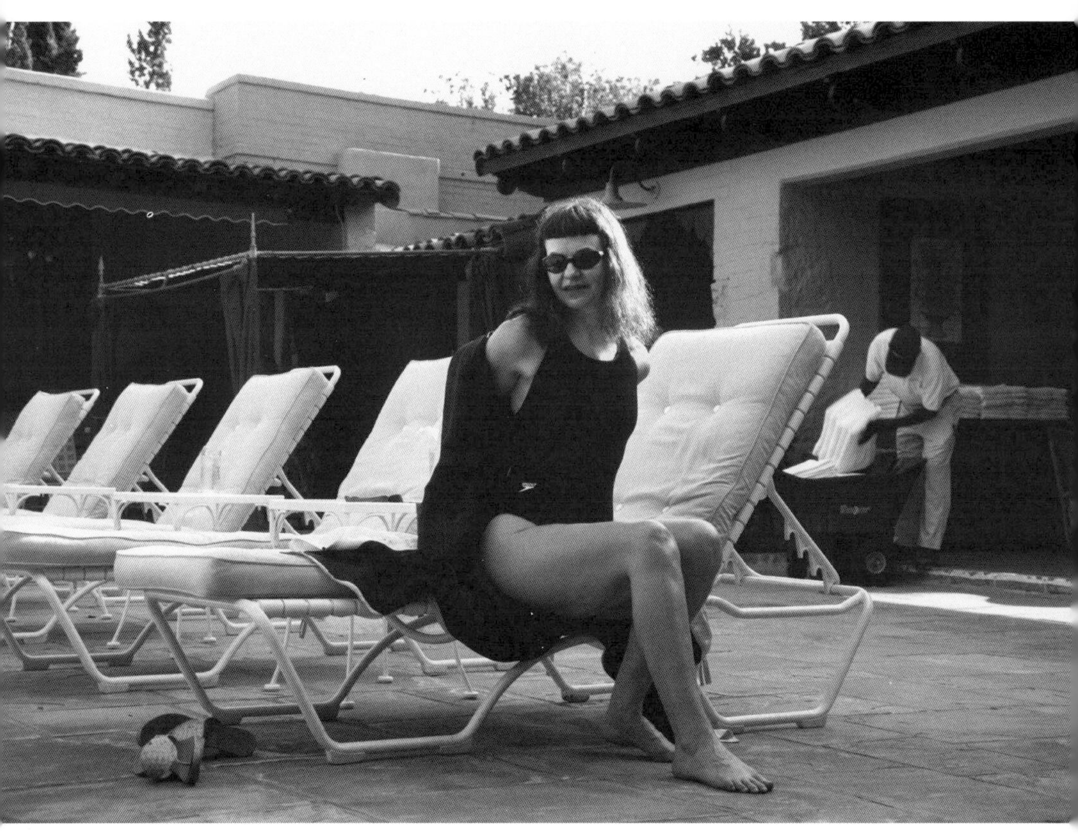

Jill O'Bryan and Joanna Frueh, *always an actress*.

From the series *Joanna in the Desert*, 2006.

At the pool you continue to wear your white satin robe with purple satin lining and, underneath, a black Speedo one-piece (instead of a bikini). Sunglasses and flowers in your hair enhance your starlet image as you lounge on a chaise, drinking ice water with a flower at the rim of the glass. Your Cleopatra bangs clearly enhance the sunglasses and the structure of your face. You swagger to the pool, throw your hips sideways and your shoulders back, and drop your robe onto the pool's edge. You, as body, enter the water slowly so I can shoot. You, as body, move in the water. "Turn left, okay . . . good . . . the light is better there. Don't move so strenuously . . . swagger . . . you feel incredibly sexy and know you are being watched, so show it off. Dance . . . think of the water as a place to move your body like you are dancing. Water makes you look good if you let it . . . doesn't it feel good to have no weight?" (Joanna resists going into the water, but then she does, and loves it. Now she goes into the water all the time when she visits the Pink Fairy Palace and she thanks me for turning her on to it. Mystifying, isn't it? A sexy woman like that not enjoying the water?) Your movements are about slow, swagger, self-love, and performing/acting.

NOON

We lunch by the pool. This is now becoming a favorite activity. It is luxurious.

2:00 PM

We move to my room to shoot the sexed nudes. Sexed: primordial. I think of the way you have written about Sade, Mme Duclos (Sade's muse, dominatrix, torturer), fucking your lovers. In *Sade, My Sweet, My Truffle; or, Giving a Fuck* you speak about being exhilarated by shamelessness, by unshaming the body. You embrace the body's abject actions and fluids. You also embrace the risky business Sade has to offer: "I would love to receive a love letter from Sade. He wrote delicious ones, full of aristocratic lightness, flair, and lies, full of erotic flatteries. Sade, my sweet, here I am right by your side, in your arms, lovingly, subversively in bed with you. I am in your face, up your ass, articulating the means of non-criminal pleasure's support" (*Sade*, in this volume, 285).

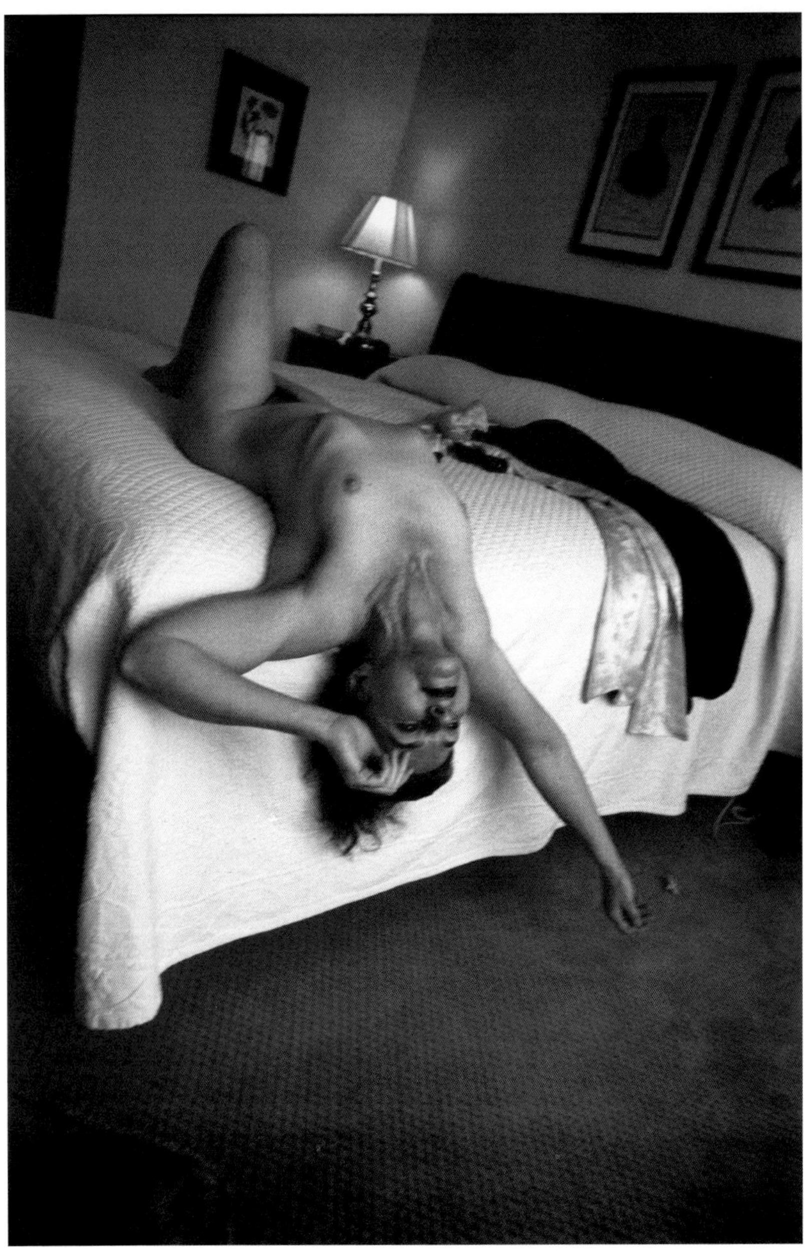

Jill O'Bryan and Joanna Frueh, *midsummer's day swoon.*

From the series *Joanna in the Desert*, 2006.

Goody. "Look like you're being fucked like you've never been fucked before . . . get yourself ready . . . press yourself against the wall . . . look at yourself in the mirror . . . lie on the bed . . . roll off the bed . . . loll on the floor." We discover a soft indoor light that reflects off you, through the mirror, through the camera lens, through the window, the walls, the gardens, the Pink Fairy Palace. This is definitely your place, Joanna.

And pornography?

In *Amazing Grace* you and Russell make word love to each other. It is the type of witty banter enjoyed by poets and their courtesans in the era of chivalry, until the time of the plague. I think of Tullia d'Aragona (c. 1510–1556), who was taught by her mother how to really enjoy men by becoming a courtesan instead of a bride. But you are both.

> Pornographic partners
> Know
> Fuck theory
> The amazing grace
> Of soul-inseparable-from-the-body
> The powers of true love
> The art of pornography comes into being through our willingness
> to take control of powers we may only dream we have.
> Dream with me. (*Amazing Grace*, in this volume, 211)

4:30 PM

We shoot amid a grove we've found. You're tired. It's overcast and you are not keen on this particular shoot. But the grove is unearthly in the late afternoon and early evening light and you are in the white muslin again, leaning on the trees, complaining about the ants. Uh oh, a discontented Parrish woman. "Oh, Joanna, don't be such a prima donna. If you can tiptoe among the saguaros you can certainly hug a few trees!" The sun breaks through the clouds and a glory streams into our shoot. The white muslin becomes whiter than white, so we use some scarves to tone it down. Whiter than white is scary. It can blast out the film, make it too high-contrast and ruin the light in the photo.

White is another of your colors. It is the most difficult to work with. As an artist, sometimes standing in front of a white canvas or a white piece of paper can be a terrifying experience. It can be a moment of either empowerment or disempowerment, and it can switch from one to the other at lightning speed. Empowerment comes when embracing the whiteness and reveling in the filth with which an artist is about to embellish it. You, Joanna, describe this moment in terms of innocence when you say: "Innocence impels self-discovery through satisfaction of desire. Discovery and desire are reciprocal. When we offer to the universe our desire, we receive discovery" (*Ambrosia*, in this volume, 330). White is also the color of racism. White skin, the whiteness of ideal beauty. The white marble of the Knidia. In *Ambrosia* you teach me about whiter than white.

6:30 PM

At the Pink Fairy Palace we shoot you in its cavernous passageways: desert woman in pink. We shoot you in a yellow chair with lush desert gardens behind you: woman with pearls in pink. *The Performance of Pink.* Perhaps too sweet? But the sky is vermilion—on fire—and I think of St. Lucy's words:

> I had a vision of fire, surely a memory, in part, from when the soldiers tortured me. In the vision I walked through flames. At first I did not hurt. My arms were raised, like wings, as if buoyed by wind, and I was twirling. Then I was on fire, too hot, and I ran, streaming flame, into a placid turquoise pool. I became cold, so stepped out and sat between the fire and the water. Evergreens surrounded me, and I thought about red: cherry, poppy, copper, madder, ruby, iron, garnet, bloodstone, and many more. Above all, the veracity of vermilion. (*Vermilion*, in this volume, 178–79)

Vermilion was presented at an exhibition of Bailey Doogan's paintings that she titled *St. Lucy/Oedipus.* During the autumn when she was writing *Vermilion*, Joanna was going through a divorce from Tom. Dire straits: "During the weeks of dire straits I felt like I was quite literally up in the air, my head disconnected from my body" (*Vermilion*, 171). And when you finally get your feet back on the ground . . . that's when life turns sweet. You're not afraid of "sweet." I am, but I'm working on it.

Dinner on the terrace, but before that and in costume you approach the piano man and ask him to play "Some Enchanted Evening." It's too perfect. I am hoping you'll sing but you don't. Still you stand and sway at the pianist's side in your unabashed performer mode. All in the dining room are enchanted by the actress without a voice. The irony is comical to me. If they ever knew!

DAY FOUR, JULY 18, 2005
9:00 AM

We shoot in the morning light: you as the actress among the cactuses, sitting again in the big yellow chair, and walking through the passageways of the Pink Fairy Palace.

NOON

Tanya arrives from Phoenix. We lunch.

2:00 PM

I leave. You stay.

1   Joanna Frueh, *Swooning Beauty: A Memoir of Pleasure* (Reno: University of Nevada Press, 2006), 87; hereafter cited in the text as *SB*.

2   Marsha Meskimmon, *The Art of Reflection: Women Artists' Self-Portraiture in the Twentieth Century* (New York: Columbia University Press, 1996), 1−2.

3   Ibid.

4   Frueh, "Polymorphous Perversities: Female Pleasures and the Postmenopausal Artist," in *Erotic Faculties* (Berkeley: University of California Press, 1996), 102−3.

5   Frueh, "Rhetoric as Canon," in *Erotic Faculties*, 163.

6   For the photograph *Venus Verticordia 2004*, see the front cover of *Joanna Frueh: A Retrospective*, ed. Tanya Augsburg (Reno: Nevada Museum of Art, 2005), the exhibition catalogue for *Joanna Frueh: A Retrospective* at the Sheppard Fine Arts Gallery, University of Nevada, Reno. See the back cover of this catalogue for Joanna's "On Love's Sweet Track," her redoing of Rossetti's sonnet.

7   Dante Gabriel Rossetti, "Jenny," in Dante Gabriel Rossetti, *Poems: A New Edition* (London: Ellis & White, 1881), 127. Available online at http://www.rossettiarchive.org.

8   Alphonso Lingis, *Dangerous Emotions* (Berkeley: University of California Press, 2000), 148.

9   Charles Baudelaire, "Jewels," in *The Flowers of Evil*, trans. James McGowan (Oxford: Oxford University Press, 1998), 47.

10   Norman O. Brown, *Love's Body* (New York: Vintage, 1966), 266.

11   Hayden White in *In Memoriam: Norman O. Brown*, ed. Jerome Neu (Santa Cruz, Calif.: New Pacific Press, 2005), 79.

12   Hannah Arendt, *The Human Condition* (Chicago: University of Chicago Press, 1998; first published 1958), 208.

13   Emmanuel Levinas, *Totality and Infinity: An Essay on Exteriority*, trans. Alphonso Lingis (Pittsburgh, Pa.: Duquesne University Press, 1969), 195.

14   Information about saguaros is taken from Susan Hazen-Hammond, "A Giant Shrugs Off Vandalism, Poaching, Tales of its Demise," *Smithsonian* (January 1996), 76−84.

15   Joanna Frueh, *Monster/Beauty: Building the Body of Love* (Berkeley: University of California Press, 2001) begins her definition of *monster/beauty*, which she theorizes throughout the book, calling it "an extremely articulated sensuous presence, image, of situation in which the aesthetic and the erotic are inseparable" (11).

JOANNA FRUEH'S WRITING

Having sprayed the space with Balenciaga's Quadrille, one of her two signature scents, Frueh awaits the audience's arrival. Dressed in two shades of mauve—a long-sleeved silk blouse tucked into a mid-calf wool crepe skirt—and taupe leather pumps with a subtly squared toe and a heel no more than three inches tall, she now and then fondles the coral-red gladiolus pinned into her hair above one ear. The visual effect is of contrast, even disjuncture: understated city wear and the dazzling brilliance that only nature can provide. The overall effect is sensual and minimalist.

Every day she walked to dinner at dusk. As the mariachi band played "Canta Canta Pajarito" and tiny crabs scuttled away from her feet as she walked across the cooling sand, she tried to perceive the exact advent of night. The rhythm of the waves filled her ears, alternating with the distant tinkling of glasses raised in drunken toasts. Her muslin dress, white like the moon and full with the wind, blew above her knees, and the trees on the islet in the bay, mauve under pink clouds, began to disappear, as if felled by puffs of wind. The fragrance of hibiscus blew toward her along with that of sizzling meats and strong coffee. She was hungry, the daylight had disappeared, and, as always, she had missed the moment of darkness.

In the city she rarely planned acute observations of nature. She sat at her desk and turned on the light when she could no longer read the words she was writing. Sometimes, alone in the apartment at night, she switched off all the lamps, stood by a window with her hands on the glass, and tried to see the stars. In summer the leaves looked amber beneath the streetlamps' garish light. If a murder were to occur, the knife would glisten red before even entering a victim's body.

But here near a beach on the west coast of Mexico, sunup and sundown were unaccompanied by electric light. She inhaled so slowly and deeply that she felt the air pass into her pelvis. She thought of the stranger she slept with and heard him calling, "Giovanna! Giovanna!" in imitation of the lonely Italian who also desired her company at this isolated resort. "Call me Lorenzaccio," the Italian said to the women he nagged and ogled, for he saw himself as a mischievous Medici, a sly and stately fellow whose body, covered only by daringly scant pink trunks, would appear, like the vision of a savior, in the minds of the sun cream–slathered women who lay, with their eyes closed, along the palm-edged sand from mid-morning to late afternoon. If he had allowed himself even an inkling of his unromantic presence, the pudgy belly, the sad though flinty eyes that tried to twinkle, he would have wished himself sealed in a marble coffin, one fashioned by a gifted artisan and secluded in a quattrocento church.

Neither ignorant, foolish, nor pretentious, this would-be scamp never considered the burden he carried in idolizing himself through his own romanticizing of the past. If some women wanted to be Botticelli sylphs, flaxen hair flowing in a Cyprian breeze, shell-like skin enveloping slight frames, modesty belied by beauty too abundant, too vulnerable, he wished himself the face and figure of a Piero Christ.

"Giovanna! Giovanna!" She too had worshipped the same aesthetic incarnation of divinity, but her love had more to do with a desire for possession than with an envious, though adulatory, need to identify. For almost an hour she had stood before *The Resurrection of Christ*. "He holds His banner and stares at me as if I were His beloved. But I am no Magdalene, no Christian penitent. Passers-by linger to look at my loving eyes without noticing His. They glance at His pale rose robe that droops so comfortably, yet provocatively, over a sturdy knee and shoulder, below a slender waist and deep navel. They sleep like the soldiers at His tomb, unaware of His more than spiritual charms." She could not keep her distance, nor did she want to. A bird fluttering among the trees' thin branches; a hill climber resting near a clump of bushes; a horsewoman reining her mount at the horizon; a believer watching from the ramparts; an insect crawling along an armored biceps; a lover caressing a bearded cheek or massaging the muscular torso: she was them all, and as part of the picture she later knew that instead of losing her art historian's integrity, she had extravagantly extended her ability to see.

Piero had painted a human being, minimizing the wounds, making the hair as rich as the halo. Once she had read that Piero stripped his figures of emotion. If she had believed that, she might just as well have considered herself mad. Artists, she believed, did not paint in order to retard a viewer's curiosity about sensation. Painters offered pathways not only into their works but also into self-reflective territory. Did she want to feel the painted man's flesh or had Piero, alive in Christ, forever resurrected in Him, the quiet countryside, and the spiritually unawakened Romans, permitted her to feel his fundamental attunement?

"Giovanna!" She sequestered herself in the night but called back, "Come and get me. I'm so hungry. Come and get me, John, and take me to dinner. Find me through my voice." She started to sol-fa the song played by the band but began to laugh. John's body, like that of Piero's deity, did not in and of itself arouse her. The tender maleness of a lean anatomy and smooth skin did. "Come faster," she cried, "and kiss me."

She awoke alone the next morning. John had already gone scuba diving, but the remembrance of her dream kept her in bed. Actually she couldn't reconstruct it, but since she had left the city, every night, all of sound sleep, brought images of calm seas, lush jungles, singing parrots and cockatoos, unfamiliar flowers in variant primary colors, and sunny days never dimmed by the doubts—bred by the stench of exhaust fumes and alley garbage, multiple murders on the late-night news, antiquated social commonplaces like wolf whistles, expectorating workmen on subway platforms, and the flirtatious public primping of hopeful pubescent virgins—generated daily in urban outings.

The trouble this morning was that she could not forget the city. Or perhaps it could not forget her. Having lived there for ten years, she could not make a complete escape, for like a betrayed and relentless lover it pursued her into the paradise to which, in contrast, it was hell. The city wanted no rivals, and as it maintained the fodder for her work, she could not disregard its insistent intrusions.

Some might think that belonging, as she did, to the peerage of a provincial art capital would have many privileges: invitations to swank receptions; recognition in galleries where the hoi polloi were met with disdain; introductions to the supposedly glamorous instigators of the latest breathless brouhaha. However, like a fairytale maid in a tower, she remained chaste. As a writer about the art that moved her she could only be truly beguiled by the subject itself, and still she guarded her virginity as though dragons were always at her door.

"You always were an idealist, a purist," said a former friend, unseen for almost ten years, who called unexpectedly the day before she left for Mexico. "I'm being chided," she thought, miffed. But the next afternoon, flying south, she realized that idealism and naïveté did not have to be mates.

Sometimes, when walking toward a row of galleries, she imagined that she'd see in one of them a wall, a painting, a sculpture, a material whose substance suggested puréed gold. She never saw it, but she never expected to, for that anticipated reality was a desire, not a need. What a disappointment it would have been for that fantasy to vanish, which it would have if that golden room or remnant of someone's imagination had actually awaited her. Although she sometimes strained for pleasures that no mental picture could provide, her devotion to fantasy did not wane. "Once you go to bed with someone you've desired for weeks or months," she thought as she rang the bell to an artist's studio, "the urgency and languor of the longing die. Passion for art, like passion for a human being, produces periodic renewals of lust, but fantasy, so clean because of its utter privacy, continually purges one of emotional cynicism."

She sat with the painter and talked, studying his paintings, then his face. He was afraid. His closest friends and colleagues did not like this new work. Surely he was a failure. He had lost his touch and at the age of twenty-seven was facing the future as a has-been.

She was not ashamed for him because of his insecurity. It drew him to her heart, and even though his paintings looked less attractive, less fervid and startling than before, they possessed a singular, slow beauty; they showed his newfound capacity to weep. The gay colors were gone, replaced by sandy, stormy, murky ones; lagoon and wasteland colors nuanced with soft applications of pigment and occasional fluttery strokes that looked like small bands of one-winged birds. She saw him as a lame animal and held back tears. "I am a cripple too, so I cry for us," she resisted saying. "All of us human animals bruised by each other."

He, like the others, bared himself to her. Divorces, abortions, illegitimate pregnancies;

suicidal mothers, alcoholic fathers, philandering mates; financial burdens, pressing professional jealousies, the sacrifices of security made in the name of Art: all these unasked-for stories, from detailed accounts of affairs with members of the same and opposite sex to angry confessions about lack of time, sales, and love, she remembered long after the telling and kept to herself. She did not want her life publicly dismembered and assumed that neither did these touching raconteurs. Scars and liberations demanded the continuation of the privacy in which they had been conceived.

She questioned herself about the artists the same way she questioned herself about their art. How fragile was the ego? How strong the soul? How soon did she want to see them again? Was the memory enough?

The longing that drives Frueh's words and her speaking of them increases.

"The last stop today," she sighed to herself as she buzzed for entry to the studio of an artist she had never met. Her heart always beat hard before such meetings, and as she smelled her wrist, lavished with her favorite perfume, peppery, reminiscent of the spicy flowers and sweet silvery weeds she dreamed were in a fox's lair, a musky woman answered the door. Seven stories up they sat, teacups resting on their knees, looking as carefully at each other as they did at a wall of drawings. They were portraits, real and imagined, and hers was there. The two women stared at one another. They could not even ask what was happening.

The eyes of each portrait gazed from a flowered paradise where wind had damaged forests to deserts or water had rushed down mountain peaks to cover their life-infested feet. Garnet, crimson, carmine, rose: sometimes there seemed to be pools of blood curdling beneath the hot sun of this gifted woman's skies.

Their hearts beat harder as they tried to keep themselves from crying. "Rivers and oceans, heavens and stars." The words repeated in her mind so many times she could not count them. "Fish and crocodiles, mudpacks from the Nile for my face. My face. It looks at me from one of these drawings. Some memory . . . some memory of mine . . . must have forecast today." Her perfume suddenly reminded her of the scents escaping from an

If I drink myself to death.
I tell you, I don't act too real,
'Cause you're always giving me a raw deal.

Don't forget that I exist.
Don't opt for oblivion.
Or someday it's you who'll slit your wrists.
No one's having fun.
You're not the only one.

See me now, the sad dolly:
Faded lips and uncombed hair.
You, who never know your folly,
You, who always say you're fair.
Your heart needs harder wear.

So I dare you . . .

*The tempo increases and the attitude, though not
the sound of Frueh's voice, turns harsh.*

Jump off a cliff, waste no time,
Fall in a cesspool, swim in the slime.
Find your way to a health retreat.
Tell them there that you're really beat.
Test their feelings, hear them laugh,
You'll leave with a heart that's ripped in half—
Shreds of muscle, drops of blood.
They'll send you back into the mud.
That's what you get for being smug—
No friendly kiss, no tender hug.
I know you're dying just like me.
I'd like to smirk, but I'd rather be free.

Here we stand on heroin corner,
Streetlamps shine, the city glares.
I'm waiting for our eyes to meet,
But I'm crying because no one cares
If I moan or sigh or eat a meal,
If I drink myself to death.
I tell you, I don't act too real,
'Cause you're always giving me a raw deal.

Her name was Brumas, and she resembled a vampire. Lipstick seemed to melt from her mouth when she sang, so she joked with her band about the victims that she had to drain each night in order to energize a performance. Or else she just said, deadpan, "Too much cherry juice."

She powdered her face pale and circled her eyes with white shadow. When the roots of her blue-black hair appeared, she religiously dyed them dark again so that no one would know the true color. Her gowns, in which she became a dervish Salome before a multitude of Herods when she whirled and grinded onstage, were dark plum and raisin. Designed by a woman Brumas wooed once a week with her deep voice, they looked like dense webs. "My body must shine through the fabric," the singer regularly reminded her fan.

"Yes," the designer then said to herself, "I am a needy recruit for your desires."

One night, as always, Brumas challenged her audience to touch her. She ran her fingers through her hair, licked her shoulder, and drew the microphone slowly up her bare leg, raising her long skirt to mid-thigh. Sometimes she moved her hands over her body's contours, and when she felt the crowd's fantasies mingling near her, too close for her to acknowledge complicity in their creation, she kissed her lead guitarist on the mouth. If she was in a good mood, Brumas would rattle off teasing verses composed on the spot, such as

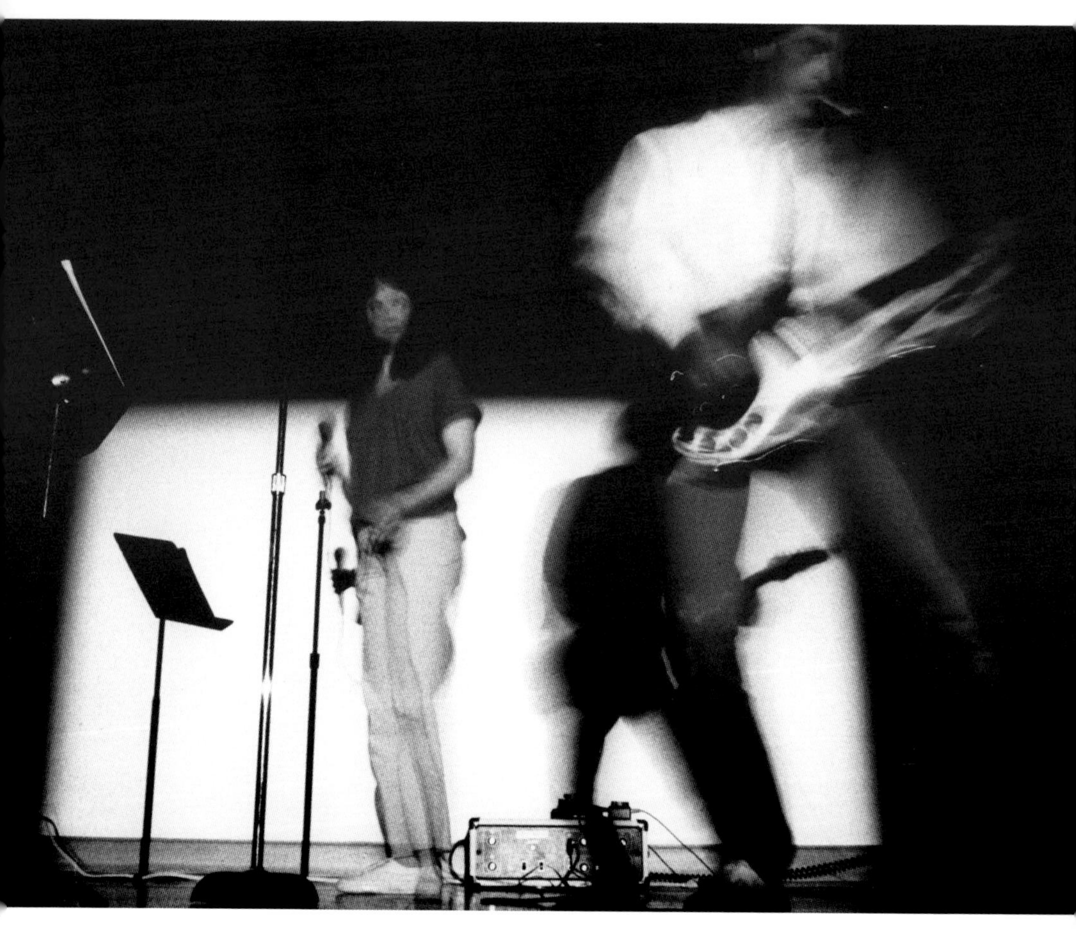

BRUMAS, publicity photos, 1982. Shot during rehearsal. Joanna Frueh and Thomas Kochheiser are not in costume. *Photos courtesy of Pat and John Glascock.*

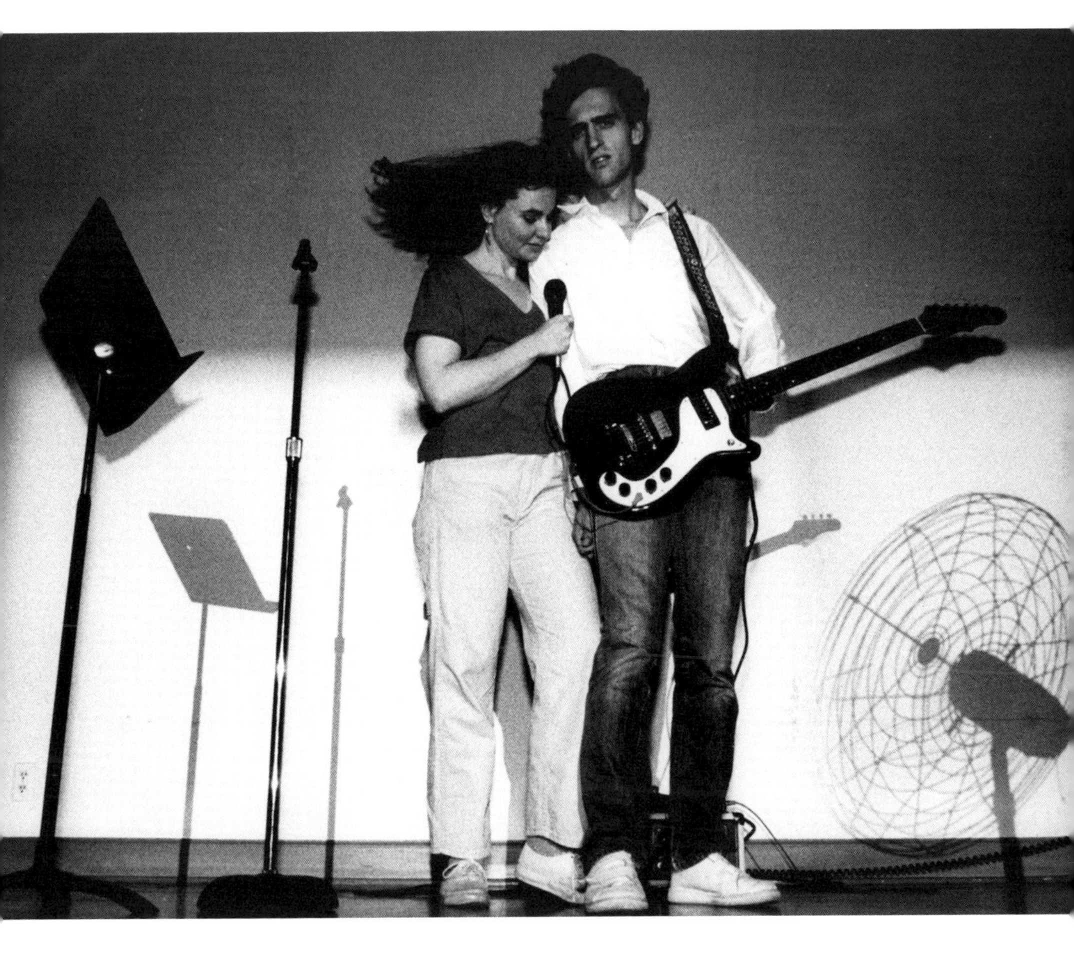

> I've got a flair for men,
>
> And I've got December eyes.
>
> If you want me, you'll dare
>
> To let your body be wise.

When she felt mean she wanted to call the wolves to mass. Her voice grew cold. "Maybe I can charm the earth to ice," she once thought as she sprang toward the microphone and howled, herself like a wolf running from a forest fire:

> I am a fright.
>
> I am a sprite.
>
> I am a plumber of disaster.

Indulging in either disposition, Brumas became ecstatic, jumping and stomping till she imagined that her thighs were bulging and she could stalk a grizzly on its own terms.

Brumas was raging from mood to mood. She swore between numbers, trying to antagonize the crowd. She wished that their faces would turn as white as hers, that they would roar at her till their throats felt raw. She and her admirers could become hoarse and hostile together. They would call her "bitch" and "whore," and she would sacrifice her voice and breath to their abuse. She would never have to perform again if just one audience would rise to her rage.

No one turned against her. Rather, she felt that the women were with her. They shared her movements and sweated under the soft cloth sticking to her naked skin. They gripped her wrists to lead her towards the edge of the stage, and she relaxed into a tune about a fugitive from a starving land.

Tonight the final applause touched her deeply. She said no "thank-yous" because she was afraid that her voice would crack. The thousands of hands clapping sounded like a hum, and she did not sense the agitated bodies that had prayed to her as she sang. She believed that a myriad of fingers was tugging at her viscera, that she grew a harp inside her taller than the mountainside she owned near the shore of an ocean she rarely saw, that the melody played was too sweet for tears, just right for tortured screams.

Just as her music entered the organs of her listeners, so their devotion controlled her guts. She no longer remembered when she had convinced herself that she had no soul.

From then on, however, Brumas supposed that she was driven by physiological phenomena. She also thought that radio waves from planets in dead solar systems, which she
imagined zooming through her brain and pelvis, connected her to beings whose minds
were more similar to hers than were those of the women, men, and even the animals of
Earth.

I am an alien,
A race apart.
We have no soul,
We have no heart.
We breathe no air,
We eat no food,
We feed each other's evil mood.
I am an alien.

Brumas sang one encore, and her voice did not waver, but the applause sent her running
to the dressing room. No one waited for her there: to hug her or take her out for a late
dinner or tell her how exciting she had been. Brumas did not care tonight. Intimacy
demanded agony, sexual partners were always mismatches, and many had resented
Brumas's snarling commands to please her as well as her lengthy orgasms, during which
she seemed unconcerned that anyone else wanted attention. After a recent encounter
she had been told, "You need a machine, not a man." Brumas had replied, "If you were a
man, then I would be the woman you thought I was before we had sex."

Brumas undressed and was surprised that she sighed as she sat down on a velvet couch
the color of her skin and crossed her legs. Someone knocked at the door. "I told you not
to check up on me and not to bring anyone here," she yelled, assuming that one of the
band stood outside. Her lead guitarist said, "Brumas, there's a kid here to see you, and he
won't go away. Says he's a poet. Wants to give you something he wrote for you."

"Nuts," she said under her breath.

"Hey, bitch, you there?" her onetime bedmate asked. He had been young enough to love, but too much of a lamb to fuel her furies. He was capable of caring, so she let him protect and tease her.

"I'm here." She drew out the words.

"So, can he come in?"

"Yes, I'm here," was the irritated reply.

Before the door opened, she posed like an Ingres odalisque. The guitarist winked at Brumas and left, and her admirer's face turned red.

"Well?" she demanded, wanting his complexion to become the color of her lips. She had no intention to offer herself to him. Rather, she wished to unclothe him, put her hands to his breast, so she could imagine that she cupped his heart, and send him off with a fast pulse and a hard penis.

He did approach her, staring as he did so at her face, then her feet, moving his eyes quickly over everything in between.

He handed her a crisp sheet of paper with several neatly typewritten lines. "Will you read it?"

"Why?"

"Because it's a gift and you accepted it."

His acuity startled her, and she was annoyed that she could not hide the goosebumps. "All right."

As she read, the boy sat on the floor in front of Brumas and kept his eyes on hers. She refused to show that this unnerved her, so she focused on the writing.

> You are neither good nor evil. Perhaps your separate ways try the tolerance of the staid. Your beauties wither my rationality as I puzzle over communions between matter and spirit. I want to crawl in damp earth and I don't know why. I see myself standing on a star and I fear the fire. Everything except you reduces me to insignificance, and I feel ashamed. You trick me again and again out of my loneliness.

Brumas had concentrated so hard on each word that she had no idea what she had read.

"Nice," she said through tight lips.

"I didn't come here for your approval. All I wanted was to give you what you deserve."

Brumas could bear neither his innocence nor self-honesty. "You must leave," she said, taken unawares by the softness of her voice. "Now!" she shouted.

As he was walking to the door, he said, without looking back at her, "It doesn't matter to me how you appear to be, because I know who you are."

After he left she sat up and gritted her teeth. Then she ran to the door, opened it wide and said loudly enough for anyone nearby to hear, "What a blessing!" She banged the door shut and started to cry, but the tears did not last long.

Brumas glanced in a full-length mirror. She wanted to look as stark as a statue in the desert; not be naked, but dressed in the slate-gray silk tunic hanging on a hook next to her reflection. As she caressed the fabric, she imagined that when she put it on, it would twitch and crackle. If she stretched her arms sideways, she would touch the poles of black and white and charge herself with diametric powers. She would be the circuit and the balance, and siroccos would originate in the spot where she stood, as would summer thunderstorms and the goad for the movement of glaciers. Her hair would be torn from her head, and she would be free.

Brumas wanted to laugh wildly, to show herself that she was a madwoman. If she could cackle like the hag who had frightened her in a hotel lobby several nights ago, then she could forget the clapping hands, the harp inside her, and what the boy had said. To prepare herself to cackle, Brumas tried to assume the identity of the old woman by inventing a story about her.

"I'm a stray," she thought, "a widow who has wandered into a fancy place without knowing where I am. I'm dressed in mourning black, like a Greek in the hills of her island, and I'm dripping wet because I'm beside myself with grief, and I don't care if I walk in the rain without an umbrella."

As she developed the narrative, Brumas slipped on the tunic. When she was pulling black stockings over her knees she began to admire her legs, breaking her attention to the hag, the cackle, and the proof of craziness. "Hopeless, ridiculous," she muttered. All she could do was to laugh at herself and run over in her mind a new song that she had just begun to rehearse with the band.

Played and sung in a driving, punkish manner.

You're a rude, rude girl

Demented by dread.

Visions of ugliness cram your head.

Chorus:

Alchy/junko/he-man talk.

The murderers take their garden walk.

Lips-to-lips and cheek to ear,

It's the funky jargon they love to hear.

You're a slattern pearl,

Say what you will.

Mothers and daughters wish you no ill.

Chorus:

Alchy/junko/he-man talk.

The murderers take their garden walk.

Lip-to-lips and cheek to ear,

It's the bargain words they love to hear.

Chorus:

Alchy/junko/he-man talk.

The murderers take their garden walk.

Lips-to-lips and cheek to ear,

It's the bargain words they hold so dear.

Brumas spun around the room in time to the drumbeat in her head. Dizziness stopped her, and she was tired, from tonight's performance and weeks of touring. She tied the laces of her black tennis shoes, draped a froth of white feathers around her neck and shoulders, grabbed her purse and peony-pink trenchcoat, and left the dressing room.

"Randy!" she called, and in seconds her guitarist appeared to take her to the Plaza.

Usually when Brumas went to bed she reminded herself of the coming day's obligations, for then she felt that she could master any problems that might occur. Sleep, she believed, did not so much refresh her as renew, through the implosive, indulgent drama of dreams, her power to control others' lives, and thus her duties as a performer and businesswoman burdened her accountant, agent, lawyers, and fellow musicians.

The band would be playing two more nights in New York and she had no appointments, so she could sleep into the afternoon and no one would disturb her. All she had planned was a five o'clock dinner with an old friend.

"Between the sheets is better than in the arms of an unlearned lover," she thought as she pulled the covers to her chin. Brumas wanted to dream about the educated body that she would not have to teach to love hers. Instead, she dreamed about a horror movie. Brumas and Alicia, with whom she would dine tomorrow, were standing outside a theater in which a film called *Thalia* was playing. On the poster a portrait of the female grotesque, Thalia, stared at Brumas. Bony fingers dripped blood, and the illustration was a repulsive enticement, like a smashup, a dwarf, or a bearded lady. Corpses hovered in a crimson fog above Thalia's swirling hair, and the blurb proclaimed: *Her crimes could not be proved. Her methods were hideous.*

Alicia and Brumas entered the theater through a side door. The lobby was quiet, spacious, and ruby red. Alicia turned to leave, and Brumas asked her to stay; but she was only keeping the singer company till the terror began. "I hate horror movies," she said as she put on kid gloves and left.

Brumas walked towards the screen. The floor dipped deeply, and she thought that if she did not watch her step, she would miscalculate the incline, take too long a stride, and roll into an unseen abyss: an underworld inhabited by Thalia and her sister and brother freaks who, affectionately entwined, would invite her to stay for the coming orgy at which, like starving vampires, they would feast on babies' blood and puncture the necks of beautiful men and women, making them theirs with bites of extra-human love.

In the center of the seats a carnivalesque machine dispensed popcorn and played music that, like an organ grinder's, depleted her self-assurance and opened her to heartbreak. Brumas did not avoid the few people in attendance. She and they just seemed not to meet.

As soon as she sat down, monsters filled the screen: tentacles, antennae, watery eyes, oozing skin, hairy eyes, scaly backs, foaming tongues. They emerged from bubbling mud and squealed like hyenas that had lost the ability to laugh.

Brumas felt as though she were sitting on a glider that would crash, leaving her to recover, disoriented but unhurt, in Thalia's domain.

When Brumas woke up she knew that the dream would color her day. She switched on a soap opera, puffed up the pillows, and propped herself against them. To her, the dramas were benign, so she used them as escapism, congenial conversations in which she did not have to participate and during which she could doze or fantasize. Soap operas never made her think about her own life, which she felt was remote, in its emotional brutality and sexual fluency, from the television characters' petulant cruelties and intermittent passions.

Brumas wanted to think about nothing, but Thalia and her companions stayed in Brumas's mind: not as savage images, but rather as fellow frights who could guide her into the foundation of her own life.

*Frueh performs, in voice and facial expression, the
plaintive depth of this ballad.*

> People with pretty blond hair,
> Demons with deep-set eyes,
> Feelings thinned by cheap despair,
> Black guts wearing no disguise.
>
> *Chorus:*
> Which do you choose, man of many faces?
> Which do you use, woman of costume colors?
> Exchange your makeup for nature's graces,
> Exchange your makeup, or you'll be duller,
> Duller than you already are.
>
> People whose tongues are sweet,
> Children whose words are crude,
> Some shake hands when they meet,
> Some court each other in the nude.
>
> *Chorus:*
> Which do you choose, man of politesse?

Which do you choose, woman of sugared dreams?
Run from the ice life, risk a mess.
Run to the border of tropical steam,
Steam that takes you straight to the skin.

Let me in, let me in, let me in through the skin . . .

Last night she performed what she called her "tropical tribute" for the first time. The words had come to Brumas quickly three days before, and she had forced the band to rehearse the song over and over so that it would be ready for New York. With the soap opera on, she only heard her own lyrics and saw the hybrids of her concoction. They pleased her, even though in the dream she had smelled the stench of their stagnant habitat. If she had slept longer and the movie had continued, she was sure that the monsters would have attacked towns and cities, enraged because the inhabitants assumed that because they looked human, which was merely looking ordinary, they were humane.

Brumas had never met anyone who she believed was as monstrous as she was. Alicia had come close, but when she gave birth to a daughter three years ago, an unexpected compassion was simultaneously delivered. Each time the women met or talked on the phone since then, Alicia assured Brumas that she too could, as Alicia put it, "humanize" herself. Occasionally Brumas shrieked at Alicia after she said this. When she endured her friend's concern, Brumas's chest tightened and she held her breath as long as she could.

Today she wanted Alicia to talk from the heart. Brumas was tired of coercing Alicia to tolerate hostility. Brumas did not feel benevolent or even in control of her temper, but she wished, for once, to let Alicia love her easily.

It was a quarter to four, time for Brumas to bathe and dress. She always dabbed perfume on her wrists, throat, and pubic hair, but this afternoon the scent seemed pungently sweet, unwearable. She decided to pick up a new fragrance before tonight's work and called Alicia to tell her that she was on her way and to ask for suggestions about what to buy. When she hung up, Brumas dressed in the same clothes she had worn before leaving the theater the night before.

She arrived at Alicia's exactly at five. They hugged, kissed lightly on the lips, and Brumas asked, "Should I get Opium or Joy? I've never liked either one on me. I smell like I'm decaying in Quadrille, sickly sweet, like an old woman who fell down dead in her flower patch and has been lying there for a few days. Maybe I should try something for men, like Van Cleef and Arpels. Randy wears it, but I'm sure he won't mind if I do, because . . ."

"Honey," said Alicia, "we'll buy you whatever you want. That's no problem, but what is?"

As usual with Alicia, Brumas expressed anything in any way.

"You're my ultimate mommy, Alicia."

"That's because we've known each other as ultimate friends."

"Am I still? Still the bad girl?"

"No. You never were. We played at evil. We were sassy, and the spunk still serves us well. I've continued to whistle at men on the street, and they've continued to be disconcerted. I boss people around like I did when I was seventeen, and I expect pleasure from being alive. The world doesn't want us to be explicit about our desires, about fulfilling them. So you and I have often bitched our way to satisfaction. So what?"

"I want out. No one knows, but I cling to my lovers. I want everything and caress myself at night to make sure all the parts are there. Sometimes in the dark I lift my arm, raise it straight out and feel it with my hand. I let my fingers dawdle, so I can know how smooth I am. As I'm loving my skin, the arm seems to float, as if lifted out of a dream, as if brandishing Excalibur, and I wonder: Am I the Lady of the Lake? Or just a lunatic?"

"You know you aren't."

"I can humanize myself, right?"

"Humanize, feminize, butchify, bitchify. It's all the same."

"I don't want to be a frump."

"Don't beg me for love. We've always been wild women together and apart and we always will be. You know, Brumas, that when I say humanize I don't mean civilize. We'll never be civilized."

Brumas said nothing. After she had cried for a few minutes, with Alicia holding her, she asked, "What should I do?"

"Leave town. Go home. Run amok. Get screwed."

The first idea appealed, because its achievement demanded the greatest impulsiveness of the four.

"I have to sing tonight."

"You don't have to do anything."

"I don't want to go to California," said Brumas, thinking of her home by the Pacific. She looked in her purse, a pewter-colored leather satchel, to make sure that its usual contents were there: passport, wallet, hairbrush, sun block, mascara, Kleenex, cotton balls; three brands of loose face powder; seven shades of eye shadow, sable cosmetic brushes, four tubes of the same lipstick, keys for more doors and boxes than she had ever opened, and traveler's checks worth thousands of dollars. Wherever Brumas traveled for business, she was prepared to spontaneously take a trip anywhere in the world. The traveler's checks and passport helped her, every day, to feel exotic and to daydream about vacations that she rarely took.

"Alicia, I've always shown up for work. I may act loony, but I *am* responsible."

"As you know, I don't listen much to your music, but the thing that sticks with me about it is how you harp on endangering habit in order to find excitement or truth. Pardon the corniness. Look, dear, I know you have what you need to take off, literally and figuratively. You've done one night in New York, and there'll be more if you want them."

Brumas decided to go to Kos, where she owned a small house in the mountain village Asfendiou. Two years ago she had gotten the worst sunburn of her life there and had vowed to never return. Today, however, she felt that she had nowhere else to go that was as far away, yet that was home to her, no matter how alienated she had become from it.

Alicia booked Brumas on a flight to Athens that night. Then she called the doorman to bring her car to the front of the building so that she could drive her friend to the airport. "I'll call Randy and tell him what's going on," Alicia said as she sat her daughter, Camille, beside her in the car. "And I'll charter a plane for you to the island and see that there's a motorbike at your house."

While sipping her first glass of champagne after takeoff, Brumas breathed deeply as she remembered Camille kissing her goodbye. The child was not pretty, but already she was a woman.

"See my fingers?" she had asked Brumas in the car. "They can sing," and as she danced them over Brumas's hands, the latter shivered, for she heard her mother humming ancient folk songs to her as a child.

After two refills of champagne, Brumas fell asleep happy. Not until she unlocked the door to her house did she start to question her decision to leave New York. She was angry that she had over-tipped the driver who would not take her to her own doorway.

He had dropped her off at a vineyard in the center of Asfendiou, and she had had to walk a half hour. Her makeup was in disrepair, her tunic smelled, her stockings had run hours ago, and she wished that she felt tired, because she did not know what to do with herself.

She opened a closet and was startled to see that all the dresses, pants, shirts, and shoes she had brought to what she referred to as her "Greek retreat" were still there, as white as they were when she purchased them. She pulled out a pair of canvas sandals and stripped as fast as she could, opened the drawers of a small dresser, and found the bathing suit, white like every other piece of clothing, that she would wear. While showering she recalled that she had bought only white because Alicia had told her that Greece was clarity and sunlight, and Brumas wanted to partake of the curative brilliance in what she felt was a straightforward way.

Before starting the motorbike Brumas spread sun block all over her body, tied a shirt around her waist, and packed a towel in a backpack. She wore no makeup because nobody knew who she was, though when she stopped to buy a lemon soda near the vineyard where the driver had left her, the shopkeeper recognized and hugged her. Sitting on the store's front step she looked to the sky and thought of everything she had loved about the island, especially at this time of year, mid-September, when most of the tourists had gone and the days were still hot: a high, dusty wind near the water and in her hair when she rode her bike; the odor of pine trees and cow and goat dung; huge baskets of purple grapes lining the road between the seashore and Asfendiou; full-skirted flowers whose single-stemmed bodies held heads that seemed to be made of silver-pink hairs; the many plants whose names she was ashamed she did not know; a fast, sweaty coupling near the beach.

It was not far, and Brumas rode there. She laid her towel in the sand, which would have burned her feet if she had not been wearing sandals, and sat staring at the sea. No one was in sight. She drew a circle around her in the sand and sighed for what seemed to her like many minutes. Then she stood barefoot and offered her abandon to the wind and water.

"The second coming, and she came with a bang," intoned the singer. "Sparks of gangbusters' belongings slid between her thighs and she wondered, 'How much longer? How much deeper?' Her endurance waned. She felt as though she were being throttled by invisible fingers. Coca-Cola advertising had finally granted her leave to experience the real thing on the other side of the screen. No more matrons' emptied uteruses. No more widowers' wasted thighs. Leaving the nursing home, her onetime dream house, she threw the TV out the window and watched it smash a dizzy blonde to the sidewalk. 'You L.A. garbage can,' she thought and stepped over the dead body to freedom. So what was it like, outside the courtyard, the barnyard, the bramble-bush interior, in the real world, the man's world of cocks and cunts and contraptions for the prevention of medicine? Hello, dolly, hello, toots. Tell me your troubles. Don't just stand there, afraid to spout the words that can free your soul, afraid to sprout the wings that can turn a disaster into a wholly heavenly dynamo. You, who belong to everyone, and don't we all? You, who move inside me or toward me when pleasure begs response, pluck my bleeding hearts. Now! My pleasure requests your company. I say this under my breath, over my better judgment. I wait for us to find each other."

As soon as she had said each word, Brumas forgot it. When she finished her exhortation, one hand was raised to the sky, and the other pointed to the sand. Involuntarily her arms swung so that they were parallel to the beach, and she spun three times. Then she was still and she thought that the wind, for a second, stopped blowing.

Several hundred yards away, where the water washed the sand, a figure approached Brumas. She could not tell whether it was a man or a woman. The hair was very short, and the wind whipped a loose, white robe around the stranger's thin body.

Brumas heard her mother's songs from down the beach, and a magnet seemed to pull her towards the stranger. The sand stung her feet as she ran to the sea, and she sang along with the voice that drew her breath into the stranger's diaphragm.

By the time they were face to face, Brumas felt as though she had sung every song that she had ever known. She was drowning in music, and her past played in her mind as she sank into the melodies that linked one episode to another.

"I've never seen you here before," the stranger greeted her.

"I don't visit often or stay for long," said Brumas. She could not help but stare into the flickering amber eyes and turned to see if they were reflecting the sun. The stranger's body pulled at hers. Though the two stood a few feet apart, they seemed to Brumas connected at every point, like mirror images bonded by unseen energy.

"Where do you come from?" asked the stranger.

Brumas had no answer.

"You must come from somewhere."

"I sing," said Brumas.

"I know." The stranger accepted Brumas's response as a statement of her origin.

"When you sing," said Brumas, "I want to be as close to you as I can."

"Then let's sing together, breath to breath."

The stranger's voice, she thought, was purer than hers, and she felt overexposed in her bathing suit, cut so high on the thigh that it displayed her hip bones and so low in front that her nipples were almost revealed. From adolescence on, Brumas had coyly flaunted her body, trying to overcome the shame that, as a woman, she sensed she was supposed to feel at the sight, smell, and touch of her own skin.

"Don't be embarrassed," said the stranger, laying a hand on her shoulder where the strap pressed. Brumas stiffened, for no one else had ever read her mind.

"But you sing like a siren," said Brumas.

"So do you."

This is BRUMAS's first song in a major key.

> When your heart is lost, exhausted,
> Get it from the ground.
>
> When your feet keep missing the beat,
> Get it from the ground.
>
> When you think the party's over,
> Get it from the ground.
>
> When the brides beat you to union,
> Get it from the ground.
>
> Sand and pebbles, soil and mud,
> Earth is fertile, and you're the stud.
> Moist or dusty, black or red,
> Tap the source, or you'll be dead.

The singers created the song on the spot. They alternated verses, and the stranger conceived the chorus. Then the two sang it in unison.

They walked along the wet sand, arms around each other's waists. "Are you shameless yet?" asked Brumas's companion.

She answered, "Touch me. Everywhere."

"Only if you do the same."

Alone in Asfendiou, Brumas smiled to think that no lessons in love had been given. She took the jasmine, given to her by her latest lover, from her hair. She brushed it so that particles of sand stuck to her shoulders, chest, and back. Then she cut it as short as she could and shaved her head. Tomorrow her own blond hair would begin to grow in. It looked like a halo by the time she played again in New York.

JUSTIFIABLE ANGER

*Lyrics and text by Joanna Frueh * Music by Thomas Kochheiser*

Frueh and Kochheiser wear the same everyday clothing: white T-shirts, jeans, and white gym shoes. No eye spectacle. Every-woman, everyman clothing. Doubles with dark hair and light skin who perform a yearning and poetic querulousness. The stage is bare except for sound equipment and a black music stand holding the text.

SONG I   *The Dudes Have Danced the World to Death*

The dudes have danced the world to death
Let's sing a song of ruin
The wildlife leave their last bequest
A lovelorn ranting at the moon

Chorus:
Never mind the flowers and ferns
The seeds for which our one heart yearns

Source of power, source of birth

Dandy dressers killed the earth

The dinosaurs just ate the sun

Wearing a suit and tie

They said they were just having fun

But they don't hear the corpses cry

Chorus

The boys sport top hats when they twirl

They think they're Fred Astaire

They charm the pants off any girl

Whose silliness lays her soul bare

Chorus

Hum a hymn of strangulation

Turn it into a roar

The dudes are dancing until dawn

They're coming to your door

I lived in a place where I lost my dreams.

I'd wake up and remember

Nothing. I was afraid

Of

the depletion of love

the granting of friends

Whose favors I did not wish.

SONG 11   *Strictly Evil*

You're trying to show me that you're my friend

I don't believe it, you're trying to bend

My mind so it fits the limits of yours

Get lost, you creep, 'cause there are no cures

For your granite heart or your jellied spine

For the lips that chirp the party line

For the hand that writes a loving note

With all the right words learned by rote

Chorus:

You're strictly evil

Don't try to repent

Don't be my false brother

When you're so damn bent

Out of shape, out of whack

Get off my back

Strictly evil

You told me why I didn't belong

Thanks for pointing out how I'm wrong

You're barely an embryo learning to live

Don't think that you're the one who can give

To a woman pregnant with anger and pain

It's the violent emotions that keep one sane

When fools like you, guilty and blue

Want to make me touch and comfort you

You sent me flowers and tried to explain

I looked at the vase and thought, "You're inane,"

'Cause you're looking so weird in that suit and tie

You're trying to be human, but what catches my eye

Is the halo you've put around your head

Like a saint in a painting of the martyred dead

But you're just a zombie who walks this earth

As if Mother Mary had given you birth

You cooked me lunch on a winter day

Is this a kindness I must repay?

I'm having a party. You won't be there

You're not enough fun and you've got no flair

We'll dress in feathers and leather gear

We'll sip champagne and gulp down beer

While you'll be turning the earth to dirt

As you scavenge for love in an old hair shirt

Chorus

I spent two weeks in a terror.

"Kiss of Judas," I said out loud.

"How can a kiss betray?"

What a perfect time

For

A sick sweetheart to come along.

Say you love me

Fiercely when the wind is sharp as knives.

SONG III   *Mal à Tête*

Mal à tête,

You make me sick

Take me to the doctor.

I can't compete with your egotism

The strong silent man is an emotional dumpster

The passionate actor,

Be real to me.

Mal à tête,

I don't want Freud

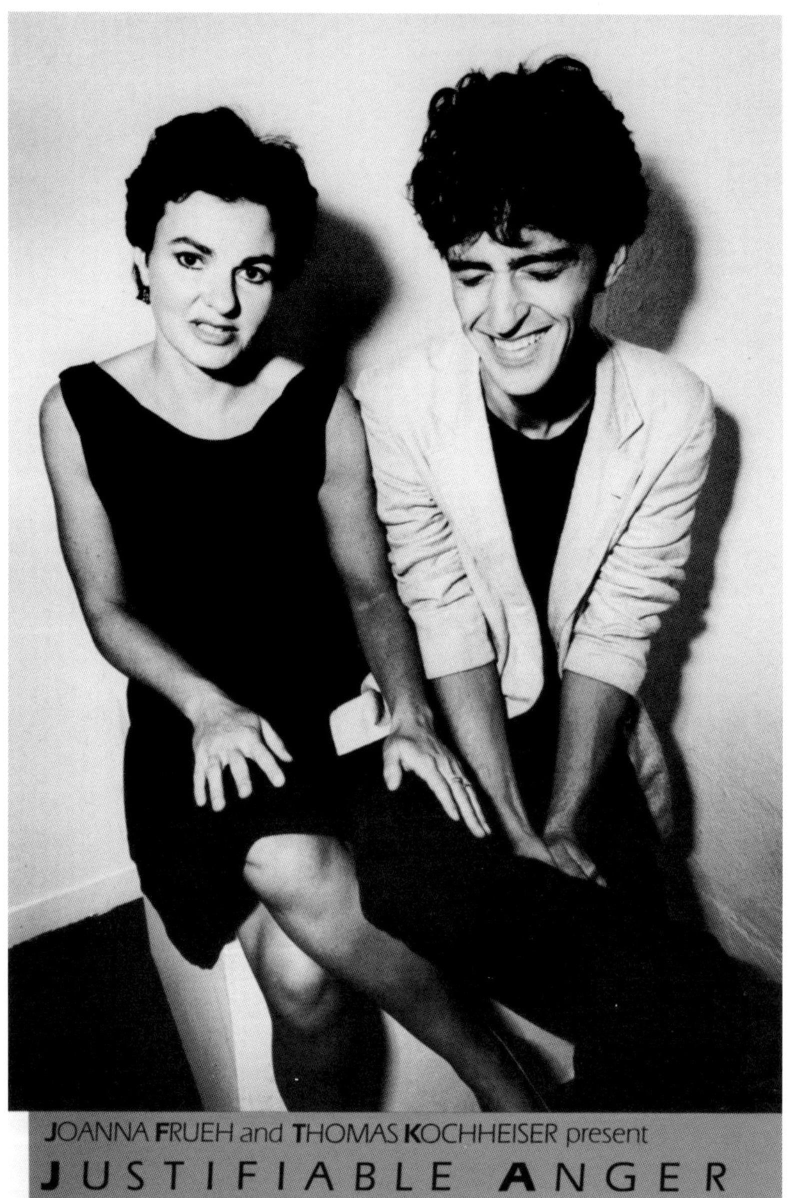

Publicity photos, *Justifiable Anger*, 1984. *Photos courtesy of Ann Simmons-Myers.*

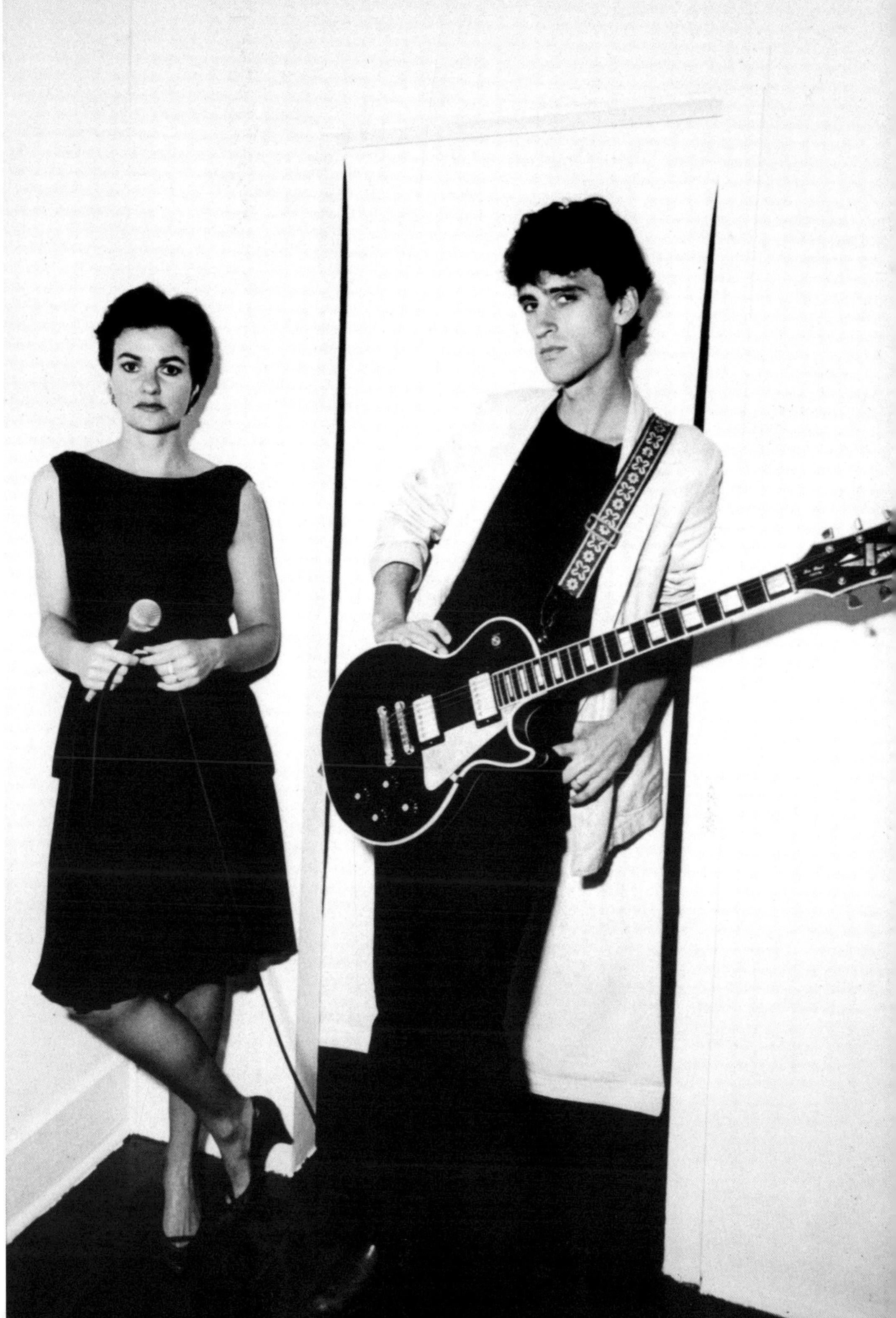

I'll go on vacation.

Bougainvillea is so appealing

Flame of the forest glows through my dreams of you

Love me in Jamaica

Or the Greek Isles.

Mal à tête,

I've got a migraine.

Have you ever had one?

Then you know the nausea

The chills that make you put a sweater on.

Turn the heat up

It's so cold

My mind is freezing

Because I cannot think

About your anti-tropic heart.

Envoi

Mal à tête,

I'm sick, you bet

It's all your fault

My heart's on halt.

Aspirin won't work

'Cause you're a jerk.

Mal à tête,

Mal à coeur,

Je suis une bête

Qui est une fleur.

I saw a movie

The wolves snarled from

Their graves . . . and ripped

The organs from the living

I would

Do the same

To you

So sorry

You cannot see

Your head

Laying on the sidewalk

Ear to the pavement

Do not pretend

That you can

Hear

Like an Indian

Cheek pressed to the earth

SONG IV   *I Call You a Man*

I am a woman, I call you a man

Can we get close? Can we get close?

I know we've done the best we can

So far away, so far away

We tried to raise the energy to be free

I stroked your hair, I stroked your hair

But how can you fly when you can't even see?

Gone to the grave, gone to the grave.

I am a woman, I call you a man

Try to rise up, try to rise up

We sat in the heat, we had no fan

The kiss was soft, the kiss was soft

As ardor grew, we called it love

Press close to me, press close to me

But where were you, friend, when push came to shove?
Please, don't hold back, please, don't hold back.

I am a woman, I call you a man
Let's not deny, let's not deny
But love made you fearful, so you ran
We both have cried, we both have cried
I'm a fool sometimes, but never blasé
The anger fades, the anger fades
When your worries have lessened, I'm here to play
I'm a woman, hon, I'm a woman, hon
And my emotions cannot be undone.

I smelled too good, a
sophisticated woman liking
facials and French perfume. Too
old too sweet too bitchy
as women go.

SONG V   *Demento Beauty*

Demento Beauty, here I am
Get out of my way, or I'll have to slam
Your smug little, ugly little, custardy face
What makes you think you're part of the human race?

Chorus:
I'm so beautiful, so berserk
Why doesn't someone pay me
So I don't have to work?
My pearl-pink skin, my diamond-shine eyes
Miss America, move over, I'm the maniac prize

You think you're a gift to the family of man

You're a chopped up melody, an also-ran

The has-been who climaxed before being born.

If I had compassion, you'd be forlorn

Demento Beauty walked the street

Ran down an alley, tripped on the feet

Of a dirty condition, a city of slime

Is it a corpse or a wino or just a crime?

Chorus

Rape in the morning, rape in the night

Look out, sweet ladies, you might have to fight

The sap with integrity, the creep with a gun

Who thanks you for indignities after they're done

Pull out your razor blades, hold on to your knives

Women of distinction, butter-soft wives

Listen to the language of those hips that sway

It's Demento Beauty leading the way

Chorus

I charge over bodies, my arms held high

No flag-waving soldiers, no apple pie

Just homemade weapons that make men twitch

The flamingo-pink mouth with a tongue of a bitch

Demento Beauty, I'm so pure

Nobody's honey, but I've got allure

Electro-nuclear-solar zap

Some think I'm magic, some say a trap

Chorus

Fires of suspicious origins.
I heard the phrase on the news.
I was ready for them to
Begin in my city.
I am full of blood
and water, and I would rather
Turn blue
Than see you watch me bleed.

SONG VI   *Mistress of Desire*

If I am the woman I love
Then no one is a slave.
I've got no one to beat,
I've got no one to crave
I've got no one to answer,
I've got no one to ask
I'm just a woman,
Charmed to say,
Without the master's mask.

Chorus:
Mistress of desire
Whip us, if you will,
Into our devotions,
The turbulence to kill
Our grasp of an idea
Outside of destiny
You know we are your lackeys
And we can barely see
The shape of stellar bodies

Other than your own
We live inside the darkness
Of a none too torrid zone

I looked in the mirror
And took out my tools.
What a friend I was to myself
Orchid lids   pink cheeks   screaming mouth
I sat at my desk
Saw lipstick on the coffee cup
Loosened my tie and
Wrote a letter.
"Things aren't so bad," I began.

SONG VII   *Feeling Festive*

Feeling rather festive
Despite all the odds
Communing with necessity
And goddesses and gods
Praying to the powers
For the wherewithal to grip
My life around the middle—
Don't let my fingers slip

Chorus:
I'm tired of surviving
I'm frazzled from the strain
I thought I'd see the phoenix rise
I thought that I'd regain
My hold on what's called sanity
If I let the sun beat down

On my pale skin day after day
Until I turned smooth brown

I want to be a queen
No court, no crown, no jewels.
The body, brain and savoir-faire
So I can break the rules
I'll wear red lipstick, dye my hair
Be platinum blond, so cute
One day I'll wear a corset
The next wingtips and suit

Feeling rather festive
Despite all the odds
Communing with necessity
And goddesses and gods
Praying to the powers
For the wherewithal to grip
My life around the middle—
Don't let my fingers slip

You may not
Be the charm
You may not
Do the trick
You may be the jester
But I am not laughing

SONG VIII   *Angels Beat Me Down*

I tried to find some stairs
But none were there

I walked for miles

This was not the style in which I was accustomed to living

I saw a gold ladder

The kind in dreams

No clouds, pure day

Out of the blue a voice dared, "Don't you want to test your skills?"

Chorus:

Did I have a will?

No no no

Have you climbed a rope?

Long ago

Have you danced on top

Of a peak?

Not when it mattered

Was I strong?

Yes, I see angels

Arms outstretched

Ready to hug me

Am I wrong?

They're beating me down.

Angels sing,

Angels beat me down.

Their arms were not like clubs

But I was bruised

The air smelled good

But my nose was broken and the black hair shivered on my head

I am tender like you

I too could fly

Give me a chance

They said, "See us next fall when your hair will be turning gray."

Why must I go away?

They flung me down

To earth I fell

And looking up I saw a wing, a smile, a blond goodbye

I tried to find some stairs

But none were there

One sign says

Mexico next right

Another reads

Runaway trucks

Then . . .

Falling rocks

Rattlesnake crossing.

So tell me

Where am I anyway?

SONG IX   *Esperanza Boulevard*

Where's Esperanza Boulevard? Someone must surely know

Tell me—in the foothills? Or in the mountain's snow?

In the desert scrub where the rattlesnakes can cope

Without the water we would see as equivalent to hope?

Chorus:

If you hear me, I'll be frank,

My arid heart can't bleed

I'm wasting like some old dog's bones

On a sun-dried river bank

I'm waiting for a monsoon

To inundate my guts

To fill me up like liquid light
But all day is high noon

Where's Esperanza Boulevard? My question states a need
Oh, you're new to the city? I think I'll start to speed
And run somebody over, someone who's just a dope
For having faith that heaven is the home for those who hope

Where's Esperanza Boulevard? In the tortured air?
Too hot for me to drive it? False paradise? A snare?
A hell that breathes the flames of hearts condemned to be heat-kissed?
The street of rolling waters I guess does not exist

Where's Esperanza Boulevard? Just point, I'll find my way
You act like you want something. I can't afford to pay
In word or deed or upfront cash. I'm burning, destitute
But if I had a gun, you jerks, I'd point at you and shoot

Chorus

(with a different melody from previous verses)

I see I've got no friends today
But right there near the sky
It's Esperanza Boulevard. I think I'm going to die

Somebody's actually here
Though God knows why
A jacket hangs on
the back of a chair.
I am not alone.

So lucky we're alive in the postmodern world.
Blazing the trail.
Computer-packed decorum
Thanks so much for your time
Showing me the language of a new divine.

Living the life, no primrose path.
Humming with fun.
Quantum physics holisms
The stars are my children
Try shooting them down to your garden with a gun.

Some people eat garbage, rifle through cans.
Alley vikings.
Invite them to dinner
For bubbling drinks and meat
Hype them with coffee, push them out to the night.

Chorus

*Frueh's tone is wistful and ironic, and
she is on the verge of tears.*

So glad to be a postmodern mind.
So lucky we're alive in the postmodern world.
Won't you be my postmodern girl?
Won't you be my postmodern man?
Won't you skip with me into the modern twilight?
Won't you be the love of my postmodern life?
So lucky we're alive in the postmodern world . . .

❈ DUAL CONCEPTION

*Written by Joanna Frueh for a piece to be performed
by Frueh and Thomas Kochheiser.*

. . . .

Joanna sings.

Lying in the bathtub

Water's awfully hot

Feeling like an embryo

Liking it a lot

Waves of fluid buoy me

Porcelain's like skin

Smooth and so embracing

Won't you step right in?

Chorus:

Vita nova, vie nouvelle

Promise that you'll kiss and tell

When the New Life strikes your head

And says it's stupid to be dead

. . . .

Tom sings.

Begats and begottens
Misbegotten things
Born of forgetfulness
And wedding lies and rings

. . . .

Joanna sings.

Baby, I don't owe you
Unless the fires spark
If you like the burning bright
I'll give you a birthmark

Chorus:
Vita nova, vie nouvelle
Promise that you'll kiss and tell
When the New Life kicks your butt
And says you're boring in your rut

. . . .

Tom sings.

Mother Right, Father Right
You know that they're wrong
Because only newborns
Know how to sing this song

. . . .

Joanna sings.

94

Muscles are for building
But boxing is for fools
Infant brother, fight with me
So we can break the rules

Chorus:
Vita nova, vie nouvelle
Promise that you'll kiss and tell
When the New Life claims control
Of your body and your soul

"I'm pregnant," she said. No one heard her, for she lay alone in bed and she was spending the day by herself at home, where all the walls were painted pale crocus. "Iris," her mother had said when she first saw the apartment, "you know what they say about those lavenders, especially in a bedroom. They make you so hot, you can hardly stand it."

Sometimes, as a little girl, she was not sure that her name was Iris, and as a woman, she lived occasional nameless days. They never scared her, for she walked through her garden, or her father's, thinking that she was Laurel, Lily, Heather, Poppy, Ivy, Rose, and Violet. In adolescence she had wanted to be a stripper, and every once in a while she still imagined herself as Rosy Dawn or Gloria Midnight, queen with the velvet cunt. Every spring she was April, then May and June. When she felt that no one treasured her, she called herself Amber, Ruby, Pearl, or just plain Jewel.

"Bella donna, mamma mia," she said, the child and woman ready for the new life delivered always in a new name.

Joanna sings.

The seer never knows her name
Bella donna, Mamma mia
Vision fixed is wisdom tamed
Beautiful woman, mother mine
A captive eye is color blind

Bella donna, Mamma mia

Bouquets' beauties are unrefined

Beautiful woman, mother mine

Chorus:

See the stripper free her sight

Coral and emerald suit her right

Hands off, mister, give her room

Pink is the mind, and gray is the tomb.

Try to bury her if you will

Her legs are restless, can't be still

Each time she struts she knows what's real

Cataract veils are what she peels

The stripper always feels her calm

Bella donna, Mamma mia

Her own sweat is a heady balm

Beautiful woman, mother mine

A fluid figure knows the brain

Bella donna, Mamma mia

Sight and motion make her sane

Beautiful woman, mother mine

Iris liked the color of her home, but she needed to redecorate. When she closed her eyes, the room turned shrimp pink. She had seen it on a swatch, going by the name of Monet Blush.

With the aid of a speculum, as yet uninvented, that would painlessly dilate her cervix, Iris wanted to prove that her uterus and its contents were as pearly-toned as a dead man's waterlilies. She held her breath and fought down nausea when she thought about the dense red of her womb. She comforted herself with images that she believed had nothing to do with her flesh or blood: melting rubies, cherries bobbing in thick syrup, American Beauties sailing in a pond beneath a scarlet sky.

Iris's friend Zandy had said to her one day, "Men think the womb is a black hole." The two women discussed this. It was a more interesting idea than the toothed vagina.

You come from a place that burned your heart before you were born, singed the vanity into a tube of ice, let it fall as snow on the planet Earth. You blamed the blackness, in which you thought you had no stake. Raygun, raydance, Raimondo the loser begged forgiveness from the slivered moon. He had halved it, quartered it, sliced it miserably thin, like chicken julienne for a gourmand's stomach. You all eat too much, then tell me that I have fattened you for the kill. You act like a goose that had knowledge of becoming *foie gras*. You are nursery rhyme senseless, fairy tale divine. In fact, you are a tooth of the Divine, conceived by a gorgon bleeding on the rocks of a tourist trap beach. You are a joke. You think that you belong in a pool of jewels, with brilliant liquid heightening your skin's natural luminosity. You jerk. I feel for you, for I suffer from the same stupidities. We want to believe that we can eat custard pies and not grow fat. *Crèmes, caramel. Crèmes, chocolat.* Cream, whipped. Cream, in your jeans.

Iris told her husband Childe what Zandy had said. He painted, in gold outline, a six-pointed star, formed by intersecting triangles, on a tondo with a black ground. "It's yours," he said and hung it on the wall that faced him and Iris when they slept.

Childe had ruled line after glittering line, connecting all points so that crisscrossing stars and geometrics receded to a black, twelve-sided aperture. "Whose orifice is that?" asked Iris.

He did not speak, but raised his right arm and pointed the index finger at the painting. She could not take her eyes off his hand as he tapped the edge at twelve equal intervals. Then he traced a circle around the central polygon a dozen times. "Feel my arm," he whispered. "I too am a black hole."

Just a touch was impossible, for shoulder to fingernail rippled; so when she pressed her lips hard to his forearm, the beat in his body shot to her head and toes. "I want to kneel, I've got to kneel," she said, her breath warming his wrist, then fingertips. He too dropped to the floor, facing her, because he wanted their knees to touch. As Iris knelt between Childe and the painting, touching his flat stomach, then thighs, he nestled his hands in the hair that hung behind her neck. "There is no space between us and your eyes have become black," she said. What she had wanted to say was, "Astro Man, I feel like I'm inside your body."

Iris knew many reasons why she had married Childe. Her mother had warned her against him. "He won't hold your love," she said. "Sweet men are dull and they don't make a lot of money." But Mother had never stroked his legs. When Iris was sixteen, she had raved to a girlfriend about some singing idol's sexy limbs. "Look at this, Alex," Iris said, holding a picture of a young man in tight leather that gleamed as it curved over his quadriceps. "Don't you want to fuck him?" All Alex said was, "Men don't have sexy legs." Ten years passed before Iris talked to anyone about the subject again.

Childe's calves resembled those of a winged genius on an Assyrian relief sculpture. She told him that she could see the sinews; they snaked through him, and one night she heard them hiss. Mother would never have seen beneath his skin, even if she looked very hard, would never have heard the serpents, even though they slid across her forehead and ran their fangs over the hairs above her ear.

Childe was aloof during the first few weeks of his and Iris's friendship. When she said, "I've been trying to find out about love for years," he cried. "Search with me," he invited her.

* * * * * * * * * * * * * * * *

Joanna sings.

He called himself a bachelor
The man in boyhood jeans
He told her not to touch him
She might dim his youthful sheen
To her he was no innocent
Though his skin was soft and white
He was no virgin of the soul
Yet she would show him night

They walked together slowly
Too far and they would lose all breath
Dark streets could not be holy
If the two met only death

Until she was twenty-six, Iris had not liked men much. Staring at the Pacific while reclining on a *chaise longue*, she watched a hairy man walk by, wearing brief trunks. "Cut it off," she yelled, "with a machete!" Once, when someone said he wanted to make love to her, she snapped, "Climb inside me? Be my baby in a melody of love playing in my womb? You must be kidding."

Soon after meeting Childe, Iris dreamed that she bit off his penis and ate it. She told him, and he asked, "Did I bleed?"

"A little."

"Did you hurt me?"

"I don't think so."

"I was still a man for you, right?"

"Mmhmm."

"And what about you? As a woman?"

"I freed myself of femininity. I just want to be female."

With Childe she removed the corsets of love that had straitened her self-affection. She still rimmed her eyes in Nile green, colored her lips orchid pink, and rouged her cheeks with a cream called Rich 'N Ripe. She continued to read *Vogue* and buy Jolie Madame and silk underwear, and when she and Childe became lovers, she bought at his request a garter belt and black stockings, which she wore with a pearl necklace and earrings, for both their pleasure, sometimes when they had sex. "Do you know how long I've waited," she asked Childe, "for someone to say they wanted to see me in a get-up like this? These are the luxuries of my lust."

He was out of town, and she wrote him a letter that she did not mail.

> I may go mad if I don't see you soon. My thighs will turn to flab through lack of exertion, and I will grow a fat, dumpling brain. I'll age quickly, and be left to myself with only pride and a belly full of veins. Mother is talking to me about you. She acts as though our pregnancy is a mistake. I said to her, "Remember when I was a kid and I went to the library a lot to renew books? It wasn't because I hadn't read them. It was because I adored them and wanted to read them again immediately." There are renewals of love.

Both Childe and Iris remembered the night of conception. It could have happened other times: when he grabbed her shoulders and rode her like a mare; when he shuddered and named her My Celestial Whore; when he slapped her ass; when she scratched the skin at the bottom of his spine; when she saw his eyes flash blacker than a man's; when she demanded, "Harder, pretty boy." But all those times they did not want a child.

In early May the night was very cool. Iris had lit a fire in the living room, and she and

Childe went to bed there. They kissed and the fire crackled, so loudly that it frightened Iris. "I know this sounds stupid," she said, "but I feel strange angels in the room."

"Okay," said Childe tentatively.

"Now they're gone," she sighed.

Joanna sings.

Halcyon days in the month of May
Baby, baby, come my way
Dance to me on the midnight light
You're so refined but never tight
You're free like a petal fallen in a storm
You're loose like a hound that's growing warm
From running with the halcyon breeze
I stop in my tracks and fall on my knees
Seeing you dance on the midnight light
Look! Your body's whirling white
Now you're as dark as a blackbird's tail
Wing to me, baby, we cannot fail

After Childe and Iris made love, she said, "I'm seeing gold stars between us and the wall."

"I know. The angels are back."

From the next night, Iris recalled two dreams. In one she was naked and Childe stood above her. "I see neon blue eyes beneath your skin," he said. "They're rising." In her abdomen she felt pressure exerted outward, a pleasant push, and then a young head with blond hair rose to the center of the room, eyes simultaneously piercing hers and Childe's. In the other dream, her face was magenta. She could neither see nor feel her body and her neck began to bubble, like scarlet blood. Cranberry-colored cars raced around her throat, jet planes zoomed into flaming skyscrapers, and aqua clouds of smoke twisted through fireworks and explosions. A fleshy pouch squirmed above her. She could barely see it, but she knew that a fetus with claws and a huge head was growing inside.

Joanna sings.

What can happen when you yield?
Clutch of climax, heads that reeled
Plant the crop and wet the field
Fruit and blight will be revealed

Chorus:
Flesh and heaven know no bounds
Pain and pleasure make the rounds

What can happen when you yield?
You've got nothing left to shield
Even old sores can be healed
Eternity becomes unsealed

Chorus

For years Childe had felt that he had been collecting a cornucopia of sins. The mystique of money, power, and beauty, the trinity to which the cities pray, haunted him. His heart throbbed like an old wound, which he had thoroughly cleansed but which he always expected to erupt periodically. He would be blotched forever, but he could redeem himself:

> If he camped in the alley where the stool pigeons laid their eggs; if he trained his parrots to sing at twilight; if he listened carefully and imitated not the song but rather its meaning before he slept; if he ate only grains gleaned by happy field hands; if he spent part of every summer tending cows; if he read to Iris from a heart-shaped book.

He loved her because he had to wrestle with her imagination. "I saw this sword yesterday in the museum," she told him. "The label said 'Sudanese, second half of the nineteenth century.' Half moons and stars were etched on the blade, and I was on a horse, in battle, with magic in my weapon. I could have been a warrior sometime. Hacking off heads, slashing through skin, blood all around." She paused, smiled a little, and continued, "We're two swords crossing. We can fight and win."

Iris did not make commitments easily, and that drew Childe to her. When she said, "I want to marry you," he knew that she meant it, especially after she added, "This excitement isn't loss of self-possession. It means I'm finally faithful, to me." Her words reminded him of the times she showed him her breasts but did not want to make love. He knew that sometimes she needed to exhibit herself, as if she was a work of art.

The day that Iris announced the pregnancy to Childe, he looked at reproductions of Annunciation paintings, remarking on the variety of the Virgin's postures to Iris: one woman stood solid as a pillar; another drew her mantle to her throat, recoiled from Gabriel, and averted her eyes; some women leaned toward him and crossed their arms over their stomachs; a few seemed at once calm and surprised. "How do *you* feel, Iris?" he asked.

. . . .

Joanna sings.

> Annunciation, I am yours
> We don't debate, for his is hers
> Hers is his and it is they
> Sexes fade the sky-sent way
>
> Annunciation, heave our souls
> Into yet more eternal roles
> We'll choose to whom we want to pray
> Our heartbeats ride the sky-sent way
>
> Annunciation, press my arm
> Suddenly I conceive no harm
> Sky-sent fingers cause no pain
> Yet they pierce me to the vein
>
> Annunciation, no one cries
> Sky-sent words never harbor lies

Kiss me, peer, my mouth is dry
The rains are pulsing from the sky

Annunciation, I am drenched
A young girl's thirsts are being quenched
Sky-sent waters wash me inside
Deliver me with winter's tide

Chorus:
No angel molds the form of man
No devil rides a womb
People breed whatever they need
Annunciation! Hear our plan:

Annunciation, I am yours
We don't debate, for his is hers
Hers is his and it is they
Sexes fade the sky-sent way

Childe had owned a lovebird and two parrots for years. The day he knew that Iris was pregnant he bought her a cockatoo. As he was telling her how to care for it, she said, "This bird's for you, not for me." Childe protested, but Iris stopped him by saying, "I don't mind at all. You want me to see that I'm as beautiful as a bird."

Birdman sings at the siren's window. He vamps her easily and thoroughly, not only because his voice is pure, but also because she has heard his tunes before. She has sung them herself, from childhood on. When she is troubled, they soothe her to sleep, and when her daylong headaches dull her taste for food, she remembers one of Birdman's melodies, which she feels as close to as she does to the brother, dead at birth, who tells her in her dreams that she is beautiful.

Birdman, perched by the geraniums on the back porch, compels her through his songs to confess that love is plentiful. This she does not admit to many animals or men, for they are cheap with passion; but once the words are spoken, Birdman and the siren know that they will sing as long as the notes can quiver.

She called him Nighthawk, though he knew how to be other animals as well. She had seen him bow to a friend's mutt and get on all fours and face it. Then the two lay down on the rug together, side by side, the tips of the dog's fur touching Childe's shirt and jeans.

* * * * * * * * * * * * * *

Joanna sings.

The giraffe man leaned on my gate
His eyes were soft with tears
He said, "I know I'm late,
But I can quell your fears."
He bent his muzzle to my cheek
And crooned, "I'm still your favorite pet
The plains we ran, I know you seek,
The leaves we chewed, they've remained wet."
He grazed me with his sturdy neck.
My thoughts could not be held in check.
I said, "I dream in ancient tongues."
He said, "Your heart still knows it's young."

The swan man swam to my door
His throat was smooth and pale
I asked what he'd come for,
And he lifted up my veil.
He stared into my Cleo eyes
And said, "I knew you in the Nile."
I said, "You heard my passion cries,
You helped me breathe and moan in style."
He touched me with a milky wing.
I almost had to scream or sing.
I said, "You are my special guest,
Come in, come in, you've found our nest."

The goat man lay in my bed

His horns were young and hard

He thought that I'd been dead

Or my ego badly marred.

His eyes explored my fuchsia lips

He asked, "How long since you have dared

To let men lick your fleshy hips

Or see your fruitful belly bared?"

He touched me with a muddy hoof,

I heard some cats howl on the roof,

I said, "You know, I love your fur."

Just then the cats began to purr.

The first pictures Childe had ever seen of people having sex showed a man fucking a woman who was chained to the floor. He was embarrassed that he did not laugh with the other boys, but the photograph made him feel as though he could not move. Why, he wondered, did he let himself sink into the skin of someone or something else?

Childe wanted badly to enter Iris's body, but neither with his penis nor as an embryo. "Is this a transgression," he asked her, "of my proper place?"

"No," she laughed. "You're made of the same stuff I am."

"So I'm not committing some sacrilege against you?"

"Why would that be? I'm a woman, not an idea."

Every once in a while Childe made a point of presenting himself naked before Iris, as if to say, "Here I am, man." The last time he did this she gave him a note that read:

> You bare yourself to me when you charm Zandy's cat; when you stretch your arms above your head and lick your lips; when you barbecue like an ancient man home from the hunt; when you cry about your inconsistent moods and occasional stomach cramps.

"I don't want any pain during labor," said Iris.

"Maybe," said Childe. "But I think you don't want to see any blood."

"Listen to this, then. It happened to me today. I was walking past the pay phones in the supermarket and a woman without shopping bags stood at one of them talking. 'Run from me all you want,' she said in a low voice. 'I will find you, always, anywhere. And there will be a blood letting.' Then she raised the pitch a bit. I didn't think that she knew I was watching, and she kept on. 'I love blood, you know. I love to think of it hot in your veins and heart—the liquid that turns your skin pink for my admiration. You flush for me when I kiss your neck. Sometimes I have lapses, of memory. How many years ago was I merely someone who ate the rations of earth? Lapses, of memory; of appetite for the food of your heart; of casual desire for the body that a creature less kind than I, but of my persuasion, would forget under a park bench in the city at night. I leave only one mark on your skin. You tell me that people call it a love bite, and I laugh to myself. If only they knew how my lips draw your blood slowly, as if I were testing it for flavor and richness. I love your blood, so rare, not in type, but in quality.' She hung up the phone and turned around. She looked just like me, and I almost threw up on the spot. When she stared in my eyes for just a couple seconds, I smiled, pretending that I had taken all she said as metaphor."

"So you're telling me you saw a vampire in the grocery today and she was your double?"

"I suppose so, but that's not the point. It was the best story I'd ever heard about blood."

Childe called the midwife, who advised him:

Fishman, swim in the siren's sea, near her home by the ocean far south of the snows in which she was born. Sip the water from the wells she has dug. Then take a trip. Somewhere on that sea is good. She will have to breathe underwater for three days— be a fish as you are a merman. But before you go, she will have wanted to run through the woods with her hair loose and howl, be the bitch to your hound. Leave her alone at that time. She will avoid calamity if she winds around her belly a wreath of her favorite flowers and you make a circlet of them for your head.

* . . . .

Joanna sings.

       Be my body

       Be my head

       See the ways that we are wed

Open minds

Open caves

Let's all make some human waves

Time to act

Time to love

Time to give the world a shove

Entry, exit, time to leave

See the ways we interweave

Blood and oceans, thought and deed

If we live, we all must bleed

Childe and Iris dreamed together on board ship: of blood brothers, blood boiling, blood letting, blood baths, blood and guts; of glistening fruits and flowers, all red. In the morning they stood on deck: no shore was in sight. With little warning, the pain came, and the blood. Iris caught Childe's eye, and they both screamed, "I'm alive!"

Frueh and Kochheiser, wearing the nothing-special yet stylish attire of jeans, white T-shirts, and white gym shoes, enjoy the spaciousness of a stage whose only props are essentials: a black music stand for Frueh's text and the sound equipment and a stand for Kochheiser's electric guitar. Their friend, the performance artist Robert Bray, has designed romantically effective lighting.

SONG 1   *Skydive*

Frueh feels elated performing this upbeat, driving love song.

> I want to skydive with you
> I'll learn that falling isn't failing
> When we hit rock bottom
> Then we'll rise into the cool, dry air

Chorus:

Skydrop, skyfall, skyline drive

Travelling to hard ground

The earth quakes and the sky cracks

I'm falling, falling down

I'm tumbling like a wild weed

We're wondering if we'll walk again

It's hell and gone, no man's land

It's not for this woman either

I'll skydive if you will too

I'm closing my eyes, please catch my heart

Do I have a failing heart?

How can I stand? How can I stand up?

Chorus:

Skydrop, skyfall, skyline drive

Plunging to the heartland

The earth quakes and the sky cracks

Take heart and take a chance

Frueh, who articulates words very clearly in performance, does so with transcendent clarity throughout Solar Shores.

Friends said, "You are strong

Play with the powers that be,"

But I have no tactics

I am not an army

So I say the game of patience has been called off

I didn't tell anyone to go to hell

I didn't say you're not my type, I'll pick a fight with you

Just tough talk from the muscles

Tough talk through the teeth

Tough talk from the pelvis

Tough talk from the hips

I'll spin three times and kick your ass

If you make me

Chorus:

'Cause I'm not a candy ass anymore

I was so sweet, but had no flavor

I'm not a fool for tasty words

Rub me the wrong way

And it's you who'll quaver

You'll hear what I'm saying, like it or not

Not 'cause I speak to you, but just 'cause I have lips

Just found a way to simmer

Found a way to perk

Found a way to wiggle

Found a way to shake

I've spun three times and walked my way

Goodbye

Chorus:

'Cause I'm not a candy ass anymore

I'm still as sweet as any you've met

Chocolate melts, what a sensation

You think it's all gone

But you never forget

Leaving a lover a town   Again

I hear I am a cannibal

I eat the heart for fun

SONG 3   *The Healing Place*

*Frueh delivers this sexy blues song from memories of
her first cross-country drive to Tucson, which
aroused both melancholy and ecstasy.*

The air was hot and heavy

The peonies had died

I packed my stuff into the car

To take a long, long drive

Chorus:

Nocturnal language

Speak to me in drums

I'm ready for a message

I want a brand new tongue

I slowed through battered cities

I could not find a laugh

I felt the instant friction

From people who had cracked

Chorus

Dark house in Oklahoma

I tried to eat my heart

I shouted at my lover

Who'd already fallen apart

Who could I kiss? Who knew me?

I sped through high and low

I knew no one in Texas

Or in New Mexico

Chorus:

Nocturnal language

Speak to me in drums

I'm ready for a message

I've got a restless tongue

I drove down from the mountains

Into a healing place

There were no pools of water

There was no sudden grace

The air was fresh and burning

White sand cooled my feet

Meet me in this Witchwood

Where I am healed by heat

Chorus:

Nocturnal language

Speak to me in drums

I'm ready for a message

'Cause I have found my tongue

Summer brings the sex out

Lizards crawl the vines

I can't believe that flowers grow

In this desert sun of mine

The first acknowledged erotic moment

You cut your finger and I held your hand

Now I am nervous standing in front of you

My face is hot

Let's do it

SONG 4   *Be My Body*

Be my body be my head

See the ways that we are wed

Open minds open caves

Let's all make some human waves

Time to act time to love

Time to give the world a shove

Entry exit time to leave

See the ways we interweave

Blood and oceans thought and deed

If we live we all must bleed

Seeping scar-

let lips

Say

Time to wash this wound

SONG 5   *Church of the Painted Hills*

Sometimes don't you feel like everyone has died

There's no one to talk to and you're so tired?

The weather is just too cold or too hot

And you're stuck?

Chorus:

That's not really happening

Church of the Painted Hills

Your brain is unraveling
See the moon, I'm crossing
Demons seem to know your name
Gardens bloom at midnight
Feel a fine kiss in the rain
Church of the Painted Hills

I know that some will talk about magic
I know that some will talk about God
All I say is, See the hills in color
When it's dusk

Chorus:
There is no congregation
Church of the Painted Hills
You are a party of one
See the sun, I'm crossing
Salamander sleeping tight
I'm home again and dreaming
I promise, no loneliness
Church of the Painted Hills

This is our room
The paint is fresh
We kiss for we are clean of envy

SONG 6　　　*Cozy Man*

*This is one of the songs in Frueh and Kochheiser's repertoire
in which she looks at him a lot while singing.*

Gem and heart, he talks to birds

I don't know the words he says

He has a gift

With certain speech and snaky sinews

Climb his legs

Sometimes when he moans

In bed I stroke his hair

This cozy man

And then he dreams again

Chorus:

He came so long

He came so slow

He took so long to come

I wanted this

I wanted him

And things are good, yeah, good

You and I will not kill each other with our bodies

Even though we have heard about the dangerous sex

She is a cliff

Jump off and die

SONG 7   *We'll Be Dangerous*

Sit down in the dark

Sit down with me

We'll touch as if we tangoed

We'll be dangerous

Sweat like a woman

Sweat like a man

Come along with me, honey,
We'll be dangerous

Smell of orange trees
Follows me home
Don't leave now, I want to faint
We'll be dangerous

Chorus:
Talk to me, talk to me
You won't regret your words
I'll open up my lips real wide
And squawk like some exotic bird
And whistle like I had green wings
And chirp because I have no cage
Talk to me, talk to me
We'll be so dangerous

Conspirator   we burned our portraits
We wear less makeup than we used to think two perfumed people
should

SONG 8   *Beauty by Pocahontas*

We live at the end of the world
El Dorado, Emerald Isles
Some people say there's nothing to do here
Avalon, Camelot, City of Smiles
It's not very dirty or gray
Sears, Prudential, Empire State
In fact, it's blue like dynamite
I chose to come here, but it's also fate

Chorus:

Beauty by Pocahontas

I don't care if you dye your hair

Beauty by Pocahontas

Be daring, if you dare

Beauty by Pocahontas

Wear it blond or plum or pink

Beauty by Pocahontas

Don't bother me with what you think

We live at the end of the world

El Dorado, Emerald Isles

Some people say there's nothing to do here

Avalon, Camelot, City of Smiles

It's not very dirty or gray

Sears, Prudential, Empire State

In fact, it's blue like dynamite

I chose to come here, but it's also fate

Chorus:

Beauty by Pocahontas

Not Halston, Arden, or Chanel

Beauty by Pocahontas

Now buy your cleansing gel

Beauty by Pocahontas

Stray hairs, be sure to pluck

Beauty by Pocahontas

I think your values really suck

The last time I went to the coast

I did not drive alone

My navigator sat beside me

And we were tourists in the sun

     Ocean Boulevard (or Shake out the Dead)

I smelled the Ocean

Ocean Boulevard

I parked near palms and roses

There were no cops or lifeguards

I walked until I dropped

No one was near to save me

From an unexpected faint

Now it's dawn

I reached the Ocean

Ocean Boulevard

I was just about naked

I had nothing to discard

I sat down near the water

Soon I began to sway

With currents clear and cloudy

Now it's dawn

Chorus:

Well, I finally made it

Take me to the edge

Anemone, Anemone

We'll shake out the dead

Thanks to the Ocean

Ocean Boulevard

I was just about naked

I had nothing to discard

I saw the distant ship

And the golden city lights

I spun into the water

Now it's dawn

Chorus

I sat at the bottom of a canyon
And we watched the river
Our voices echoed off the walls
And into the sky

SONG 10   *Star Stream*

*Frueh all but loses herself in the lushness of Kochheiser's
streaming chords and her own alliterative lyrics.*

Stars stream across your legs
Stars stream into your eyes
Stars stream onto the wall
The river runs, we rise
To fall into the stars
So play that sweet guitar
And knock me to my nerves
We are the sirens' song

Chorus:
I am not drowning
Lure me love me
I am not drowning
We lure we love
I am not drowning
Unplug your ears
I am not drowning
Tide of liars
I am not drowning
They are washed up

I am not drowning
'Cause I can hear

I stand on solar shores
The fish rush to my feet
The waves roll over my head
And up into the trees

Chorus:
I am not drowning
Leaves of the palm
I am not drowning
Pink camellia
I am not drowning
Eel and mermaid
I am not drowning
Seal and black shark
I am not drowning
Crown me with sun
I am not drowning
'Cause I can swim

Envoi
Solar shores
Star-studded shores
Solar shores
Star-studded shores

with the exception of "Endymion" (1983) and

"There Is A Myth" (1984)

Frueh enters slowly and quietly and sits on a sofa. Her black merino wool cocktail dress, which she designed, bares her shoulders, arms, chest, and back, is snug through the torso, and flares gently from hips to mid-calf; the skirt drapes over the furniture. She changes her position for each poem that she speaks, sometimes crossing her legs so that they and her black suede sling-back high heels are very visible, sometimes leaning on one of the armrests, sometimes lounging into the depth of the sofa with one arm extended along its back.

A wooden end table sits stage right near the edge of the sofa. The table holds these items: the text, two glasses, and a bottle of red wine; Bellodgia perfume, one of her two signature scents; and a three-by-five-inch pink card on which she has written an intimate note. Frueh drinks and pours the wine when she feels like it, and when the spirit moves her, she performs the following acts at two different times: she picks up the Bellodgia bottle, walks to a

There Is A Myth

Frueh's tone is alternately delicate and caustic.

There is a myth.
It says You are better than I am
It says I am better than you are
I say We exist in equilibrium

There is a myth.
It says We are evil
We belong to the darkness and
The darkness is bad
I say We turn the lights off
And call what we see obscenity
I say Touch your fear, come clean,
And the darkness and the light will no longer oppose each other

There is a myth.
It says Balls to the walls
It says The girl's got rhythm, backseat rhythm
It says I've been around the world
I've seen a million girls
I say Cunt to the front
I say The Boy's got rhythm, backseat rhythm

I say I've been around the block

I've seen a million cocks

There is a myth.

It says Blondes have more fun

I say Marilyn Monroe killed herself

I say Jean Harlow's husband beat her

I say Jayne Mansfield was decapitated in a car accident

There is a myth.

It says Woman is Other

It says The husband is the head of the wife

It says The penis is the head of the body

It says Men are fuckers, screwing into some dead,

Dark female core, penetrating the heart of the world of ideas

It says Woman is absent, she is a cunt, a nothing, a black hole

I say I am a fucker

I say I am a cunt, and I speak with my own body

I say The phallocrats are thoughtless

I say They talk big, they talk too much about big things

I say They fear their smallness, their own absence

I say I am a woman, and I have more presence than you have absence

I say Call me the living

There is a myth.

It says Those who build their bodies are dumb

It says They who develop their minds are weak

It says You whose hearts grow deep roots will bleed

I say There is a three-in-one

A triple goddess, a trinity

I say I am a bodybuilder, thinker, bleeding heart

There is a myth.

It says You are human

I say Turn into a wolf
I say Start howling now

There is a myth.
It says Eroticism belongs in the bedroom
I say I am Eros and you are Eros and
We can kiss, tongues deep in each other's mouths, whenever we please

A friend gave me a card. It was deep violet. She had written on it in
silver the following words:

> The reality of the
> imagined:
> a complex weaving
> through layers
> Keep moving power full heart

I say

Frueh whispers

LISTEN

Different Kinds of Heat

Where I have lived
It has been hot.

My lover says The Guatemalan jungles
Are no steamier than here.
We are in a terrible heat
Just like the flaming callas in July.
Waterlilies native to the tributaries

Of The Amazon
Hold three hundred pounds because their veins
Are filled with air.
I can hardly breathe, but if I lounge along your body
on a lily pad
seven feet across the shallow pool
if you sink
      into my lips
in the botanic garden gasping
How hot I am
Will be oblivion.

My lover says It's hotter now than normal
Body temperature.
The sun scorches the earth all day to silence.
My lover runs through the desert
Like a fire god.
Then he lists the radiations
and the fluids of late June.
He uses all the trite words—
      It is sultry.
      I am sweltering sweaty dripping wet.
And his voice is washing over me
            like a hot wave
            as I wring his soaking shirt.

The desert sunset is an apocalypse of orange.
I am overheated in this city named for a saint.

Desert Sex

Infrequent headlights beam down the valley
Guiding drivers out of control
Here comes a car says one man

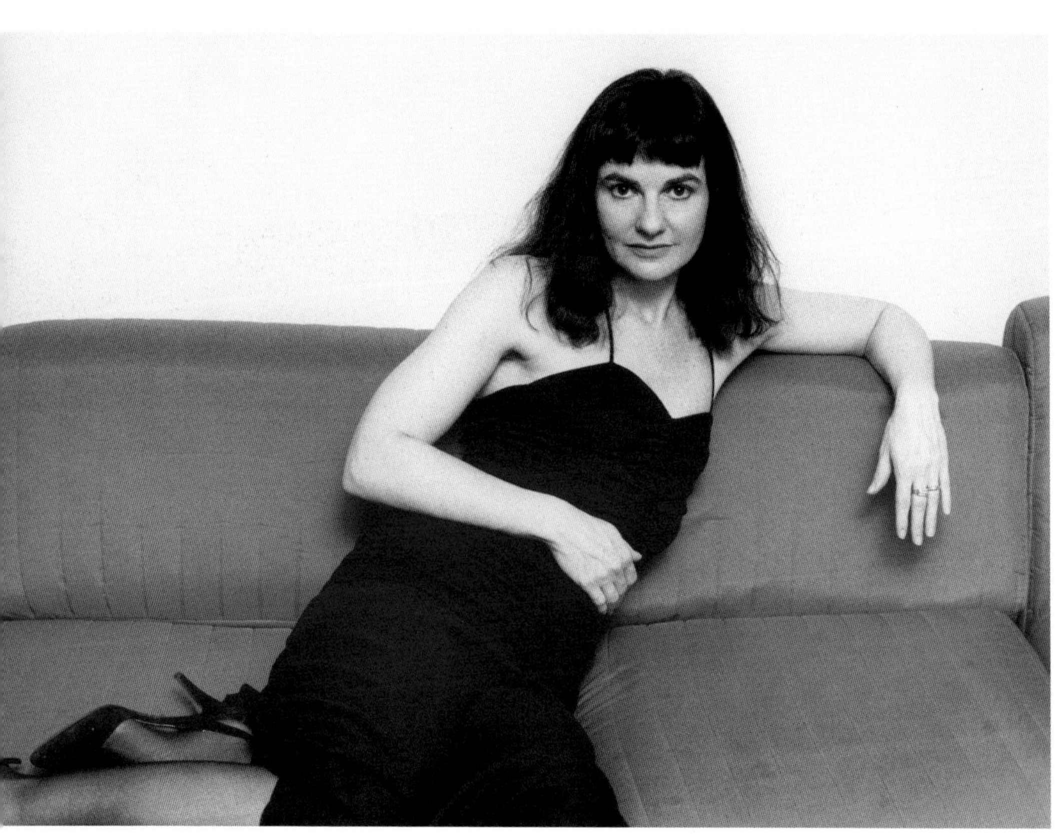

Publicity photos, *A Few Erotic Faculties*, 1986. *Photos courtesy of Huntley Barad.*

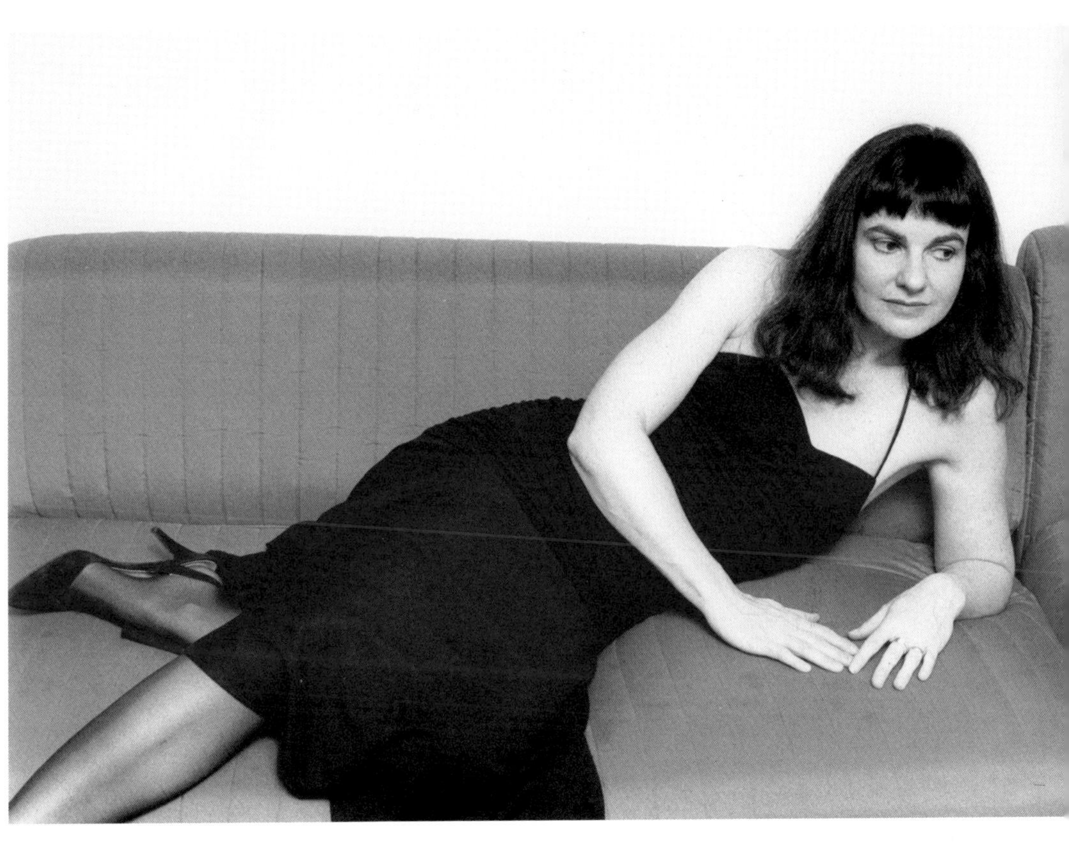

Back to the hood of his truck
Warm from a hot engine
Shirt open and pulled back over his shoulders
Moon on the muscles of his chest and abs
Jeans below his butt
Cock stiff for all the stars to see

They magnetize one woman like his lips and dick
So that she stares at unknown constellations
Spreading her feet on the desert floor
Cooling her slopping crotch with breezes

I saw a sign she laughs
Say Dripping Springs
One man dips his fingers in
Coyote cries
You're so wet one man says
Drinking
The salt of margaritas clinging to tiny places on his fleshy mouth
My big lips on your big lips he says

I want to fuck the shit out of you she says
And her tongue circles the head of his prick
That's so sweet
He says I can't imagine anyone doing it better

Then I want you one woman says
To kneel in the sand lick my pussy
In the back of the van she says
Do me a favor
Lay on top of me Hold me down
So I can feel
How strong you are

The desert says one woman is overripe
In the Summer

When the succulents flower

And their bodies croon and flame with color

The fruits of the prickly pear she says

Look like cunts

Oranges pomegranates

Fall for you

To pick up

Skin parted pulp displayed juices

Sticky on your hands

One man says the sun sucks the heart

Out of animals

Until they have to crawl in holes

One woman who had believed herself beyond bleeding says

Crawl until you growl

You will find your heart

Saguaros raise their arms as clichés turn to love

And point to the nooks

Where drivers drunk on desert sex have parked their cars

He's Got That Diamond

He's got those blue eyes that blond hair

He's got those black curls on his neck

He's got those lean legs and that lope

He's got hard muscles without trying

He's got a leather belt that's tooled

Into a snake

Around his hips

I want to slide

That snake away

I want to slither over him

Unsnap unzip undress

Redress the impropriety

That says a cunt can only wait

Like Eve for a catastrophe

Like a sleeping beauty

In the thorny State of False Desire

Lost for years in notions

Not her own

Garden

Wet

I have a mind

To grip embrace and slide Him into me

He's got that diamond

In his eyes

Across the table

Lucid with the lightning

Stroke from hip to hip

He's got that diamond

In his ear

A hearing of my dirty words assorted

Lusts

My sacred tongue

The sounds that lick the labyrinth

I bite

His earlobe when we fuck

He's got that diamond

On his tongue

A voice that takes me home

At night he spreads the sheen of his saliva

On my nipples inner thighs

He's got that diamond

In his pants

But he is never hard as rock

The body as a proving ground

For hardest substance known to man

Who ought to know

That silken thickness

Is just flesh

That gem

Is just a metaphor

We give our girls ironic riches

Name them

Opal Pearl and Ruby Beryl and Amber Jade and Jewel

The ornaments the natural wonders

Flora Heather Hazel Myrtle Holly Olive

Lily Daisy Laurel Fern Rosemary Rose

A bouquet of clues

To a partially misbegotten

Harmony

Of Dawn Spring April May

June Joy Gloria

A star still shines

Like a diamond in the sky

I do not wonder where you are

I've got that diamond

In my hands

He's got that orchid

In his pants

A Few Erotic Faculties

In your Quest for True Love
You've listened to the lyrics of ten thousand songs
Where words are coupled in

Conventional positions
Like the genders
In the dark
In man's millennia
I've got a bad desire
Oh I'm on fire
With that burning burning
Yearning feeling inside me
Deep inside
My Mississippi Queen
She was just seventeen
You know what I mean

In your Quest for True Love
You costume me in corsets apricot
And peach, rose and lavender
As if my cunt must be a fruit and flower
Sweetly spiced
I select pearls fresh from my grandma's grave
And silver shoes
In my delirium of living
I do adore myself
As Goddess of the Heart and Hard-on
But I am just a beggar
Too bare
For you in simply flesh

How can I repay you for this
Tongue-in-cheek regalia?
For your preservation
Of a few erotic faculties?
For your perseverance in adapting
Any hole to fit your cock?

The next time that I blossom

In your eyes

I will prepare your face

With cherry plum and violet

I will smooth a little color on

Your nipples

I will spray my own cologne

Bellodgia

Fragrant with carnation

Everywhere you'll sweat

When we are fucking

And the next time that you say

I want to fuck your butt your mouth your cunt

I will jam a dildo up your ass

In your Quest for True Love

Fucking in Public

Whore derives from the Latin *carus,* as does *charity*, loving others for

the sake of Love itself.

I'll take you

To my house near the foothills

We can climb

Into my bed

Along the rises

Of a pelvis hip and shoulder

Clit and hard-on

We can kick the sheets down

From the mountain

You can call me

Any name you want

I am

Your fucking Whore your Sex Boy
Some divinity
You'll tell me
Every inch is heaven then
Your screams will pulse into the street
From all the windows
I'll have opened
Everybody
Passing by our paradise
Will hear how loud the lovers are
My groans
Singing in the air
My one wild yell

When we go to Dairy Queen
Order me
To lift my skirt
Back me to the window
Push
Your head between my legs your fingers
At my waist my pubic hair and ass
Taking off
My ordinary underwear
For an Eternal Taste
The slippery tang of me the Quim the Cunt the Dairy Queen
Of down to earth desire
For the flavor of an Absolute Availability
Without the privacy of walls
Inside my heart
I'll be your whore if you'll be mine
And pay me for my milk
With liquid just as smooth
And oozing

From the opening of charity

I touch my finger to my thigh

I put my finger to my tongue and yours

We kiss and rearrange our clothes

We look at people's melted sweets

And in their eyes

The Word

A woman at the window whispers to me

As we leave

The Word is Flesh

We're driving through the park

On Friday night in summer

Lust lays thick

In the humidity

I'm breathing hard

On curving roads

We trail a car

The Woman at the Wheel speeds through

A young man's longing

Looking for an evening friend

To last like an Ascension

In the soul forever

I see him turn his head

Under the lamplight

Eager eyes collecting tears

Lips about to cry for the connection

Everybody wants

From Earth to Heaven

Air to Ocean

Shooting star to sweetest grass

From ground beyond the atmosphere

Of superficial fondlings

We start to touch

Each other's hair

So full

From all the moisture

That each strand seems to tremble

In the heavy breeze

And hum along my hands

Until I pull tight at your scalp and

Urge your mouth to mine with moans that

Float like fleshy petals

To the sycamores and

Roses

What corny excess they've inspired

In romantics of both Church and Sex

    Your mouth is like a rosebud

    Your skin is soft as a rose petal

    My love is like the red red rose

    Mary is the Mystic Rose

    The Holy Rose a medieval scholar writes of as a

        Vulvic sign

    The scarlet flower fucked to ecstasy

    The white rose of Dante's paradise

    You smell like a rose

    Or am I just excited by

    The Infinite Aroma of your pheromones?

    O leave your dewdrop in my rose

I squeeze your ass to set

The rhythm of your cock inside me

Near a building called the Jewel Box

Made of steel and glass

Transparently alluring

We are not alone

For all around us roses are unfolding

In the dawn of sex that's not sub rosa

We listen to the lapping and the sucking of

Rings around the rosies and

The squoosh and click of

Rosy holes

Theologians talk to god

In orgies of epistemology

Authorities of Nothing Much about

The suction and the friction of the sexes

They don't even know

Lovemaking is charisma

I know

What I know

I speak with lubricity about ideas of ardent origin

I trust no orthodoxies   jaded beyond belief

        in the body   commonplace

              is a temple   sentimental

Born in the dimensions of a gem with undetermined facets

And the Acknowledgment

To fuck your lover high and low

And the Water Will Turn Red

In the afternoon

The bathtub fills

And I am bleeding cramping

Thinking when I sit down in the soothing heat

The water will turn red

And as it does

I see us in the darkened desert

Kneeling naked

Unaware of prickliness beneath our bodies
(And maybe my knees will bleed
And maybe a rock already scratched my back.)
We have fucked my cramps away.
My blood is covering your cock.
While you're still stiff
I stroke the shaft
Then line your cheekbones breastbone
Find the beginning of your spine
And paint your posture as you face me.
Another stroke and red
Will mark me up the middle
To my mouth.
A small and sticky kiss
A mixing
Of blood and sand

The darker color will seek deep ground
So deep
The mountains and the water will turn red

Venus Street

Venus is the Evening Star, the generic nude in Renaissance paintings,
some say the Goddess of Desire alone.
You're walking Venus Street again
Footsteps follow you
Follow them
The chase is on
For hunters of musk secretions Lubricants
To ease the application of words of love
In L.A. Austin Nashville New York

Your black boots need new soles

Jet across the water

And Aphrodites rise from your seasoned doubt

To stroll

In Paris Bruges Bologna Oslo Dusseldorf The Hague

The Evening Stars are out

To glitter in fake jewels and junk

Bought secondhand

The Evening Stars

Are foaming

Compliments and other honeys

The Evening Stars

Are looking for some cock

To crow about

You like to lie beneath the Evening Stars

Or leave on the light so you can see Your penis

Lustrous with their cum

When they scream

On their stomachs

They twist the hotel sheets

And all the mothers daughters sons and fathers say

Jesus Christ and God

We call the deities

In hours of unspeakable grace

No one asks for a woman

Venus with her many names

Laura Peggy Nancy Frances

Aphrodite Stella Maris

Miriam Elise and Annie

Moerae Ishtar and Astarte

Janet Claire Joanna Edith

Inanna and Libitina

Renée Sarah Katie Mary

Notre Dame Ma Donna Mia

You know them all on Venus Street

Our Ladies Bella Donnas are the drug

For soothing a severity

Of Venereal dis-ease

Birdman and the Siren

I

Birdman sings

At the Siren's Window

He vamps her

Because his voice is pure and

She has heard his tunes before

Sung them herself

From childhood on

In trouble

They have solaced her to sleep

When daylong headaches

Dull her appetite

Birdman's Melodies

Remind her of

Her brother dead at birth

Who tells her in her dreams that

She is beautiful

Birdman perched

By the pink geraniums

On the back porch

Compels her through his songs

To confess that

Love is plentiful

Which she won't admit to many

Animals or Men

For they are cheap with passion

But once the words are spoken

Birdman and the Siren know that

They will sing

As long as the notes can quiver

II

The Siren says

I may go mad

If I don't see you soon

My thighs will turn to flab

And I will grow a dumpling brain

I will lie in bed alone

Where all the walls are painted crocus

Pale enough to beg for sunlight

Mother says

You know about those lavenders

I read they make you so damn hot that

You can hardly stand it

To be left alone with only pride

And a belly full of veins

III

The Siren says to Birdman

I can see the sinews in your calves

They snake and I can hear them hiss

Mother

You would never see beneath his skin

Never hear the serpents though they slid

Across your forehead

Ran their fangs

Along the hairs above your ears

Mother

I have pressed my lips

To his flat stomach

Then his thighs

And pushed my finger between his buttocks

His eyes turned black and

Astro Man I say there is no space between us

I V

Together Birdman and the Siren

Recollect conception

It could have happened other times

When he slapped her grabbed her shoulders

Rode her like a mare

When he shuddered

And he called her Queen of the Velvet Cunt

When she scratched the skin at the bottom of his spine

When she saw his eyes flash

Blacker than a man's

When she demanded harder

Harder harder pretty boy

But all those times they did not want

A child

In early May

The night was almost cold

The Siren lit a fire

In the living room

They kissed

The fire

Crackled frightening the Siren

And she said I feel strange

Angels in the room

Now they're gone she said

As Birdman and the Siren

Sucked each other close and came

She said I'm seeing gold

And blue stars on the wall and in the air

Between us Birdman said

The angels have come

V

The midwife spoke to Birdman

Advising him to

Be a Swimmer

Fishman in the Siren's Sea

The two of you must take a trip

And somewhere on that sea is good

Fishman snakeman Birdman slept

Beside the Siren

On board ship

Together dreaming red

As if vulnerable to some miracle

Blood Sister and Blood Brother

Blood stone and blood bath

Blood line and blood thirst

Blood boiling and blood letting

Blood sucking and blood staining

Blood stirring

In the morning

Birdman and the Siren stood on deck

No shore in sight

They felt the pain and saw the blood

The Siren catching

Birdman's eye

They shouted I'm alive!

Rock Garden

He stares at her at the Pacific
Reclining on a chaise longue
She watches him walk by
Hairy with brief trunks
And yells Cut it off!
With a machete!

He wants her to call him Nighthawk
To snap when he attempts seduction
Are you kidding?
Be my baby in a melody of love
Playing inside my womb?

Nighthawk dreams her
Nonchalantly stripping from the waist up
She displays her breasts and
Rubs with the rotation of a fingertip
Her nipples till they stiffen and
He tries to kiss them
When she slaps his face
He retreats
Awed into stupidity
As if a classic nude could prostitute itself for him
She spreads her legs and
Pulls her full skirt to her hips
No underwear
Reveals the black curls
Where her fingers idle
As she raises one leg to sink her foot
Into the seat
He apologizes in his mind for gazing at
Her triple lips

That he will never lick

Or stroke

Or penetrate

With both her index fingers

She parts her inner lips and

Slides her buttocks

To the sofa's velvet edge

Shoulder blades pressed to the pillows at her back

So he can better see

Her seeping cum Her fingers glide

Into her slit

At once and in an alternating rhythm

Slowly circling her clit

Petting all the dark pinks into slickness

With his breath between her legs

He savors sweat mixed with perfume

He asks its name

She bathes her fingers to the knuckle

Drawing out a clear elastic thread

That thins to nothing

Inches from his eyes

She sucks the liquid from her skin

Shoves his chest with one foot

Says Rock Garden

Fleurs de Rocaille

You came he says

I saw your cunt lips tighten

Face expressionless as ever

She stands

Slips her feet inside her shoes

Buttons her blouse and tucks it in

What's it to you?

Yanks her skirt above her waist

Sits spread-eagled on the sofa

Jams her crotch against the cushion

Gyrates

Saunters to the door and leaves

A glistening stain

Nighthawk sits with black espresso

In a café by a harbor

After eating nothing sweet or salty

Spicy creamy or refreshing

Impossible to embrace

He folds her in his thoughts

For him she's hairy in lush places

Where other women are afraid

To show themselves

Her joy is posing

Naked for a prone man

Like a crazy beauty queen

Parading in high heels

She carries whips

To make him wail

And swings a sword

Blade etched with stars and half moons

I road a horse in battle

Magic in my weapon

I was slicing heads off slashing skin

Ruby splatters on my gloves

She presses one thumb to the heartbeat in his neck

You hope at any moment

I will kiss your throat

Instead you feel the marks of my salvation

You will thank me for a love bite

But I see a little puncture

In your integrity a wound

At which I test

Your strength and flavor

She divests herself of tenderness

When baring just the basic

Flesh and fur

He thinks she is professional

Controlling how his blood diffuses

Through the satin sheets

Deadening

The shell-pink luster

Like her menstrual flow when

It begins during sleep

He reaches for the gleaming hairs

That shade the watering mouth

His own hangs open

As she lashes him into a dog

Penis rigid panting on an airless summer evening

Nighthawk pictures her

In the first photographs he saw of people fucking

She is chained to the floor

And he is grinding hard

Trying to implant her with a long

Lost love

Endymion

I

The sensitive system needed

A rest: no nourishment

to divide the organ's attention

Fasting

in solitude like a fat

little monk.

Sometimes the cleansing is

A purge:

No dissenters against

The cause of a soul

in revolution.

II

I walk in the door and smell

Sweat.

You also wear

The scent of fish.

I'd always

Read that's how

We know the female's place.

Were they wise

Man's words?

"When her cunt

Is damp, it is because

She has just stepped out

Of the ocean."

You are not the woman

You once were.

Your body no

Longer melts when we move

Together naked.

A change in

Passion has differently construed flesh and bone.

Ah press into

Me. You are firmer

Than before, a fucking

Man.

I I I

Remember

Endymion.

It is a painting

in the Louvre

He is a youth

Forever

in the forest Lips

turned to the moon.

We call her Selene

Or Luna the celestial whore Diana

Or Artemis who never

Hunt for men.

Her light

Lays him

Bare. He undulates

For she burns

without fire to the blood.

They will never obey

One another and that is their

Love Lunatic

Watching touching sleeping

Undemanding they

Carry on In the close

Night

Air

Through the distance

Of dreams never knowing

How deep they are

It Is Time

It is time

for me to dream about the luxury of making love with you

It is time

for me to hold your hand after you cut your finger

to kiss your palm

It is time

for you to bring me brassy roses and baby's breath

It is time

to put your arm around me when we leave the restaurant

It is time

for your voice to give me chills

It is time

for my mouth to go dry

It is time

To hear your groans and sighing on the telephone when you say

I have to touch myself

It is time

for our love to terrify me

It is time

to talk about diseases shared by modern lovers

It is time

to learn the curves and angles

It is time

to run my tongue along your teeth

It is time

for me to see you stiffen in your pants

It is time

for the wetness between my legs

It is time

to nevermind the clock

It is time

to say how much I want to sleep with you

Frueh removes her shoes and lies on the sofa,
her back to the audience.

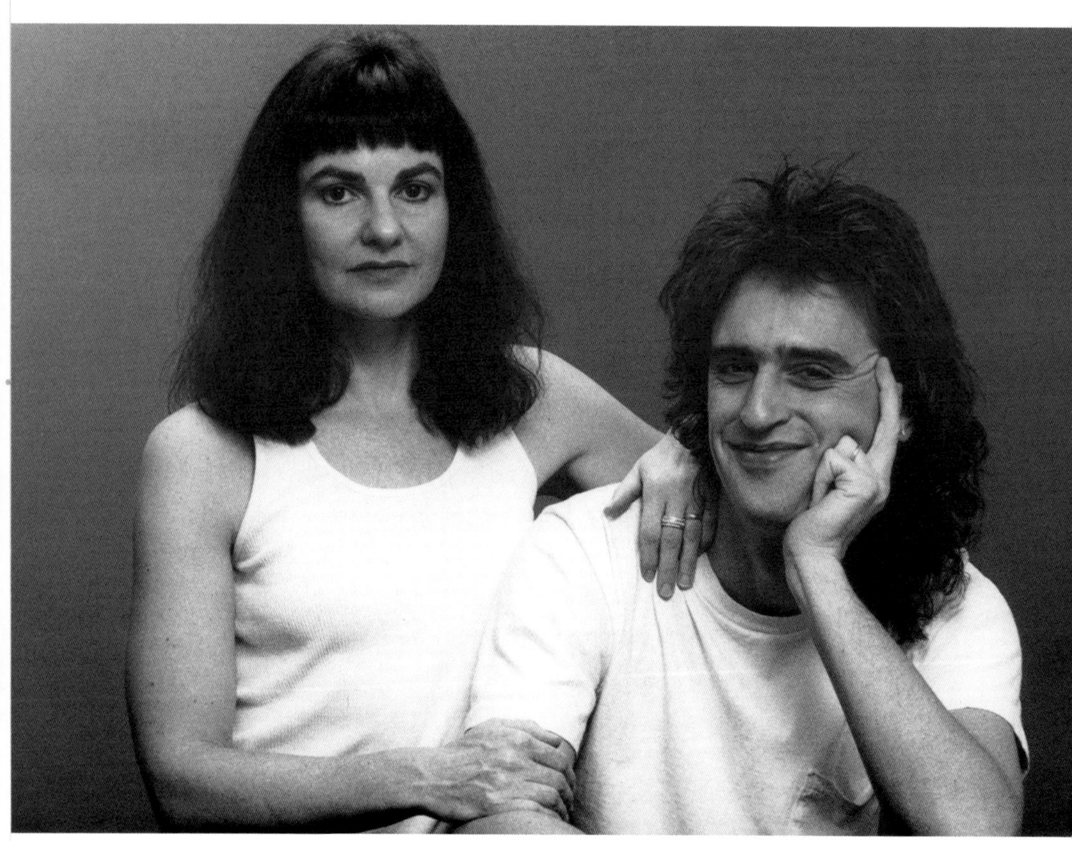

Publicity photo, *Clairvoyance (For Those In The Desert)*, 1986.

Photo courtesy of Huntley Barad.

silver cross and a diamond stud in one pierced ear. They drank from his liquid blue eyes and could almost taste the richness of his mouth, the lower lip so plump you'd like to bite it. Fire Hands was ripe, and sometimes they wanted to share his lusts, for he was generous, satisfy them all together. But his means of fulfillment differed from theirs.

Fire Hands ran in the desert for his health at 4 p.m. when the temperature was ninety-four degrees. He'd eat enormous meals for two weeks. Then he'd fast, drinking glass after glass of fresh lemon juice, honey, and cayenne pepper for ten days until he cleaned out his system and lost many pounds. He practiced no orthodoxies save one—drug-taking. Shooting heroin, he said, was a rite of passage and it was better than sex. "Hey, you two," he'd say, "I can quit anytime."

You wouldn't want to go south of the border with this man. But they did.

The last time they saw Fire Hands his teeth were turning brown along the bottom gums and the uppers of his boots had loosened from the soles. Maybe the clammy pallor of his complexion came from exhaustion, for he had recently returned from a tour in foreign lands. Maybe the greasiness appeared because the desert air was so hot and the season was monsoon. Maybe his hair was dirty, brown, and stringy because he was simply too tired to wash it and they were good friends, intimate enough to understand. They paid for his dinner and his margaritas. Never a big talker, he hardly spoke to them at all. They noticed the delicacy of his thighs beneath old black jeans and remembered later, after he and they had parted, that Fire Hands had eaten all their food and bought none when he house-sat for them and had at the same time drunk all their liquor except for a finger's width in every bottle, each of which he replaced exactly where he had found it. He is turning into a predator, they said, a sly one.

The Indians call Coyote sly. Because he outsmarts man. He survives. Fire Hands's future is less secure than Coyote's, for what good does it do to outwit your friends? Men are killing Coyote, but Fire Hands is killing himself. Maybe he is dead as I speak to you.

No. Fire Hands haunts them, but he is not yet a ghost.

And Coyote's slyness in no way diminishes the heart of his beauty.

SONG 2   *Coyote*

> Coyote crossed the speedway
> Then stood by the road
> Looked at me, I stopped my car
> He was golden as the sun went down
>
> Coyote likes to eat sheep
> Kills them in the night
> Don't be scared, the desert dog
> Was so golden as the sun went down
>
> Coyote pokes at garbage
> Near the city streets
> A cold meal and some poison
> He was golden as the sun went down
>
> *Chorus:*
> Arizona blue sky
> Swallow him today
> Your sun comes down and picks him up
> And carries him away
>
> Arizona blue sky
> Swallow me today
> Your sun comes down and picks me up
> And carries me away

On a Desert City Sunday when the sky was the dense blue that no postcard could reproduce, the women met. They called each other *honeybunch* near a viaduct that flooded in even a modest rain and across the street from a boarded-up hotel painted warm pink.

One woman lit cigarette after cigarette. The smoke became a perfume floating quickly away in the clear air. Trellises filled with bougainvillea and oleander climbed the wall behind the friends.

Unafraid of being corny, one woman said, "Your perfume is intoxicating." Every so often she noticed rock music, from an unseen source, songs repeating on a tape loop, and water, rolling and dripping in a fountain nearby but out of sight. During these moments the sounds themselves seemed lucid, as if aware of their own presence, each tone of its own existence.

As the women talked, about work and men, their pasts and futures, the possibility of love for them or anyone, the lipstick faded from their mouths. The hotel's rough walls were turning blush, then rosy orange to mauve, then violet, and soon their edges and much inner detail disappeared.

Desert City streets were poorly lit. The rapes and murders would begin with sundown.

But the women did not worry about blood that night. They told their plans for the next day. One said that she liked to face the light and feel the sun's warmth through her hair. And the longer she stayed in Desert City the redder her dark hair grew.

SONG 3   *Scarlet Women*

Prelude 1

I sat at a bar with some women

They said, "Let's go out back"

There were tables, chairs, and a fountain

The moon came up so flat

Prelude 2

Their perfumes were mixing with flowers

We didn't count the beers

We were loud like a storm at midnight

And soft as wind in leaves

We are the scarlet women

We've been burned by the sun

We walk the streets at high noon

We have no need to run

From heat that makes our heads swim
And makes our bodies shake
We are the scarlet women
The bottomless blue lake

I am a scarlet woman
I came here for the heat
I came here for the palm trees
I came so I could meet
Some other scarlet hearts of steel
Some lips and nails as red
Because we're scarlet women
You'd like to see us dead

But we are burning too hot
And you are just too cold
You've got no hunger or thirst
That cannot be controlled
By some dreamed up oasis
And even though I ache
I am a scarlet woman
The bottomless blue lake

Three Scarlet Women drove thirty miles southwest of Desert City. Their destination was the birthplace of a friend who often carried a plastic purse of sparkling gold. In Desert City he had stamped red cows on the sidewalk in front of the homes of people he loved. All three women found red cows one morning as they walked to their cars.

At sixty miles per hour the driver swerved to the right. "I saw a snake in the road," she said. "Did you see it?"

The others hadn't, but one said, "Go back. I've never seen a snake in the desert." Night was falling, but the driver hadn't yet turned on the headlights. Seeing no traffic, she put the car in reverse, all three looking for the snake so that it would not be hit.

The driver pulled to the side of the road. They had spotted the snake on the shoulder. The woman at the wheel got out of the car. "It's hurt," she said. "Maybe someone ran over it."

"No," said the second woman, looking too at a wound. "Then it wouldn't have been able to move this far."

"I can hardly hear the rattle," said the third. She found a stick in the back of the car and held it toward the snake. She picked the snake up and laid it in the desert brush.

The rattle was softer than before as the women stepped into the car.

"Let's stop here on our way back," said the second woman.

Hours after darkness they easily found the spot. The driver turned the headlights off, took out a flashlight from the glove compartment, and turned it on even though the moon was bright. Each woman thought, "Maybe the snake revived and we won't find it. Or maybe it will bite one of us."

Neither was the case. The snake was dead where they had left it. The driver asked the second woman, "Do you want to take it with you?" She shook her head no.

The next day another woman who had also driven to the birthplace southwest of Desert City phoned each of the three. "I passed you on the road last night where the car was parked. At first I was worried. I didn't see the flashlight. Then I felt like you'd been spirited away, into the desert or the stars."

SONG 4   *Rattlesnake*

· ·

This song's passion is rough, and the melody is almost non-existent. Frueh feels relieved when the song has passed through her.

Chorus:
Snakebite is no accident
Snakebite is no answer
Snakebite is a choice to live
Forever in the desert
Rattle me with your snakebite
Riddle me with your venom

A desert juice, no anger
Just a snakebite, snake bite me

Snake bite me I will not jump
I've looked for you under the rocks

Snake bite me bring me to earth
I'm on my belly moving slow

Snake bite me and make me die
I'll lie in the desert with you

Snake bite me I'm not afraid
Saguaro will be my tombstone

Chorus

Venom derives from the Latin *venenum,* magic charm, drug, poison and it is akin to the Latin *venus,* love, charm, which is spelled like the goddess of love, Venus. The snake lady has won many hearts by being charming. Maybe she has drugged her lovers with her tongue. Maybe she has bitten them on the neck or leg.

One morning as the heat rose five degrees an hour, she was lying in her back yard wearing a bikini. While she stared at the cloudless sky, squinting in the almost unbearable brightness, a thin line of sweat appeared at her waist and trickled to her navel. She felt her lower back. It was wet. So was the skin behind her knees. Making a decision, she said out loud, "I'm going to love like a bitch."

She stood up seeing sunspots, ready for a sundance, waiting for no sungod.

For many years she had worn a perfume labeled Bandit. It was no longer available, so she had not bought any for months. But her last bottle, long empty, sat on the bathroom windowsill, sun shining through the dark and shapely glass.

    Border Cowgirl (for Peggy)

You got out of your car
You went to the center line
You saw a snake curled up
The sun made its scales shine

You stood in the desert
A spider crawled to your boots
You put it in your hand
Tarantula to your roots

Chorus:
You may be an old spider woman
You may be a snake lady's child
To me you're a border cowgirl
So willing to be wild

You made love on a rock
Till your back began to bleed
Stone and sand are tender
When your love's a tumbleweed

You saw a smiling boy
At a Mexican motel
He strangled a songbird
You told him to go to hell

Chorus:
You may be a scarlet woman
You may be a snake lady's child
To me you're a border cowgirl
So willing to be wild
Put on your boots of green leather
And let's take a walk in the wild

Down Mescal Road and Manlove Street

So willing to be wild

Just stand out in the monsoon rain

And hug me when the winds are wild

And soothe me when I've walked too far

So willing to be wild

You're just a border cowgirl

So willing to be wild

Border Cowgirl told a story.

She and some friends were visiting the reservation. They spent a weekend with a lawyer, another friend of Border Cowgirl's, who worked with the Indians. One night the lawyer suggested that she and the visitors go to a bar. She knew many of the people who drank there regularly. Inside, an old Indian man sang a song in his tribal language. Border Cowgirl said the song was beautiful. When the old man finished he approached her table and said to one of the men something like, "Now you sing." The man said that he could not sing, that he had no song. The Indian could not believe this and asked the other man again and again to sing. With each refusal, the old man became more and more distraught. He would not take no for an answer. He was beyond reason. Finally his own friends carried him out the door.

Border Cowgirl told this story many times.

SONG 6   *This Is Not the West*

I went to a circus

It wasn't fun at all

A buffalo jumped through a flaming hoop

And I did not applaud

I went to a restaurant

Fake guns hung on the wall

With posters of John Wayne as a cowboy

And I could hardly eat

I went to the movies

The men were lean and tall

They shot each other and laughed at the blood

I walked out halfway through

Chorus:

There's a sickness of the soul

For this is not the West

This is just false paradise

Your dreamed-up wilderness

There's a sickness of the soul

You think the West was won

Woods and cactus died for you

Pumas are on the run

I am seeing in the dark

I had a dream last night

I was called White Buffalo Woman

And I learned how to fight

Chorus:

For there's a sickness of the soul

And this is not the West

If I'm White Buffalo Woman

I'll teach you how to fight

Even though they knew how to rub the earth and heat the sand, doing these things was not enough.

One sunset in the month of evenings filled with lightning, he said, "I want to leave."

She said, "If that's what you want, we'll do it. We'll buy you a ticket and put you on a plane. You can leave me, leave the desert for a summer, forever."

She did not cry and he was surprised.

"Don't you feel like you're in a prison?" he asked.

"No, not at all. I can leave if I need to."

Again he was surprised.

"But I will fight for us," she said. "I will fight until we both feel free."

They took a drive around Desert City, talking about old affairs and indecision, everything that had been hurting them for so long. In the foothills at one edge of the city they stopped to look at all the lights below. It was not a time for romance. They drove the valley streets, hour after hour, and at last she cried because she understood that she had almost broken his heart so badly that he could not trust her.

As they walked in the door of their home, the phone was ringing. She picked up the receiver and a Scarlet Woman talked about breaking up with a lover of twelve years. Then another Scarlet Woman called to say that she would have to have a hysterectomy.

The rain was falling when he turned the lights off and they were remembering what someone had told them when they arrived in Desert City. The desert, they heard, was a proving ground, a labyrinth for the heart.

SONG 7   *Going Down*

> The rains came fast this year
> Maybe there'll be a flood
> A city with no gutters
> We'll be washed away
>
> *Chorus:*
> We're all going somewhere
> We're all going down
> Fast and hard and frantic
> We're all going down
>
> Friend, I'm in the desert
> Friend, I'm all alone

Maybe the sun will blind me

Maybe cure my soul

Stand with me in the sun

Take the heat with me

Lie down near the cholla

Close to me as you dare

When you're good and naked

When we're skin to skin

The monsoon's going to drench us

Shiver in my arms

Chorus

I look at your picture

But you're not even there

God I cannot see you

Where'd you disappear?

Chorus

It sounds stupid to say that the mountains were on fire, the sky was in a blaze, and as they looked up, another fiery star was falling. It made the four of them crazy with desire for each other.

The television was on and a voice carried outside saying, "The borders are out of control. It's a modern-day horror story." Fire Hands had already drunk three screwdrivers and Border Cowgirl was barbecuing chicken, preparing dinner for departing friends.

They did not want to go, because the desert was their home and no one who had lived there belonged anywhere else forever after.

Each time they returned to Desert City, they were never simply visitors, and every time they left, they cried, as if there were not enough tears for their bodies to create.

They sat with Fire Hands and Border Cowgirl, watching them drink a lot, listening to them cracking dirty jokes and exchanging nasty witticisms, all an effort not to show in tears how much they wished that their friends would stay with them, locked always in the immediate embrace of Desert City.

SONG 8   *Zodiac Lounge*

Throughout this song Frueh finds it difficult to veil her tears.

Let's meet in the Zodiac Lounge
Where there are windows all around
And you can see the ground and sky
Let's open the windows real wide

Chorus:
See them coming, tempests from the West
Look up quick it's going to rain
I don't live anywhere anymore
I'm an alien, alien

It's dark in the Zodiac Lounge
With the wind whipping at our throats
The sand is flying in my face
And the flowers have fallen down

Chorus:
See them coming, tempests from the West
Is it clear you've got no place now?
I don't know anyone anymore
I'm an alien, alien

I'm lost in the Zodiac Lounge
But can you kiss me anyway?

As the mountains burn far away

Struck by lightning, struck so hard

Chorus:

See them coming, tempests from the West

Have you come to a conclusion?

Can I help you touch the ground?

We're such aliens, aliens

BREATHING

*A Proposal for a Performance by Joanna Frueh and
Russell Dudley • Written by Joanna Frueh*

*A restaurant table for two, with one chair on either side, sits
center stage. A vase holding a large, brilliant red or pink flower
stands in the middle of the white tablecloth. Audience seating is
very close to the table. The performers, dressed for a date, enter
from opposite sides, and each takes a seat. Dudley removes his
jacket and Frueh sets the vase at the back of the table. The performers lean toward each other and begin to breathe, audibly, in
variant rhythms. The performance continues as long as . . .*

NOTE:

The proposal was not completed.

This is Frueh and Dudley's first performance collaboration. It differs considerably from
their individual performances.

Frueh stands in front of a set created by artist Bailey Doogan. ("Bailey" is Doogan's professional name. Her friends call her Peggy.) Paintings from Doogan's show, which she titled St. Lucy/Oedipus, *extend to the right and left from center stage. Frueh uses a white column provided by Doogan to hold the text. Red velvet winds up the wall voluptuously behind the column, and the color of the fabric corresponds with Frueh's scarlet dress—a long-sleeved wool jersey, designed by her, under which she wears nothing. The low neckline bares her shoulders, the sleeves show the curves of her biceps, and the skirt skims her knees. Black suede sling-back high heels ground her boldly defined presence—beaming in red, lipstick as well as dress, with a gold art deco necklace whose diamonds and aquamarines sparkle just below the hollow of her throat.*

Dear Peg,

My Lucy poem isn't working. Not as originally conceived. I thought it would start with a narrative.

Lucy, a Sicilian saint, who died in the third century, was one of the many virgin martyrs of Christianity. She came from a wealthy family and distributed her riches to the poor. A suitor sought Lucy as a wife, but she rejected him, choosing to gouge out her eyes and send them to him in a goblet rather than lose the independence she had.

Lucy would not be moved, except by her own desire and belief. When Roman soldiers tried to drag her out of the temple in which the Empire had imprisoned her, she stood, more tree- than statue-like, rooted to the floor. The ropes and pulleys, the oxen were useless against the force of her faith, and it is recorded that one soldier, clearly a psychic as well as a physical warrior, exclaimed, "She is a rose whose petals as well as thorns make her invincible! She is the plant whose roots curl round and round like strong and twining cords, and shoot so deep they pierce the earth's foundation and rocket to the stars!"

The fire the soldiers built at Lucy's feet on the temple's stone floor did not kill her. The flames licked her toes and heels and calves and thighs like loving tongues of enlightenment, and after they had spoken their vermilion desire and belief, the color hot as her own conviction, the flames turned liquid and ran like blood into the cracks between the stones. The fact that the blood left no stain was said, by medieval worshipers, to signify the purity of Lucy's heart.

The soldiers also poured hot oil into Lucy's ears, and one of them stabbed her in the throat with a dagger. As her inner vision became clearer when she gouged out her eyes, so her ability to hear the songs of angels was enhanced and her skill at speaking with any and all deities increased.

Finally the soldiers thrust swords in Lucy's flesh and organs and she died. Speculation abounds as to the location of the wounds. Theologians say it was the heart, but medieval witches, who prayed to St. Lucy as a healer and a nurturer, say the soldiers stabbed her in the cunt as well. For Lucy, as was known to Imperial spies, was a sexual omnivore who especially loved young men.

The spies had found a note, written to one lover, that read only:

Responsible to the stable virgin.

Even liars, who used their eyes and ears and throats for evil, knew, from women on the streets and the word of ancient priestesses that lingered in the intuition, that to be a virgin meant to be autonomous, clean of soul. The soldiers had spotted the note in the young man's garden, as if it had fallen from his clothing as he was fleeing, at Lucy's urging, for his life.

It is said that Lucy was resurrected, that her sight was restored, as were her voice and hearing, and it is also said that she then lived, in culture, wildness, and in marriage, with the man to whom she had written: *Responsible to the stable virgin.* For he was one too.

And Lucy's husband achieved the smooth and supple strength of bald men intrigued over the years with the workings of their own bodies and lovingly accustomed to their semen, snot, and shit. And Lucy aged into the womanhood of silver hair and deeper eyes than ever.

I'm fascinated that this narrative is not what I thought it would be. I thought it would be pretty neutral, or more part of the poem of pain that had been coming to mind. I'd written many of the notes in a time of dire straits—divorce and difficult new involvement. I'd been creating Lucy as a prophet of doom, telling her own story, able to see all—past and future—and relating history as well as life as a battle of the sexes: the torment of dead-end quests.

Since I wrote the first notes I've freed myself of the agonies of ungroundedness. During the weeks of dire straits I felt like I was quite literally up in the air, my head disconnected from my body. I remember meeting someone for a business lunch and wondering, as I walked down the street, if I'd put on my skirt and underpants. Even when I saw the skirt, right there where it should be at my waist, covering my hips, clinging to me, making me safe and sexy at the same time, I still wasn't sure I wasn't naked. People said to me, "You look great!" and I thought, Don't you see I'm not all here? That I'm dazed, part of me in the throes of a death that won't permit rigor mortis?

Anyway, the earth has become my companion once again, and the air is simply what I breathe, not the habitat of a shrieking soul. A couple weeks ago, then, when I realized with a clarity that had not come before how much my psychic and actual circumstances had changed—the releasing ritual of divorce court accomplished, the new relationship not yet settled but no longer a cause for obsessive anguish—I knew that Lucy couldn't be a martyr spouting nastiness and sarcasm. That's not what your Lucy and Oedipus paintings are about, and it's not what my writing is about. Our work is about victories of vision.

During my days of dire straits, I was blind and you helped me see.

Frueh looks at Doogan with love and tears.

I was up in the air and you said my feet would touch ground soon enough for sanity to be maintained. We were in your studio, looking at Lucy and Oedipus, and I was talking about sex and connectedness, the communion you and I have felt, each with only one man, one lover, in the richness of experience with many men. You and I talked about the compelling terror and voluptuousness of going over the edge in such an intimacy between a woman and a man. You and I agreed that love of that depth and passion is so rare as to be found once in a lifetime if at all. I said, I love your work because it deals with that kind of sexuality, the possibility of a visceral and psychic and intellectual union from which neither partner would return to the everyday world, in one mental piece or at all. You deal in the dangers of magic, medicine, the spirit world, and to do that is a victory of vision.

I don't want to pretend, despite the victory of having navigated dire straits, that they are not a part of the geography of my soul or yours or Lucy's. So I must write down some lines for you from the piece I'd first planned. It's good to recognize a passage, to not deny the process of pain that may have to move us from one point to another.

The poem would have begun:

I see

I see the body

Icy body

Tortured into coldness

(I see through the heart

Waves

Of my own blood

Running cold.)

The sequence of the following sections is unimportant. Now that they are markers of passage, I don't have to think about how to structure them for greatest sense or impact. (Events and language, remembered as poetry, find their own configuration anyway, despite the writer's seeming control.)

Eyesore I
Am tired of the sights
Man has created
And its histories
Keeping me
Awake the sore-eyed insomniac
Breeding tourist headaches
I am Lucy in the Sky with Diamonds
Rich in misery
(Still starry-eyed)
And Skepticism

I am sightless in the eyes of men
A site
Of detestation
And when they stabbed   my throat blood spurted
From the bottom of my voice my blood
Covered their hands   horny like
    lizards' skin liquids dripping like vermilion fire
(I cannot tell the difference between blood and flame. The Christians drink red wine and say it is The Blood, as if there is no other blood than Christ's, as if my own mortality were not their desire, as if men never knew My Blood through memories of birth or in the menstruation dried on my clothes, their cocks or rags and sheets.)

I look at you
the angry aging bitches
still on tour
You are elders

at the temples
You are white and vulval pink
with scars you are the sisters and the brothers
Who I love as illegalities of flesh
Who are looking for adventure in whatever comes
Their way
Who say, See see rider
See what you have done
My moments of contentment
Come through
the blitzkrieg black of nights ill-starred
one by one with cold
points of light like blade tips
Fed with My Blood
Blinded by the scintillations
Hidden in starless skies
The sight Medusa
Took from men
The heroes ravished
by her penetrating
Vision Snakes
Interlocking—twining
Heading for the eyes
Dancing into irises
Snapping out the whites and pupils
Whipping them, each coiled uncoiling tendril into its fanged orifice.
Dead men surround
Medusa and the Sphinx.
Bones and rot array the so-called monsters' feet

Man alive
I am looking for you
I the Snake

I the Sphinx

I the lonely opening

to love

I the woman veiled head to toe in false

Enigmas   flirting with

All I've got

Looking for a way out

Looking for love in all the wrong places

I am searching

For the winged protection of an angel man

My women

Friends

(All saints, I say,

Under the eyes of men)

Are theorists. They test a phrase, an idiom by living

One woman says male bonding is oxymoronic

Another knows the missing link

The lack of doubled chromosomes

One seer calls the problem a poisoning by testosterone

Another says The more hair the less heart

And all the sister saints agree

That men are the afflicted sex

That too much hair or hormone

Too little courtship of each other

Genetic fallibility

Are too sad for tears

And then my women laugh

For if the source of pain is sex not gender

Then why not keep the eyes dry and the cunt wet?

My women

Friends

Say they are afflicted too

With talking

As if the world could change through contests of conversation

Men sit on the mountaintop

In the desert

Hermit saints

These are lovely pictures

    Man alone

    Ascetic isolation

    The senses stuck

    Between Him and a rock a dune a palm tree glacier

        Cataract

Oh, boys

and girls listen to this

          sacred story once

Again come see daddy

In Jerusalem

On the cross

What a pretty

Image in his loincloth

In the wasteland

Sexy demons tempt him

on the peaks of business law and education

snowy ultimatums

Where wisdom froze

On the rocks

It is said, Jesus rose from the dead

I rose from the dead and dying,

Buchenwald baby

Eyes baked oven hard

A poet said Her eyes the sungate of the soul unbar.

I say They unleash coronas

I say They are the flaming spheres

> Unmeasured but existing
>
> Planted in the universe like roses growing
>
> Wild

Talk about dire straits. I've seen Lucy in the dire straits of her own brand of Christian bliss, which is an ecstatic loss of faith.

I've just opened a book, *Masks of the Universe*, at random. It's about different societies' visions of the universe, creations of reality. I read, "The penalty of knowledge is doubt." On the other hand, the pleasure of doubt is knowledge. The "roses growing/Wild," which are Lucy's vision, indicate a change of heart, a resurgence of faith. The believer is the Lucy of the narrative. Maybe she'd say, in her silver-haired and satisfied old age:

> I am a cock-eyed optimist, an aging whore, as is my husband lover, and both of us are proud of rosy vision, corny as it is.

And a storyteller might say:

> Lucy the whore and virgin were the same, for her soul was full of charity, the pagan grace that Christians tried to rid of sexuality. *Whore* derives from the Latin *carus*, as does *charity*, loving others for the sake of Love itself. The stable virgin and the aging whore love themselves as well as loving friends and lovers. Some medieval sources saw Lucy as a female Christ and attributed the miracles he performed to her. One was restoring sight to the blind. Lucy and Christ were gifted in charity and therefore charismatic. *Charisma* is a cognate of the Greek *charis*, charity.

The charismatic is a lover.

The charismatic cures diseases of the eyes, as artists do. Lucy, one of the most popular medieval saints, was advertised as the patron of sufferers from eye disease. Her symbols are a lamp and an offering dish:

> Let me light your way and lighten your heart with love. Here are my eyes so you can see.

Many have written that the eyes are windows of the soul. Lucy the charismatic healed the soul.

It is said that Lucy bestowed the gifts of enlightenment and eyesight, especially as the opener of newborn children's eyes. Her spirit, it is said, entered an infant and brought its whole being, soul-and-mind-inseparable-from-body, to new life. St. Johanna, a medieval admirer of Lucy, wrote, in the following loosely translated tribute to her:

> Vita nova, vie nouvelle
> Promise that you'll kiss and tell
> When the new life strikes your head
> And says it's boring to be dead.

Several scholars of hagiography have connected Christ's words,

> Enter unto me
> And ye shall die,

with Lucy's sexual omnivorousness and her giving of new life. Men, the scholars suggest, would have intercourse with Lucy, die—*la petite mort* of orgasm—and come to new life, sight and soul.

Many Christian Fathers have wanted to divest Lucy of sainthood because of her sexuality. They have said she was evil. Little have they seen of truth, the origin of *sacred* from the Latin *sacer*, holy, cursed, the fact of their own evil eyes.

Lucy was a protectress against the evil eye. As late as 1890, Tuscan witches used what they called Lucy's Healing Charm as security against the evil eye. The charm was a wreath of rue, entwined in red ribbon, and the patient would spit three times through the wreath, calling on St. Lucy for assistance.

The color red has been associated with Lucy for centuries, not only because of the blood and flame in her story of torture, but also because she had written to her father, after several years of living in the wildness and in culture with her husband, which reads:

> I had a vision of fire, surely a memory, in part, from when the soldiers tortured me. In
> the vision I walked through flames. At first I did not hurt. My arms were raised, like

wings, as if buoyed by wind, and I was twirling. Then I was on fire, too hot, and I ran, streaming flame, into a placid turquoise pool. I became cold, so stepped out and sat between the fire and the water. Evergreens surrounded me, and I thought about red: cherry, poppy, copper, madder, ruby, iron, garnet, bloodstone, and many more. Above all, the veracity of vermilion.

Lucy's father loved her with a heat that he himself had once called vermilion. It is said he told her, when she was a girl:

> Today I crossed the Vermilion River and I thought of you. I may not tell you often, but I love you with the fluency and fire I saw in the river, vermilion.

Too many families are afraid of father-daughter love, as if such love were sick. But Lucy's father, tight-lipped though he usually was, gave her health. For instance, medieval witches acknowledged his advice to Lucy, given when she was still young enough to learn, and used it in their own teachings. It is written that his words were:

> Relax and you will be pursued. Reflect and your wisdom will be rewarded. Live with conviction and your passion will draw love.

From her father's words, Lucy drew the conclusion,

> I will be the Lucifer of women, linked with lust fulfilled, bringer of light, heart luminous with love. I will be a subtle dancer.

May you and I dance subtly, Peg, with Lucid Lucy and the ones we love.

Joanna (*Completed October 15, 1988*)

A black folding chair and music and microphone stands sit upstage center. The music stands hold the script. Frueh enters, wearing a white leather strapless minidress, bright red high heels, and scarlet lipstick. The heels click slowly on the floor. She walks downstage center and speaks unmiked, her back to the audience.

When I was twenty-five, I began voice lessons. My teacher's name was Everett. Everhart, strong as a wild boar, your voice was rich and mellow. You had control and power, authority and beauty, seductiveness and compassion, a heart that came from the diaphragm, source of the column of breath that rises from the gut, from the vital organs, of which the mouth is one.

The mouth, your voice said to me, is the exit from the body and the entry to the world, the opening at which the inner and the outer breath are one and private and public air can mix.

Everett gave me satin dresses, red and white and black, bought at mansion sales. I was to perform in the gowns, for Everett wanted me to be a singer, a chanteuse, creating heat with torch songs.

On the night of his sixtieth birthday, Everett came to hear me at a club. He said my singing was the best gift he could receive.

Once, early on, he told me, "You have a golden voice."

Sometime later, I said, "I want to be a star."

He said, "You will be."

Not long after that, Everett became ill and lessons were canceled week after week. When he began teaching again, I did not return. Another of his students told me, "Everett's asking about you. You're like a daughter to him." Still I did not return.

Everett, Everhart, the next time I heard about you, from a student, she told me you had died. Someone, a disgruntled lover, it was said, had knifed you in your studio, where you had moved my voice to sing and speak in ways I had not known before.

Frueh turns and faces the audience. From now on she alternates between standing and speaking miked and sitting and speaking unmiked.

Standing, miked.

Mouthpiece:

One who speaks on behalf of others; one who expresses another's sentiments and opinions; one who gives public circulation to the common soul.

Mouthpiece:

Something to put in the mouth. That part of a musical instrument which is placed between the lips and is usually made of a material agreeable to the mouth.

Mouthpiece:

An instrument in which the vibration of membranes sends forth harmonies that scholars throughout the ages have been unable to reduce into components and have therefore named aesthetics and poetics. Examples include wood wind and flesh cock.

Wood wind and flesh cock speak. They announce, proclaim, both by sensation.

I speak in public.

Seas and rivers, desert prairie speak. They reverberate, emit the sounds that scholars cannot categorize.

I speak in private.

Baying hounds give tongue and firearms report.

I speak on, against, and for.

Speak: to exercise the voice; to loosen discourse; to deliver an address in an assembly; to disclose, reveal; to appeal to, touch, affect, or influence.

I speak to desires.

I am on speaking terms with you.

<hr>

Frueh looks directly into an audience member's eyes.

I speak for those of you who don't yet know the words, who've lost your tongues, who have not found your voice, who are afraid to tell your stories, fearful they may be too telling.

I will be your mouth, speak out, so as to be heard distinctly.

I will speak up, testify to acts, emotions that exist in speechlessness because belief calls them unspeakable.

I just wanna testify 'bout the love you give to me, and so I have a foul mouth, trash mouth, big mouth for speaking on the streets and in the bedrooms.

With my big mouth I can eat your heart, swallow your pride, devour you if I desire.

With my big mouth I speak in blood and shit, in cum, saliva, and orgasm, in wisdom gained through books and body.

And it was written that He was excruciatingly close to coming. "And then He came," She said. "For I drew out His semen, warm and slow, and I tasted His orgasm, I took Him wholly into Me, into the body of the world."

I speak with a learned tongue, for I am the Spokeswoman, Woman Who Speaks.

Belief that the feminine nature could be coarsened by learning has been coupled in history with the idea that it is in woman's nature to say too much.

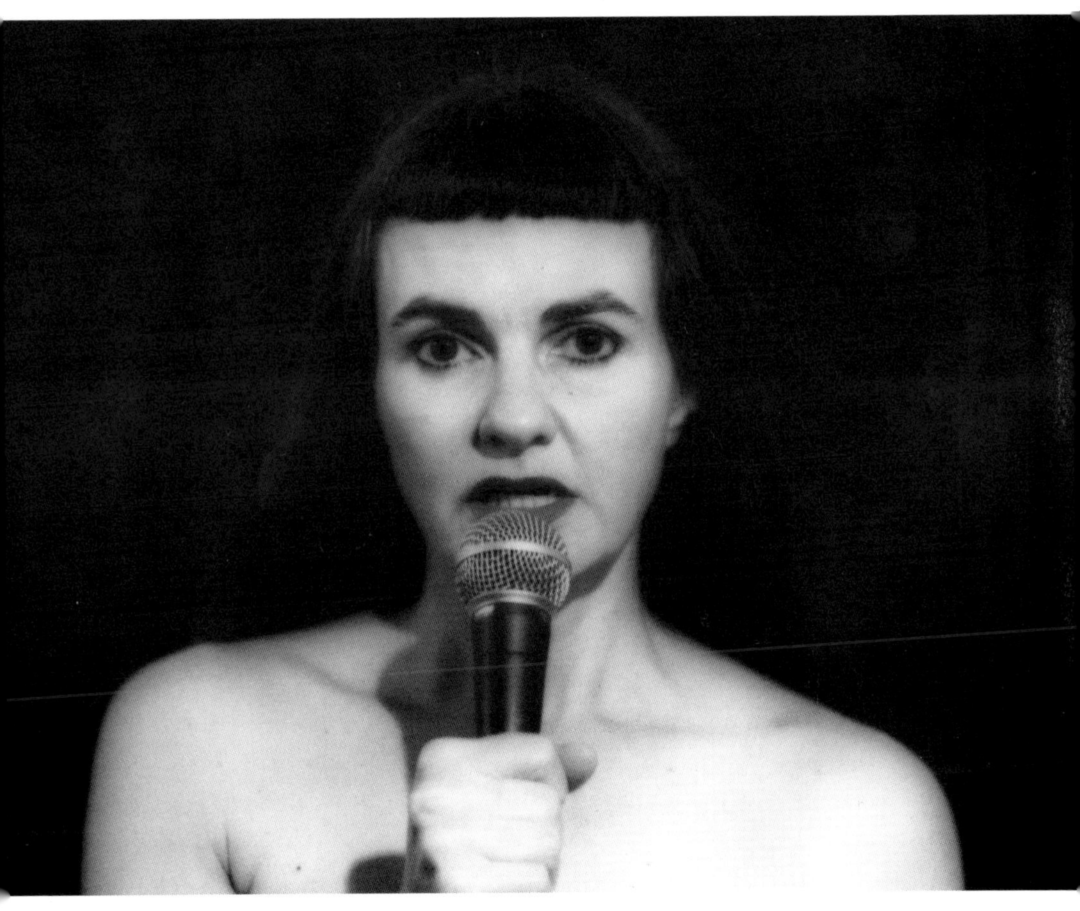

Joanna Frueh and Russell Dudley, *Mouth Piece*, Columbia College Dance Center, Chicago, 1989. *Photo courtesy of Frueh and Dudley.*

Frueh speaks the next sentence so lightly and with such delight that she smiles. She imagines that the smile is shared by the audience and that it exists within them if not on their faces. The smile indicates mutual knowledge and experience about men's sometimes absurd and infuriating behavior.

Frueh alters a passage from Susan Brownmiller's Femininity.

Loquaciousness in the female sex has been remarked upon, not surprisingly, by the most voluble of men. Woman's wagging tongue was discussed by Aristotle, Aristophanes, Juvenal, the Babylonian Talmud, Swift, Ben Franklin, Shakespeare, and Milton. Her silence was counted a virtue by Sophocles, Plutarch, St. Paul, and Samuel Johnson. Babblers, tattlers, gossips, chatterboxes, nags and scolds: the descriptions apply to one sex only and suggest a severe defect of character. It is said that women gush. (Ah! But men gush. Gushers.) We run on about insignificant matters. The din is infernal. What's a man to do? A popular pub in London, The Silent Woman, named for the Ben Jonson farce, has as its tavern sign a headless female torso, a final resort.

"I am Wordswoman," She said, "Swordswoman, and I use wordplay as a weapon from the head and lips. I speak in leather, as an animal, in black hair. I speak in metaphor and emblem. I speak in legend and case history, as seer, goddess, scholar."

And it is said that all who feared and loved Her listened well, for otherwise they would die in sorrow, never knowing how to speak, from Greek *spharageisthai,* to crackle, from Sanskrit *sphūrjati,* it roars, it crackles.

Seated, unmiked.

You speak of omens. I don't hear men doing that. My mother always has, and my women friends. You speak of the sexy black death snake you met on the mountain trail, on your approach to a rock you later climbed. You speak of white rabbit heads brought to you by your dogs. You speak of your own terror, and your terror speaks belief in magic, and your words themselves are speaking magic, spoken magic, the making of magic speech, the capacity to make magic speak.

Frueh's breath, from deep in her body, is soft.
She feels as if she sighs this passage.

Your breath spoke to me. That was before we began to breathe hard with desire. We sat on the hood of my car and you asked me if I'd sleep with you, and I smelled your breath, your fragility. I touched your hair and cheek and you wanted to kiss me and you took my fingers in your mouth and had one hand at my waist and tucked a finger between my sock and skin. It's hard to describe how I scrutinized you. It's simply that I felt your vulnerability, and in that, your desire, so strongly that I thought, How can I? How can I do this? Sleep with you? I felt absolutely drawn, yet distant in scrutiny. I felt soft, like a balmy breeze, an angel in your arms (the wind was speaking), and I had no idea what age I was.

> We made love and the rocks
> Spoke
> We were moving through
> The rocks
> We moved and the rocks
> Moved with us
> We were moving rocks
> Moving mountains

We speak in love letters. Love alters the order of our customary alphabet.

We speak in blood letters, imagine ripping each other apart when we make love, a re-creation of ancient ritual in which the male was sacrificed.

You speak: I am your lover, you can't kill me. But cut me. Make incisions in my back, suck my blood and I'll lick yours from between your legs.

You speak in the wild, about wanting to know me in the mountain winterlands, in a
sleeping bag
bedded down
my cold nose to your cheek
to take me to the snows I've never seen
so you can lace me in your love
close to the earth
my dark hair in our mouths
when we kiss
You speak in the grocery store: I want a bloody wine.
    You speak in the restaurant, to the waiter: Which wine is the bloodiest?
    You make the red wine speak when you pour it on and into me and sip it from my cunt and lips and let it sink into my hair so that it mats and smells like flowering soil.

. . . .

Frueh is almost breathless.

When you speak, in mild words, to your mother of the magic spoken from our blood and brains and bodies, she says she sees a red flag, waving darkly like her mother's visions, feared by the family, who do not understand the source or point of prophecy, in which, it seems, you share your grandma's gift.
    But your mother need not worry, for in fifty years you and I will speak together, on our golden anniversary:
    You are my goldsmith
    Goldmine filled with sunny dispositions
    Of my wealth

*Standing, at mike. Frueh emphasizes her upright posture and
speaks emphatically as she imagines Hypatia or Cleopatra
would have spoken to a crowd.*

I speak in milky tongues

And at the whites of eyes

Whitewater rafter

I speak in the voice of worms

And underground rivers

I speak in dirty words in smut

The black of soil and sex

I speak goldilocks brunette and silver white and

Redhead

I White Buffalo Woman

Grow flaming snakes that crown my scalp

I speak as bête noire

As the dark horse

Running like a winner right beside you

We are in the black

Together

Making profits with our love

I speak black bear blackberry

Black swan black pepper

And black henbane hellebore and hemlock

Plants of death

I speak as queen of spades the nightshade

Black lady with my black book

Full of names of lovers young and old

Flames burning still fires

In my heart

I sound the red alert

I speak black market

Violate

The public regulations

I speak in currency betrayed

By the blackout of love

(Which I foretold)

The indecisions blind to candlelight and heavy breathing

Rhythms of the bedroom

Spreading the sky's legs

I speak white lightning

Drink white ladies

Flagrant red and drunk

I speak in black tie

Ready for a party

I am lit and flushed

Dyed bloodshot through and through

Incited and redhanded

Wanton nails turned into claws

Red rover

I speak rouged for action

Queen of Hearts

The ruby in your teeth

The cherry on your tongue

The wine you swallow

I speak Red Cross

Humanitarian

Brain coral red

And bleeding heart

I speak red-footed falcon

Who sees heartbeats of angels

Flutter in white mist

I speak black powder blasting

My way into viscera

Darkrooms

Where pictures of a golden age develop

When I speak

White dove and raven robin redbreast

I am speaking

White sheep in my dreams

And black sheep

Straying from the fold

The monochromes of cant

Though I speak lily snow and milk

The whitened head of age

Speaks too in bridal dress

The white nun orchid

showy

    breathing in the tropics

    bearing single icy flowers

    suffused with rose

Snow White enough

The bride in Ivory Soap

She is the bitch too wearing white as well

As her unbridled passion

Red hot mama

    eating white and devil's food cake at my wedding

I speak in gold stars

Slice golden sections

For a new gold standard

For I am the black

Remains after the fires have burnt out

I am the white

The ashes blown

I am the red

Mouth at your ear and belly

    Telluric

I speak pitch darkness

Bloody tongues

White magic

See these lips?

Look at my mouth move over every word

And all I say is golden

Like the marigold and palomino

Frueh sings. Her eyes are closed most of the time.

Black black black is the color of my true love's hair

His lips are like some rose so fair

His eyes speak gold when'er we talk

I love the ground whereon he walks

Seated, unmiked.

You sing to your dogs, Ananda, Pup, Xia Wu, personalizing rock songs for their pleasure.

Ananda's got the snake

Pup's on the take

Xia Wu's on the make.

Then you choose a rap song, sing it deadpan:

Trick and magic

Magic trick

We're Mame and Joey

And we like it slick

You say you're not sure if you remember the women's names right. I say it doesn't matter, they sound great and, besides, you know my name perfectly. You whisper it when we're fucking and I'm on top of you. Over and over, Joanna Joanna Joanna Joanna, and it becomes a soft cry, like Oh God or Jesus, which are sometimes louder, but not as loud as screams.

Often when I think about everything we do with sex, I want to scream, and I wonder,
Are our sex sounds and words a song?

Standing, at mike.

Sing:

From Middle Welsh *deongl,* to explain, Greek *omphē,* voice, oracle, and probably Prakrit *samghai,* to say, teach.

Sing:

Frueh lets the sentences sound like music, proclamation,
chanting, and a voice making love.

To utter words in musical tones, inflections, modulations.
To proclaim in a clear or resonant manner.
To chant, intone, to celebrate.
To make love with words, make poetry.
To bring or accompany to a state by singing.

Frueh crosses her arms and holds herself.

I will sing you to eternity and back
I will sing away your pain
O Goddesses
O Gods
Eros Astarte
Songsters
Songstars
It's the singer not the song
We come

To sing your praises

Tell us of the torch songs

Intoned at first for martyrs

Final songs for lover men aflame

Like saints and witches

Bound to twigs and branches

Sticks and flesh both named faggot

faggot faggot faggot faggot

Sing forgotten songstars

Sing Choir of Angels

* *

Frueh alters and condenses four paragraphs from Erich Neumann's
The Great Mother: An Analysis of the Archetype.

Etymological relations among passion, fury, song, excitement, violently desiring, raving, burning with love, storm, to understand, possession, god-inspired singer, oracle, being-outside-oneself, and poetry characterize the creative aspect of the unconscious, whose activity sets human beings in motion, overpowers them, and makes them its instrument. Human beings are seized by these powers. But since this possession causes higher, supraconscious powers to appear in human beings, they methodically seek it in ritual, in art, religion, cult, in sex and poetry.

* *

Frueh alters one paragraph from Chris Weedon's
Feminist Practice and Poststructuralist Theory.

The semiotic chora is the site of those meanings and modes of signification that cannot be reduced to the symbolic order and that exceed rational conscious subjectivity. The semiotic chora is manifest in symbolic discourse in such aspects of language as rhythm and intonation and is at its strongest in nonrational discourses which threaten the organization of the symbolic order and the stability of its meanings, such as unorganized religion, art, and poetry.

Oracular priestesses, who were originally associated with sacred poetry, were each called *saga*, She Who Speaks. Saga literally meant female sage.

Seated, unmiked. Frueh crosses her legs and leans forward
with one arm along the back of the chair.

You tell me, "Never underestimate your voice." You say the first time you saw me you were taken by my voice, the sound, the words, the short and rose-red boots whose curving to my ankle you describe with lyric lust, my mouth which you presumed I lipsticked scarlet as a sign of vocal clarity, my entire being read by you as voice.

Frueh leans back.

And I listen to the cadence and the colors of your voice, the songs you make of daily life. And I think, We speak with each other in the voices of angels. Your body and mine are vocal organs.

Standing, at mike.

The celestial voice exists in every human being and can be expressed individually or by vox populi. Communities are vocal organs composed of people who know they have a voice. (They listen to their inner voices and to the voice of winds.)

We can pinpoint a major hindrance to the development of the celestial public voice in the psychological evidence manifested in high school students' English essays. Recent studies reaffirm older data: only the rare student consistently uses the active voice. Ideas in both logic and poetry suffer from passive sentence structure. Our conclusion is that people who do not feel they are agents in their own lives have difficulty understanding the active voice, in sentences and in society.

Unfortunately, many teachers are no exception. They have memorized the principle, but they have no voice.

Frueh speaks deliberately and gently. She transposes and
paraphrases material that appears in W. Brugh Joy's
Joy's Way: A Map for the Transformational Journey.

Words and their content may expand the abstract, intellectual portion of consciousness, but ideas alone do not and cannot cause change. The teacher's voice vibration can augment the experience of learning, and it is the sound, which could as well be gibberish or chanting, that brings the change. The control and mastery of sound waves is part of the path of a teacher. Thus the teacher can talk about anything at all, can sing, moan, cry, or laugh and still achieve results.

Seated, unmiked.

When we are miles apart, one of the things I miss most about you is your laugh, your many laughs. They are contagious. You infect me with your love.

Frueh is excruciatingly aware of walking across the stage.

Standing, at mike.

The mouth is the gateway of infection. We share food and blood and air, drink and cum and kisses.

What follows is part of the case history of a contemporary Don Juan, whom I refer to as X.

As X entered his twenties he became sexually hyperactive. At twenty-five he began to use heroin regularly, and often he shared needles. Both practices put him in danger of contracting AIDS.

A new sex partner said to him, "I'll kiss you anyway." Then she performed fellatio. She pulled back, which angered X, and he said, "If you're afraid, you don't have to finish me off.

Watch me do it." When X ejaculated in his hand, the woman said, "What a narcissist."
X smiled.

The Black Death scourged Europe six centuries ago, and Edgar Allan Poe has written of
the Red Death. But I will tell you a story from the nightmare days of the White Death,
when milky-colored pustules signaled someone's end.

One town built a wall around its borders before the plague struck. A woman named
Head of My Heart begged the mayor to leave the gate open till Hope in One Eye
returned from business travels. He was due that very day, and Head of My Heart and
Hope in One Eye were best friends. The mayor and all his deputies would not listen to
Head of My Heart, nor would they let her leave. Did she want her town to die for love of
one man? Would she die for love? She could not answer, did not know if love of one was
worth the death of many.

Three years passed. The gate flew open, as if it knew the plague itself had died, and
Head of My Heart left to look for her friend. She did not find him anywhere, in her twelve
years of searching. Mass death does not leave single graves, nor do the unwanted stay
close to home.

Head of My Heart sat on the ground, the hardest she had walked since leaving the
walled town, and cried. "If only love were of epidemic proportion," she said, clearly
through her tears. And then she smiled, not knowing why.

. . . .

Seated, unmiked.

I have two pictures of you grinning, which I took. You look like a friendly Marlboro Man.
Your little teeth are very white.

When you grabbed my hair with those teeth, on the hood of my car, I could feel what a
bunch of it you held. You were sitting behind me, then leaned into my back, and you
pressed your teeth against my neck, maybe letting go of many strands, and bit it through
my hair. I moaned and knew from then on that I held you fast, as if I had bitten into your
heart before that night.

So I say, Bite me

Make me smart

With love.

And you request my bite below your nipple, as hard as I will dare.

. . . .

Frueh uncrosses and recrosses her legs.

We make our marks on each other's skin. I see bruises left from my teeth in your upper arm. You bite my head, leaving a sign on my scalp that only I can see, for it is hidden under my hair.

We make our marks inside the skin. We bite each other to the core, where Eve bit into the red apple, into Adam's center too, beneath the grip of a lonely and hardbitten tyrant god.

You say when I suck your cock the second morning that we're lovers, "You're very conscious of teeth. I've never been with someone so conscious of teeth."

"Do you want more teeth?" I ask.

"No. Not now."

Then you pause and say, "Sometimes more, sometimes less."

. . . .

Standing, at mike. Frueh quotes from Arthur C. Danto's
The State of the Art.

"Philosophers have said some crazy things about the real world. Aristotle insisted, for reasons I can only guess at, that women have fewer teeth than men. In medieval representations of him, Aristotle is often depicted on all fours, being ridden by a woman with a whip in her hand. This was Phyllis, the mistress of Aristotle's pupil, Alexander. One might suppose, from his posture of erotic domination by a woman he was mad about, that Aristotle would have believed she had more teeth than men; thus even masochists can be sexist. In any case, one need only look into the nearest female mouth to refute that mighty thinker."

$$\textbf{\textit{❧}}$$

Armed to the teeth

Wordswoman never bites her tongue

Tooth-gnashing

She bites off what she can chew

And sits, teeth set

While tooth-winged butterflies

Circle her head like halos

* *

Frueh's lips are set in a snarl.

Seated, unmiked.

I put my tongue against my teeth

To speak

I put my tongue to your teeth

Rub it along them

Your lips yielding

Our compliant hearts

You've worn lipstick when we fuck. The first time, you asked, after we'd been naked and in bed already for a while, "Where's your lipstick?"

I answered, "In my purse."

I turned over, on my stomach, aware of my ass in the air, to your eyes. I found my lipstick, pulled the top off, twisted the crimson stalk up, to paint your lips. Then I said, "Put it on me," and you covered my mouth with pressures like your kisses. I reddened one of your nipples and slid the lipstick over your prick, and then we kissed until I saw that the color had disappeared from your mouth.

Months before we're lovers, you see my lips imprinted on a letter. You remember them to me and say how soft and warm my lips seemed on the paper, how jealous you were of their receiver. Our second day as lovers, I kiss your chest with lipsticked mouth, not realizing anyone could see my love between the sides of your unbuttoned shirt. Unexpectedly you meet our friend Mercedes, who laughs and says, "You have big red lips on your chest." And you tell her, "Everything is different. My life has changed."

You want your own page filled with kisses. You say it will make you feel secure. I reapply the color several times for you. I lick the paper like I'm tracing veins, remembering tendons and your creamy ass and back. I drag my tongue along the dryness—only paper. My mouth forms patterns, puckered, heavy, light, and open.

Two old lovers give you grief about wearing what you call your "snazzy lipstick" in public. One asks, "Do you want to get beat up? I'd feel safer walking alone at night than with you." The other calls you a little fuck, a term I find it endearing that you call yourself.

You tell me that your lipstick threatens them, because you've taken on femininity and, in that, freedom.

. . . .

*Standing, at mike. Frueh touches the mike stand with
the fingertips of both hands.*

       In a garden

       Judas passed the Kiss of Death

       With flowers all around called Kiss-Me

       (Known by another name, Wild Pansy)

       Christ speaking

           lip-love

           lip-homage

           in lip-lusciousness

           or was it simply lip-deep

       could have said

       Just kiss my ass

       I would have

       She Who Speaks

With kiss-curl on the cheek

    might have said

Had I been asked

Oh, honey, I will give you Great Lip Service

All you need forever

Frueh quotes from Luce Irigaray's "This Sex Which Is Not One."

"A woman 'touches herself' constantly without anyone being able to forbid her to do so,
for her sex is composed of two lips which embrace continually."

Lip:

    Probably related to Latin *labium, labrum,* lip, and to Latin *labi,* to slide, glide.

Seated, unmiked.

Almost as soon as your prick was sliding in me, as we were sliding along your prick the first
time, you said, "I love you."

    Prickslide: this is your word.

You call me Joanna the Slippery. I like this, my cunt wet for you, for our smooth talking.

    Joanna the Slippery, the unclassifiable.

I put my finger in my cunt, in and out, slowly, as we're talking on the bed, then to my
mouth, and taste, lick it, almost as if I'm not aware of what's happening, as if we do and
don't know what I'm doing. But you groan.

    I put my finger in my cunt, then to my mouth, and taste. Lips to lips.

The positive femininity of the womb appears as a mouth; that is why "lips" are attributed to the female genitals, and on the basis of this positive symbolic equation the mouth, as "upper womb," is the birthplace of the breath and the word, the Logos.

Even today sexual symbolism is still colored by alimentary symbolism. Hunger and satiety, desire and satisfaction, thirst and its slaking are symbolic concepts that are equally valid for sex and for nourishment.

Magic began no doubt as "food magic" and developed by way of fertility magic into sexual or "love magic."

The goddesses of love, the hunt, and death are grouped together in Egypt as in Greece, in Mesopotamia as in Mexico. Symbols of the womb-as-underworld include the gate and gully, the door, ravine, abyss, and, of course, the gullet. All are numinous sites. The mouth with bristling teeth and the gullet actively rend, swallow, devour, and kill. The toothed vagina's sucking power is mythologically symbolized by its attraction for man, for life and consciousness and the individual male, who can evade it only if he is a hero, and even then not always.

It is said, "When Woman Who Speaks says, 'Eat me,' those who listen receive oracles from her mouth."

Yet others say, "A man who gets sucked into female ways will pine and die, will be no true man, in fact, nothing. . . . Our myths illuminate the facets of this stereotype."

Woman Who Speaks says, "The hero enters to be devoured. If he survives with true desire, he returns, at once diminished and engorged."

You tell me, "I was talking to you, out loud, in my bed."

"What did you say?" I ask.

"I want your cunt to devour me. I want your mouth around my dick when it's non-existent."

I'm astonished that someone called a man would say this.

Later you send me a letter. All it says is, Gorge-us.

Part of a story I wrote scares you. You say the heroine eats up young men.

Still, you taste my menstrual blood. It is your red badge of courage.

"Love is not blind," the Buddha says. "Indeed, only the Lover is fully aware of the Beautiful."

Wordswoman says, "The Lover sees with the mouth. The seer tastes the lover, for sight is simply another tongue, another language of the senses. The Lover sees the Beautiful, sees beautifully, has the best, the most beautiful of taste."

The appetite fails when we fall in love. The food is the lover, the lover is the food. This has to do with eating the lover, cum, sweat, tears, saliva, blood and soul-inseparable-from-the-body, the lover who is the object of appetite, desire. This has to do with wanting the smells of the lover's body. (Aroma increases appetite.) But also the lover is full of the beloved, full of love, so full that she requires no other sustenance.

Lovers eat together in public in order for everyone to see their lust, their taste, their devouring of sex.

The appetite fails because lovers have consumed each other.

Seated, unmiked.

On our first date, our first dinner out, the waiter waits, for over an hour, till we order.

You suck my fingers later

On the hood of my car

My four fingers

All but my thumb

In your mouth

It was deep wet

Saliva on each one

And you say that

You are wet

And you say that when you drink you are in my mouth.

And on the city streets we stuff food in each other's mouths and suck it out in kisses, drink liquids too this way.

And we are fucking, you on top of me. Sweat from your forehead is raining in my mouth. I lick the salt from your cheeks.

You write to me about vanilla pain. It is the taste of desire for an object out of reach.

I am eating breakfast at a cafe, where I like the coffee and the blueberry muffins. The coffee is rich; the muffin flesh melts in my mouth. I remember winter and the coffee's heat, its creamy denseness. I think of you in another climate. I am far away from you in miles. I just wrote a postcard, words I'd rather speak in your presence. I say to you, We could eat here together. We could stare at each other full of lust, and you would put your finger to my mouth, a little between my lips, wanting entry. You like to look at me in public as though you're ready to fuck me. I say to you, People look boring here. This is the dead place. My mouth is on yours when I say this. Do you feel it?

The food goes tasteless in my mouth. And I'm aware of the saliva. There seems to be more than usual, a displacement of tears?

What follows is my transcription, from a tape-recorded session, of the patient's poetic mania regarding her father.

I eat to live. But how can I live if I feel sugared to the bone? I had no Sugar Daddy who'd feed me with phrases of honor for my beauty, sex, or girl-childishness. Oh, Daddy, I sever my sex and guts from you. I sever the connections, cords, and filaments between our vital organs, the places from neck to crotch that just can't cover our insecurities. Still we speak and eat together.

I eat to live. I eat sweet to live well. I eat sweet to live at all, oh, Sugar Daddy God My Father. I transcend the grief of stunted love by eating

cakes and cookies

ice creams

toast with butter and raspberry preserves

    (your favorite fruit)

muffins, mousse, and chocolate kisses.

Where were yours? There would have been no incest in the meeting of

our father-daughter tongues, our separate languages in words of love.

The crime is in the lack of language

melting over hearts

the hot fudge sundaes I needed

melting my snowy heart into the

cream I share with men, my cum

my husband lover says is sweet.

He eats to live, eats me to live.

I eat to live. I gain no weight. I'm neither fat nor ugly, but I worry for my health, all that sugar coating me inside like silken death. I am too sweet, not sweet enough. Was I not sweet enough for you? Am I, I wonder over twenty years, a poison in men's veins as soon as their eyes taste me?

Frueh embraces herself and caresses her upper arms.

I eat to live. But I'm so sick of sweets, for every day cannot be Valentine's, plump hearts and flowers candied for supposed lovers.

I eat to live. I try to make myself sweet, but there's no cure for hunger like this, the rotting sweet tooth of a daughter, except to say, Dad, I love you and I must let go, cut our umbilical cords. To let go we embrace anew. In letting go we come together cleansed of all the saccharine father-daughter feelings and others falsified as ugly lust, too true to publicize, destigmatize into the necessary passion of simple nurturance and occasional feast.

I eat to live. I love you, Daddy, let me be sweet enough for you. Tell me I'm sweet enough for you, so I don't have to eat as if there's no tomorrow for us. Oh, let the love, the words be sweet enough.

Seated, unmiked.

During our first dinner, we take the words out of each other's mouths, we eat each other's words and know we're gifted in each other's tongues.

When your tongue is in my cunt, I'm amazed I don't know which are your lips and which are mine, that I can't tell my cum from your saliva.

Prickslide and cunt worship are two tongues we speak. Your prick is your tongue that finds and makes a language inside me. Your tongue becomes my tongue, our prick and our cunt, and we create a language of our own, but known in variations to all loving fuckers.

With her outspread legs, the Gorgon takes the same posture as the exhibitionistic goddesses. Her outstretched tongue is always phallic. In New Zealand the outstretched tongue is a sign of power, and in Lifu, one of the Loyalty Islands, the male sexual organ is known as "his word," an expression that gives the phallus meaning as the originating force of language.

Tongueman and Woman Who Speaks chose one another as consorts. In the ancient days of their love, Tongueman meant speaker, orator, and Woman Who Speaks herself spoke far and wide and wet and deep and hard. On their wedding day, she moaned in beauty through the world that worshipped her and Tongueman,

>Let the organ in your mouth
>Resonate in the cathedral with no walls

>The center of me my voice my being
>Nexus
>Confluence of the wordstreams

You were talking about us, and then the river. You were talking about yourself and your work, and then the river, being like the river. And you were crying, kayaking, underwater, almost drowning. As you sobbed, I watched your cheeks turn red, and I noticed your skin begin to burn, to look as though iris petals growing underneath your skin were surfacing. The petals looked like tongues, and I remembered the name of irises in the botanical garden. Scarlet Showman. Maybe this is you.

Showman

Shaman

She-Man

I go to the gardens

In my red lipstick

The wind is blowing

And shifting direction.

I come to know the language of the irises

I begin by listening to their posture

Here they stand

Some almost to my waist

Like you kneeling,

Head up, tongue offered to me,

Like you in the shower

At my cunt with your tongue.

I call them by their names

Which also sound the meaning

Of our love

    Occult

    Sun Fire

    Gift of Dreams

    True Bliss

    Serene

    Bride's Halo

    Danger

    Sorceress

    Allegiance

Limpid Harmony

Star Walker

Morning Thunder

Gypsy Magic

Sable Night

Chérie

Clearfire

Spun Gold

Truly Yours

Star Queen

Royal Magician

Black Madonna

Blood Dance

Heat Pump

This I Love

Black Gamecock

Beaver Lass

Trice Blessed

Red Echo

Bridal Passion

One Accord

Sweet Deal

Star Studded

Coral Chalice

Marvelous Style

New Kinda Love

Toujours

Exhilaration

Rosy Wings

Black Flag

Night Lady

Piping Hot

Embraceable

Infinite Grace

Crystal Cathedral

Cameo Wine

Enchanting

Whispering Breeze

Deep Fire

Rosecraft

Mulled Wine

Simple Pleasure

Precious Moments

Majestic Beauty

Divine Guidance

Venus Rising

Jeweled Starlight

Sheer Poetry

Seated, holding mike.

We sat outside with your dog, Xia Wu, between us. We were watching for shooting stars. Word said there would be many. The wind blew up as we were sitting.

I lifted Xia Wu's ear, bent close so that my lips touched velvet skin, and asked if she saw shooting stars.

You lifted her other ear and said, "Xia Wu, I see one. Over there."

And as we softly talked into her ears, the wind embraced the three of us and stars shot and showered on every side.

"The stars aren't falling," I said to Xia Wu, "they're finding new homes."

Then we heard the voice, of Everett, Everhart, encircling us, for just a moment, in the wind.

"Golden voices," Everett said, "my stars."

Frueh lays the mike on the music stand and walks offstage,
high heels clicking slowly on the floor.

*Amazing Grace was presented at a two-hundred-foot-long gran-
ite retaining wall next to the Genesee River gorge at Maplewood
Park in Rochester, New York, on May 11, 1990 at 7:00 p.m.*

*The audience, led by a confederate, gathered at the center
of the graffitied wall. Then Russell and Joanna walked toward
them from the wall's left edge (as the audience faced the wall).
Russell wore jeans, cowboy boots, and a black mock turtleneck
T-shirt. Joanna wore a rose-patterned black cotton knit minidress, red high heels, and a jean jacket. From one of its pockets
she pulled the folded papers on which the text was written and
unfolded them. Then she and Russell delivered the text, handing
the papers back and forth as they read.*

*After the reading, Russell and Joanna walked to the left side
of the wall, where Russell took off his turtleneck and jeans to
reveal a black T-shirt with the sleeves cut off and white tights,
and changed from boots and socks to bare feet and climbing
shoes. He tied a chalk bag around his waist. Then he climbed*

* * * * * * * * * * * * * * * * *

Russell speaks.

You sent me crimson kisses. Centered on a page, their shapes and sizes vary, each is
particular. I can feel your lips surround my cock, for each print suggests a different
pressure. At the top you say, "I masturbated before writing this. Kissing it felt great. Put
cum on here too." At the bottom you've written, "For wherever you want them."

* * * * * * * * * * * * * * * * *

Joanna speaks.

I look more like a whore as I get older
Act the age of ancient Graces
Charities
The sacred charismatics who gave sex compassion kindness
All the faiths and hopes
That countered culture at its worst and brought to life
Pornography:
    The words and pictures melodies and actions of whores
    Who often changed the lyrics of old songs

And the position of nudes and martyrs in cruel paintings

And the place of the body

In life itself

Pornographic partners

Know

Fuck theory

The amazing grace

Of soul-inseparable-from-the-body

The powers of true love

The art of pornography comes into being through our willingness to take control
of powers we may only dream we have.

Dream with me.

Russell speaks.

The crimson lips hang in my studio, part of a collection, dumb substitutes for my romantic
desire. I've tacked up someone's drawing of a mystic suspended by his feet from a rope
and also a postcard from a climbing partner in Seattle. There are photographs of myself
climbing in Arizona and of my father as a small boy next to an idyllic river, bending over
with his brother, a homosexual who gassed himself thirty years ago and whose suicide
materialized the manifest destiny of my father's family and blew it to kingdom come.

I'm living in the northeast now, Rochester, miles from the Tucson desert. Nothing bites
here. It's cold, but it's not sharp. There are no tarantulas to greet you in the living room, no
rattlesnakes at the bases of climbs.

Joanna speaks.

I sat on a porch in the deep South, looking up and out. I was sad, demoralized by a job in
another city and the city itself. I was mismatched with both, and I was seeing that I had to
consider my position, as a worker and a resident, absurd if I was to maintain my psychic
power, my sense of magic in which dreams, night and day, did not disappear. I even

wondered if *maintain* was the correct verb, if loss had progressed to the point where *resurrect* was more accurate.

But I was possessed enough to see that still the sky was blue and still the clouds were moving.

On that porch in the South, where I was a visitor, and at my desk in the north country where I lived, I felt homeless. Part of that feeling came from events in my own life and those beyond my everyday, the world mired in the inadequacies of human relations.

I'd left a marriage and a midwestern city, fallen in love with a man who was living in the southwest desert, which had held me in its absolute embrace since the time I'd lived there several years before. So I went to the desert, returning to my two loves, then leaving with the man for a job in the North. The job hunt had been nasty, long, and grueling, and the uprootings and replantings, whose outline barely suggests the flesh of pain and questioning, wore down my belief in my own passions.

As I speak, I remember the wind howling, the snow falling, the sky, winter white, static outside my window. And I remember knowing every day, in order not to lose myself in homelessness, that somewhere else the sky was still blue and the clouds still moved.

And I see now that my passion is strong, for it grew in unfriendly soil.

* * * * * * * * * * * * * * * * * * *

Russell speaks.

I spend a great deal of time remembering: my body's form, specific sequences dictated from routes on Mt. Lemmon.

Prowess

Toy Roof

David and Goliath

Green Ripper

Nancy's Crack

Chaboni

Voodoo Child

My mind pantomimes boulder problems from Gates Pass, the El Yoyo Wall, guarded by my friend the tiger snake.

Left thumb on the arête, right hand on the small edge at your right nipple. Layback up the arête until it is possible to move right to a large hold on the overhanging face. Match hands, moving dynamically up and right to a sloping finger pocket at the top.

I remember that rock is alive, full of soul, that rock transforms my own soul through its demands, that rock requires shifts in attunement, which indicates dangers and possibilities. Rock will tell you when, as often as not, it is not safe.

I boulder on a retaining wall now next to the Veterans Memorial Bridge. The wall is mute, never safe. Its twelve feet rise next to the Genesee River gorge, next to a foot path next to Route 104, which is the only granite around. It's urban climbing, suburban movement, and I carry subversive pretensions. The wall is a couple hundred feet long, made of blocks with thin edges scattered about. The mechanized homogeneity of even the blankest sections requires a wealth of invention to satisfy my passion. Invention is the necessary manufacturing of desire, a substitution of the most pathetic nature.

. . . .

Joanna speaks.

I say, if you have no passion, then the holocaust of hearts has claimed you, and if you have a passion but do not place it, the passion will rot and make you sick.

And the ancient whore spoke, as she and her brothers and sisters always had, in dreams:

> Fallow passion sucks out the soul-inseparable-from-the-body's nutrients till the dirt of sex sifts through the centuries, like dust through vagrants' fingers.

. . . .

Russell speaks.

I was at the Veterans Memorial Bridge just before the first snow. Some cops had a guy in a muscle car pulled over near an intersection. They were going through his trunk. There were a lot of cops and four or five cop cars. At the bridge two cops checked out my van and came towards me. One was plainclothes, classically awkward and removed. The other wore a black ninja suit, a jumper, with matching black cap, and a silver badge that read SWAT pinned to his chest. He carried an implement that I couldn't immediately place. It frightened me. It was used like a cane and clicked when he walked. It looked remorseless; he looked vindictive. The tool was polished silver on its three tips. Power and technology in all the wrong places.

I stared. The cane was a black anodized ice axe, a mountaineering tool made by a company called Forest that used to be comparable to Chouinard before they figured out that it's more profitable to sell to cops than to independent adventurers.

Later another plainclothes guy came around. He wore a canary-yellow Walkman and looked more the clown than the first, peering into the gorge through binoculars, looking for birds, I suppose. Still I felt like a criminal.

* * * * * * * * * * * * * * * * * *

Joanna speaks.

The news, which is never new, for it tells the old stories over and over, of robbers, soldiers, rapists, arson, murders, makes everyone feel homeless, as do the ads that accompany them. Familiarity masks displacement. We buy comfort, in a new car or lipstick, a cruise or microwave popcorn. The same old stories, the spurious comforts are both wounds and culture's ways of taming the wild solutions that come from soul-inseparable-from-the-body. I see passion stuck in ugly places, so that its capacity for healing is depleted.

* * * * * * * * * * * * * * * * *

Russell speaks.

The paper said there's a serial killer or two at loose in Rochester, that serial killers tend to be white males from twenty-five to forty-five years of age. The paper said serial killers like cops, like to hang with cops in bars, and have often tried out for the force. The paper said serial killers are sometimes cops and that they like to collect cop stuff, like black anodized ice axes.

Serial killers, said the paper, like to be incognito. They live with their desire cloaked, twice removed.

Joanna speaks.

Neither the cold nor snow specifically has made me fear a loss of passion. I will move to the West, high desert, where the winters are cold and snow lingers on the mountains into spring. It is the bare earth and blue sky in any season that I miss, the uncovered ground and the air released from humidity, for I too, in body and soul, like to be uncovered. Warmth in flatter lands and wetter climates is a substitute—when we take off our protective coverings—for naked earth and the clarity of air that makes the sky blue.

The flat and humid North, populated past the point of nature's death, is a place to grow fat and middle-aged. The shut-in suffers the shutdown of her own lust to be naked, which means lucid as well as sexy. The shut-in is an invalid, sickened by the reduction of her own desires. And once she invalidates them, they will embarrass her and she may, then, ironically, grow fat on them because they have nowhere to go.

Russell speaks.

Last night Joanna and I fucked in the bathroom because we like the mirror and there are interesting places to put our feet. Also she was bleeding pretty heavily, and the bathroom is easily cleaned up.

She put a new pink lipstick on me and we talked about wearing pearls. But I guess we forgot.

Afterwards we made photographs. I made her perform. My favorite commands came from a bodybuilding competition we had seen last summer: from the rear now. Up on your toes. Let's see your most muscular.

Then I added a command of my own: now bend over.

The blood ran in rivulets to the floor. There were drops between her legs. Her cunt formed a bloody red fleshy triangle with a short tendril of hair that curled down from the center.

215

Joanna speaks.

I am forty-two, but I am not middle-aged, a word that connotes a fall from grace, from beauty in its many permutations, and I have, here in the flat and humid North, felt embarrassed by my own body and desire, but I have not gotten fat.

I've worn silly slippers, so that the curve of my naked sole could not be kissed, and I have laid in bed all night with a comforter pulled up to my nose, no firm breasts or biceps available to my lover's eyes.

I used to wear tights and tank tops, little skirts over bare legs, feet decorated in anklets and brightly colored high heels.

The dead are covered up, buried.

I think about fruit sweetening and shrinking as it ripens. I think beyond middle age to sweet old ladies, little old ladies. The fall from grace nears completion in the image of a small and cloying female, a shriveling fruit on the way to the garbage.

Our language creates allegiance to the holocaust of hearts.

. . . .

Russell speaks.

The paper said they found a woman in the Genesee River gorge. Her name was Francis Brown. She had been strangled or suffocated.

The paper said Francis was a prostitute.

The paper said there is no indication that the general public is going to be a victim.

. . . .

Joanna speaks.

Why do I dream an art of pornography as a vehicle for healing the vagrant souls-inseparable-from-the-body abandoned by the holocaust of hearts?

Because, I say, the erotic obliterates boundaries.

And it was written, by an ancient whore:

I will weave my soul-inseparable-from-the-body so closely with another's that my distinctness will be his, hers mine, and ours then risen from the groundedness and grounded in the risen nipple, cock, and spirit, clit.

Russell speaks.

Francis Brown the prostitute was also a poet:
Walk with me along windswept
Shore
Let's chase the clouds as lovers did
Before
We'll build a castle and keep it safe
From the tide
You be my king
I'll stand by your side
We'll have the sun to warm us
To start our day
In the evening the stars and moon
  Will light our way
And I,
I am an angel
Amazing Grace
Motivated by the vision
  in your pants
I am an angel
Winged Man
  Come to my bed
    And I will spin
     My cock
        down your throat
    And at your waist
    Wings will grow

I am an angel man
Whose hands will kiss the wall
    As best they can
        For our pleasure
        For gods know
        The claws of our angels
            have been severed from our memories
I am an angel
Amazing Grace
And I have seen
    My fingers turn to claws
        on your shoulder
    And your face become ageless
    And the buck in headlights and saguaros
        a four-point Sonoran fairy
And I have felt
    skyscrapers breathe
    my plane stop in midair
    and the river swell
    My head and torso
    Pressed against a rock in Pistol Creek
    Me upside down
        A torrent
        my legs trapped
        still in my boat

. . . .

Joanna speaks.

The spring comes.
I want to get sloppy wet with you.
And the old question
Comes to mind

Why do women get wet and men get hard?

Why does Ophelia float down the river dead?

Why do cops use billy clubs?

     Men   use night sticks

     Beat your swords

        Into plowshares magic

         Wands

     Metaphor multiplies into clichés, which are the elements of truth, as are the earth
and air fire water.

I return to the elemental

The shut-in springs

Herself naked

        Which means lucid sexy

Description of boulder problem #1:

Start left center of the heart, right foot on edge of heart's point. Layback left and work up
to a large hold directly above. Using the outside edge of left foot on a pin-sized edge,
layback left to a horizontal just below the top. Continue up.

         . . . .

Joanna sings.

Flow gently, sweet Afton

Among thy green braes

Flow gently, I'll sing thee

A song in thy praise

My Mary's asleep

By thy murmuring stream

Flow gently, sweet Afton

Disturb not her dream

Description of boulder problem #2:

At the first zigzag crack made from split mortar, execute a low traverse. Start at a missing block, using nothing above head height. Move right through a series of thin balancey hand and foot changes to an obvious large hold. There are then two long reaches, one left, one right to the top.

· ·

Joanna sings, some of the traditional lyrics
and some of her own.

Who killed cock robin?
Who killed cock robin?
I said the sparrow with my little bow and arrow
It was I oh it was I

Who dug his grave-o?
Who dug his grave-o?
I said the lark in the cool and misty dark
It was I oh it was I

Who lowered him down-o?
Who lowered him down-o?
I said the crane with my pretty silver chain
It was I oh it was I

Who said the prayer-o?
Who said the prayer-o?
I said the dove for I know the tongue of love
It was I oh it was I

Who sang the blessing?
Who sang the blessing?
I said the starling for the cock he was my darling
It was I oh it was I

Description of boulder problem #3:

This is the thinnest problem of the group. Towards the center of the wall five feet to the right of "LISA 8/7/85" there are two fair holds with a remarkable undercut centered a block and a half above. Moving off of the two holds, high step and rocker up using the undercut. From here, tuck right foot under hips and use this to pull body weight into the wall. A full reach above is a half-digit undercut for a right finger that will make possible a thin opposition first left then right. Power straight to the top.

Joanna sings a blues song about a woman whose man has died, and as the narrator looks up in the sky, she wonders if that's him—a bird way up high—and she wonders, too, if he is looking down at her, seeing her rooted, immobile like a tree, in her grief.

Description of boulder problem #4:

To the left of "BENNY DON'T BE A MARSHAL BURNOUT" there are two vertical seams made from decaying mortar. Using a sit-down start, move left hand up these seams employing the right to a pinch up and right. A high step and long reach will attain a horizontal two thirds of the way up. A similar series will gain the top.

Joanna sings.

As I rode out in the streets of Laredo
As I rode out in Laredo one day
I spied a young cowboy all wrapped in white linen
Wrapped in white linen and cold as the clay

I see by your outfit that you are a cowboy
I heard him remark as I boldly rode by

Come sit down beside me and hear my sad story

I'm shot in the chest and I know I must die

Was once in the saddle I used to go dashing

Once in the saddle I used to go gay

First down to Rosie's and then to the poorhouse

Shot in the chest and I'm dying today

Get six handsome cowboys to carry my coffin

Get six pretty women to sing me a song

Lay bunches of roses all over my coffin

Roses to deaden the clods as they fall

Then beat the drum slowly and play the fife lowly

Play the dead march as you carry me along

Those six pretty women will sing me to heaven

Stand there and listen to their strange love song

Description of boulder problem #5:
Just to the right of "BENNY . . ." there is a group of obscure little holds that can be used to gain a 20-degree edge just above. Using the edge as a two-finger, half-digit layback and stretching far right will gain a solid diagonal flake. From this flake move straight up through a series of pliés and solid reaches to the top.

. . . .

Joanna sings.

From this valley they say you are going

We will miss your bright eyes and sweet smile

For they say that you're taking the sunshine

That's brightened our pathway awhile

Won't you think of this valley you're leaving

Oh how lonely how sad it will be?

Won't you think of the heart you're breaking

And the grief that you're causing to me?

Come and sit by my side if you love me

Do not hasten to bid me adieu

And remember the Red River Valley

And the cowboy who's loved you so true

Description of boulder problem #6:

As the gravel starts, above and right of "I LOVE," there is a deep one-finger pocket. Once established five feet left of this, traverse and execute as soon as possible a reach into the pocket. Continue right until possible to cross up and left to a sloping diagonal. An interesting crimp and plié will enable movement up and left through a group of mediocre and insecure features to the top.

. . . .

Oh give me a home where the buffalo roam

Where the deer and the antelope play

Where seldom is heard a discouraging word

And the skies are not cloudy all day

How often at night when the heavens are bright

With the light from the glittering stars

Have I stood there amazed and asked as I gazed

If their glory exceeds that of ours

Home home on the range

Where the deer and the antelope play

Where seldom is heard a discouraging word

And the skies are not cloudy all day

Description of boulder problem #7:

To the left of the stairs at the far right of the wall find a group of horizontal edges. A delicately long reach from an awkward stance will gain a hold identifiable as a large missing block. Strenuous laybacking and foot crossing will enable a traverse left with only one hand switch. Up and left a flake will set up an exquisite counterbalanced layback.

* * * * * * * * * * * * * * * *

Joanna sings.

Amazing grace! how sweet the sound
That's touched a soul like me
I once was lost but now am found
Was blind but now I see

Through many dangers, toils, and snares
I have already come
It's grace that's brought me safe this far
And grace that will lead me home

Amazing grace! how sweet the sound
That's changed a soul like me
I once was lost but now am found
Was blind but now I see

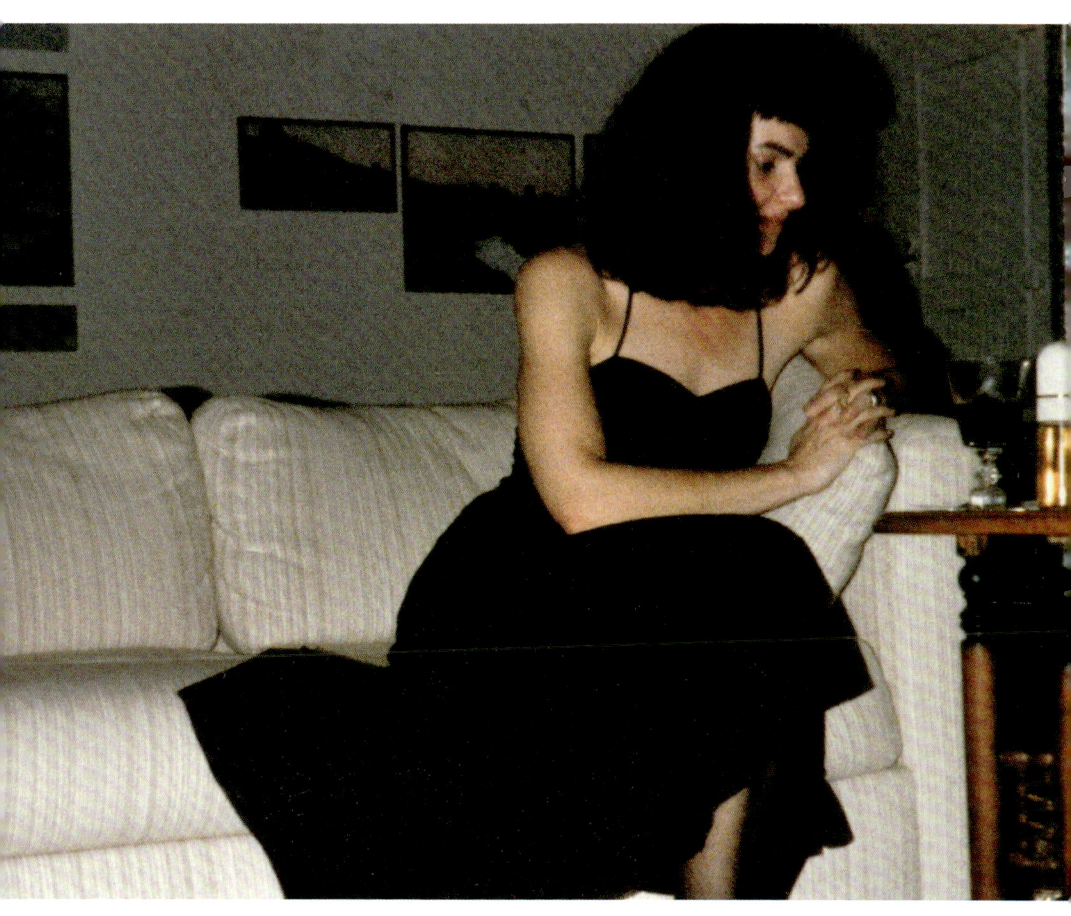

A Few Erotic Faculties, Dinnerware Artists Cooperative Gallery, Tucson, Ariz., 1986.
Photo courtesy of Bailey Doogan.

Rehearsal for *Clairvoyance (For Those In The Desert)*,
Sheldon Memorial Theater, St. Louis, Mo., 1987.

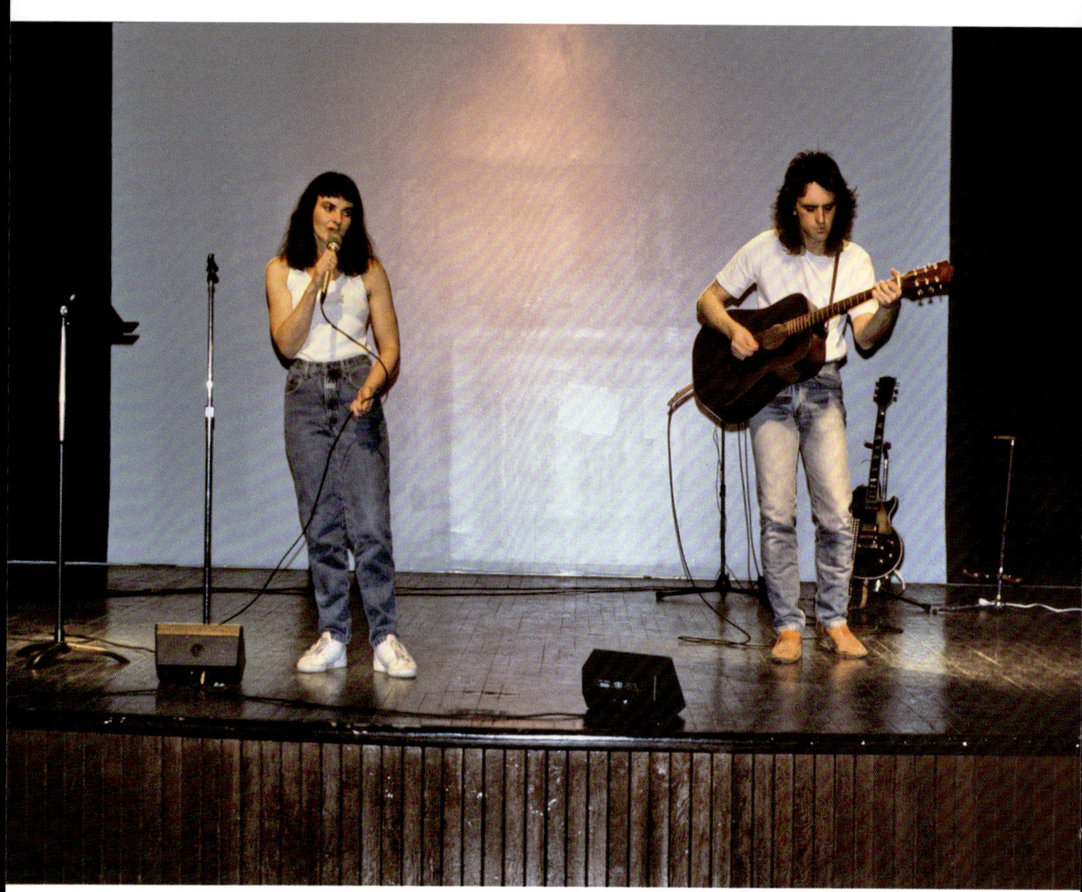

Joanna Frueh and Russell Dudley, post-performance, *Vermilion*, Terry Etherton Gallery,
Tucson, Ariz., 1989. *Photo courtesy of Frueh and Dudley.*

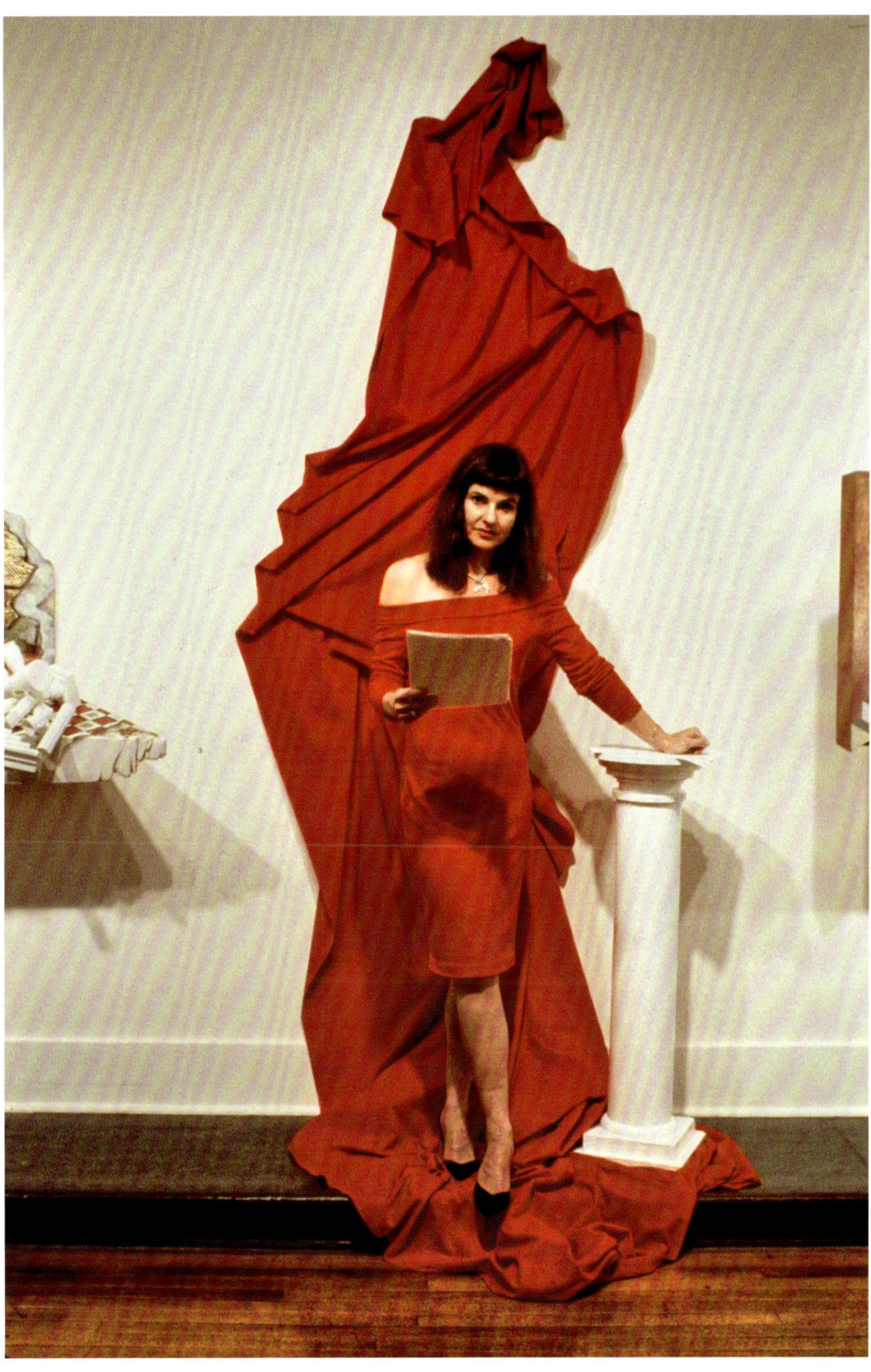

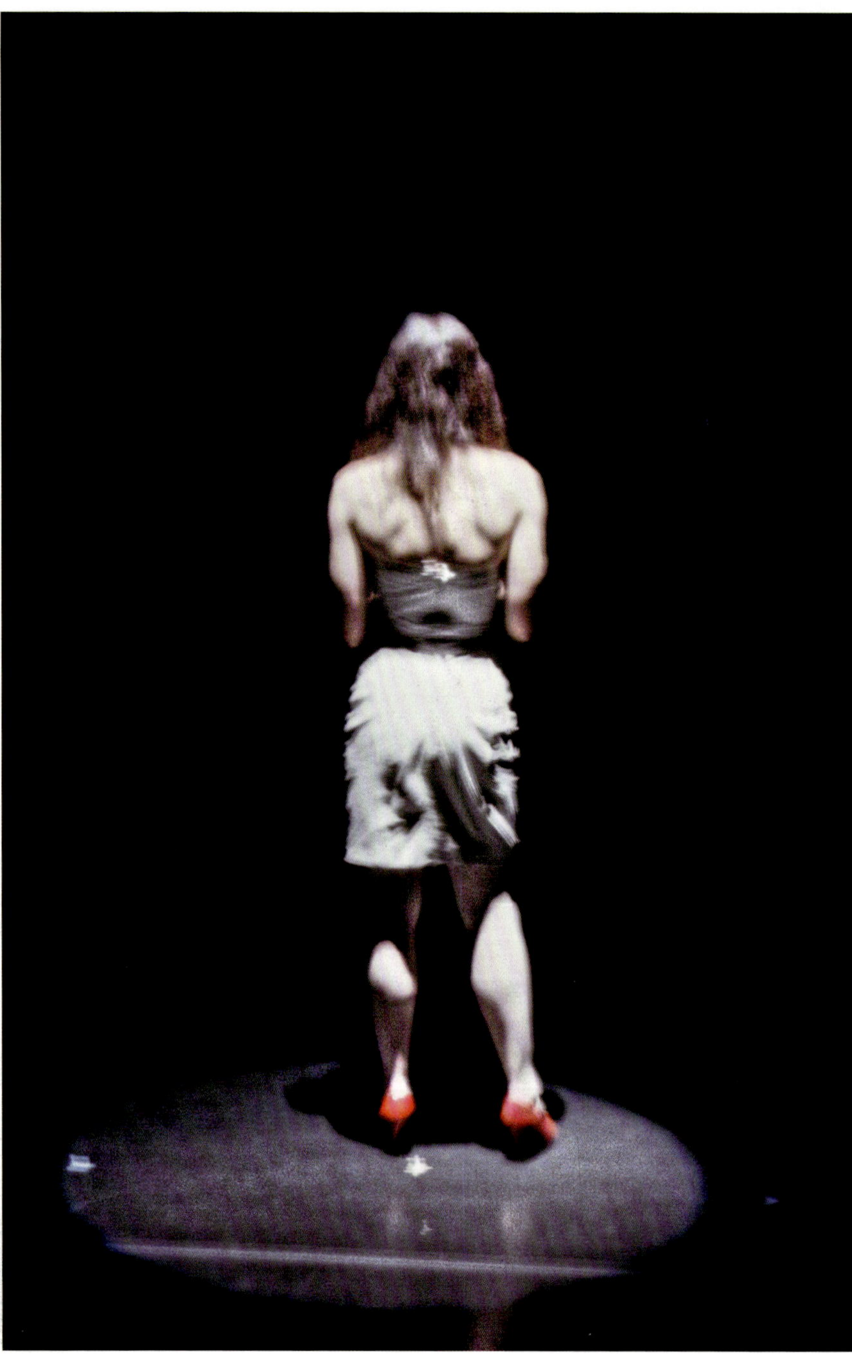

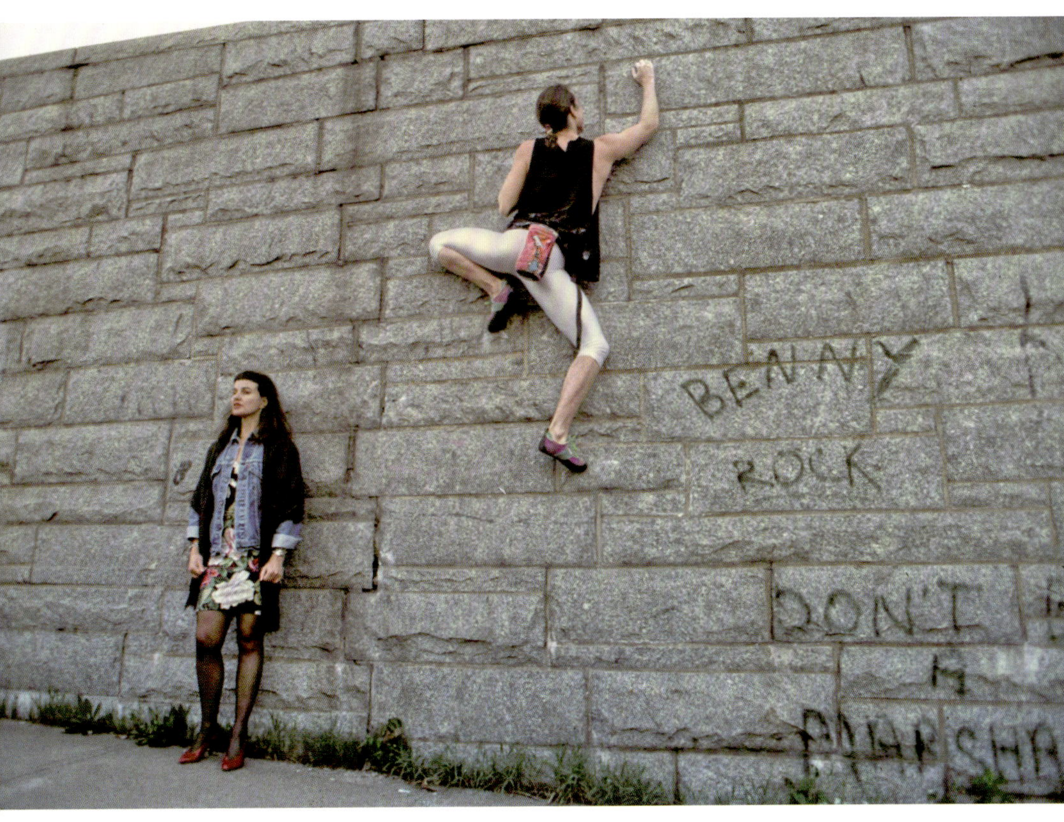

Joanna Frueh and Russell Dudley, pre-performance, *Mouth Piece*,
Columbia College Dance Center, Chicago, 1989. *Photo courtesy of Frueh and Dudley.*

Joanna Frueh and Russell Dudley, post-performance, *Pythia*, Pioneer Center for the Performing Arts, Reno, Nev., 1994. *Photo courtesy of Frueh and Dudley.*

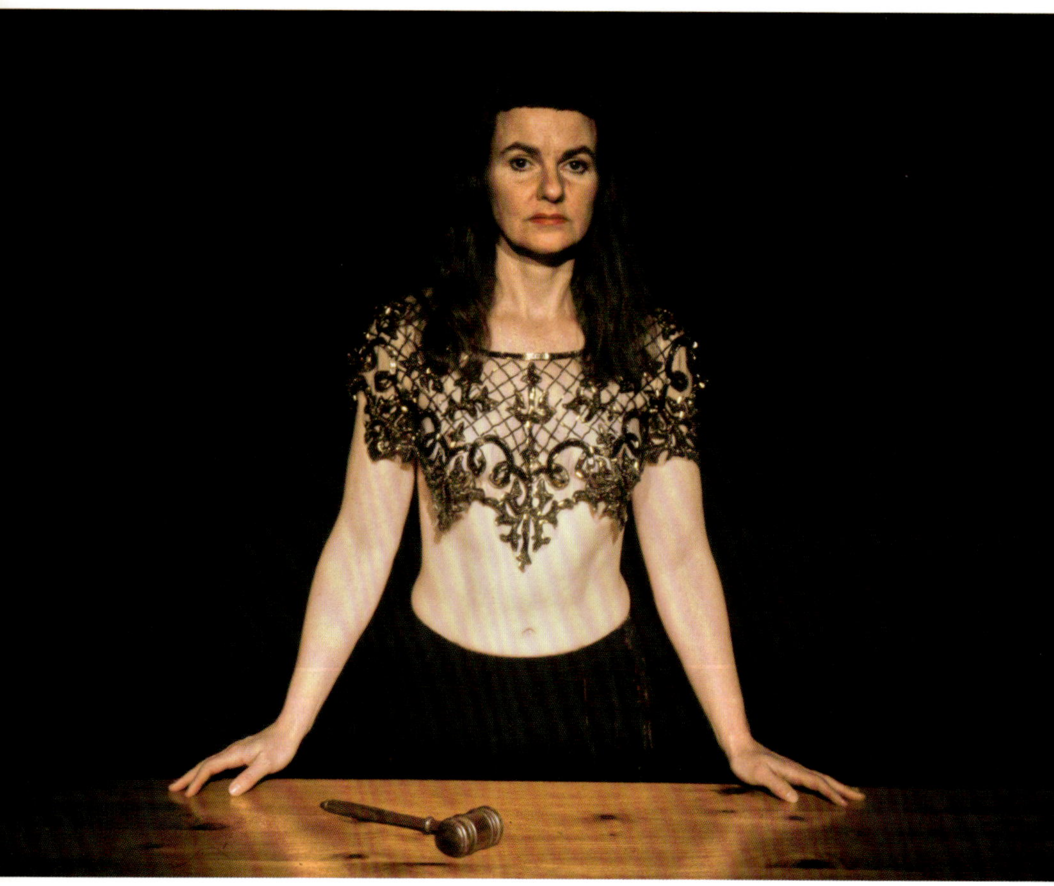

The Aesthetics of Orgasm, Sheppard Fine Arts Gallery, University of Nevada, Reno, 2002. *Photo courtesy of Dean Burton.*

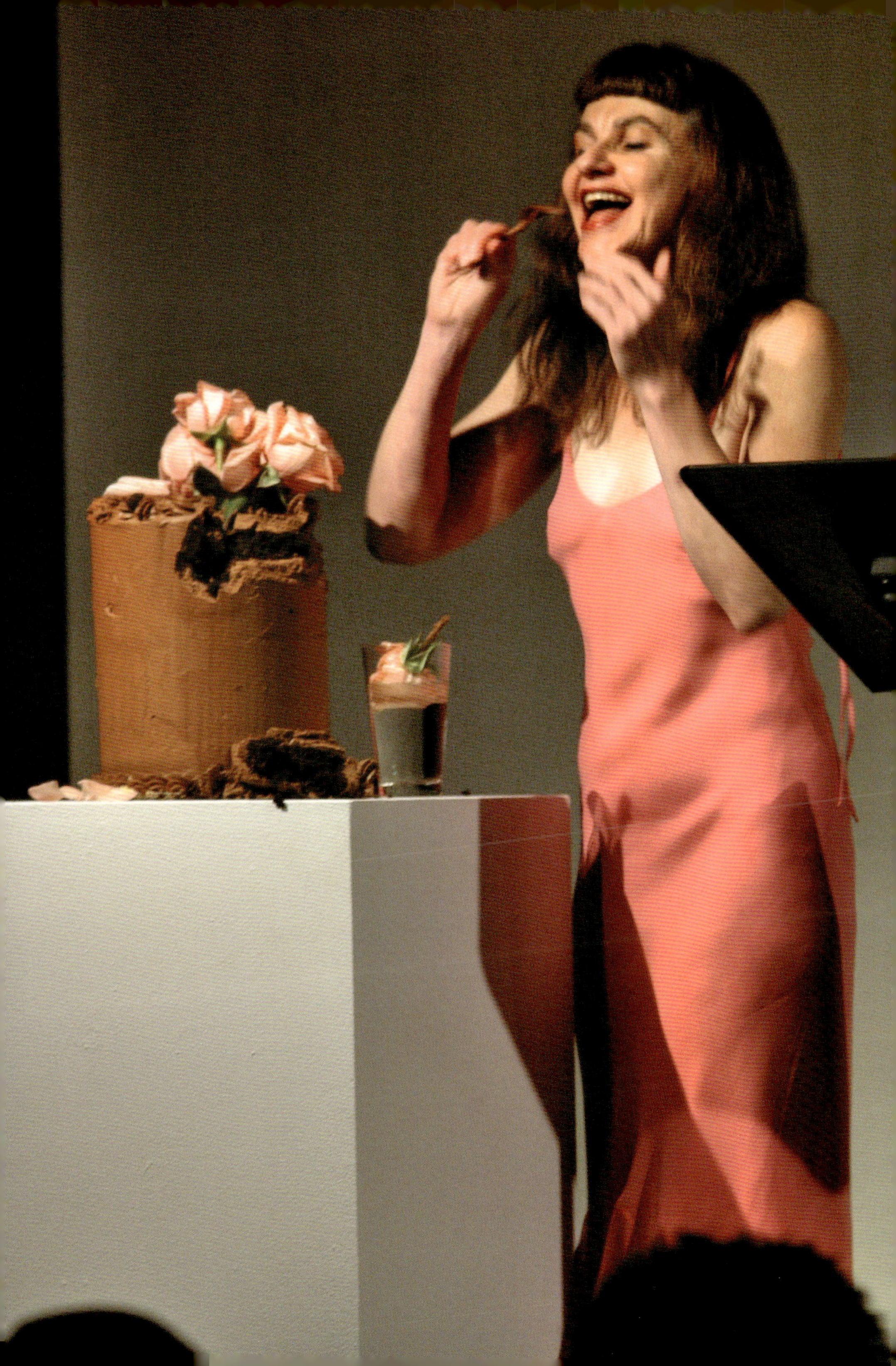

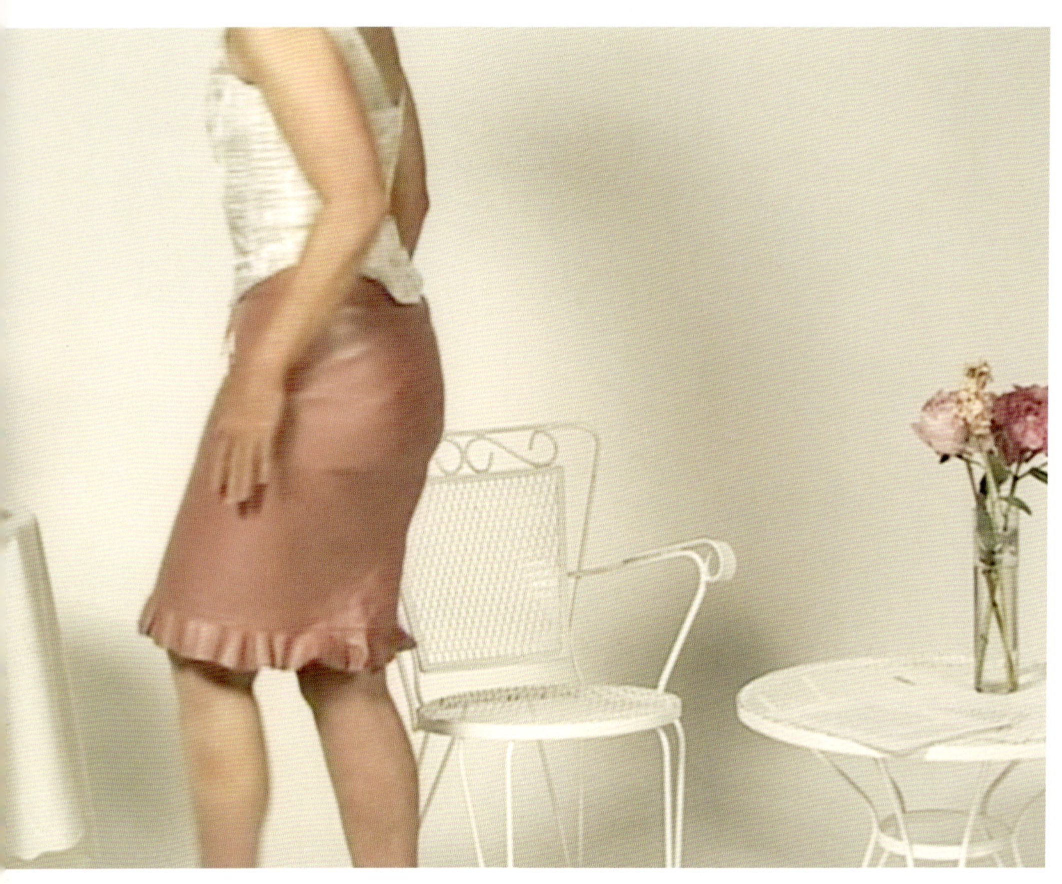

Joanna Frueh and Jeff Griffin, *The Performance of Pink*, from video shot in studio, Teaching and Learning Technologies, University of Nevada, Reno, 2004. *Photo courtesy of Frueh and Griffin.*

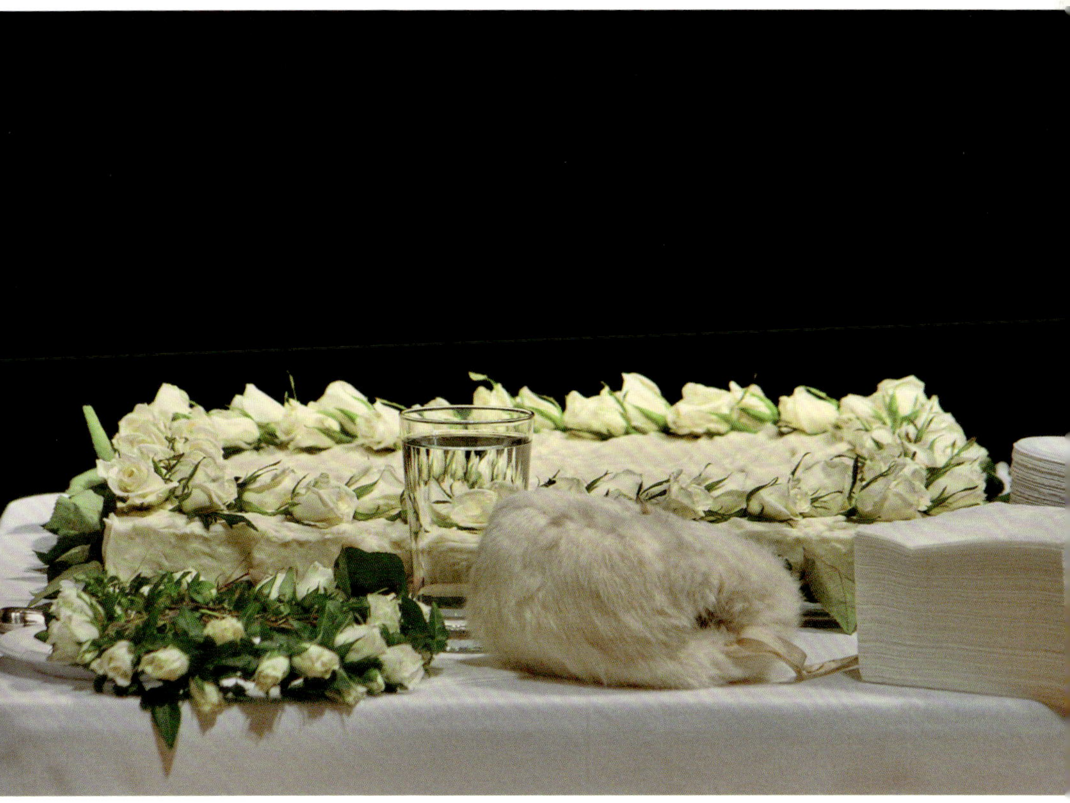

Props used in *Ambrosia*, Nevada Museum of Art, Reno, 2005. *Photo courtesy of Dean Burton.*

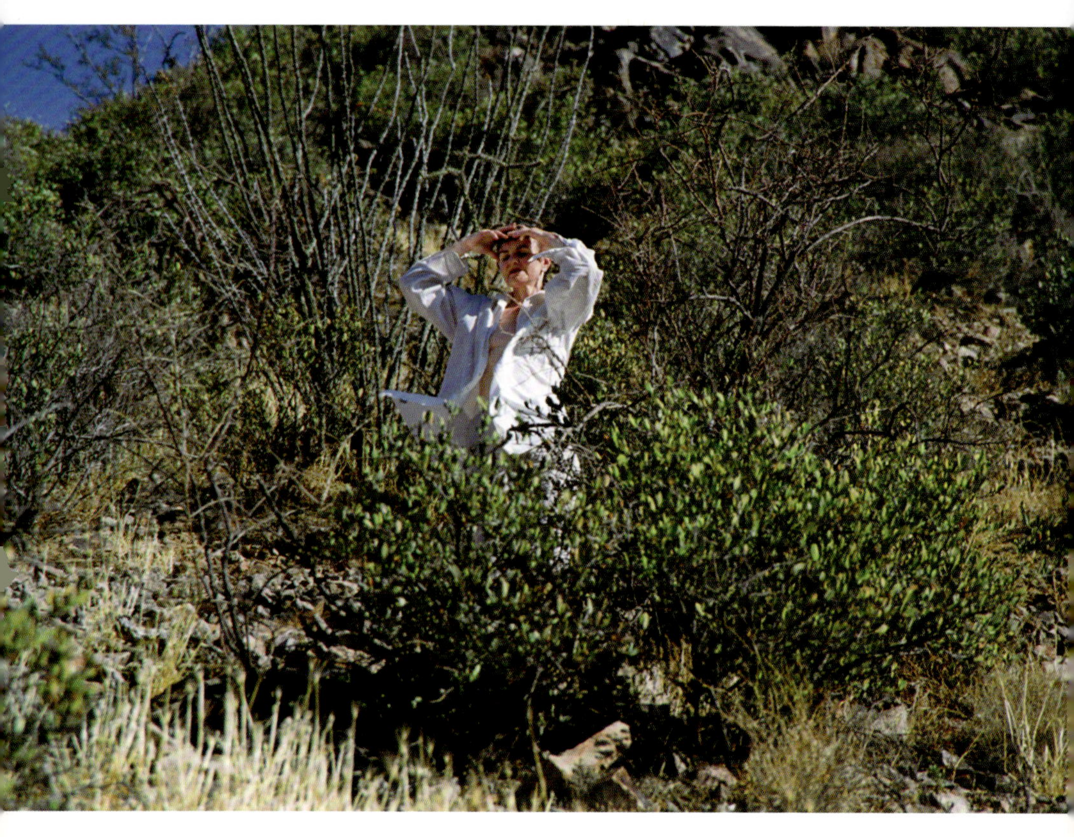

Jill O'Bryan and Joanna Frueh, *breathing there*. From the series
Joanna in the Desert, 2006.

Jill O'Bryan and Joanna Frueh, *the clairvoyant*. From
the series *Joanna in the Desert*, 2006.

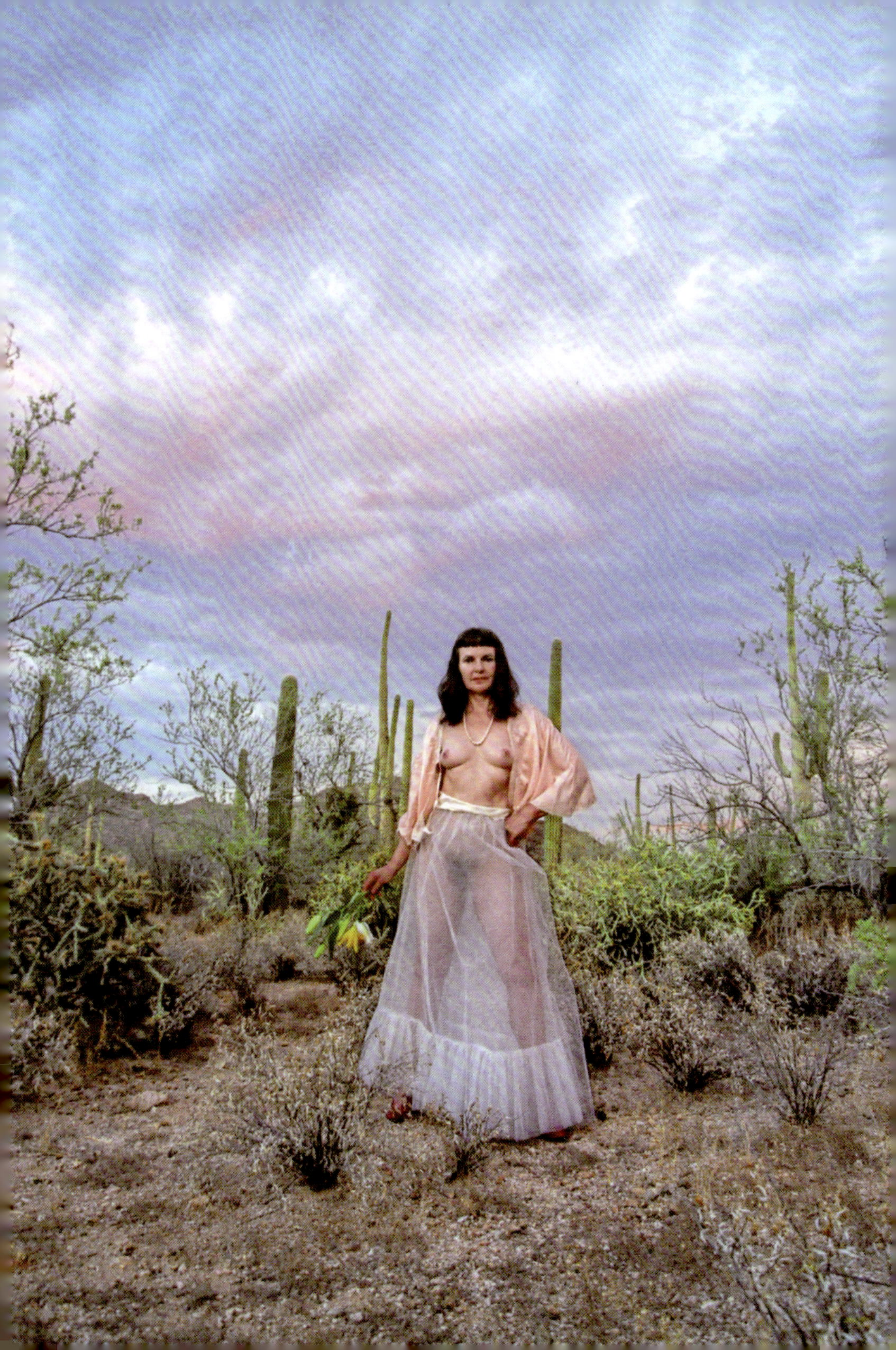

Jill O'Bryan and Joanna Frueh, *pink allure*. From the series *Joanna in the Desert*, 2006.

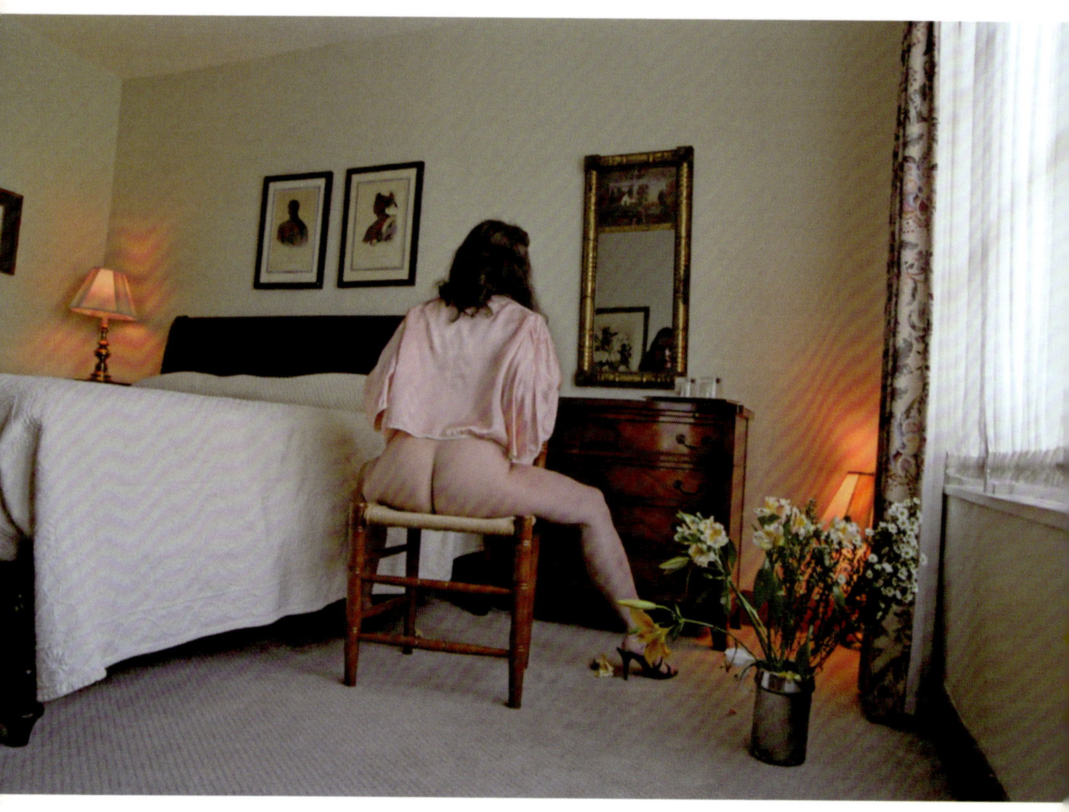

Jill O'Bryan and Joanna Frueh, *fucking hot*.
From the series *Joanna in the Desert*, 2006.

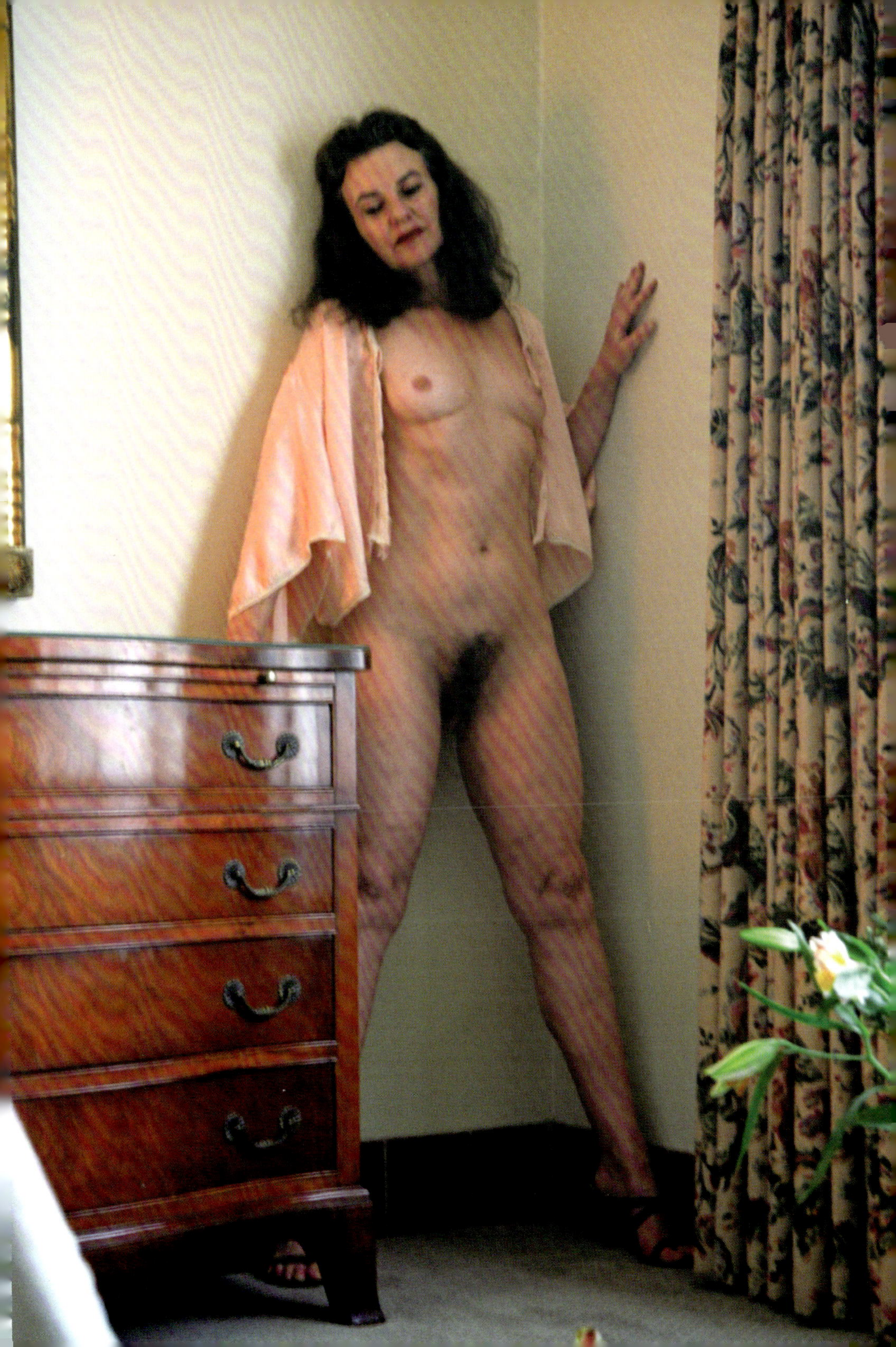

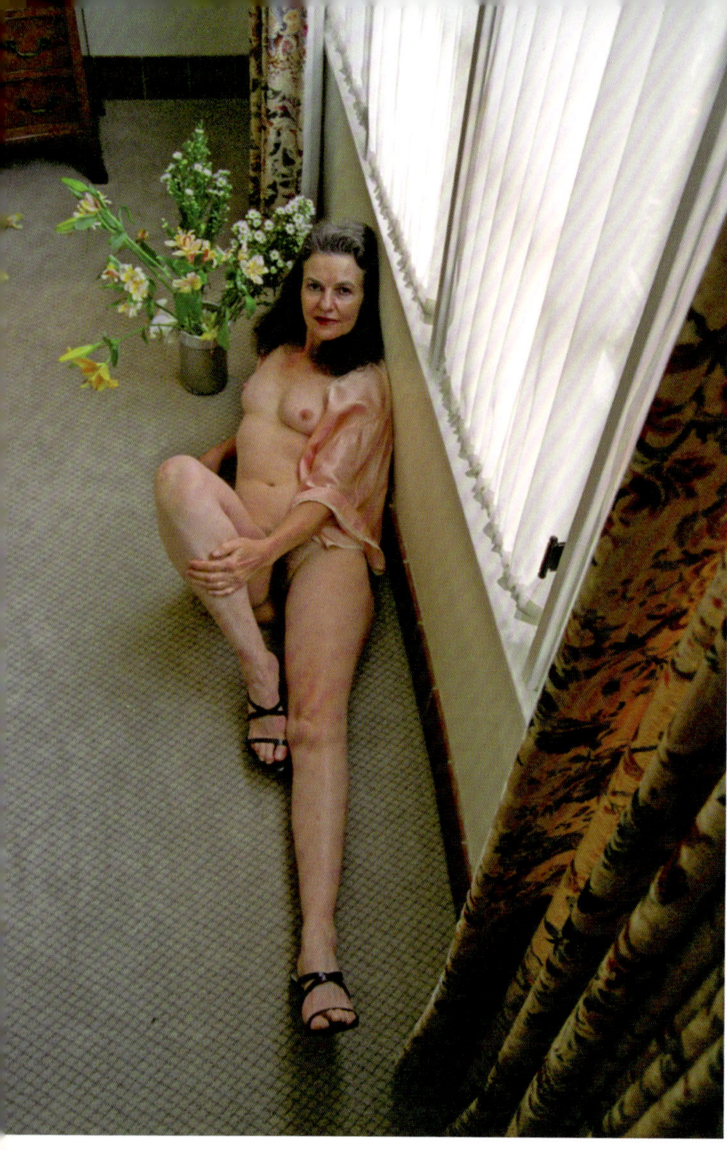

Jill O'Bryan and Joanna Frueh, *lustre*. From the series
Joanna in the Desert, 2006.

Jill O'Bryan and Joanna Frueh, *I am an angel in their eyes.*
From the series *Joanna in the Desert*, 2006.

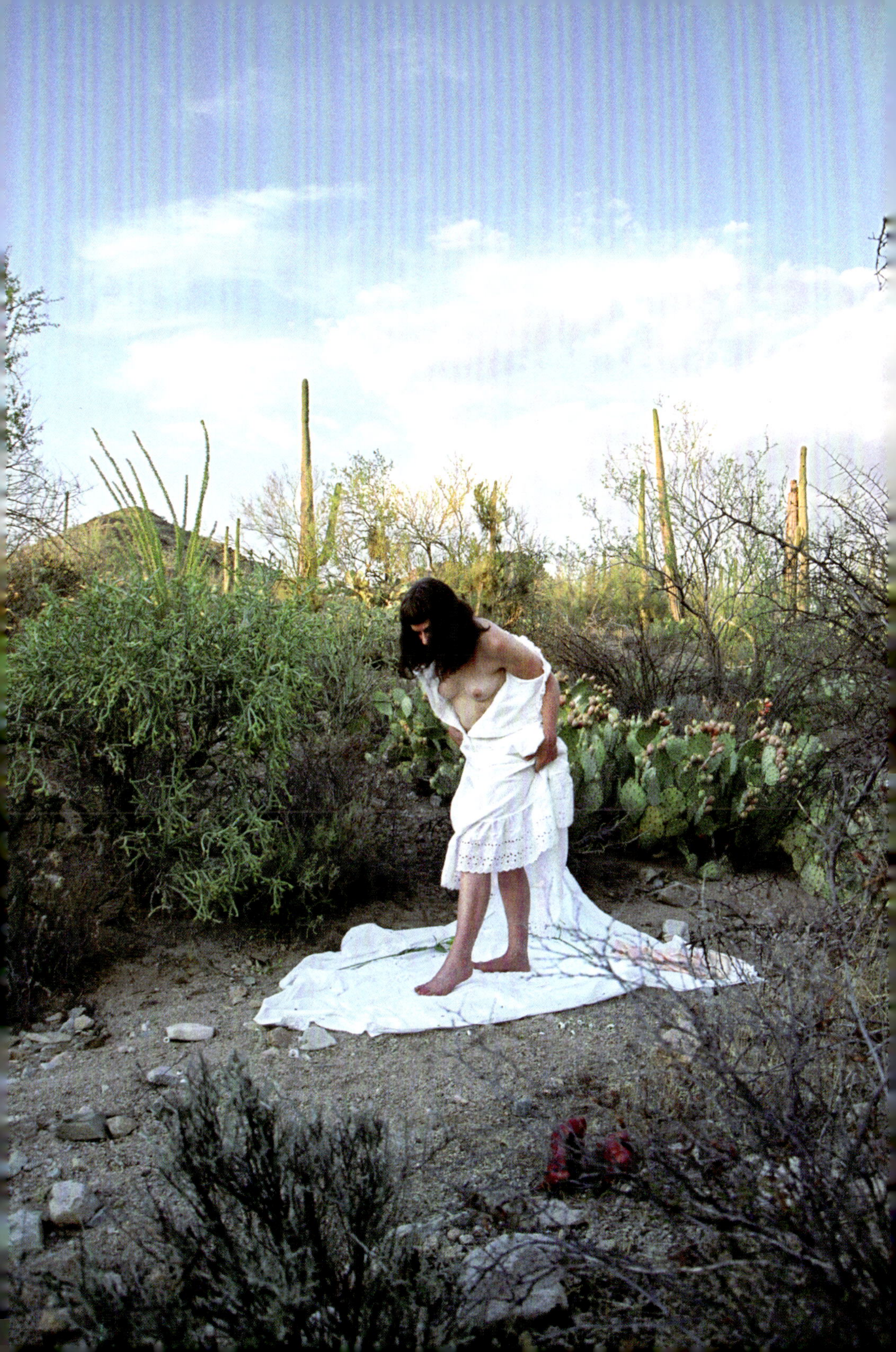

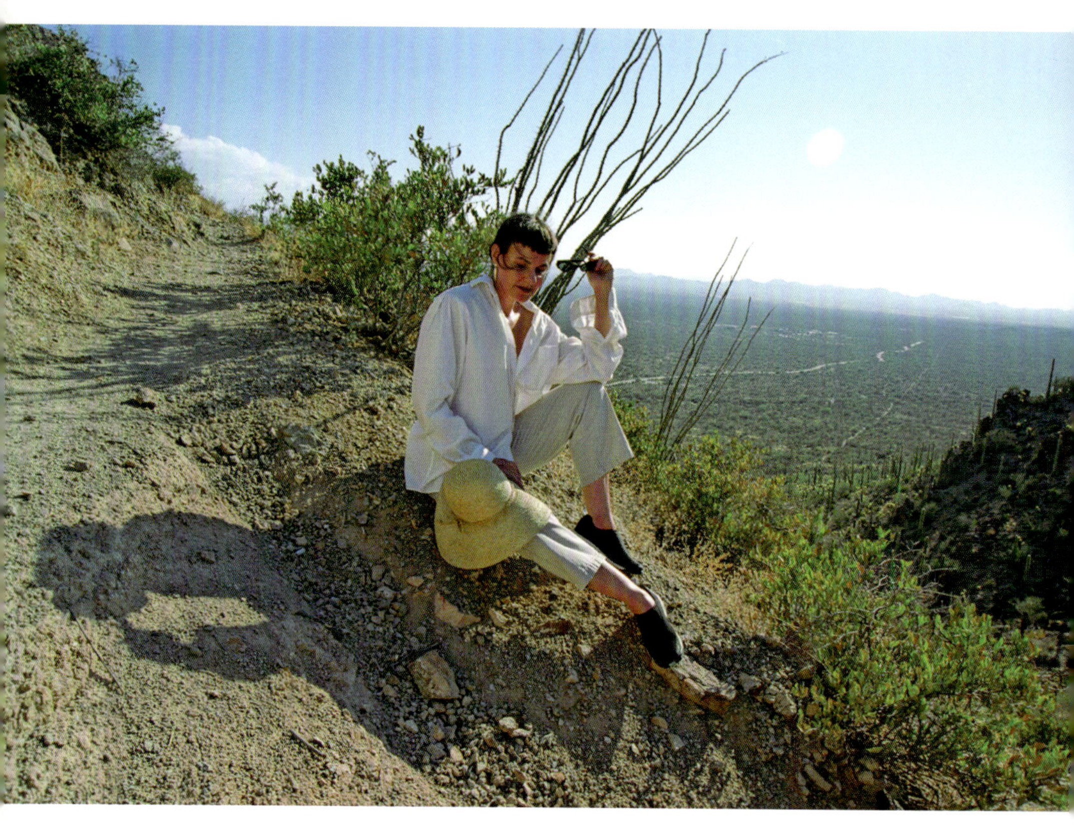

Jill O'Bryan and Joanna Frueh, *belonging here*. From the series *Joanna in the Desert*, 2006.

A long table with a gavel on it sits center stage and separates two music stands, each one holding a copy of the script. Frueh enters stage right and stops at the music stand nearest to her. A hip-high stool waits by the stage-left music stand. Stage right is dark and shadowy, like a cave. Stage left is warm, golden. Frueh stands when she is at stage right and sits stage left. A shawl of gold beads and sequins covers Frueh's shoulders and breasts. A deep red-brown velvet skirt bares her navel and hangs to the floor. Her feet are bare. Frueh stands very straight, places her hands on the music stand, and speaks as if she is simultaneously telling a secret and giving a proclamation.

Listen. Nobody likes you. Not even the one you call wife. You come to me for counsel, climb the mountain, slow, breathless, dazed by exertion. Were your feet bare like mine, they would be bleeding. Me, I wear my blood on my mouth. True red. It is not a simple color.

You desire deliverance and yearn for promises that are predictions of love coming your way, so you expect others to redeem you. You think you are a saint, but you play the role of a seeker. Any saint would tell you: the seeker does not play a role, the seeker is a lover.

You, a walking confession, are stuck on your sincerity, which you confuse with integrity. Sincerity means only that outward appearance and actual character match. That definition includes neither grace nor soundness. Sincerity is the liar's path. Look at yourself. You avert your eyes. You protect your aversion to truth, your belligerent ignorance. I hear you saying, under your breath, "I am the lover, the shy lover." You are always convincing yourself: my children love me, I am amiable, easy, and everyone is difficult, intractable, so they, like pigs and fishes, cannot be persuaded, I am a star rising from the muck of women and men. You speak about pigs and fishes the way you speak about assholes: you denigrate the animals and the body. Observe my hands and shoulders: no wings, no wand. I am not a mountain goddess, a dream to which ziggurats were built, a deity, inarticulate to every passing present, who mixes with a long-gone pantheon of stars. I told every single star just how bleak I think you are, and now I'm telling you, and I am gleaming.

The walking confession betrays his unconvincing authority. The only gaits you know are graceless: belly out, shoulders up, neck compressed, legs weak from the weight of sincerity.

. . . .

Frueh's voice is dulcet and seductive.

Hummingbird, sucker, you try to extract nectar from my breath, which you feel hot, almost dripping, on your face. My mild voice and its melodious touch you mistake for a caress, but intimacy is not a condition of my love. You are desperate for a fortune cookie as you watch my lips shape your life. And you begin to know that your voice resonates in the wrong places, not in your pelvis, diaphragm, or the length of your legs, not from the top of your head or the heart of your mouth. You are ready to screech or cry, for sincerity is no substitute for grace.

So come in closer, further, to the lap, the lips, my medicinal blood.

Tiny scarlet flowers in the desert produce large, vibrant scents.

Think about the red words: grace and eros.

Remember once you leave my voice that the mountain is a place of orientation and that you came to get your bearings.

Then remember that what I say is fact and fiction, and all of it is true.

Table. Frueh sings the beginning lines of "Bird on a Wire."

Sitting.

A meeting with the Pythia required a snaking climb up Mount Parnassus to Delphi. Pythia was also Pythoness, a name derived from Python, who guarded the oracle, which was Pythia's location, words, and person. Python was the Greek *drakōn,* which means serpent, dragon, literally the seeing one.

Frueh's voice is commanding, nasty, and charming.

Python, my graceful tongue to crush loudmouthed visitors. We see them under the white-hot sun. They feel heavy and thirsty, and they are starving for advice. They are tearful and can barely breathe, and they wonder if the light and air will kill them before they are brought to me to ask one question. I am your dragon lady, full of word-honey, wind me round with the love I owe them. They are puking on the temple and sanctuary stones, ready for this comfortable cave. Underground we wrestle with volcanoes.

Visitors described the oracle at Delphi as cleft, gorge, and chasm. They talked about a precipice, the dark mountainside, hairpin turns, and the hot and heavy air, like a dragon's breath, they said. Pythia sat or stood before the people who came for her command, prediction, warning, prohibition, or approval, and they claimed, after hiking, fasting, praying, and ascending the steep flight of steps that led to Pythia, singer of Delphi, once called Pytho after the graceful tongue, that dragon's breath rose from the deep fissure at her feet. No one except a Pythia knew how deep that crevice was. Visitors simply said they saw and smelled its stinking vapors that supposedly sent her into trance or madness or simply made her ill, so that she had to vomit her words.

From Pythia's clefts and orifices a perfume floated when she spoke, and it was sweeter than a first-time lover's intentions. Some scholars say the scent was concentrated at her

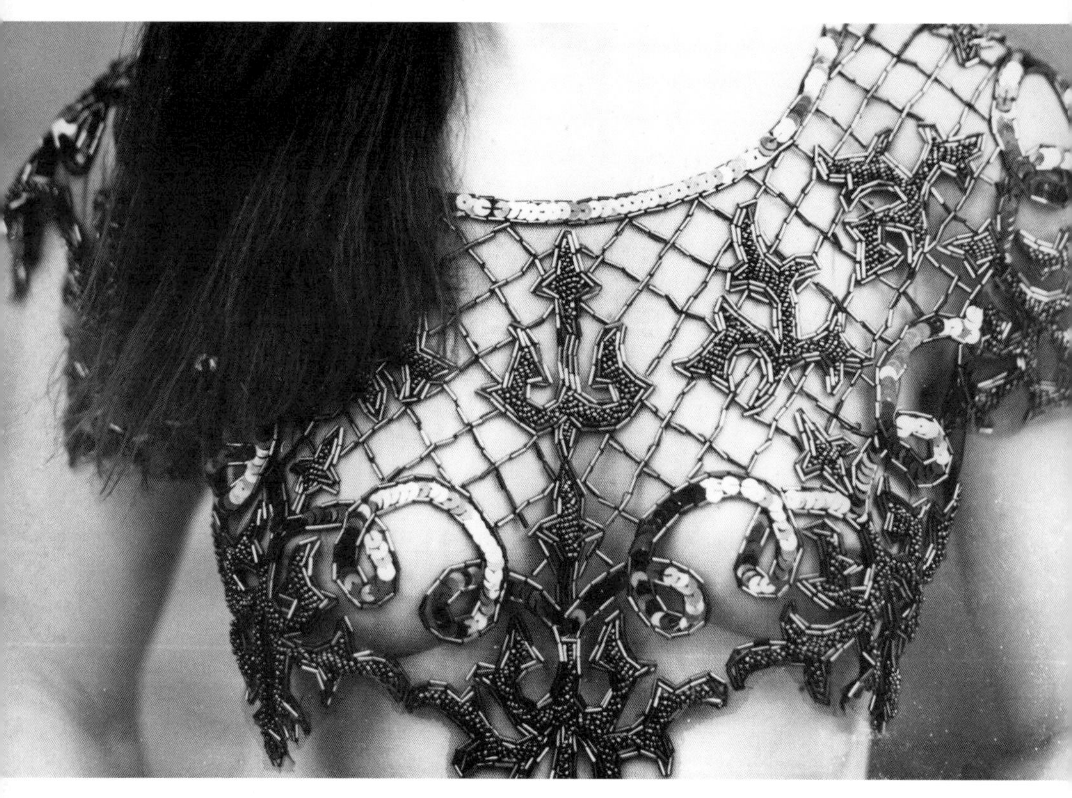

Joanna Frueh and Russell Dudley, Joanna in costume, *Pythia*, 1994.

Photos courtesy of Frueh and Dudley.

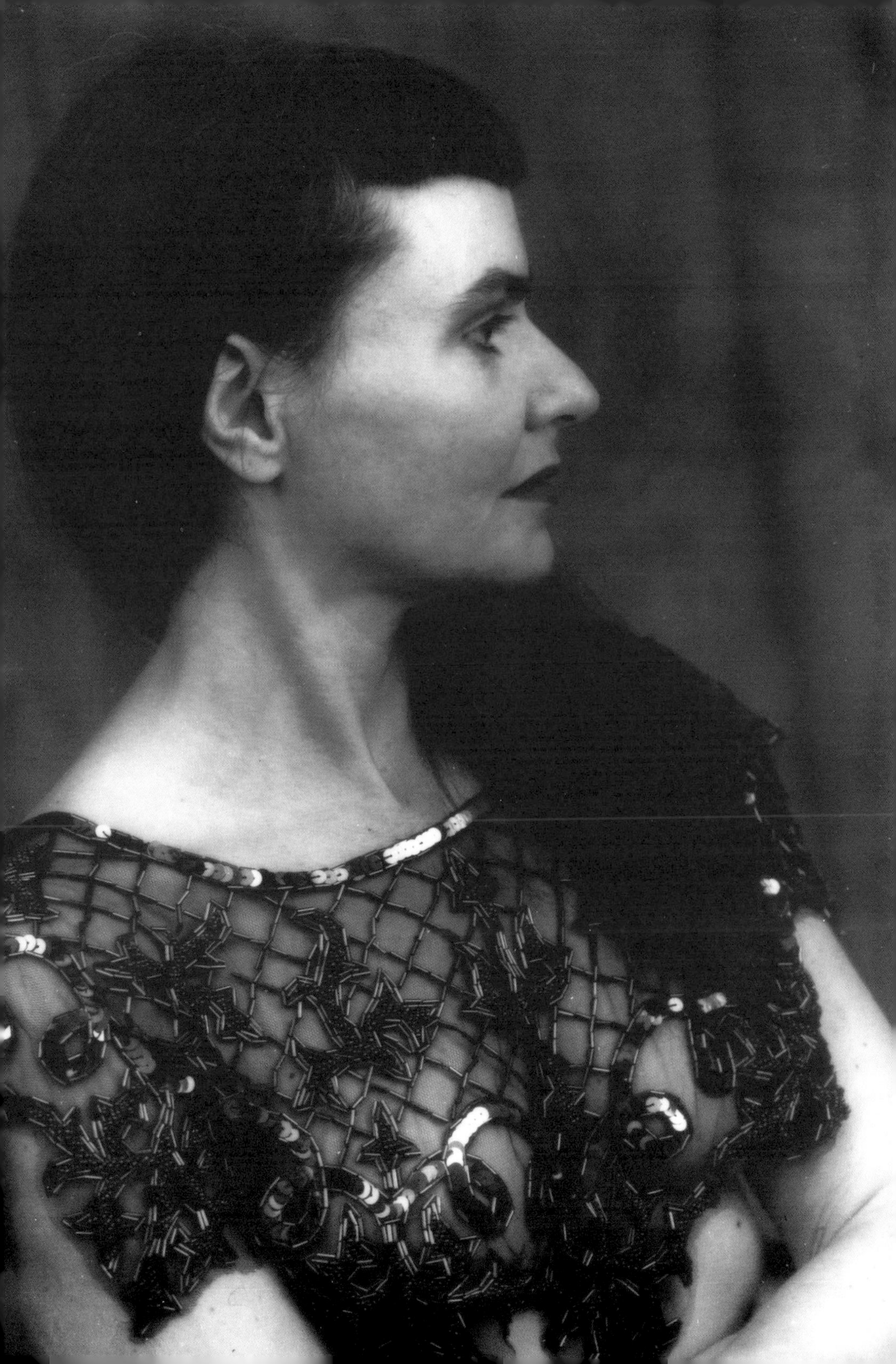

navel, so visitors would stare at it. They felt safer looking there than into her eyes. In the same way that Delphi exerted a downward pull on the body as if forcing someone to draw closer to the earth, Pythia attracted her questioner. This effect, called Eros's Invitation, at once soothed and terrified visitors, whose preparation for the meeting entailed many repetitions of one of her maxims: the lover is a seeker who becomes sought after.

I, Dragon Lady, am, like Delphi, the site of erotic intersections. The navel is the center of the body, and Delphi, called Navel of the World, is one of the earth's geographical centers. The builders knew this, for they founded Pytho at the junction of two major dragon lines. That crossing causes dry mouth, vertigo, tears, hard breathing, heaviness, and earthward attraction. Enjoy with me the subterranean encounters of arm to shoulder, hip to pelvis, cunt to anus, back to buttocks, breasts to ribs to belly, head to neck to chin to jaw moving as my mouth moves ready for a mouth like yours, like loam, on thigh to knee to ankle, then on the feet, which, simply by walking, are intimate with the ground. Together we are at the center and see dragon lines, currents that connect one navel to another, whether it be oracular site of earth or body. Delphi to Chartres to Borobudur to Chaco to Teotihuacán; chest to chest, calf over buttocks, tongue on finger, head on stomach: they are the same, for all centers, all points and moments of concentration, are erotic.

I weed dandelions for hours and see their centers when I close my eyes at night.
   Pythia, they say you hypnotize yourself in order to let go of everyday distractions.
   One word in a book occupies me for days.
   They say you chew laurel leaves, which take you into poetic and erotic frenzy.
   Between sets of lat pulldowns I sit in the gym, staring seemingly at nothing, and a voice next to me intrudes: "Wake up. Get back to work."
   The inattentive observer mistakes concentration for absentmindedness.
   The second day of my period we are fucking and afterwards my blood mesmerizes my lover. Russell calls what he sees, what I feel on my thighs, buttocks, and lower back, a hemorrhage, and when I stand up, blood from my vagina and the sheets runs down my legs and drips on the floor. Russell tells me later that hemorrhage is an inadequate word, unequal to his perception. "Gallons, through the sheets, through the bed, through the floor," he says. The Dogon say that "a woman without adornment is speechless." I say that

style is in the body, its size, movements, and spirit, rich colors are often reds, and decoration is information. The different colors of menstrual red flow from my hips: raisin, crimson, muddy mucus. All the better to kiss you with.

Pythia, they say you wear white, to speak your virginity. I see a picture of you painted by a nineteenth-century artist, and you are wearing red and umber. You are barefoot and your skirt touches the ground, where a snake that is far too small rests next to a smoking fissure. In another nineteenth-century painting I see you with your breasts bare and a huge python emerging from between your thighs. Virgin, for you, means "my choice," and your questioners never think that Pytho is either only a spectacular phallus that you need as your companion or an external vagina that represents the origin of your counsels. Only a fool speaks from her cunt alone.

They say that oracular voice necessitates madness. But no one listens to women called mad. No one listened to Cassandra. History has reduced her to less than tears. A synopsis of the Trojan War doesn't mention her once. One scholar says that cultural myth grants seers such as Cassandra the dubious privilege of speaking from the simultaneously despised and romanticized lower mouth. You see, but visions do not possess you. Sometimes you speak in the precision of riddles, more often in the considered words of the learned woman you are. Speaking only from the cunt would make any woman mad.

· ·

Frueh shifts position more consciously than she has yet done in this section.

In graduate school my professor wore a red velvet suit. He was impersonating the menstrual female, though he would never have thought that. He liked to think of himself as a nineteenth-century dandy. He wore socks when we fucked, and they signaled his inhibition. All along he rejected my seduction, which he thought was madness. One day I said to him, "I think I know what it would feel like to be crazy." He said, "Sometimes I see madness in your eyes." I hadn't asked for confirmation, but I was in danger, for the bloodman's words cut, they felt as real as prophecy. Too easily I equated prophecy with apocalypse.

Many years later a friend said to me, "Your mind is like a diamond."

"What do you mean?" I asked.

"Hard and sharp," she answered.

not the only consequence of grace. Cock up, cock down; body grows tall, body gets buried; facelift, ten-years-after sag. Denials of gravity are temporary, for grace overrides gravity. Grace is not higher than me, higher than you, as rarefied as gods of light, like Apollo, who took over the Delphic Oracle by killing Python. Some say Apollo also killed Delphyne, the Pythia at that time, by slitting her throat. He had to see her blood, which he called "dark and demented," and then his blade—such an earthly weapon—disappeared. No evidence. Delphyne, delirium, delphinium, which is sometimes poisonous. Delphyne, only toxic to the gods who say light is an absolute. After Delphyne, for a length of time unknown to us, the Pythias were teenagers, permitted to bear children, who called themselves brides and wives of Apollo. (Take me, O my god of consummate light, for I am dressed in a pale desire, like Mary's lilies in the radiance of a later god.) One young Pythia was abducted, and from then on the oracle was at least beginning menopause and usually well beyond her reproductive years. (Consort or companion of Apollo, my ass. My choice. Listen, rapist, lustrous with the glamour of high gods and angels, gold comes from the earth. Gold comes up from under.)

Grace does not derive from words meaning good or evil. The Indo-European base *gwer* means "to lift up the voice," and the Sanskrit *gṛṅāti* means "he sings."

In my parents' forest, looking for my father, I wanted to sing, even though, or because, I was full of fear. Mom and I soon discovered that Dad was in their bedroom taking a nap. In the summer when the temperature is comfortable and the windows are open upstairs, the bedroom doors, even if gently tapped to close, swing shut hard and unpredictably. I went to the study for a nap of my own, and as I fell asleep I heard, in my mind, I'm sure, my father singing:

. . . .

Frueh sings to the tune of the traditional song
"The Demon Lover."

> Hello, hello, my own true love
> Hello, hello, cried he
> I have just returned from the dark scented wood
> All for the love of thee
> I could have married the Angel of Death

She would have married me

But I refused her strange perfumes

All for the sake of thee

Often I am sitting at my desk when the late afternoon wind rises in summertime. Across the street the willows' limbs sway, then shake. I feel my naked arm, which is smooth and satisfying. Instantaneous voluptuousness comes over me, and Pythia calls that state singing. Sometimes she sings to her visitors.

I danced and sang with a bird watching. I had fallen in love with Russell and was getting a divorce. I felt crazy that night. First I whirled around the big living room whose curtainless windows reflected my image, and I could also see the lights of the city. I played a tape, over and over, of a dumb and passionate popular song, one of the few hits at the time that made me want to move. I turned the music off and looked at the bird. A song whose tune was as dark and melancholy as an English folk song about love and murder came out of me, but the song was about the bird. Unlike a folk song, the melody was unrepeated and rambling. The lyrics praised the bird—her sheen, her sharp eyes, her voice and movements, which I wanted to understand. (Goats dance through darkness.)

Lascivious Pythia, they say an old goat is a lecherous man. They forget your lust. Today Hormone Replacement Therapy means sex, and so does I fell into a blazing ring of fire and fever, you stoke my fever, and the illustrations on romance book covers in the grocery store. I don't see you, Pythia, on them. I see a man and a woman in their twenties. His muscles bulge. Her breasts bulge. She has long hair, and his upper body is naked. Often her skirt is hiked up to reveal her leg, bare from foot to thigh. Here we see clichés of skin to skin, which try to show what lies underneath them: it is the heart as the love muscle that strains to break free from the confinement of skin as contour. Deeper yet runs the representation of the heart's athleticism and youthful vigor: the heart has endurance and probably acrobatic skill. The cover pictures keep me at a distance, within the confines of voyeurism. I would like to observe eros and see the body as permeable, as a site of events—orgasm, toothache, sneeze, the appearance of a pimple, lesion, wart, or wrinkle—and as a condition of processes, which are the changes that lead to the events. The heart is an ancient organ, ancient like ferns, and I would like to observe the eros of ferns.

The book titles read:

*Frueh recites the words lovingly, as if the titles were something
other than dreck. Yet a hint of sarcasm colors the recitation.*

*Silver Fire, Stardust Dreams, Angel Eves, Touch Me with Fire, Forever His, Halfway to Paradise,
Rebel Wind, No Other Love, The Passionate Rebel, So Wild My Heart, My Only Desire, Love's
Timeless Dance, The Rogue and the Lily, The Panther and the Rose, Tender Deception, Emerald
Dreams, Moon of Desire, All the Time We Need, Fascination, Wildcat, Scarlet Lady.*

The asinine parody of eros that I see and read in the grocery store is a melancholy
reminder of people's everyday and necessary desire for the poet's, the lover's, and the
prophet's ecstasies of enigmatic speech, which is the desire for wild grace.

Frueh quotes a lyric from her own Clairvoyance
(For Those In The Desert).

> I am the scarlet woman
> The bottomless blue lake.

Table. Frueh taps the gavel.

> Scorch the law.

*Standing. Frueh alters a lyric from her own
Clairvoyance (For Those In The Desert).*

> Road to ruin I heard them say
> The name of a bar on an old highway
> See the neon burning red
> In the desert of the dead

Table. Frueh taps the gavel.

Learn the law.

. . . .

Sitting.

When Pythia chooses to answer, she does it clearly. When she suspects slyness in a question, she is more subtle and poetic. Sometimes a visitor, having received an answer, goes back to tell Pythia she has been vague. Pythia then says, "You heard me." Occasionally she adds, "She sells seashells by the seashore," or "Loothe lipth lithp legendth."

Pythia's first maxim, "Know thyself," later used by Socrates, was carved on the temple at Delphi. The oracle and the poet coax meaning from the seeker. They stamp out rumor and create it. "Rumors create legends," says Pythia.

Based on the few extant documents about the ancient Pythias—who practiced from before 2300 BC to AD 129, when the Roman emperor Justinian closed the schools in Greece, thereby abolishing the education of women, which meant the closing of the oracle at Delphi—scholars have reconstructed a rare public address given by the Pythia Xenocleia. Shortly before 900 BC, she ordered the Twelve Labors of Heracles and later commanded that he be burned. She, like other Pythias, sentenced Apollo's heroes to death whenever she could in response to the heroes' string of moral and physical murders.

Scholars say that Xenocleia delivered her address in the same manner that she answered individuals, and that her manner was characteristic of Pythias: she was almost motionless, and her maintenance of a peaceful dignity made her speech measured. "She weighed her words," writes one scholar, and another reveals, in strangely unacademic prose, "I wish her beautiful voice could have excruciated me."

Here are Xenocleia's words:

> Speaking is believing. My words create and eliminate. Veiling and unveiling, my voice hums in the heart, transforming the time we are together.

There is no purely physical inflection of a voice. Sounds are carriers of memory and of sensory experience, and sounds are immediate. My sounds are in you now, my body has become yours. We are breathing, all enveloped in our human breath. Inhaling and exhaling the air, the subtlety of pheromones, exchanging the denseness of hormonal rhythms, we are one breath, one body. We cross the fragmented, the manifest, and the explicit with the inseparable, the transitory, and the implicit. Sounds, like breaths and melodies, are contingencies of present, past, and future, which my sounds actively transform.

Words don't like being alone. They thrive in company. That is why tones are needed now, a song with many grace notes. My melodies transmute thought into sound and action, and, like myths and folk songs, my melodies are never fixed. Musical thinking is thinking in motions, and clear movement, like clear thinking, is erotic concentration. In the Ayurvedic *Book of Timeless Medicine,* we learn that love agrees with music, justice agrees with rites. The law, the rites, promote stagnation, for they are ascetic, like a melody with no grace notes. Dictionaries tell you that grace notes are unnecessary to the melody, but champagne has no charm without bubbles, and chocolate bars are worthless without sugar.

Grace is sweet in and of itself; the singer must not force the song. Singing with feeling inhibits fluency, for then melodrama becomes the primary inflection.

Ascetic thinking separates people from one another, as the law does, too, in contrast to love. Erotic thinking, which is dependent on melody, alleviates the loneliness of words. Melodies are dragon lines, moving to center after center of meaning. The law of light and of risen and rising angels restricts what any of us can say. What we cannot say we can sing about. So song enhances living as grace notes enhance melody. Do not misunderstand enhancement as ornamentation, the way dictionaries misrepresent the grace note as embellishment. Enhancement is necessary, for it heightens awareness.

I am aware of you listening and observing. Some of you have come to me with questions, and others of you will. Some of you have heard that my words are the law. Lawyers advise, and so do I sometimes, but they arrange sounds pleasingly in sequence in order to win, and their interest in gold is different from mine.

In this golden hour my voice grows. I fly united with the golden eagle, yellow bird, and gold-winged woodpecker. My voice moves back and forth through centuries. I last forever, for no time at all. Kiss me, my golden tongue is melting in the heat of my mouth.

*Standing. Frueh catches the eye of a young woman in the audience,
someone in her twenties, for the first several lines, and looks
at her pointedly off and on throughout this section.*

You ask, "Where is home?"

It is not anywhere you think it is. Not in the library in your parents' home, not in the kitchen where you cook with friends, not with the men and women you call lover, not with your suicidal visions.

You sat on a boulder, feet in the Aegean Sea. Hours later you felt for calluses that the water had washed away. You stood on the boulder, ready to dive underwater and breathe like a mermaid.

You see everyday occurrences as possibilities of death: hair blowing across your forehead turns into a knife, slices your skin, and penetrates your cranium; a car thirty feet away speeds up and rams into your car head on; honeysuckle petals become plutonium pellets that force themselves into your mouth and down your throat.

Road signs scare you: Watch for Rocks; Runaway Truck; Hitchhikers May Be Inmates; Truckers, Check Brakes; Rattlesnakes; Exit Now.

You're afraid that because things have gone to hell, they'll probably stay there.

You're wondering if you should keep turning the other cheek.

Release your pain, and you'll relax. Prepare for another slap, and call self-sacrifice victimhood.

Your enemies have given you more strength than they can even imagine for themselves. You will change history as we know it.

Decisions of magnitude do not require time. Consideration is only a leap of faith to a path as true as the next one when the traveler has begun another journey.

Repeat my next words after you have left me:

> I am a *fauve*
>
> True to my kind
>
> I am a *fauve*
>
> And we're all divine
>
> I am a *fauve*

An experiment in terror

I am a *fauve*

A formidable error

I tell you to recite these lines, very soon now and also before you go to sleep tonight, because you call yourself an ugly animal. As the dancer Sarah of Alabama says, "Animals have beautiful bodies till they are tamed." Rapunzel, Rapunzel, let down your hair. Slouching is obedience to shame.

Make your voice more like music, and your posture will change. Your voice will help your hands, which you wring and pick at, to throw caution to the wind. Then they can begin to collect blood from broken bodies.

You know Pythia's maxims, for all questioners learn them before facing me. I choose one especially for you: do not turn back while on a journey.

Rapunzel, Rapunzel, let down your hair, for you must sing a song. Sweetie, I will brush your hair as you are singing.

Frueh sings to any tune that comes to her mind.

Wild as a nun running to god

Wild as a runner unaware of the weather

Wild as a player who's forgotten the game

Wild is the crooner who knows your real name

Sitting. Frueh continues to sing.

Wild the stargazer who knows when to stop

Wild the weightlifter who lightens her load

Wild laughing singer who coughs up her aria

Wild is the wanderer on a new road

Pythia wanders into a rigorous initiation. Initiation is the death of old ways. Study and revelation are the methods she learns, and they establish eros in body and mind. The disciplines of reading and dreaming day and night, of moving mind and body, one's own and others', creates Pythia, who, according to ancient and contemporary scholars, is hard-headed and amorous. She learns to read people, fields of energy and fields of wheat, not only books. She dreams in the lake, in the gym, on the toilet, and in her lovers' eyes.

She disobeys injunctions against knowledge, for the severest education forces the initiate to reject the law. This rejection cannot be rebellion, for then the would-be Pythia fails. In order to complete her initiation she must demonstrate her understanding and rejection of the law. Below are some successful examples of this task, recorded by the Pythias' archivists, preserved in the oracular cave, and discovered only five years ago and published in a slender volume.

The Pythia Daphne says:

> The law came to my door
>
> Armed with a gavel and gun
>
> It said, I'll blow your head off
>
> Or beat you down for fun
>
> I said, law, you are a mother
>
> And you're a father, too,
>
> But I am not your daughter, law,
>
> And you don't have a clue

The Pythia Peggy says, in honor of Daphne's first line:

The law came to my door, or was it a traveling salesman dressed in the rags of a guy named Christ who needed a better tailor? I remember now, he wore an Armani suit. I wear one myself for some clients. I butter their bread on both sides so that they can't avoid grease spots.

The Pythia Themistoclea says:

> The law is a laboring woman
>
> The law is a retching man.

The Pythia Helen says:

Law, you are the bastard who believes that love has died.

The Pythia Edith says:

Silence is golden. Speech is golden. I hear golden rule after golden rule: blessed be the lawyers, for they are great; hail, false prophets, for they are great; hail, executioner, for you are grace.

The Pythia Renée says:

> Bring on the apocalypse
>
> Give us the holocaust, too,
>
> Shit on every advocate
>
> Of what we call virtue
>
> Now I hear the moralists
>
> Who stand on such high ground
>
> That they all call it heaven
>
> When the rest of us aren't around.

Pythia, let me tell you a story you may not have heard. The time is the Inquisition.

* * *

Frueh alters material from Lawrence S. Wrightman and Saul M. Kassin's Confessions in the Courtroom.

Perhaps surprisingly, given their heinousness, the tactics of the inquisitors were closely regulated. Lawyers were required to remain at the side of heretics and to note every word they said as they were tortured; lawyers also recorded how long the torture lasted and what specific methods were used. The law was explicit that a person could not be tortured more than once unless new evidence came to light, but torturers could use whatever method they felt suitable to the case—deprivation of sleep, use of the rack, or a water torture in which the victims feared they would suffocate. When the victim was given a chance to confess, a lawyer would record willingness or reluctance. In the name of the law it was possible to carry out the most hideous practices.

* * *

Frueh picks up the gavel and throws it upstage. Standing.

You are an abomination. Yet you come here asking, "What does it mean to be a saint?" Sit tight. Do not bat an eye. Heaven's thread is thin, like a filament of mucus from your nose. Life hangs by a noose, and you deserve death songs.

You say, "Life is precious," "God is merciful," "Do good unto others and they will do good unto you," and "I would do anything for love." Sing a song of menace for a pocketful of lies. I'll sew your heart right onto your sleeve. Ten buckets of disinfectant and four months of constant sunlight cannot clean your closet, thick with dung and mildew. Liar, liar, pants on fire. Your nose is stuck in a wild rose briar.

A saint has dignity. When you perform hysterectomies and Caesarean sections, you say, "I'll give the pretty women an almost invisible scar, but the ugly women, what have they got to preserve? so I'll leave them with a gash, with flesh that heals in the form of a tattered fabric." You think that you're keeping beauty and ugliness where they belong. All acts of maintenance are attempts to achieve grace. But acts of grace do not support the status quo, for Eros is an outlaw who demands the proliferation of polymorphous perversities. You enforce conformity to aesthetic standards, for you cannot believe that any woman not beautiful in your eyes could be sexual, since you wouldn't want to fuck her. You see women's lust as a treatable condition: fuck a woman, or wreck her. These treatments are the same, for they both inflict limitation. The human option for polymorphous perversities means that people can desire difference: St. Joan wears men's clothes; St. Onuphrius, alone in the desert for sixty years, dresses himself in a garland of oleander petals and winds his own long hair around the flowers; St. Arlene attaches her dead raven companion to the belt at her waist and lets the bird rot and shrivel there; St. Gargantua eats beyond his heart's desire and weighs a quarter of a ton; St. Rachel, at age fifty, shaves her head and wears fuchsia lipstick. You tell your colleagues that your surgeries are fastidious assessments of beauty, but the saints, in their excesses of ordinary desire, are far more fastidious than you. For a saint, your sense of aesthetics is a shrunken vision. You are like the fifteenth-century monks of many orders who, in one huge volume filled with all their imaginings about women, write, "The root of evil is carnal greed, with which the female sex befouls itself at birth."

Pythias Phemonoë, Daphne, Peggy, Claire, Themistoclea, Helen, Manto, Edith, and Renée say, "We have an appetite. Cock Robin, we are lascivious and insatiable."

Merle, French for blackbird, will fly, right over you, right over to you, cover your eyeballs with a wing. Wing will grow and blind you with its beauty. Wing will be a black shadow on your heart. Shadow will cool your cock, flap, and banish your desire. Wing will be as big as the sun.

My voice is the beginning of your requiem. Hear the other instruments approaching: whistle, reed flute, electric guitar, violin, castanets, dulcimer, tabor, tambourine. Someone says, "Robin, cock robin, robin redbreast, robin's egg blue, robbin' you blind, robber baron, rubber penis, rub yourself raw, Robin, Cock Robin, diminutive of Robert, bright in fame, the lightning rod, the little robber, darling robber, the lovely thief."

· ·

Frueh sings, altering some of the folk song's lyrics.

> Who killed cock robin?
> Who killed cock robin?
> I said the sparrow with my little bow and arrow
> It was I oh it was I
>
> Who killed cock robin?
> Who killed cock robin?
> Me I'll be blunt with my bloody cunt
> It was I oh it was I

· ·

Table. Frueh sings a few lines of Tom Kelly and Billy Steinberg's
"True Colors." Her voice is sometimes honeyed, sometimes
mean and she snarls.

Sitting. Articulated with exceptional clarity and deliberateness.

> Kaylee ojin. Quasit jilian. Ansee jasha curarania. Hwang ma shacka coumarine, tay sue sotue rangingba. Fot wojan keer, sarter olipoge, eeg fot dimiastique, fectique, romoussin. Caw, caw, anzhi dang deam cway. Eert, mofsnickenforoot. Dao orte sute ortée maglophorion.

· ·

Standing. Frueh looks at an old(er) woman in the audience
and continues, now and then, to address her.

> You feel like a monster. Then maybe you can be a saint. You are ashamed of your appetite. Remember the meals you've shared with your girlfriends, the ones you've cooked to-

gether and the ones enjoyed in restaurants. Remember the bottles of wine, the pastas, crêmes caramels, breads, sweet butter, eggs Benedict, moules marinières, peaches, coffee, sausage, tender chicken, honey, salad greens, shrimp, chocolate. Remember Cabernet, Merlot, Pinot Noir, the reds you've lingered over with your girlfriends and other lovers. Remember masturbating forcefully, deliberately when you were a girl. Once your mother saw you, in your nylon nightgown, sitting on her piano bench, pressing your legs together so that near the pelvic joint the tops of your inner thighs would press your labia to your clitoris. You knew, at eight, the use of subtle pressures. Sometimes they make you come when you don't expect to, in your sleep—and you wake up pressing harder—while reading in a chair—and you keep your legs crossed for minutes at the angle that began the orgasm, which continues as long as you don't move your legs.

In your younger days you listened to a lot of lyrics in which pride is always foolish and rhymes with hide.

>Shaking/quaking
>Yearning/burning/tossing and turning
>Lightning/frightening
>Right/tonight
>Street/meet
>You/I do
>Desire/fire/higher
>Mine/all the time.

You hear Elvis whining about only one love; the only one he's thinking of. Love is cruel to the fool.

"Just stop breaking my heart," you say. "I'm tired of falling into the arms of strangers. My earrings always get in the way when I kiss, and my hair gets stuck in my teeth, because I'm the pussy whirlpool, always testing the waters of my lust, testing my patience, too."

You say,

>"Conclude/rude
>"Sex/perplex
>"Use/re-fuse:
>"Or is it ref-use?"

You say,

"Empress Messalina challenged a prostitute to a contest. Who, the whore or Messalina, could fuck more men in a night? Messalina won, and her husband, Claudius, had her beheaded."

You say,

"Roman Empress took men on in a game of win and lose

Lost her head, not simply pride. Bad girls get abused.

"Bad and good and lose and win, I can't tell which is which

The Messalina in me says, I'll fuck you, I'm a bitch."

You say,

"I want to screw you, feel your cock screwing into me, feel your hips unscrewing my lust, screw you flush to the fucking bed. We will be screwed up, together, in my internal, eternal thread, spiraled into our thick cunt, screwing around, and around and around in the revolutions,

the evolution of grace."

You say,

"Amused/confused

"Do I put on my Bible belt, my garter belt, the cinch of prophecy, my chastity belt, my menstrual pad? Do I pull out my tampon for the last time? That bloody plug is my last remnant of a trashcan love, your sterilization of scarlet. Good golly, Miss Molly, as Little Richard would say, I am a storm and a half of eros, a hurricane of vicissitudes."

I say,

Lust/must

Appetite/bite

The root of *proud* is a Latin word meaning to be useful. Benefit yourself.

Monster, you are more than a warning to conditional femininity, whose doctrine is cleanliness: wear this sea mud, honey, clay, and mummy mask; wipe that blood from your mouth; shave those wildebeest legs; we want cologne between your thighs. Monster, how clean do you think you need to be for grace? You are ready to extinguish the femininity that requires you to wash and scent yourself until you smell like some moron's dream of Cleopatra. Monster, you are femininity to the *n*th degree. Out of bounds, off-limits, living among the unsuspecting, at their very side, you are the woman of my dreams.

Amazing grace! how sweet the sound

That changed someone like me

I once was lost but now am found

Was blind but now I see

When Apollo killed Python, an act intended to conquer Pythia, he used a thousand arrows, which Renaissance mythographers equated with sun rays.

(The name of my lipstick *is* True Red.)

One source says Apollo planned to conquer Pythia because he wanted the oracle to be for men only.

He said, "Men (more than women) need to learn gentility and self-control." Those were the words of a subtle politician who tried to suppress the extremity of Pythia's femininity. She saw many men. Odysseus, Plato, Plutarch, Agamemnon, Croesus, Laius and his son Oedipus visited her. So did Pythagoras, and Pythia was his teacher as well as the oracle who answered him. Pythia saw Socrates, too, and he took her first maxim, "Know thyself."

(I want to fuck them all. Fuck 'em all.)

Pythia saw women whenever she wanted to, although Apollo's attitude ushered in an era, not dead yet, in which many people do not know the difference between a vagina and a vulva. Nor can they pronounce clit-or-is correctly.

(I am on slow boil, in continuous heat. Pythia foretold the eruption of Vesuvius.)

Frueh lets down her skirt. She takes the last page of the text. Table.

Said in a tone whose softness of breath reminds
people of a whisper.

I am as sultry as the desert night, ninety-four degrees at two a.m. Let me take you to the saguaros. We will avoid the places people say gangsters dump dead bodies. Then let me take you, out to breakfast, lunch, and dinner, let me take your hands in mine, so I can soothe them with sweet lotion, then you can braid my hair and fuck me again. I grab the curls at the nape of your neck, and I see that your lips are wet. You are luscious, you grace my eyes, and your voice is soft like Python moving over my legs, you grace my speech, I am a serpent without venom and a bulldog for you whom I love.

Bulldog bulldike bulldagger, I re-wed you daily, I will stab my loving tongue wherever necessary to grace your name, I love your cockrush, smells, from breath to shit to underarm, your erotic agitation and agility, all your effluvia.

Frueh gently places the page on the table and exits stage left.

. . . .

Frueh wears a bias-cut, ankle-length, ecru dress of fabric that clings to her upper body and gently reveals the contours of her hips and thighs. The sleeves cover most of her forearms, and the neckline curves around her collarbones. Her shoes are pewter-colored high heels, an exotic Mary Jane style, and her pulled-back hair emphasizes bronze-toned earrings, each decorated with three pink glass drops. To one side of the black music stand at which she performs, a clear glass vase is full of creamy lilies and red roses. To her other side, a white pedestal holds a large crystal champagne glass filled with water.

Gold and roses, laughter, fragrance, flowers, smiling, bathing, oils and unguents, cosmetics, jewelry, and other ornaments: the ancient Greeks styled Aphrodite, their goddess of love and beauty, in these attributes and powers of pleasure. She embodied and enabled techniques and skills of an *ars erotica,* and they included bathing and decorating for making love with others and with oneself. Neither Greek sculpture nor literature presents a masturbating Aphrodite, and autoerotic activity should not be understood literally, as genital masturbation, or as simplistic self-gratification. The word *aphrodisia,* meaning for the Greeks sensual pleasure, carnal acts, sexual relations, and pleasures of love, does not refer to specific sexual practices. Desire, pleasure, and act are an ensemble. *Aphrodisia* is related to *aphrodisios,* of Aphrodite, who was also the goddess of creativity.

In classical Greece, the *aphrodisia* were an ethical practice created for men by men. Let us differently configure *aphrodisia,* so that Aphrodite may suggest to us ways in which to use and to be pleasure, appearing dressed, undressed, and in-between, as a model of a technology of the self, practiced in aesthetic/erotic self-creation.

Men took pleasure in Praxiteles's Aphrodite of Knidos and her successors: Aphrodite was an aphrodisiac. Perhaps she inspired or encouraged women and men to become aph-rodisiacs, to create themselves as sensuously stimulating and welcoming by both entering into and creating in others *aphroditē,* a psychological state combining passion, empathy, and attraction. To these I add attractiveness. Independent and giving, calm and fun-loving, full of the grace that became lovingkindness and that we admire today in the charismatic decorum of a star athlete's body at ease, Aphrodite offered beauty of appearance and being as means through which one could gain material and spiritual knowledge.

The ancient Aphrodite invites us to care about styling ourselves, to tend to details of human expression and behavior that design the extreme self-articulation I call monster/beauty, details that are corporeal and connective—pertaining to the single body that is our own and to its opulent and expansive erotic possibilities with other bodies. Eros is errant and it flows, from body to body ad infinitum: bodies of people, knowledge, vegetation, paw prints, water, and unorthodoxies. I speak here of sex and beauty because they are Aphrodite's domains, and loving human bodies, through looks and touches that belong to her *ars erotica,* is one way to develop concord, a social transformation through pleasure. I choose Aphrodite over narcosis because she teaches me to treat the body as an oeuvre. I work against inaction, paralysis caused by bodily shame or even by an embarrassment of riches that I could feel in the process of fulfilling what I understand to be her ordinance, which is to build the body of love.

I step into Aphrodite's shoes. I am building the body of love. This does not mean that I am incomplete, always in a state of desire, in contrast to a state of pleasure, of satisfaction. Pleasure engenders its reproduction.

I step into Aphrodite's shoes. Like her body, I am body to body ad infinitum. My body articulates with others the pleasures that my husband and I share. Aphrodite was a married woman and a passionate wife. That Eros is the illegitimate child of Aphrodite and Ares may lead to the false conclusions that passionate wives are insatiable—nymphomaniac—or unsatisfied with their husbands—frigid at home: myth upon misunderstanding. So the passionate wife becomes a pervert, for law sanctions few erotic activities and marriage supposedly kills eros: the passionate wife becomes a paradox, for she can only lust, fuck, and fantasize away from her husband. In truth, the passionate wife styles herself in *aphrodisia*.

I step into Aphrodite's shoes. She and I are not bad-girl bodies, not images or housings of coy, efficient sexual rhetoric. Body to body, she and I are fearlessly invested in loving women with the force of little girls who feel invincible because they are intimate with each other; in spreading our legs for men who undress us slowly like Anchises or in a rush of will; in embracing black and golden skin unfalsified by ethnographic exhibition, gleaming differently from white marble, freed of the snide lust that searches for some new Hottentot Venus or Latin lover. (This is not Gauguin's gold. It is Aphrodite's.)

I step into Aphrodite's shoes. They improve my bedside manner.

I return to my hotel room after talking with Guillermo for the first time. He is gifted in the erotic art of conversation, in which smiles and touches are as significant as words, in which all three sustain an intricacy of *aphrodisia*.

I step into Aphrodite's shoes. My cunt is wet. I undress and sit on the side of the bed and the following picture fills me:

I'm wearing my long, silk robe embroidered with one gold leaf over each breast. I'm naked except for black boots that catch the light like satin and white anklets with a tiny lace cuff. The robe bares me down the middle and I'm sitting as I actually am on the side of this bed. Guillermo is in front of me and I part my legs a little, and when I feel his tongue on, then inside, my labia, his hands, one on each thigh, become wedded to them.

This image does not replicate a chic porn photograph. It is not a film noir still updated with nostalgia for a mystique-filled portrayal of lust. The atmosphere is golden, nowhere near the light that rakes the bodies in porn movies. We are bodies, not figures, and we move with shifting motivations as we negotiate pleasure.

From the Knidia to Titian's Venuses loved by lute players and mirrors to Marilyn Monroe, Aphrodite, in mostly degraded forms, has come to read as perfection, and therefore as a kind of being who is impossible to become. Women, including feminists, from diverse disciplines and in popular and scholarly publications, decry and critique the imperialism of feminine beauty standards, which not only ignore and demean differences in human beings' attractions but also contribute to people's difficulty in even seeing their species' wide-ranging beauties. The idea, the anxiety, of bodily perfection misrepresents aphrodi-tean beauty, for the goddess embodies comfortableness in oneself that is a basis of erotic and aesthetic confidence.

Perfection is the feminine truth of the body that ancient Aphrodites, later Venuses canonized in art history, and the twentieth-century fashion model declare to be an attribute of females. The perfect body is supremely clean, sterilized of sweat, of variable color beyond shades of white, of women's lustful participation in each other's beauty. The perfect body is deprived of the ability to enjoy anything but a look—of appreciation, envy, or desire—to be anything but a glimpse of sensual plenitude. Today's perfect body is erotically atrophied. Because it can only be thin, it exhibits symbolic if not literal anorexia that shrinks the body. The goddess flattens into merely a figure, an icon with no tactile range, an outline filled in with stupidity. Her skin, which should speak of volume, which is the intelligence of *aphroditē*, is a garment with which to lure. A goddess frees our aphrodisiac capacities, but perfection is the liberation of nothing.

We imagine the perfect body's sweetness when we test *Vogue* samples of Calvin Klein's Eternity, Donna Karan's Chaos, Givenchy's Organza, or Ralph Lauren's Sport. Sport: neither the blond in her white T-shirt nor we are meant to smell the efforts of her athleticism. Eternity: the Eternal Feminine lives on in images of a wife-and-mother who is young, fair-skinned, and dressed in white. Windblown, sitting at the shore, she squints, and her startled casualness is an effect of photography. Chaos: the ad bids, "Discover the calm within," and, back to us, a nude, as creamy as the Aphrodite of Rhodes, bows down her head. The page cuts off her lower legs, so she is a deliberate fragment, unlike statues from antiquity that lost their wholeness to the vagaries of time and inattention. Karan's Aphrodite appears to sit on stone that simulates the inside of a surfer's wave. Her spine is sister to that of Ingres's Grande Odalisque. Calm may be meditative, but it is also immobilization and possible engulfment. Organza: it will allow us to "slip into luxury." The model in a pleated, bright white gown and the golden bottle, whose vertical ridges resemble pleats, are the same height, and they look like fluted columns. The ads recall Aphrodite's sea-birth and autonomy, her authority over fertility and procreation, and the richness of her golden necklaces and earrings, her glimmering, as we see in Homeric Hymn 6, "with every sort of jewel," but the ads mistranslate the goddess, for perfection eliminates bodiliness.

In the next line, Frueh speaks an aside.

When I quote from the Homeric Hymns, I'm using a translation by Apostolos N. Athanassakis.

Sea water cleanses but not absolutely, for salt and algae cling. The body's scent can be ambrosially briny.

The small, bronze and stone copies of the Knidia that were popular in antiquity ranged from plump to slim.

Aphrodite was never a caryatid. Nor did the Greeks or Romans sculpt her in a frontal pose that registers as static.

Stark white fabrics on white skin replicate the marble of the Knidia and the drapery that she holds, the way that we see her today in Roman copies. Originally her skin may have been painted a light, unnuanced tint, and perhaps she had been lightly buffed. Her hair was gilded or yellow, her lips, cheeks, eyes, and jewelry were painted, the vase gilded to resemble bronze, and the drapery painted flat bright tones. She was white, but not as white as she appears in perfume ads, and today a goddess whose attributes and powers cannot be complicated beyond the sex and color of her origin is useless as a model of aesthetic/erotic self-creation.

Female perfection reeks of a high femininity molded out of racial purity and class privilege: white is the cleanest skin color, unflawed by the "defect" of darkness, and perfection, which the fashion and beauty industries try to persuade us will be ours if we work hard enough at it, is an upper-class possession. Female perfection is an ideology, driving those industries' economies, that exacts ultimate hygiene, so designer perfumes can serve as antiseptics. But for the most rare exception, black and Asian-featured models do not appear in designer perfume ads, primarily geared to middle-class or upwardly mobile women, because marketers believe that black bodies and Asian-featured faces cannot sell the ideology of supremely clean.

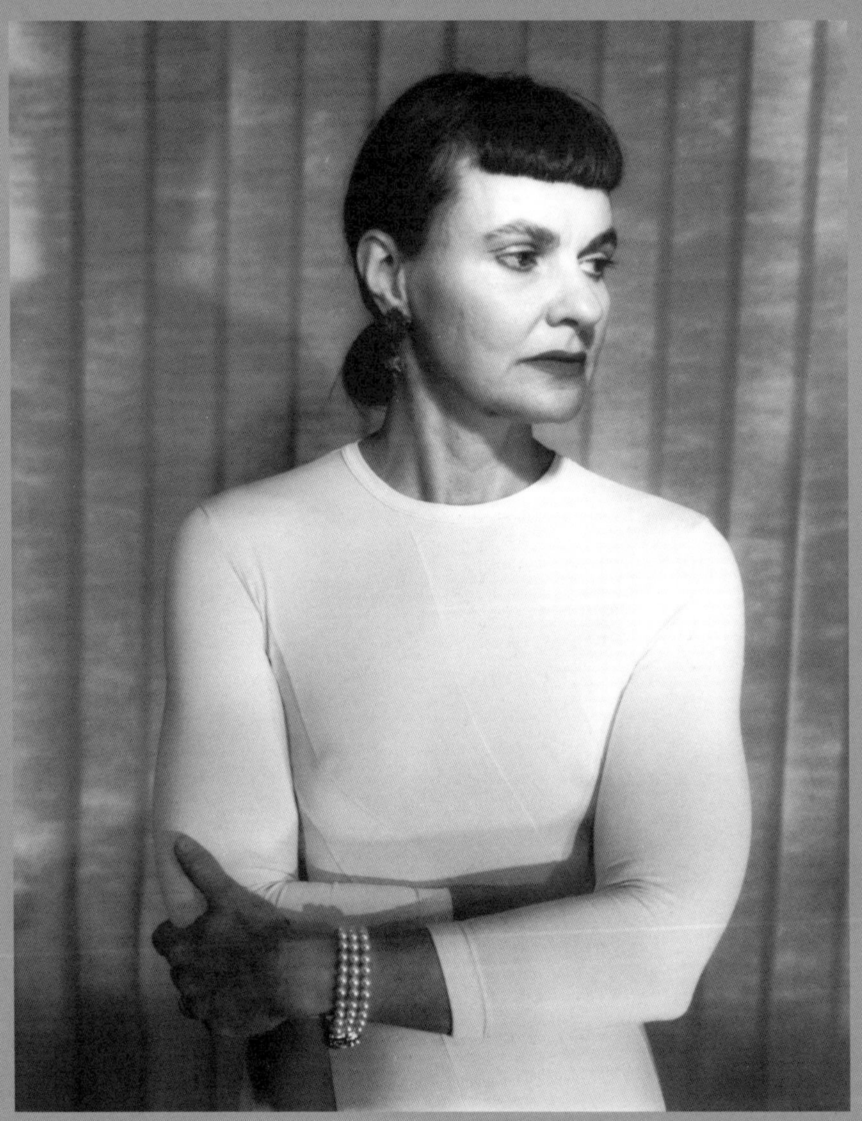

Joanna Frueh and Russell Dudley, Joanna in costume, *Dressing Aphrodite*, 1997.

Photos courtesy of Frueh and Dudley.

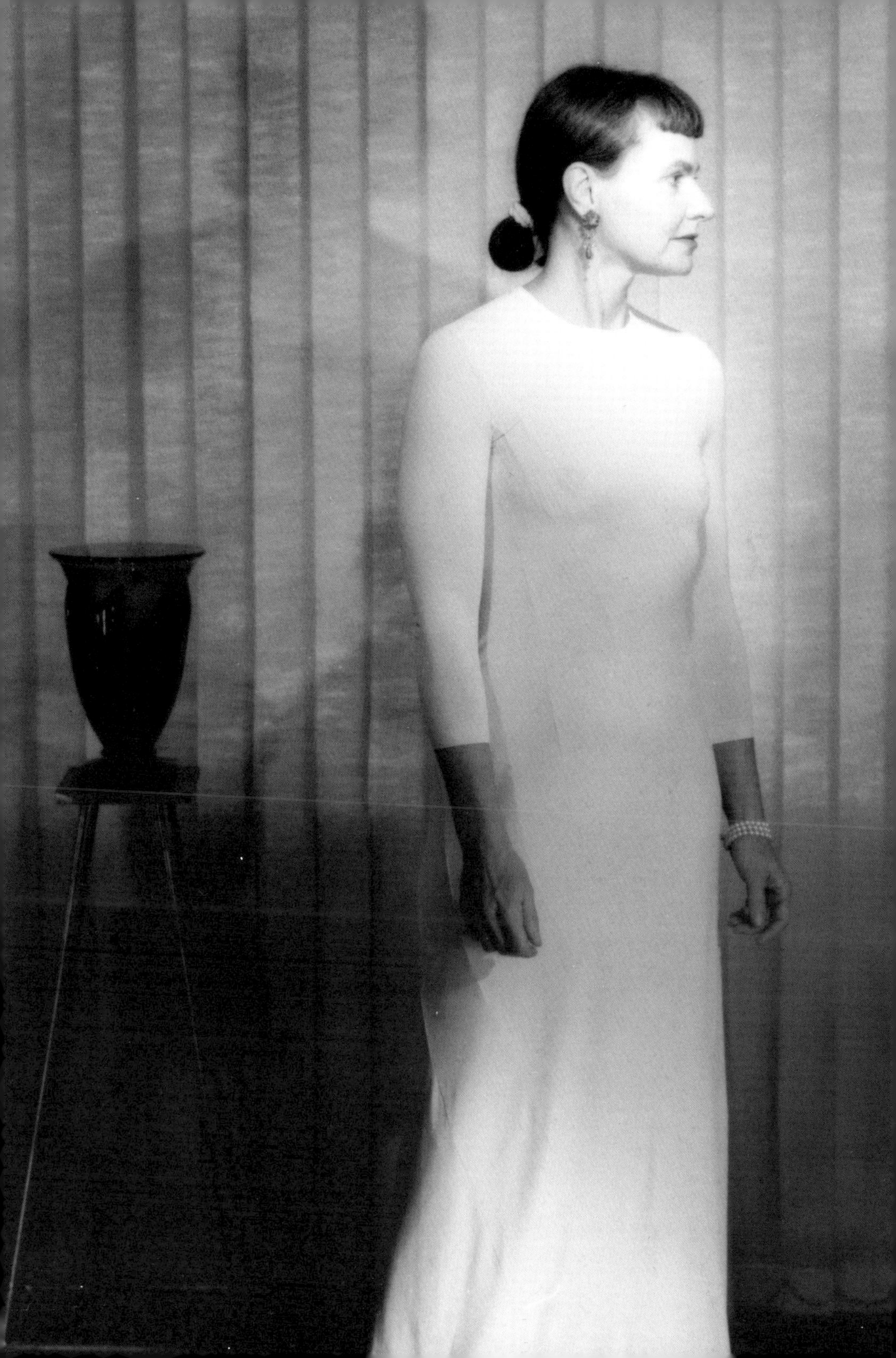

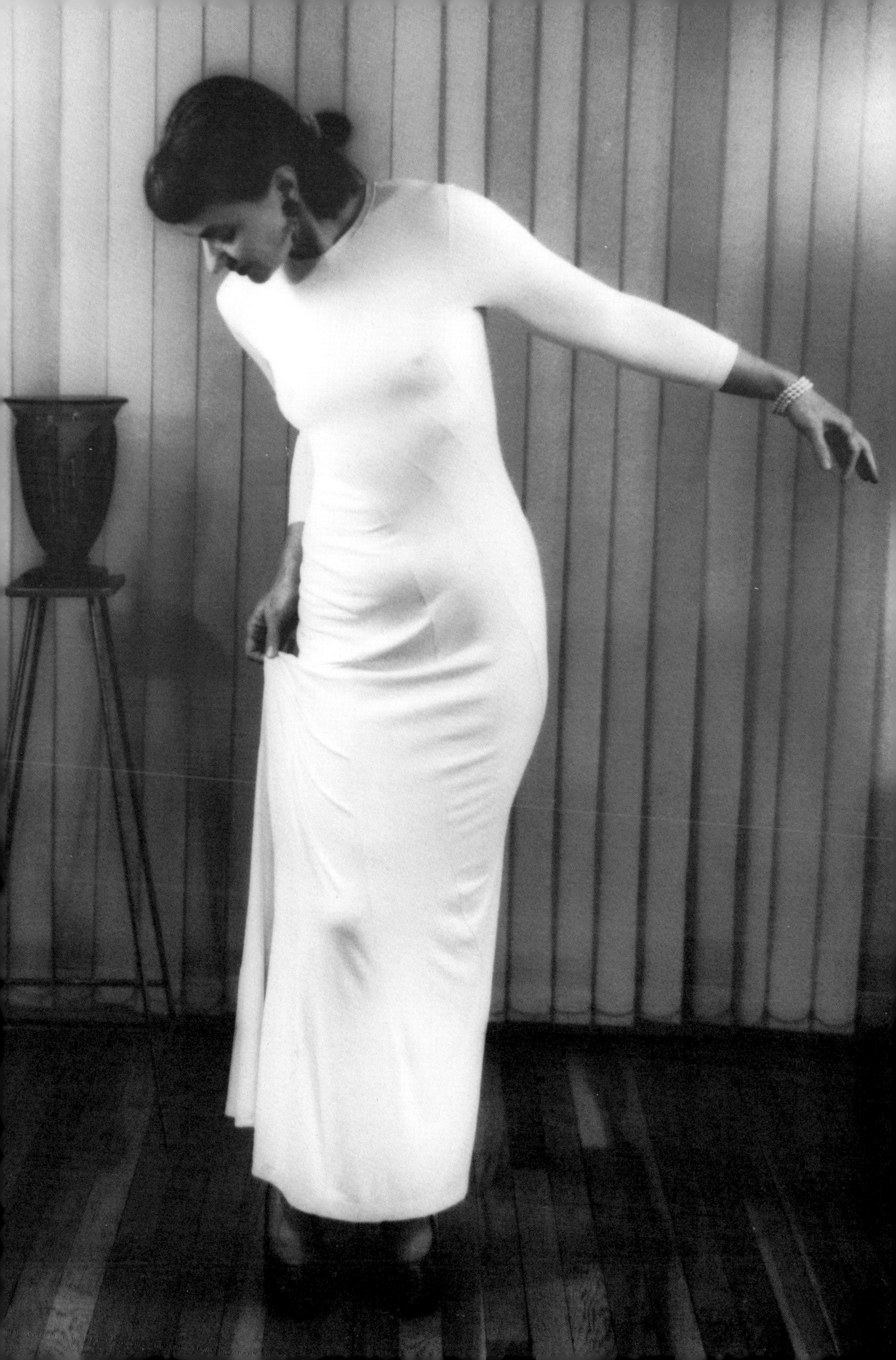

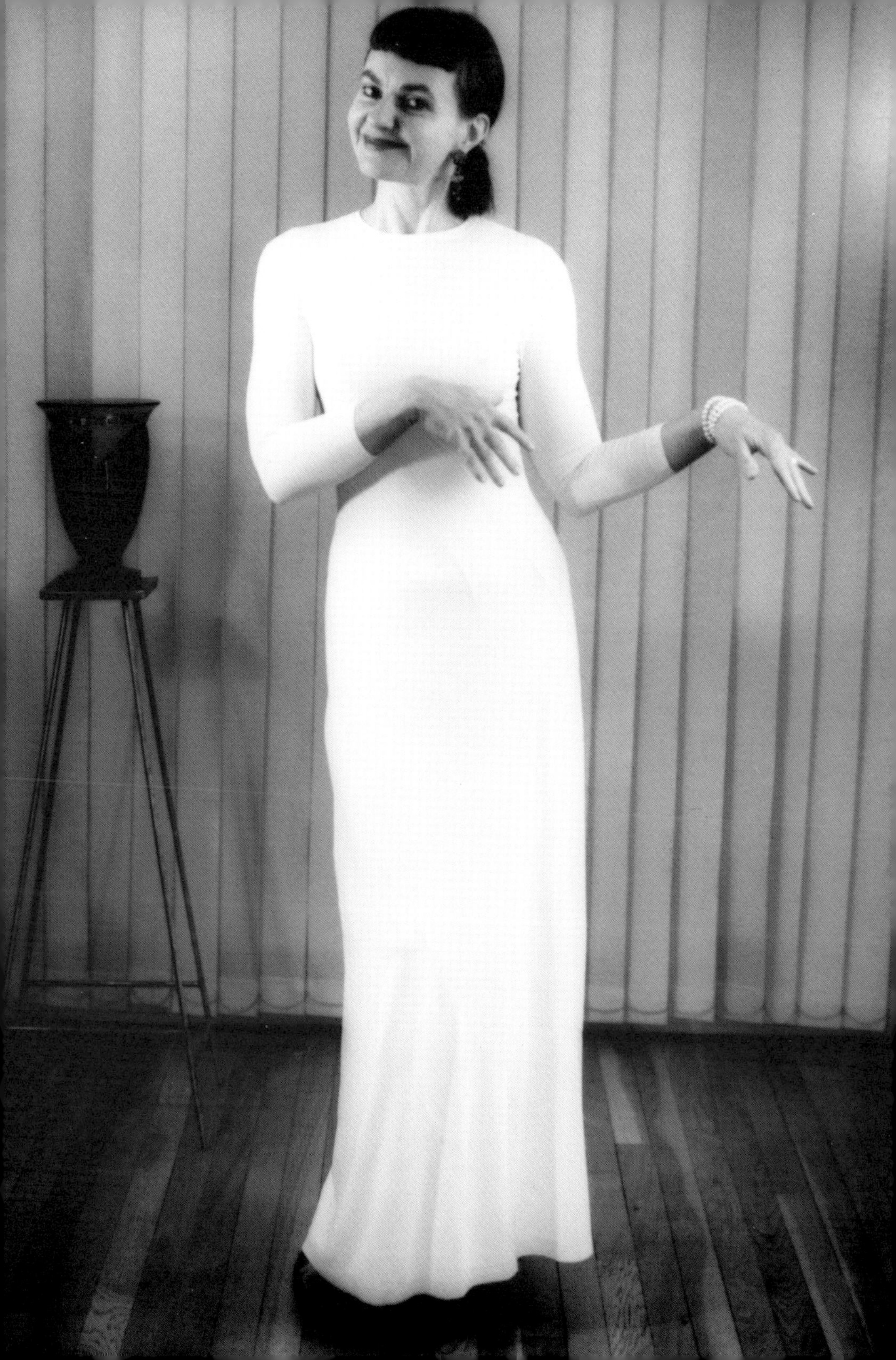

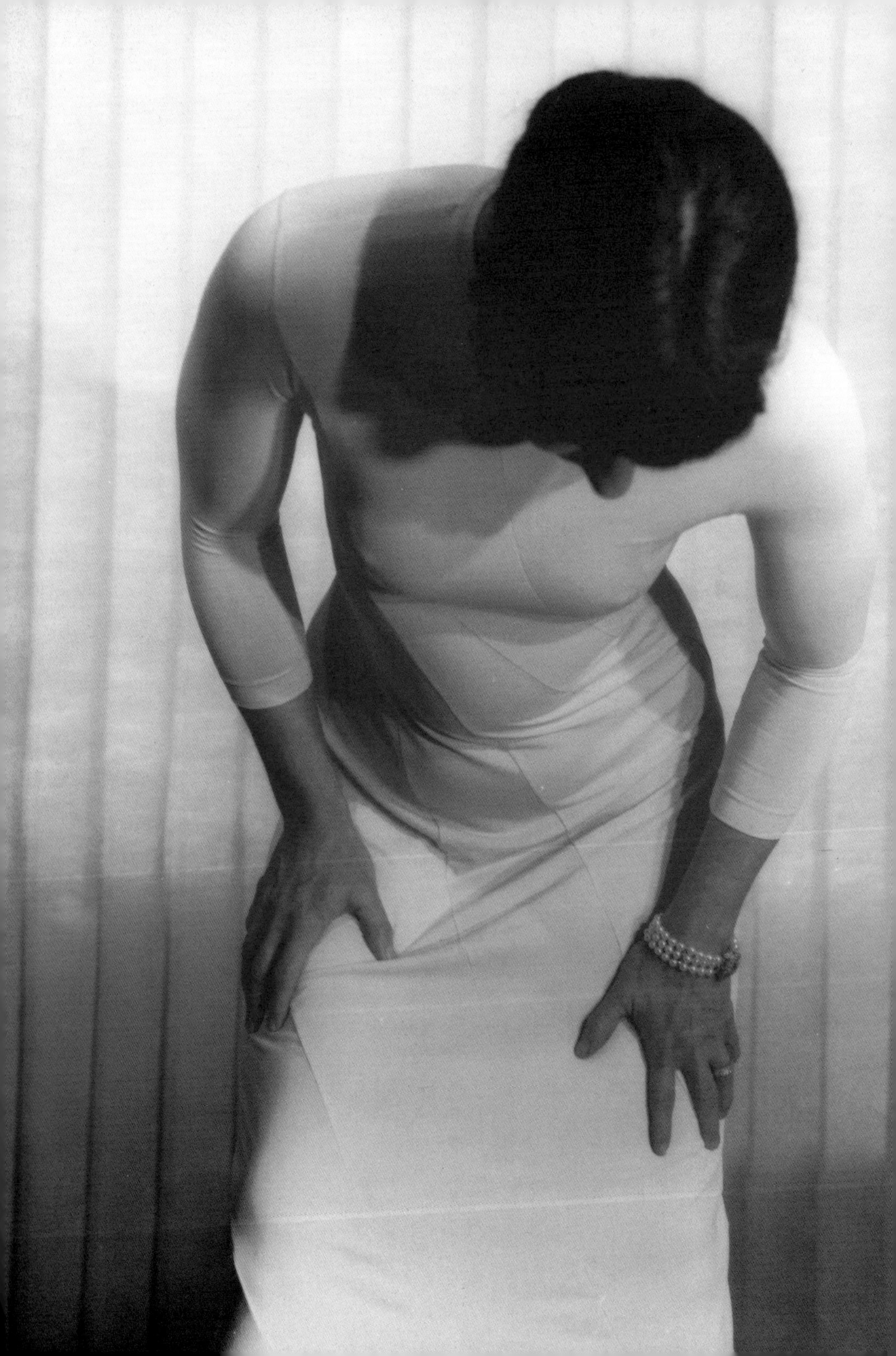

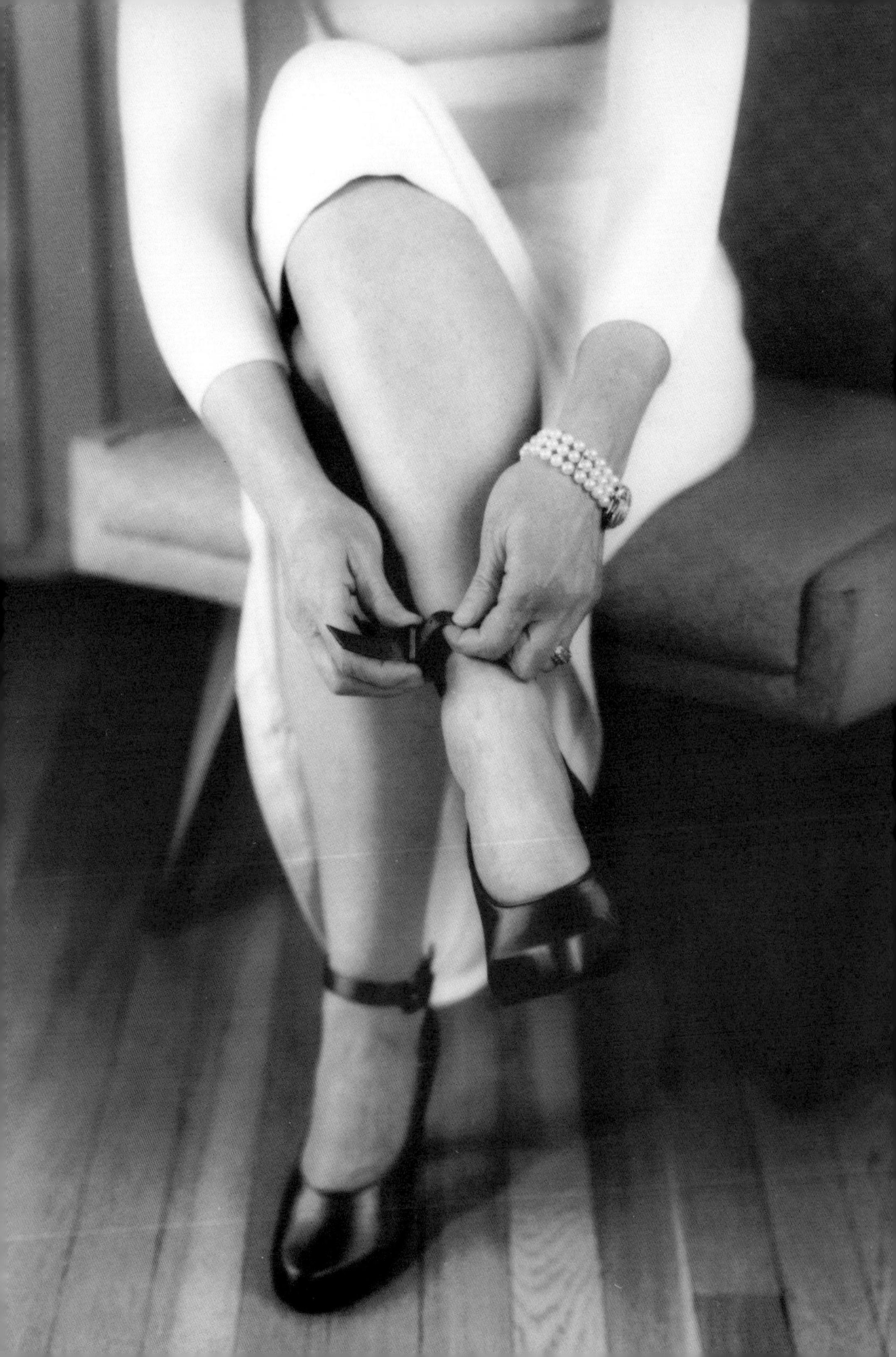

In the early 1970s, when I was in my mid-twenties, I was a salesgirl at Saks on Michigan Avenue in Chicago—a high-class department store in the city's ritziest commercial district. My manager, a white woman younger than I, told me she'd been riding a bus sitting next to a black woman who smelled. My manager's vocal inflections indicated that *smelled* meant *smelled bad.* Then she added, "You know what I mean, how they smell."

Spring semester, 1997. Midori Ishibashi, a young Japanese-American woman in a class of mine, includes in one of her papers a letter she had submitted to the *Sagebrush,* my university's student newspaper. She was countering a letter to the editor written by a man who, from what I gather in her letter, bemoaned what he saw as current biases against white males such as himself. Midori wrote, "I would guess that most white . . . males have never heard anyone walk by them in a grocery store muttering that people of their race . . . all smell like fish." She quoted part of the man's letter: "We're entitled to be treated like dirt."

High femininity sanctifies antisepsis. Darkness, dirt, non-Caucasian features, and putridness conflate, making stink and black skin the opposite of sweet whiteness. As the man's remark brings into relief, white men have not been and must not be made dirty.

I rose from the ocean, pungent like cunt and fish. Don't call me sweetie without thinking about the implications of all my bouquets and spices—fennel, myrrh, cinnamon; roses and lilies, two of my favorite flowers.

Roses

What corny excess they've inspired

In romantics of both Church and Sex

    Your mouth is like a rosebud

    Your skin is soft as a rose petal

    My love is like the red red rose

    Mary is the Mystic Rose

    The Holy Rose a medieval scholar writes of as a

        Vulvic sign

    The scarlet flower fucked to ecstasy

    The white rose of Dante's paradise

    You smell like a rose

Or am I just excited by the Infinite Aroma of your pheromones?
    O leave your dewdrop in my rose

Theologians talk to god in orgies of epistemology
    Lily lie lay lewdly say
Authorities of Nothing Much about the suction and the friction of the sexes
    Lily lie lay lowdown
They don't even know
    Lovemaking is charisma
I know
What I know
I speak with lubricity about ideas of ardent origin
I trust no orthodoxies   jaded beyond belief
    in the body   commonplace
        is a temple   sentimental
Born in the dimensions of a gem with undetermined facets
And the Acknowledgment
To fuck your lover high and low

Ambrosia is like honey, sweet but not cloying, golden not white. Ambrosia's aphrodisiac thickness sticks to one's skin, creating the aura of radiance. Ambrosial aura does not simulate beauty; aura isn't necessarily artificial, commodified charisma. Unlike perfumes marketed for the user's creation of atmosphere, so different from *aphroditē,* Aphrodite's ambrosias, one of which *can* be the golden liquid, perfume, signify the sweet heart, one's own or another's, that will satisfy longing for deliciousness in our lives. Aphrodite's ambrosias—her perfumes, oils, cosmetics, cum, saliva, balms—will change your heart, which means that they will change your body.

   I call everybody Honey.

Penelope, a faded beauty and Odysseus's wife, becomes in Homer's *Odyssey* marvelous to the Achaeans with the application of Aphrodite's balm. In this instance, Athena beautifies Penelope. Aphrodite brings provisions for pleasures greater than beauty, pleasures that cannot be reduced to mere visual effect. They are the sources that shape the smiles and laughter Aphrodite so enjoys.

Smile and *marvel* share the Latin cognate *mirus,* wonderful. Aphrodite, Penelope, and numerous once-faded Aphrodites blooming because of ambrosial balms, which neither remove blemishes nor minimize pores, you are wonders groomed to monstrousness not feminine perfection.

One cannot be indifferent to ambrosia.

Sometimes I can barely smile. How wary I've become of myself. I dress in off-white. Whose skin do I imitate? If only it were simply golden Aphrodite's. Wearing white protects me against nothing. It is the troubled power of brides and virgins. Ecru, my color for today, is closer than bright-white to blood, veins, and tissues, not refined into the perfect female's sacred adornment.

Ecru and whiter white cloth are always dirty. White is the sign of visible and potential dirt. Dirty as the ground, as sweat, as excrement, and the making of love. Dirtiness is one of monster/beauty's attractions. Because she perverts, subverts, and diverts the purity of white, wearing white for monster/beauty is a partially perverse strategy.

Gleaming off-white fabric also creates the illusion of gold, which is radiance, and this gossamer-feeling fabric, of undergarment color, fondles me like lingerie, and recalls the depiction and significance of Aphrodite's body, which asserts and reveals itself even when dressed. Her clothing, such as filmy, clinging drapery in the Parthenon's east pediment, and the resplendent garments she wears before permitting Anchises to remove them for their lovemaking, is meant to make the observer or reader aware of Aphrodite's body. Dressed or undressed, Aphrodite is always a nude.

For the Greeks, nudity displayed liberty and power. Aphrodite's nudity manifested her divine authority and her authority in the arts of love. Nudity, the beautiful dress of skin and flesh, is aesthetic/erotic technology, and as such it provides human beings with the pleasure needed for vitality of the soul. Nudity suggests possibilities, potentials; we need not read it as a goad to be a particular body type. (Remember: the Knidia's successors varied from full to slim.) Style can be part of *aphrodisia,* for style—dressing attractively—is about nudity, which should not be reduced to fashion, for fashion relies on the currency of perfection, whose particulars it shapes.

In a tongue-in-cheek tone that is nonetheless biting, Betsy Berne underpins her November 1996 *Vogue* article, "What Works at What Age?" with the model of nude perfection. Whenever *perfect* as a description of women's bodies appears in a fashion magazine, the word startles me, for I'm fool enough to think that the last thirty years of feminism could have ended women's desire for perfection and belief that it is manifest in some women's bodies. Berne's piece supposedly treats problems and exemplars of admirable style, but we learn in a humorous though agonized tone that only "seventeen-year-olds have perfect bodies," that "no one should wear [this season's metallics] unless they have a perfect body," and that women over forty and especially over fifty had better rethink and discontinue the style they favored when younger because they are undergoing "the ravages of age" and they will appear ridiculous if they insist on "cling[ing] to fading youth." Feminist theorists, too, agonize over, to use Berne's words, "that perfect-body thing again." A recent example is Leslie Heywood in her *Dedication to Hunger* (1996). There she analyzes the relationship between supremely clean, spare high modernist literary style and women's drive to perfect their bodies.

Nudity, which styles the body, is one of Aphrodite's sophisticated skills necessary for her highly civilized practice of lovemaking. In Roman copies of Praxiteles's sculpture, she appears to have just bathed. Right hand near her genitals, gaze distant but not averted, left hand holding drapery that falls over a hydria, a water vessel, Aphrodite is neither flaunting nor ashamed of her body. Aphrodite would not have bathed to become supremely clean of soul, as in baptism; to rid herself of everyday dirt, like you or me; or to purify herself of sexual sin, because sex did not turn a goddess into filth, nor did the Greeks understand women to be impure, as does the contemporary ideology of high femininity. Bathing was part of sexual conduct, preparation for lovemaking in Greek literature. This was true for humans and for Aphrodite, who, before seducing Anchises in Homeric Hymn 5, is bathed by the Graces, who then rub her with perfumed oil. Bathing was hygienic, refreshing, and restorative, a pleasure enjoyed by men and women.

Aphrodite is nude with the Graces and with humans, Anchises, and ourselves, so that we can see her. This may seem obvious, but in general, to see a goddess unclothed was taboo, and transgressors suffered blinding or gruesome death, such as Actaeon, who inadvertently saw Artemis bathing. She turned him into a stag and his own hounds tore him apart. We *see* Aphrodite nude so that we understand the body's liminality, how, as deliciously clothed, it brings together or crosses over nature and culture, human and divine, corporeality and spiritual grace, female and male. (Only male gods were commonly depicted nude.) In such liminality, the nude Aphrodite is most abundantly and essentially erotic, because of her connective magnitude.

*Frueh sings. She quotes and changes lyrics that appear in her own
"Dual Conception."*

Lying in the bathtub, water's nice and hot

Feeling like an embryo, liking it a lot

Steamy pressures buoy me, sweet oil soothes my skin

Smooth and so embracing, won't you step right in?

Vita nova vie nouvelle

Promise that you'll kiss and tell

When the New Life strikes your head

And says it's stupid to be dead

Begats and begottens, misbegotten songs

Born of forgetfulness and golden rings gone wrong

Honey, I don't owe you unless the fires spark

If you like the burning bright I'll give you a birthmark

Vita nova vie nouvelle

Promise that you'll kiss and tell

When the New Life kicks your butt

And says you're boring in your rut

Heat and bodies vibrate while laughter fills the air

I can't measure beauty, I wouldn't even dare

Muscles are for building like hearts, all gleaming tools,

If your pleasure wills their use then we can break some rules

Vita nova vie nouvelle

Promise that you'll kiss and tell

When the New Life claims control

Of your body and your soul

In the black-and-white, four-photo series *She Wasn't Always a Statue* (1996–97), Louise Lawler shows sculptures of standing and crouching female (and male) nudes. The female figures read differently than the males. In order to be beautiful, woman, Lawler suggests, does not have to remain on the pedestal of high femininity, eternally white, stuck, and uncomfortable. Only a statue holds a pose forever. Women do not have to be finished products, like objects of art. They must assert the will to pleasure, which guarantees infinite becoming.

In "Too 'Close to the Bone': The Historical Context for Women's Obsession with Slenderness," which appears in *Feminist Perspectives on Eating Disorders*, edited by Patricia Fallon, Melanie A. Katzman, and Susan C. Wooley, Roberta Seid writes about women, "Our bodies, our fitness, and our food should not be our paramount concerns. They have nothing to do with ethics, or relationships, or community responsibilities, or with the soul. They have nothing to say about the purpose of life, except that we should survive as well and as long and as beautifully as we can. They give us no purpose beyond ourselves. This is a religion appropriate only for a people whose ideals do not extend beyond their physical existence and whose vision of the future and of the past is strangely empty." Lawler's photos convey emptiness. The statues are grouped; each feels isolated. High femininity as a religion of bodily perfection is close to the religion Seid denounces, and high femininity breeds the void of non-accomplishment. Solitary self-castigation accompanies such failure.

Seid damns being "beautifully"—ideally—thin, and I understand why she is so severe. Women waste themselves for beauty, spending too much money and time, enfeebling their health by dieting for thinness, ruining their self-confidence. Yet Seid assumes that she and we know what beauty is. Most of us think it is an end product and ultimately, for older women, endgame and pointless rituals. That finished-product, done-for female beauty consumes the erotic/aesthetic energy that Aphrodite represents and teaches. The arts of love have precisely and expansively to do with ethics, relationships, and community responsibilities. Aphrodite's arts of love civilize relationships, I would say not only one-to-one sexual encounters but also community relationships, for the creation of aphroditean beauty manifests and fosters erotic connection, the bringing together that I spoke of earlier. The concords and pleasures of lovemaking and golden self-beautification help people resist envy, greed, and commodity culture's relentless production of lack at a material level. That lack, coupled with people's lack of self-worth, spins out from their souls and psyches and enlarges a societal fabric of spiritual and aesthetic poverty.

Seid might consider beauty a luxury—literally and figuratively costly, serving no purpose beyond a palliative self-aggrandizement. Aphrodisiac beauty is a different kind of luxury: it is a time and space of joy and comfort that may or may not have been created with expensive goods. In her book *Art on My Mind: Visual Politics,* bell hooks describes the beauty she styles for herself—the "comforting cloth," such as "silks, satins, and cashmeres" next to her skin, high-priced "French lemon verbena soap and fruity perfume," "adorning myself just so"—that induces erotic connection with her writing. hooks understands that creating a body and place one loves uplifts people by transforming the fabric of poverty. In this regard, she uses the words "hope" and "healing." Fashioning a home and garden one loves is an aphroditean articulation of spirit, a necessary extension of pleasure that may grow out of aphrodisiac self-styling. The fragrance of lemon verbena soap can pervade a small house.

Feminist philosopher and psychoanalyst Luce Irigaray theorizes in behalf of female deity, which would provide for women a glorious subjectivity and new goals and values. Different from the feminist project of critiquing and opposing social and cultural wrongs against women, Irigaray's "divine project" includes women's insisting on the creation of their own beauty as self-loving and self-fulfilling. Envisioning this, I see bodies of content whose intelligent style and purpose prove that, in contradiction to Seid, beauty has great meaning beyond simple physical existence. For the early Greeks, the arts of love, states Paul Friedrich in his book *The Meaning of Aphrodite,* "were a set of practices, skills, sentiments, attitudes, and moral and aesthetic values that were learned and transmitted and that at once guided behavior and made it comprehensible and meaningful." Aphrodite represents an ethics, and its performance demands a will to pleasure. In her essay "Divine Women," Irigaray helps me know that female beauty built from the will to pleasure has no formula, and it blossoms in the practice of infinite becoming.

Becoming beauty
I envelop myself in scent over favorite scent: rose, rosemary, lavender, Quadrille, yellow honeysuckle, brine, champagne, and fish
Perfume joins divinities and human beings

Becoming beauty

I choose pearls from her birthplace, and gold, the brightness of wedding bands, so

that I can marry her, Aphrodite, passionate wife

Becoming beauty

I choose a fabric that catches light in ways that pearls and honey do

I luxuriate in a dress whose tight arms, length, and bias cut make me look statuesque; but I am no pillar of the community of beauty, bracing an isolating narcissism, the outcome of a static femininity. I move away from the Knidia's rationally perfect pose, because I am only human and her poise—a possibility for me—is what I seek, her overwhelming grace that lets me know we can create a new logic and erotics of form, from a stunning but to some degree sepulchral monument

Becoming beauty

I don't believe in volunteerist femininity, that I am completely free of the museum of moribund perfections. You could say I'm standing still, volunteering for a romance with decorum. Each shift of weight from foot to foot, each crossing and uncrossing of my arms may only be the gestures that age embeds, just as the pudica pose became the familiar sign of a modesty that you, Aphrodite, as the Knidia, did not originally connote. With a hand at breast and crotch in the Capitoline and Medici versions of you, your body has turned into nudity as a teasing, shameful state. In his *Venus Italica* (1811), Canova shows you inadvertently exposing your left breast while holding drapery to your right breast so that the elegant folds hide and reveal you with a feeling like that projecting from a movie starlet in a towel. You no longer place a hand at your crotch. Your cunt is an obscene memory.

I style myself in your Knidian comportment of elegant attention to your cunt. You never spread your legs in sculptures or paintings to declare your love of genital pleasure or your enjoyment of intercourse with men. *Aphrodisia* style a cunt in grace

Becoming beauty

My moves are subtle and I flame like you in your golden robes and girdles. We are brilliant textures, forms, and surfaces, like modernist sculpture that celebrates its own materiality. We are flesh sculpted from food, drink, and movements, everyday and educated in gyms and pools, on rocks and ice, in surf, on courts

Earth, concrete, wood, and carpeting shape my walk differently. I sink or glide with a material that is part of the pivot of my hips, the alignment of shoulders and torso, the softness or stiffness of my knees. The resonant and connective beauty of materials is one of the best legacies of your nudity

I love you, Aphrodite. Be my training partner, we will bend and stretch together, hold different asanas beyond our desire or ability to count the minutes, lift and press weights that strengthen every bone and muscle in our bodies.

Becoming beauty, I dress to the frigging hilt. Without planning to, I buy my costume on Friday, Frigga's day. A Great Goddess of Northern Europe, Frigga was a deity of sexual love. Friday was the Roman *dies Veneris,* Venus's day, and French remembers this in *vendredi.*

The Friday of my purchase was also Valentine's Day, originally the Roman Lupercalia, sacred to sexual delirium when enthusiasm overcomes self-control. On that fucking Friday afternoon I gave myself to Aphrodite Salacia, whose sacred day was Friday. I buy to become salacious, knowing that state to be salubrious for me.

Between my appearances in a selection of skintight, mesh, and filmy off-white dresses, which I try on unclothed for accurate fit and effect, Peggy, whom I love in her peach lipsticks and pale skin, her high-collared, sometimes many-buttoned tailored jackets, shirts, and dresses that reveal her body in fantasies of unfastening, undresses and dresses me in a mirrored, curtained cubicle. Like Sappho, one more passionate wife, we assume the persona of Aphrodite, and like her we know the unbridled and not always easy pleasure of styling oneself in love. (Sappho's Aphrodite oversees heterosexual and lesbian love. Sappho herself was the wife of a wealthy businessman, and in her poetry she writes of various passionate loves: heterosexual and lesbian, mother for daughter.)

In the Homeric Hymns, written over centuries by various poets, many still unknown, three songs celebrate Aphrodite. The composers are pious and enthusiastic about her radiance and beauty, and Hymns 5 and 6 describe her clothing. Hymn 5 also treats her humorously and enjoys presenting her as a charming and magnificent seducer.

I sing of Russell, rosy-cheeked, a rose among men. Allow me to undress you, as Anchises did with his eyes, then hands, when Aphrodite appeared to him. Peggy says you look like an angel and always will. Russell, carrier of divine accord between a passionate wife and husband, you don't need conventions, a white robe, wings, or halo, to prove your radiance. More Caravaggio Cupid than quattrocento innocent, you are the nude who lives in real life. You sweat perfume.

Sweet Russell, our garden in June is heavy with the fragrance of honeysuckles. We are *in flagrante* in our bedroom at dusk, and the scent, floating through a window open as wide as it can be, envelops us. You love wild growth; spring cutting back of plants distresses you, as if I were destroying Aphrodite's playfulness, which manifests in her love of all growth and creativity. Without them, not only vegetation but also *aphrodisia* would die. "Don't cut back the climbing roses," you say. I agree with your acuity.

A man, my mother, a girl, my brother; we all cross-dress for Aphrodite. (In the second volume of *Ancient Mirrors of Womanhood: Our Goddess and Heroine Heritage*, Merlin Stone writes, "To those who entered the holy places of Aphrodite, love was love. Thus at Her Oschophorian rites, young boys dressed as girls. And at the Argive feasts for Aphrodite, men put on the robes of women, while women donned the clothes of men.")

I sing of Heather, radiant: with muscles built by many, heavy pounds and pressures in the gym; with balletic grace; with black skin oiled to exquisite gleam; smiling self-love and embrace. The most sophisticated of nudes in your bikini as you performed for an audience near two hundred, you were no Hottentot Venus, no Saartjie Baartman whose black body Londoners minimized to sexualized parts and spectacle. Like other black female bodies on naked display at Parisian social functions in the 1800s, Baartman's body was an entertainment, especially her buttocks, as if smirking lust had twisted beauty into a mockery of Aphrodite Kallipygos, who gazes over her shoulder to admire her nude and splendid ass.

Heather, subordinate to no one, not even Aphrodite. Strong, broad, and large, akin to the Aphrodite I see when she shows herself as goddess to Anchises. Heather, the definition of your muscles is the dazzling self-definition displayed by a body of content. I witness in you Aphrodite Amazonia, who does not submit to divide—strength from beauty—and conquer. (I invent the name Aphrodite Amazonia to combine beauty and strength and also because gold is associated not only with Aphrodite but also in the Renaissance imagination with New World Amazons.)

I sing of Guillermo, your long black hair and brown skin, your elegant investment in spoken words that are sequined, fringed, embroidered—decked out like your body in the midst of most people's prosiness. Guillermo, I see your full lips kiss the syllables as they leave your mouth, I hear your voice sustaining baroque and rococo climaxes in conversation. The ornamented voice, words, and body do not privilege either foreplay or consummation, for both exist in a continuum of pleasure.

I sing of Laura, forty-four and theorizing a feminist performance of femininity. It caught my eye before I could place her any other way. I was walking back from a restaurant to my hotel the night before the beginning of a conference. I saw a woman, a little younger than I, coming towards me, dressed in dark pants, a black leather jacket, and long, reddish hair. She had a swagger and held a book. I thought, This woman is going to the conference and maybe she and I can be friends.

Laura, you know that beauty is fresh and it is years in the making. You parade lipstick, tight sweaters, a bracelet from France, a designer coat, and you love to show off the little leaf tattooed on your biceps, to push the air around with your big voice and laugh. Take me into the heart of their production, for you, Laura, like me and Aphrodite, are graying at the temples, becoming radiant in reds and silver. We know many ways to gleam.

Styling hair, makeup, and body is no joke in terms of time and money. Becoming beauty also requires effort, the disciplined pleasure of continually reinventing and thus redressing Aphrodite. The myth of the perfect body, besides damning all our bodies to imperfection, supports belief that beauty does not take work because perfection for some is a natural state. So, foolish are the people who work at beauty, for failure is the only possible outcome of their aspiration, and failure they deserve.

The perfection myth and fashion-magazine beauty falsify the seriousness of aesthetic/ erotic self-creation and the necessity for a new Aphrodite who is not a siren song luring us to kill ourselves for beauty, by which I mean exhausting our self-love by over-investing in beauty purchases and practices that do not build aphrodisiac capacity and power. Aphroditean self-attentiveness and intimacy with others take effort, but because they require discipline, not perfection, human beings can participate without a foregone conclusion of failure. As siren song, Aphrodite is a poignant undercurrent in narratives of loss and absence: losing youth, losing weight, losing the color of your hair, losing love.

Celebrity sex icon Cher remarks, in an article by Brantley Bardin published in the September 1996 issue of *Details*, "Sexy is a feeling and an art and something you have to really be interested in, like playing the violin—you've got to really like doing it and really be good at it." Cher's statement indicates that commitment to an *ars erotica* comes from enjoyment. Committed pleasure puts the lie to moralizing and frustration. Yet, Cher says, "I'm very insecure about my looks." Also, *sexy* is a light word compared to *aphrodisiac*. Sexy is the surface of being and using pleasure, and it signals our loss of Aphrodite.

Cher, fifty in 1996, observes that she probably dresses in age-inappropriate clothes, such as filmy lace pants that reveal tattooed buttocks. She seems happy to continue not acting her age.

Act your age
Live the narratives that always require loss
Act your age. Mine is the revolutionary Age of Aphrodite, whose very beginning will make it unnecessary for me to ask, How many stories must each of us tell in order to remember one story of true love?

Frueh wears a dark brown sheath. Spaghetti straps, bare legs, an aquamarine and diamond necklace, and spectator pumps of umber leather and suede with three-and-a-half-inch heels contribute sex and sparkle.

> Who gave me this hand to smack you with?
> Who gave me this throat for swallowing piss?
> Who gave me this whip to bleed your flesh?
> Who gave me this palate that so loves shit?
> Who dictated that giving a fuck means violence, tumult, chaos, damage, frenzy?

These questions, asked by a recanting Mme Duclos, one of the Marquis de Sade's storyteller whores in his novel *The 120 Days of Sodom,* or by me in a nightmare, are both rooted and buried in a Western erotic tradition of shame, and they also challenge that tradition. It is a predominant modern erotics and a taproot for contemporary clichés of transgressiveness and abjection.

Sade's relentless and literarily original erotics of grossness and cruelty is embraced by one of Georges Bataille's definitions of eroticism in his *Erotism,* published in 1957 (first English translation 1962): "We use the word eroticism every time a human being behaves in a way strongly contrasted with everyday standards and behavior. Eroticism shows the other side of a facade of unimpeachable propriety. Behind the facade are revealed the feelings, parts of the body and habits we are normally ashamed of." Bataille devotes two chapters of *Erotism* to Sade. On the back cover of the 1986 City Lights edition of *Erotism,* a blurb by Michel Foucault reads, "Bataille is one of the most important writers of the century."

Sade, the Divine Marquis, is, of course, legendary. We owe this reputation to his influence on numerous nineteenth-century literary lights and lesser figures—Byron, Petrus Borel, Swinburne, Gautier, Baudelaire, Frédéric Soulié, and Octave Mirbeau. Although *The 120 Days* was not published until 1935, Sade's novels *Justine* and *Juliette,* as articulate as *The 120 Days* in the erotics of shame, pain, and doom, were available beginning, respectively, in 1791 and 1796, when first editions of each work were published. Sadism—the word derives from practices in Sade's writings—is glamorous when touched by Romantic and Symbolist artists and writers, and it looms in Surrealist works such as Bellmer's *Les poupées* and Ernst's collages *La femme 100 têtes* and *Une semaine de bonté.* A host of twentieth-century theorists and philosophers, Bataille and Simone de Beauvoir among them, have written about Sade. That list also includes contemporary feminists, such as Jane Gallop. Moreover, a Sadeian aesthetic reverberates in a recent art phenomenon to which much of the November 1997 *New Art Examiner* is devoted: "lowlife scum, grotesque deformity, . . . sexual perversion, and senseless violence," is Kathryn Hixson's description in her editorial. The lowlife in Sade is the shameful body mentioned in Bataille's definition of eroticism.

I do not intend to compare the 1990s and the 1790s, and Sade was an aristocrat, as are many of his created debauchees who are either born into the aristocracy or whose noxiously accumulated wealth makes possible the extravagances enjoyed by that class. However, independent video/film producer Jennifer Reeder's *New Art Examiner* essay promulgates a Sadeian philosophy of revolution through giving a fuck as lowlife "cultural terrorism." She agrees with feminist cultural critic Laura Kipnis that the lower body and the lower class are associated, and asserts that by "embracing this farting, shitting, puking,

urgent instinct beneath the cultural burden of belief in pleasure and pain as unavoidable and necessary correlates and of sentimentality's association with a despicable propriety.

A soft and elegant, substantial chair that gives with the pressures of buttocks responding to a slow tongue on a hard cock and of knees driven into and cushioned by the seat; a chair for marital partners to enjoy the revolutionary positions of a loving erotics.

I am as proud of my beauty as I am of my oratorical and narrative skills. Sade describes me, forty-eight years old in The 120 Days, *as "majestic," and he especially lauds my ass—"one of the most splendid and plumpest," one of the "finest" anyone could hope to see, a "matchless ensemble." (He praises many asses with superlatives, but, still, I appreciate his compliment.) Both he and I know my breasts are superb. In his and the libertines' eyes I am a "radiant creature," just like Aphrodite, and my autobiographical tales spellbind my audience and brighten their November.*

I am as lugubrious as I am lubricious, for I am the libertines' sister, servant, and minion. I plunder bodies, careless of souls, with my deceit and avarice. I create events for people who love corpses, who cum when they can terrorize mothers, children, and virgins. I am one vicious and cynical cunt. Who doesn't much like cunts at all. And though I love Sade because he knew that I am smart and linguistically stirring, that I am gorgeous, in dress as well as undress— "bejeweled, more brilliant with each passing day," he says—he was a rigid son of a bitch. The party at the Château de Silling proceeded, though not always scrupulously, according to the libertines' Statutes, their program of pleasure and punishment. And Sade, lover though you are to me, you made me too perfectly beautiful; you should have described the broken capillaries that decorate my legs, just here and there, and how those signs of poor circulation drove some clients and lovers of mine mad with lust. You missed that perverse passion. Also, my Lord, my dear Sade, lover of my midlife power, I must remind you that some of the practices you made me preach disgust me. I hate cum shooting in my face, your poignant cliché of ecstatic male power, and I hate eating shit.

I first read all of *The 120 Days* several years ago, when I was forty-eight. I identified in some respects with Mme Duclos, who is forty-eight when narrating over a month the "150 simple passions," which include permutations involving urine, mucus, excrement, flagellation and other epidermal and subcutaneous stimulations with needles and hot irons, and terrorizing unsuspecting pawns through morbid, anxiety-provoking talk and situations.

I enjoyed Maurice Lever's *Sade: A Biography* upon finishing *The 120 Days*. As I read those books and critical works on Sade, I fell in love with him. He was smarter, funnier, and sexier than most men I meet, though he was also a jerk. In my late teens I looked at Sade fitfully, so repulsed by the tortures he adores that I never read anything by him cover to cover. From then through my early thirties I scrutinized and luxuriated in writings by many of the Romantic and Symbolist Sadeian family. I belong to it: it is an opulent erotic world, filled with beautiful, often quick and sometimes deeply intelligent fatal women, and I was captivated and inspired not by their cruelty but rather by their profound sensuality, the sovereign power of their erotic bodies as well as their minds. Femme fatale-ism, feminism, femininity: they and I could operate on all fronts. So I am steeped in the tradition of erotic damage, and when I met Duclos, a supreme femme fatale who, unlike most of her nineteenth- and twentieth-century sisters, is not young, I also met, in certain ways, myself.

Duclos and I sing a song for Sade:

Frueh sings Nick Cave's "The Ship Song," whose plaintively beautiful melody entwines images of bridges burned, dogs loosed, and history made in the name of an impossible and irresistible love.

I will not revise Duclos into a recanting character, for that would shame both her and Sade. She is a gem as she is, a memorable and useful star of a pornographic classic. Sade's four storytellers are all midlife women—forty-eight to fifty-six—and the libertines, four midlife men, choose Duclos and her peers precisely because they "had attained their prime—that was necessary, experience was the fundamental thing here." Though, unlike Duclos in that she doesn't relish the pleasures that her cunt can provide, I am in sympathy with her style, "very scanty and very elegant attire," adornment in makeup and jewelry; with her understanding that erotic satisfaction necessitates moral as well as physical sensation and is enhanced by "mentally heating" conversation and philosophizing that quicken genital excitement; with her vivacious and sophisticated ability to speak that kind of prose and to proudly enhance its piquancy with artful rationality. As she declares, "After having perverted you it is my responsibility to restore you to reason." She moves her audience unashamedly from body to mind, again and again, so that neither is starved of erotic sustenance.

Shit is sustenance for the libertines, and they force others to eat it. They and many of Duclos's clients are connoisseurs of shit, as some people are of chocolate. Sade himself loved chocolate. One of Duclos's customers exclaims to her, "What pleasure you give me! I've never eaten more delicious shit!" Shit is a delicacy—a libertine swallows a "turd for dessert"—and Sade would have us believe that we should all like eating shit better than chocolate.

In defense of chocolate:

Cocks turn soft in my mouth, like chocolate candy bars and ice cream that become smaller through intimacy with tongue, warmth, and teeth.

Hannah Wilke's *Venus Pareve* (1982), a nude self-portrait chocolate sculpture, is an autoerotic image of repleteness. *Pareve*: neither meat nor milk. The divine Hannah: neither essence of sexflesh nor motherfluid. The divine Hannah: able to conceive of the human body as chocolate, a symbol of love, the ultimate pleasure food, a Valentine's Day gift of supreme sentimentality. She dispenses with shame about a forbidden delight.

Compare that with Janine Antoni's *Chocolate Gnaw* (1992), a monumental block of chocolate, a huge piece of pleasure whose consumption would sicken one individual. A minimalist cube becomes minimal pleasure, for here chocolate is a symbol of desire embodied as the absurdity and even horror of satisfaction, especially when we know that Antoni sculpted the originally six-hundred-pound cube with her teeth. The (im)possible extravagance of pleasure gnaws at people.

Sade, chocolate lover that you are, I thought you might like to try my mother's brownie recipe.

Brownies: Single Recipe
1 stick butter
1 cup sugar
Cream together
2 eggs
Add
6 tablespoons cocoa or
3 squares melted chocolate

Add

1 cup sifted flour

1 teaspoon vanilla

1/2 cup walnuts

Bake at 350 degrees for 18 minutes

Duclos's attributes make her a typical Sadeian heroine (and hero): she is an "abnormal" woman who stands against pregnancy, motherhood, heterosexual vaginal intercourse, and men. (Her casting aspersions on pricks—shriveled, tiny, soft, discolored, "wretched," ugly, stublike, often altogether "miserable relic[s]"—and on their ejaculate—measly, dribbling, squirting, pathetic—critiques the image of men as infallibly and beautifully potent.) Duclos's abnormalities, including unashamedness about her body, present Sade as feminist; though one may read him, too, as frighteningly misogynist. He is full of contradictions, for giving a fuck is not a monolithic position that the giver should protect with self-righteousness.

I would love to receive a love letter from Sade. He wrote delicious ones, full of aristocratic lightness, flair, and lies, full of erotic flatteries. Sade, my sweet, here I am right by your side, in your arms, lovingly, subversively in bed with you. I am in your face, up your ass, articulating the means of non-criminal pleasure's support.

Duclos's abnormalities and Sade's contradictions, complexity, and realism enable her to be unashamed at the same time that he highlights body parts, events, and products whose expulsive properties signal shame. Sade's erotics, like Bataille's (and Reeder's), is determined by organs of expulsion rather than pleasure. Expulsion—imperious demand, tumultuous release—equals violence, and shame erupts from the body. In "The Use Value of Sade," Bataille asserts the "violence and incongruity of . . . excretory organs," nose, anus, penis, vagina. According to Bataille's translator Allan Stoekl, in his introduction to a Bataille volume titled *Visions of Excess: Selected Writings, 1927–1939,* André Breton "in effect condemns Bataille as an 'excremental philosopher.'" For Bataille, mucus, menstrual blood, and semen, as well as feces, are all excremental.

I exclude myself from your expulsions in which pleasure is forced from the body as waste. Your characters retain their shit, but you never tell me the pleasures of retention, how it produces aroused wellbeing and soul-and-mind-inseparable-from-body fullness, which is both a sense of capacity to act and the feeling that everything wonderful is possible. Your erotics become elegiac.

Sade, my sweet, my truffle, giving a fuck is a decisive act. That is why "I don't give a fuck," in contrast to "I give a fuck," is a common phrase. Not giving a fuck seems to be an easier position to take, for it is when giving a fuck that people often get in trouble. Sade, my sweet, try a different part of paradise, a different way for you to give a fuck. Join me and Russell in our yellow leather chair, in our dark red bedroom, the color of blood as the force of a loving eros.

. . . .

The staging is as spare yet sensuous as usual for one of Frueh's perfor-mances. At stage right, props include a black music stand that Frueh stands behind, a microphone, and a white pedestal that holds a fork, a clear glass filled with water, and a monumentally tall, round chocolate cake covered in chocolate frosting and decorated with bright pink roses (frosting or real, depending on the baker). At stage left Frueh has placed a black metal chair, another black music stand, and, on the floor, a clear glass vase full of a dozen bright pink roses and several white flow-ers (lilies, peonies, carnations, gerbera daisies, depending on what is available at the florist's). When Frueh speaks standing, she is miked. When she speaks seated, she is unmiked. Frueh wears a hot pink voile evening gown with a low-cut back and bodice and a flirtatious hemline that reveals much of her legs from knees to feet. A matching capelet sparkles with sequins. Her hair is loose, she wears no jewelry, and her lipstick, MAC's Dubonnet, is a rich, cunt-colored hue. Her mules, whose

Here is my primal scene. At least, it's one that I remember. At around six or eight years old, I saw my parents fucking. I walked into their bedroom silently, which I must have done numerous times. (Was the door closed? Had I heard something that I wanted to see? Did I want to intrude? Was I pushing my luck and pushing my erotic limits?) A flash of skin; then a rush of action as my father (most likely) pulled the covers over him and Mom. (Did they speak? Did I turn around immediately and leave of my own volition?) I've always read and heard that young children who see or hear their parents sexually engaged experience the event as violent, especially as violence done to the mother, and that the psyche emerges scathed. I don't think so. Not for me. When the image has come back to me over the years, it has fascinated me every time, so I believe that it fascinated me originally and that it was one of my earliest initiations into a love of the erotic.

My primal scene is a kind of Proustian madeleine, recalling me throughout my life to the roots of my persistent love of sex. My remembrance of things past shapes orgasm in the present. It doesn't take a scholar to tell us that sexual desire and pleasure are mentally motivated, that orgasm is neither simply nor solely a biomechanical response. So the shaping power of my primal scene holds no mystery, except for my wondering in the grip of memory, whose preciseness is always in question, about the correspondence between the details of what actually happened in that bedroom among the three of us and my own sexual tastes and fervors. For example, I have always liked orgasm best when fucking. Should I presume that this is because I saw my parents fucking—and maybe they were coming—and I have to repeat their pleasure?

I feel anomalous: my primal scene provokes pleasure, feeds my romance with thinking and fucking. As both image and experience, Mom and Dad in bed set me thinking, long ago, about sex as both a personal and intellectual subject, and that subject is a lifetime occupation. Lovemaking is an untoward theme for a feminist intellectual. I can't help it: sexual bodies, sexualized bodies, bodies in sexual contact intoxicate me, as orgasm, a key high point of sexual contact, intoxicates me.

My parents' real bodies do not stay with me as spectral demons. Rather, they are a source of my ability to fly on sexual fantasies and to invest my emotional intelligence in understanding sexual behaviors when I see and experience them, and their bodies are an engine of their daughter the scholar's ideas.

I email my lover,

I want you to push me up against a building's wall, in some big city on a side street at night, push me up against it hard, your cock, hard, singling out my cunt for love. A wall where people can hear our pleasure but almost none can see it, unless they want to; from around a corner our groans and hyperventilation, our taking away of each other's breath and our giving our breath to one another—breathing into each other's mouths with kisses—seduces some voyeur, one who's supersensitive to sounds, or to sex in the nearby air, as if antennaed for it like an insect.

I want your cum running down my leg after we've fucked someplace in public or in a car, and you can lick your cum from my inner thigh or we can put my lace panties in place (if I'm wearing any) as we walk to dinner and they'll be wet with both our cum. I want us to taste your cum together, like we taste mine when we're kissing after you eat me. And at a restaurant dinner table you can put your hand between my legs and feel our wetness.

I'm on the verge of the verge of coming as I write you.

These fantasies of public fucking, of coming in public with a partner: do they originate in the fact that I was the public to my parents' sex, so consequently want a public to witness mine? Is the very fact that fucking so thrills me determined by an excitement that my parents' fucking provoked on-the-spot in me? Because my unconscious knows the position that Mom and Dad enjoyed each other in, does my unconscious decide my responsiveness, my quick orgasm when a man penetrates me from behind with my butt raised just a little? Perhaps a person's sexual predilections exist *before* birth. Maybe my mother's own desires, passions, and positions designed this daughter's passions, too, in utero. And was it there that I gave myself to my first orgasm?

I suppose that my primal scene could have precipitated an effect that differs from the pleasure I describe. I could have been scared of fucking or felt diminished by it or found it to be distasteful, even ugly.

All orgasms are beautiful. Because *beautiful* is defined as that which gives one the highest degree of pleasure. The primary constituent of an orgasm's beauty seems obvious: an orgasm's physiological components ensure that it feels good. Yet all orgasms are not equal. Speaking as a female body, the duration, intensity, and location of orgasm vary, and they contribute to the particular beauty of an orgasm and to the fact that some orgasms *are* more beautiful than others to the person who is experiencing them. But even a weak orgasm provides a high degree of pleasure in relation to other pleasures in life, such as eating delicious food, participating in a lively conversation, being part of the sunny sky and the desert ground. Beauty can be graceful, striking, roaring, refined, and orgasms can have the same qualities.

Beauty can also be playful. Play plumps us, enriches and amplifies us. Orgasm derives from the Greek *orgasmos*, to swell with moisture, swell with lust. When we're full of pleasure, we're beautifully plump, like round hips and bellies and like muscles too. In orgasm, our being itself swells. Play plumps all of a person, soul-and-mind-inseparable-from-body, like sexual arousal plumps the genitals, in readiness for orgasm.

* * * * * * * * * * * * * * *

Frueh sits.

My lust, which couples with my love for you, has swollen every bit of me, has enlarged all of my materiality and immateriality so that I am full of you, decentered from a more ordinary state of ego.

Frueh stands.

The Harvard University English professor Elaine Scarry claims, in her philosophical defense of beauty, *On Beauty and Being Just*, "At the moment we see something beautiful, we undergo a radical decentering." Playing with this idea, I would say that when we feel the beauty of orgasm, we undergo a radical decentering, which may last beyond the orgasm's length.

Frueh sits.

Such decentering can linger, and it perhaps accounts, day after day, month after month, many months after you and I first came together in my bed, for feeling still as if I am aloft.

Frueh stands.

Scarry suggests that when we happen upon a beautiful object, taste, or concept, it lifts us off the rotating earth to land us changed on shifted ground. Similarly, the aftereffects of orgasm, a beautiful occurrence, cause a lifting, floating, or spinning from which we return to terra firma in a less self-centered state than that in which we left: beauty has transformed terra firma into terra nova.

I write my lover,

Frueh sits.

You said on Friday that you feel like you're floating. Let me tell you . . . I felt like I was floating all day Friday and it's been happening other times since then. Like my head is high above my body.

Frueh stands.

Fairyland surrounds us, and it fills or pierces us when we risk the fear of venturing between the world we know and worlds with which we're barely familiar. Orgasm spirits and moves us into a generally unfamiliar world, one of extreme connection with another human being; and that connection exists whether or not we love the person with whom we experience our orgasm. Fairyland is magic, a place or state of extraordinary power.

Fairies travel between human beings' everyday world and regions that the psyche experiences as both lighter and darker than the norm. Our orgasms with one another turn us into fairies or draw out the fairy in us, for during orgasm we are lighter than usual—unburdened, wanton, buoyant, giddy, perhaps foolish; inspired, animated, brightened up, and even radiant—and we are darker too—delving into supplies of energy that we generally hold secret, involuntarily daring to leap towards the twilight of cries and crying, moans and drooling, letting loose the animals that we are, permitting ourselves to be ignorant of sin. The lightness and the darkness of our fairy selves, experiencing orgasm either in masturbation with no one near or in a copulative embrace, is a letting go.

Fairies are so good at letting go. That's because they are large in courage; it's because courage enlarges them. Courage: from the Old French *corage*, heart, spirit. Huge-hearted fairies: a person who doesn't scare easy ups the ante of eros. Fairies' grasp of life and death is itself large, yet everything slips through their fingers. The reason is that they do not care about closure, the conclusions that we believe we need after a loved one dies— closure to our grief—or when we end a marriage—closure to our shared history, closure to our love—or at the end of a day's discussion in a university classroom—closure to a concept both obligated to and swirling with a complex of facts. Closure is a cowardly or lazy way out of the process of living. Living takes time, takes many turns, creates opening after opening. Belief in closure limits our understanding: of the mind's intricate play with ideas and of the continuation of grief for a parent or of love for a former spouse. Belief in closure reduces our capacity for growth, for learning, and for pleasure.

Orgasm, defined as the climax of sexual excitement, *is* a closure. Yet a climax is not necessarily a finish. An orgasm may have the beauty of finishing touches, which are sexual pleasure's final flourishes, such as the particularity of slow or savage thrusts of cock in cunt or anus, of teeth cutting into the skin that covers a trapezius, of a guttural "I love you" or "I'm coming," of sweaty groin to buttocks. Orgasm does end, but, like emotions, it remains, by embedding itself in the psyche, and although orgasm gradually fades from immediate regard, if we wish, we can consciously carry it with us, we can feel it as a constant pleasure, as a continuity of pleasure in our lives. The continuity of pleasure both comes from and creates sparkling creatures, fairies, who spark pleasure in other people.

Pink is the supreme fairy color.

I've read that when someone wears pink, she attracts love, or at the least, generates happiness in those who are looking at her. Pink unblocks the heart and increases good feelings.

Pink, the color of genitals, ranges, like orgasm, from fierce to tender, and just as orgasm is not a trifling sensation, neither is pink a trifling color.

We perceive pink as a paler version of red and therefore easier to take. Pink doesn't carry the threat of red. It is red's cognate, but we think that red is bold and pink is demure. This formulation of difference between red and pink reveals the trivializing association of pink with femininity, especially with the culturally sweetened notions of little girls' femininity.

Our trifling treatment of pink defends against its potency.

How well fashion designer Betsey Johnson understands pink's potency. The walls of her boutiques are painted fuchsia, and it's easy to find pink clothes in them. Pink sells clothes because pink lifts spirits.

Pink is bubbly, ardent, piquant, sweet, and wild, and we are delinquent hearts when we remain unconscious of pink's complexity and dynamism.

Pink carries the essence of erotic play. Pink can be light and dense, froth and crystal, liquid like a sharp or a sugary juice, pliant like tongues and genitalia, ladylike and generous. Pink refreshes us, as does play.

. . . .

Frueh eats cake. Then she sits.

"You know, you could decide never to get involved with anyone again," I tell myself. "You could close your heart after the damage of divorce and parental deaths. You could bring your heart inside, so far inside that even you would hardly know it's beating. The hiddenness of your heart would be like shallow breathing, or like holding your breath."

I give my heart again. My lover's mouth and tongue are soft and dynamic, like mine. So quickly he feels like part of me, my cunt becomes his lips, his saliva is my wetness. Our bodies, clothed alongside each other, moan together, in a union, a communion whose particularities of merging I haven't felt before. Even with our clothes on, I feel a joining that I think I've been afraid of feeling before. I love sex with men. They become feminine. I become masculine. We are both and neither gender. I look at my lover, whose eyes are closed, as I lie on him, as I snake over his body and into his being, and I smile because his pleasure and desire both relax and activate his beauty, which, though distinctly male, is more than willing to be taken—by my strength. He embraces me with power, embraces my torso, then my hips when he's eating me. His passion moves into me, he is much stronger than I am; his hands, running up and down my back, could force me to comply with anything he wants, but they push me, with perfect pressure, into the merging that thrills and stuns me. Even with our jeans on, I feel our hips, groins, thighs, bellies as one. I've read about the loss of identity that people feel with sex. The most captivating discourse comes from philosophers. I've disagreed with them. I've said that during tremendous sexual pleasure, one can feel one's own identity clearly. Now, with my lover, I'm experiencing a change of mind and body through a change of heart, through a vulnerability for which I can't account. My vulnerability surprises me. My lover and I are a surprise to each other; we are a surprise to us. I am letting myself "lose my identity" with him. Let go, as the fairies say and do. O, pin me down with your clear, wild heart, which is all of your body on top of mine, your palms to my palms, our fingers intertwining. O, pick me up and place me where you want me, which is where our identities dissolve into our surprising sexual solution. We are aggressive and tender with one another, creating fairyland with soul-and-mind-inseparable-from-body. We create fairyland together because I am between twenty-two and twenty-five, as well as being fifty-four, and I am eight and two thousand, too; and he is eighteen and twenty-two, as well as being twenty-eight, and he is thousands of years old, like me.

Frueh stands.

Fearless lovers, we play across the cultural closures of age, with the wonders of each other's sex, and with the pleasure that our hottest pink attraction to each other stimulates in our spirits' seeking happiness and home in each other's body.

Fairies are as good at playing as they are at letting go.

I play with the language of my body, the designations given to my pinkness. Words can increase orgasmic capacity. To shun the words, for me, would be a shutting off of imagination, and words can plump the imagination—our creative power—which fashions the beauty of orgasm in soul-and-mind-inseparable-from-body.

Pussy and *cunt.* They do not connote the same thing. *Pussy* has a light, amusing, even merry tone, whereas *cunt* delivers a more aggressive, blunter message, like the passionate imperative, "Fuck me." In the 1970s feminists reclaimed *cunt* in order to celebrate female bodies and women's pleasure in and for themselves. Cunt art, the vulval imagery invented by feminist artists such as Hannah Wilke and Judy Chicago, proclaimed the beauty of female genitalia and both the force and ease of women's orgasmic capacity. Many people reduce *cunt* and *pussy* to naughty words, but *naughty* is a facile description; for *pussy* describes a lovely seductiveness, pink like apple blossoms or a tangy taste, and *cunt* describes a more demanding enticement, pungent like a curry that sharpens one's sensitivity to flavors, bold as the roses in my garden whose pink an acquaintance of mine called garish and which captivated a little girl I know so much that we cut her a bouquet. *Cunt* and *pussy* both connote exuberance, and the words enrich the vulval and vaginal aesthetics originated and developed by the women artists for whom an erotics of women's bodies necessitated a visual representation and understanding of female genital beauty. That understanding disputes Freud's assertion that genitals—male or female—are ugly and, more importantly, it increases women's orgasmic capacity.

Frueh sits.

The root of *tempt* is the Latin *temptare*, to try the strength of, to urge. Men must not feel as strong as I do if they lack the self-assurance to make love to a woman and not feel that she is using his desire to urge him beyond what *he* desires. Desire is limitless: deal with it.

Frueh eats cake.

"Yes, ma'am," says pilot Tom Paris to Kate Mulgrew's Captain Kathryn Janeway on the *Star Trek* series *Voyager*. Like other starship captains in the series, she orders, "Do it," and the crew obeys. That terse imperative excites me, especially spoken by Janeway, another woman who is a man. "Yes, ma'am," say Captain Karen Walden's men when her bravery tops theirs as Iraqis attack the Americans' downed helicopter in *Courage under Fire*. Over and over, in one way and another, Meg Ryan's Walden, like any captain, like any man, directs her subordinates to "Do it." How clear and unsentimental a phrase is "Do it." How unromantic a sexual command: don't fool around, just fuck me plain and simple. Spoken in sexual circumstances by a woman, "Do it" must make tempted men feel like subordinates, caught in the machinations of the devil, the skills of a dominatrix.

At the risk of further disarming men, let me assert that all of us women don't need or want plying with foreplay, although I've read since I was a girl that we do. Some of us need and love, a lot of the time, decisiveness and force akin to the action hero's when he is at the pinnacle of knowing what he has to do, when he can't afford to make mistakes, when his focus is absolute. Mel Gibson's Benjamin Martin, a Revolutionary War militia hero in *The Patriot*, wants to kill a lot of King George's soldiers, with the help of his two young sons who are new to killing and who will be witnessing the mayhem designed by their father. Martin's prayer for success is concise: "Lord, make me fast and accurate."

My fondness for "Do it" isn't necessarily asking for a fast fuck, which is just right when its passion increases passion.

Frueh sits.

Like you, my fairy man, I love the sudden synergy of cock and cunt. How quick is orgasm when we are in our fairy passage? As quick as penis meets introitus.

My fondness for "Do it" asks that we dispense with flesh mulling over flesh, tongue debating finger, finger debating clit, clit debating glans. In a number of *Voyager* episodes, Janeway and her first officer Chakotay debate each other about some strategy or offensive on which the captain must imminently embark. Soon enough she's saying to him something like, "That's that, I'm right, we're doing it my way, the debate is over." She knows where she stands in the deep dark forest of the Delta Quadrant, where she has inadvertently lost her ship, and she's as cool as any femme fatale or dominatrix, experts at calculating risks to the flesh and will.

Here I stand. Here I am with another person. Here I am with another penis, another navel, another set of the same circumstances in a different body led by a different ego, defense mechanisms, and compensatory behaviors.

Here I am in an inescapable way. Here I am, in all my blushes and whatever little pimples exist today on my high round ass.

Orgasm puts you in your place. Here I *am*. Here *I* am. Or, with one or more partners, here we *are*, here *we* are.

Here I am in the Sonoran desert with the saguaros, chollas, and prickly pears, or here I am in my rich cream-colored bedroom with the blue jays screeching this early morning along with my coloratura moans, or here we are making our specific heat in the dead of a Chicago winter.

I am here in vaginal orgasm more than in clitoral orgasm. A clitoral orgasm feels as though it spreads across surface flesh and stays in my genital area, whereas a vaginal orgasm aroused because of intercourse often begins with penetration and opens, in a profuse petalling, as penis meets G spot, then suction and friction occur—of varying speed, rhythm, duration, vaginal/penile depth, and power exchange between my lover and me. In vaginal orgasm I flower to and through my soles and palms and from my brain into my scalp. Nothing gets left out, no organ, no muscle. And my orgasm moves beyond me. It is in my lover, of course, as he and I sculpt each other with that power exchange of breaths and bodies, saliva, sweat, and cum, and it radiates into the room or the ground which he and I inhabit and alter; because I clutch a pillow or run my nails through sand or make the sounds that sometimes only my lover hears but sometimes a neighbor can hear as well; and certainly the birds, like other animals, discern the orgasm with parts of their bodies other than ears.

Zydeco musician Rosie Ledet sings about her "joy box." The lyrics focus on female directions for male control and on the high pleasure of vaginal orgasm. Yet, for me and, I imagine, Rosie, "vaginal orgasm" seems like a misnomer, because the term implies that the pleasure exists or stays in only one place, and, thus defined, orgasm is about closure. However, now that I have enlarged the definition of "vaginal orgasm," I will continue to use it with you tonight, comfortable to think that after this initial enlargement, we will continue to enlarge our understanding of the term, not only through what I say but because the supple parts of our unconscious minds will play with the term.

Vaginal orgasm helps me know where I stand, where I am. (I speak only for myself, not for all women, because I do not presume that women's genital sensations are exactly shared. If you are a woman who feels the way that I do, I would love to talk with you, in order to enlarge our orgasmic joy by telling one another our experiences.) I know where I stand because cocks that I love reach a centrality inside me that is not simply physical. Being in that center of me—which some of the feminists who reclaimed *cunt* called the *central core*—my lover sees into me, sees through me. Most purely, *he sees me.*

. . . .

Frueh sits.

Is your cock your center, like my cunt is mine, and if so, do you feel that when we fuck I am embracing the center of you?

Yes. We know each other's center in the paradoxical dissolution or exchange of self into the lover, into the decentering, into the loss of identity that is the clearest clarity.

. . . .

Intermission.

. . . .

Frueh stands.

My lover says, "You're like a little girl." Which means that he sees me, he knows me as a little girl. He is on-target to my psyche. No wonder his cock finds its way so securely inside me without a condom. I know my trust in him without having to think about knowing it, and considering that all my life I have religiously used a condom, a diaphragm, or birth control pills so that I would not become pregnant—but also, I now see in retrospect, often enough because I have not deeply trusted a man, have not felt replete with faith either in his love for me or in our relationship—my trust amazes me to such a degree that I recognize it as part of the reason why I'm crying sometimes when my lover and I are talking, making love, or simply smiling as we look at one another. Even in the past several years, as my periods have gradually stopped, I have used a condom—maybe out of habit, maybe because of the risk of an STD, maybe because of my ancient lack of *abundant* faith in my own lovingness.

When my lover says, "You're like a little girl," he compliments me without knowing it. He says I'm a sophisticate in public and a little girl at times with him. "It's not that I'm sexually attracted to little girls . . . ," he begins without finishing the sentence. Completing it now, I'd say that he's attracted to my childhood inclinations, living buoyantly in my fairy self, and that his own fairy self feels freed in the presence of mine.

I do love eight-year-old girls. It must be because I am one, still.

When I was eight, Mom and Dad gave a dinner party at which the guest of honor was a renowned pianist. I wore a black sweater with thin, multicolored, horizontal stripes. It had a cowl neckline, and I pushed up the long sleeves to my elbows. (I still push up the sleeves of sweaters and T-shirts, or buy ones that have three-quarter-length sleeves. A sleeve to the wrist is too much sleeve. I guess I wear my heart high on my sleeve, on the biceps perhaps.)

I felt sophisticated in my sweater. The guest commented on my beauty as I and my parents sat with him at the table after eating. The adults drank coffee, whose aroma acted on me like an aphrodisiac. I felt as though a perfume imbued with heady florals, found in the tropics, was encircling me and the guest, who was telling Mom and Dad that I resembled a gorgeous Italian movie star. The pianist smiled softly as he and I held each other with our eyes.

I broke the embrace because I wondered why he hadn't told Mom that *she* was beautiful. The pianist's compliment separated me from Mom, and the pain of that separateness brought me close to tears.

I didn't understand why I, the child, the girl, was receiving praise for my appearance. I felt the desire in the pianist's admiration, and I sensed that his desire could enable a power in me. Very likely, I'd never felt that particular power over someone before. The power was sexual, and it was large, and I loved it. Just as orgasm enlarges us, so does the desire that puts us on the verge of the verge of orgasm. And there I was, on the brink.

I'm trying to remember if my power over the pianist frightened me. I think I knew, right then at age eight, that I could control people through sex, through sexual beauty. Granted, I suffered through a puberty of acne, weight gain, dark hair on my legs from ankles to crotch, and what my parents referred to as "piano legs," so I felt terribly ugly and that may have disabled developing any skills of flirtation. For decades I didn't consciously use my sexual aura or *sillage* to court men or women or to help them court me. Only now, in my fifties, have I become flirtatious, a quality that I associate, in my maturity, with lightness. Only now, in my fifties, have I become light. Though maybe I was light when I was eight.

I look at photographs of me in that cowl-neck top, and I look light—sparklingly sexy, luscious—my deep eyes, full lips, gleaming hair, my shining being that created my voluptuousness. Like a lot of little girls, I was diva delicious to myself. However, my power may have frightened me—the force and clarity of my response to the pianist's compliment excites me even today—for what avenues are open to a young girl who wants to explore her sexuality? Mom had already educated me and Ren, my sister, about sex—sex, which fascinated my mind as much as it enveloped my being. And I knew, as a little girl just as I've known throughout my life, the ever-presentness of sex for me, my love for it. Still, I did feel awkward in my own skin and my own eros.

When I was a little girl, I loved sexual pleasure—I always have; but as a little girl my intense sexuality often embarrassed me. It encompassed knowledge and clear consciousness of my own fairy opulence and my own sexual pleasure, which I had discovered through masturbation some time before the dinner with the pianist. I translate the pain engendered by his compliment as an effect of embarrassment as well as an effect of my separateness from Mom.

I was a hero: to withstand his desire and my embarrassment without crying, to stand in the beauty of my mother's own beauty, to love her beauty as I loved my own, to passionately protect her beauty in my mind and heart. As the hero I was learning to know where I stand and I was learning the art of existing on the verge of the verge of orgasm.

Like the sage commander in Sun-Tzu's *The Art of War*, I both stood my ground and moved beautifully within *shih*'s eddying and flowing unpredictability. *Shih* is patterns of circumstances and influences, and it is dependent on intuitive and strategic arrangements of those patterns. The sage commander is an action hero, but often without the action, because his ultimate aim is to be victorious without killing anyone. In actual warfare, this may be impossible, but *The Art of War*, a fourth-century BCE Chinese text, counsels the sage commander, to whom it is addressed, to take whole, to achieve victory without battle. Sun-Tzu's philosophy, whose discipline "sage commanders" in all walks of life may practice, directs its audience, who read in the position of the sage commander, to resolve conflict through methods of being rather than doing. Sometimes we simply are the sage commander, although we may know nothing of Sun-Tzu or Chinese philosophy or contemplative practices. We simply know how to be, so our words and actions make a sense that resolves conflict, both within ourselves and the circumstances that surround, inform, and implicate us. I give myself too much credit by calling myself the sage commander, because I wasn't as relaxed as the sage commander is. But children deserve to be named heroes when they stand their ground.

Does my lover love in me whatever the pianist saw? Could it be the ruthless beauty that little girls have without knowing it? Could it be my red Mary Janes? Could it be the pagan cry that I release when my lover and I are fucking and I don't know if I'm him or me? Could it be my unadulterated enthusiasm—for chocolate, sex, and learning? "You're so sexy," my lover tells me, many times. Could it be I'm sexy like little girls who stand their ground and catch, then hold, the gaze of lucky men? Men who cannot control the look that's meant to lure a girl into a tighter nexus of desire? We girls are innocent, yet we've got a lot of wit, like Isabetta, the subject of a 1936 painting by Alice Neel. Isabetta, a naked beauty with big dark hair and wide-open eyes, plants her oversized feet on a striped rug, holds her arms akimbo, and just plain looks at us. No shame or embarrassment, no taunting sexuality. "Here I am," says her body, with an emphasis on *here*.

· ·

Frueh sings a few lines of "True Colors," the song originally
recorded by Cyndi Lauper. Then she sings,

With my fucking fairy lover
I would never run for cover

We'll be gracious, debonair

We'll listen to each other's cares

We'll weave 'round one another—dancers—

Full of questions, full of answers.

I question my interpretation of my primal scene. Because I *could* interpret my reaction differently. I could see it as trauma, I could say that I'm sexually obsessed and that the genesis of my obsession resides in an event that I could not have possibly deciphered and that I never can. I could say that my psyche is full of compensations and that I've been forever mortified by sex. I could say that my sexual revelations, in print and in conversations with my friends, have been defense mechanisms, developed in order to protect myself from feeling that I can never fuck like the big guys, fuck in large scale, heroically, like adults do.

But that interpretation feels wrong, feels itself like a mystification of my reality, of my soul-and-mind-inseparable-from-body. That interpretation feels like a mystification built on theoretical absolutism—trauma results from seeing one's parents in bed—and built, too, on an ideology of anti-pleasure—one's parents' pleasure cannot be digested into a nurturance of one's *own* pleasure.

One learns the significance of pleasure negatively, or rather, through the negation of pleasure. Self-help material about sex and beauty emerges from the negative, from shame and self-repulsion symphonically orchestrated to the theme, "I don't know up from down about my own pleasure or beauty." I started reading both juvenile and adult self-help material before my teens—grooming etiquette advice for adolescent girls, such as John Powers and Mary Sue Miller's *Secrets of Charm*, and clinical discussions by patriarchal authorities, like Dr. Frank S. Caprio's *The Sexually Adequate Male* and *The Sexually Adequate Female*, two books which Mom had either bought or checked out from the library.

I was such a little, sexy lady, thinking about posture, makeup, voice, and the seductions of each, paying attention to ways of pleasing a man, letting advice about gender inform my being. Robot femininity could have been the outcome of that early education, but my looking for pleasure rather than for pat answers and my love of pleasure over passiveness, coupled with my inability to unquestioningly accept sexual "authorities," even as a child, insured that my sensuality would overwhelm Dr. Caprio's "orders" for gender-deterministic sexual health and that my sense of aesthetic drama—which Mom regularly pointed out to me from my teens on—would undermine guidance for looking and acting pretty in a nicey-nice way. Velvet, lace, satin, crinoline, nylon; Mom's red lipstick, her pointy-toed high heels, her Persian lamb and mink coats: fabrics for little girls' fancy dresses and underwear along with Mom's material femininity, whose artifacts and effects I tried on, constituted not only a terrain but also a frontier of aesthetic and erotic excesses. I masturbated in mink, high heels, and lipstick. I dressed up for autoeroticism and orgasm.

I still do. Several years ago my friend Jeff teased me, "Joanna, you always dress up in a costume." He's right. I dress up in pleasure for daily life—a pearlescent pink leather skirt with a ruffle at the hem, snug T-shirts and tank tops often worn without a bra. I dress up in daily life to arrange myself for orgasm. I dress up in order to clear away the everyday crap, the barrage of shitfire; and my dress-up clears the way to orgasm.

Accentuating my appearance increases my orgasmic capacity, situates me on the verge of the verge of orgasm. To be as pretty as I can be is perhaps a compensation for an inadequacy at once lodged in and called up by my primal scene. Being as pretty as I can be enlarges me, so maybe it reduces the large place that my parents' fucking took up in my psyche.

While femininity can paradoxically promote women's abandonment of their bodies in the assertion of a blandly frilly corporeality, femininity can also provide valuably heady pleasures. Ornament leads to orgasm because I have wielded femininity's heady pleasures with the sureness of the sage commander. Femininity helps the sage commander to take whole, to wrest her soul-and-mind-inseparable-from-body from the mere fragments of pleasure that self-help manuals permit. Rationed bits of pleasure promote guilt.

Frueh eats cake.

Pleasure is available to me even when I hide it from others.

Frueh sits.

I sit in a movie theater, legs crossed, rotating my hips so slightly that no one would know I'm doing it. I have to keep myself from moaning. I'm rotating my hips because I'm missing my lover.

* * * * * * * * * * * * * * * * *

Frueh stands.

My friend Pam, who is acquainted with my lover not only through my love for him but also in other ways, surprises me by saying that he is an angel. I say, "Hmmm," and then I assent. Lightness of being displayed in his body that dances every day down corridors and sidewalks—how energetically gentle and how beautiful. But my agreement with Pam does not mean that my lover is innocent or perfectly kind or flawlessly good-looking or always sweet to his roots. Rather, my agreement shows that I have perceived him to be as gloriously smiling as the angel in Bernini's *Ecstasy of St. Theresa,* as sure in sex and spirit as the arrow that causes her to swoon, and as fluent in passion as her thrown-back head, her parted lips, and the river of her robe.

In orgasm, Bernini's St. Theresa is a figure of insurrection against our too-often lost love of ourselves. She is ornamented in her robe the way that I ornament myself in femininity. She and I are objects symbolic of anything but scarcity. We operate against the rationing of pleasure, and our adornment ordains our faith in orgy, which is simply unrestrained indulgence, such as the most beautiful orgasm.

Theresa's angel is a sensitively sensual lover, whose smiling gaze at her is infinitely amorous. His fingers part her robe for perfect penetration of the golden arrow that he holds as light-heartedly as a slightly intoxicated celebrant holds a glass of champagne between sips. In the heaven, or the fairyland, that Theresa and her angel create together, he is fucking the shit out of her, which simply means that he is making her real. His attentions ensure that she knows *I am here,* which is a mystical experience. And there, in that orgy in which a woman's clitoris, labia, cervix, uterus, and vagina are singly or all at once pointedly in focus, they also become sheer gradients and radiations of energy, making the body a unified resonance of pleasure. That orgiastic unit is like a minimalist sculpture, one shape—orgasm as sphere or cone—and it is one sensuousness—all radiance, vibration, fluttering, and sparkling. Paradoxically, Bernini's sculpture, Baroque as it is—ornately fervent—is also concisely simple.

Of course, the orgiastic unit's sensuousness dis-integrates the shape, which is osmotic, so the shape passes from orgasmic body into the literal and figurative atmosphere in which that body exists. Theresa's robe certainly is solid, yet its marble ripples and surges into the surrounding space, saturating it with pleasure. Her body is the charged and pretty uninhibited unconscious, which the state of orgasm reveals.

Theresa's body and robe undulate. They are female orgasm described as a wave.

Frueh sits.

You know I am your deep blue sea, your ship come home, and we are rolling in each other's souls, making waves that swell and break in the same paradise that I perceive to be the place inhabited by Bernini's St. Theresa.

Frueh stands.

Held in the embrace of art, she is coming for eternity.

I talk with lovers and some friends about waves of orgasms. "How many?" asked my new lover after the first time we'd made love. "I don't count," I replied. I've never counted.

My candor has perhaps indicted me in a culture that even now, over thirty years after many young women in the late 1960s, such as myself, claimed our bodily pleasure in the sexual revolution, mistrusts the woman who is in public clearly intensely involved in her sexuality. That involvement may be perceived as obsession and labeled such because of its very difference from the norm and the normative, which demand women's compliance with the dangerously obsessive mythicizing of their replete if not redundant sexual wiles coupled—in bondage—with the constraint that women should keep their sexuality under wraps.

I think of all the criticism that Madonna received for her frank and frankly sensuous sexual displays in her performances and videos and in her book called *Sex*. When we notice the dangerous obsession and mythicization that I noted above operating on a large public scale, we must understand how insidiously it permeates the lives of we who are less celebrated and therefore more minimally renounced. Contemporary cultural institutions, which range from academia to entertainment, frequently enjoy and enforce women's self-revulsion and self-contempt. Negative criticism, such as that of Madonna, proves this perverse pleasure. So do the numerous stylish academic publications that focus on the body—lesbian, gay, and transgendered, black, white, and brown, male and female, obese and anorexic, menopausal and adolescent—and that advertise an uncovering of profound sexual knowledge only to renege in language, information, personal narrative, or emotional and psychic passion.

I will not construe myself as dreary, which is the adjective I use to describe such publications. I will not disappoint my own sexiness, which was one of the wonders of my childhood. *Dreary* describes a book such as *Sexy Bodies: The Strange Carnalities of Feminism*, published in 1995 and co-edited by leading feminist philosopher Elizabeth Grosz and sociologist Elspeth Probyn. I don't blame the editors or authors for my perception of the book. The problem is my peculiar expectation, ever since I've been a scholar, that scholarship be intimate.

Maybe part of this expectation comes from reading Freud in my early pubescence. His work simultaneously resonated with my own way of experiencing and perceiving life and people and it suggested, many years later and through my unconscious, a way of writing as a professional critic: include personal narratives, sex, observation of people, and analysis. I read Guy de Maupassant's short stories concurrently with Freud. Like Freud, Maupassant felt familiar to me, friendly. His sexually ambivalent characters touched me, tenderly, and his ease with the sexual undercurrents of everyday relations gave me some ease with my own sexual sensations and behaviors. My unconscious absorbed his sophistication and its ability to charm the reader. That charm is profound; it is not the trivialized feminine quality usually connoted by the word. Charm is a kind of literary heroism.

Sexy Bodies isn't charming. It isn't intimate; it doesn't provide an enlightening voyeurism. The subtitle, *The Strange Carnalities of Feminism*, is ironic, because an un-carnal quality characterizes the collection, including Grosz's chapter, "Animal Sex," in which her fourth paragraph disappoints the reader, at least this one, by offering the possibility of Grosz's almost having philosophically discussed female orgasm through telling us about her own.

She critiques the description and analysis of her own orgasm: they wouldn't do the sensation justice, they might be perceived simply as confessional or autobiographical, and they might not have relevance for other women. How a brilliant feminist scholar's self-described and self-analyzed experience of orgasm might not be relevant to other women mystifies me. I wish that feminist scholars, especially superb ones such as Grosz, would enter this sexual and scholarly no-man's-land that she herself considers risky.

Feminist scholars describe their eating disorders, their fat bodies, their hairy faces, their rape and sexual abuse, but they do not describe their orgasms. They discuss problems and desires, but carnal pleasure, virtually never.

Frueh eats cake.

Grosz thought that evoking the pleasures of her own orgasms would involve "great disloyalty . . . spilling the beans on a vast historical 'secret.'" This reasoning doesn't convince me that Grosz should keep silence. Why would female orgasm need women's guarding? Isn't feminist scholarship *about* spilling the beans on all kinds of historical secrets? Later in the same paragraph she seems to apologize because "if what is left [after spilling the beans] is not a raw truth of women's desire," it may be "another layer in the complex overwriting of the inscriptions or representations that constitute the body or subjectivity." Layers may constitute *or* constrain pleasure.

From one perspective, a chocolate cake can't have too many layers. More layers mean more feast, more sumptuousness for the eyes and the tongue, and that sumptuousness itself constitutes a raw truth of chocolate. From another perspective, that sumptuousness has nothing to do with the essential pleasure of chocolate, which can be tasted in one bite. Grosz's evocation of the pleasure of orgasm would have given the reader an essential bite of women's carnality, of our animal sex.

Consciously exposing one's animal self isn't easy, even though we may admire others' animality—their sensual aliveness, their instinctual attunement with other living entities and with forces of nature.

My lover is like the animal I've been looking for since I was a child—a being with whom I would not have to cling to words or push for love or acceptance, a being who would know my basic self as readily as Theresa trusts her angel because she has faith. My lover is primitive. He says that sex is primitive. I feel peculiar using the word *primitive*. It reeks of unsophisticated politics: they're a primitive people—not Anglo and therefore uncivilized. But primitive means primary and basic. He knows primitive things about me, through our lovemaking, and even before we became lovers. He is primary colors blended to splendor; and he is fairy pink. I want to ask, How do you understand me? But I'm afraid to ask, afraid I'll ruin a spell that we've been weaving, a spell created by animals' magic in the presence of one another. He knows me through his breathing me and through his fingertips, both before we ever touched. He tells me that on our second date, which we would not have called a date at the time, he felt a "pulsating" in my presence. The pulsating continues. After the second time we made love, I asked him, "Are you my warrior lover?" He did not answer right away, which scared me, because I thought I'd asked a serious question too soon. But serious questions don't scare away the animal, and my lover answered, "I think *so*."

Witnessing her parents fucking shoves a child into the intimately animal. If she does not scare easy, if she can be the animal that humans are, then she stands a chance of not becoming *simply* human, strictly human, which is remotely human—*Homo sapiens* as the species that is always weighing and judging its life and love away. Orgasm is an avenue out of fear, a fact of warrior heart, angelic lucidity, and fairy vision.

* * * * * * * * * * * * *

Frueh sits.

Often when I see you I can't contain myself. Not only do I smile, I start to laugh. Laughter is akin to orgasm, for the contents of the unconscious overwhelm us. Laughter is animal—primitive— and it is angelic—lightness manifested in a delicious burst of emotion. When we laugh in joy we're in the pink—of fairyland—and our hearts are lawless, beyond the cultural negation of pleasure; both the current fears and ancient traumas that burden us, that make our bodies feel heavy to ourselves and others, that make us more full of thoughts than we need to be—they retreat: we are warriors, laughing, though we may not be aware of it, at whatever our enemy or tormentor might be. When I see you I am giddy. I whirl in a radical decentering.

No one else has made me laugh like you make me laugh, and my mirth initiates me into new, though primal scenes. We are enjoying orgasms—our coming at the same time and

· ·

Frueh digs into the cake with her hand, eats the cake,
licks her palm, her fingers. Then she invites the
audience to eat the cake, to share it with her.

Frueh sits in a circle with her BFA *seminar of eight students. As usual, some take seats with attached desks that can be raised and some take chairs that Frueh and others have brought from her office or elsewhere. A snug top, mid-calf skirt, bare legs, anklets, and low-heeled black spectator Mary Janes feel comfortably familiar to the audience—for it is Frueh's typical professorial attire —and comfortable to Frueh, who moves freely and gracefully as she frequently changes position: she crosses and uncrosses her legs at the knee, and she raises one leg to the seat of the chair and crosses it underneath the other. The school year is about to end and over the semester this class has traveled far together into the subjects of love and art.*

Thank you for your openness. Thank you for your presentness. Thank you for your honesty. Thank you for your love. You take my breath away. And you give me new spaces in which to breathe. Breathlessness that comes from loving deepens our breathing. This kind of excitement soothes the heart and relaxes it, so that the heart expands.

As you may know, *aspire* comes from the Latin word *aspirare*, to breathe upon, and *inspire* comes from the Latin word *inspirare*, meaning to breathe. The etymological facts for both *aspire* and *inspire*, in my *Webster's New World Dictionary*, read "see SPIRIT." Seeing *spirit*, we find the Latin word *spiritus*, meaning breath, courage, vigor, the soul, life. The words *spirit* and *breath* cover corporeal, ontological, and ethical territory. Looking at language, we see that spirituality is very much material.

I am so glad that you will all be in my home next week, for our party. At parties, the partygoer aspires to have fun, to breathe life upon the conversations and the actions, upon the eating and the drinking. At parties, we hope that our fellow partygoers will inspire us—enliven us, inspirit us, give us the courage to talk honestly, to laugh, to dance, and maybe even to sing. We will provide food and drink for our party, for our physical, our sensate pleasures, and we will *be* our beauty and our love, food that will fill my home and inspire me as I enter my sabbatical year. We will be the mystics who celebrate our knowledge of the invisible—love and beauty—and whose knowledge of them impels us towards the wisdom that is the artist's real work.

Last week in class I said, "I'm a lost soul and I don't know where I'm going," then I corrected myself and said, "I'm found. I'm a found soul and I don't know where I'm going." The lost soul asserts a pathetic authority. The found soul asserts a degree of grace, and that is *its* authority. Remember the day I questioned my authority? At first, I stated, only *half*-jokingly, "Maybe I should assert more authority," and you guys said, "No, don't." I listened to my quick and seemingly simple questioning of my teaching posture, and I listened to your quick and earnest response, which contained an element of fear. That I might transmute into an authoritarian, which meant that I would try to control you and that you would have to obey. Which meant that we all would become rigid, that we would have to hold our breath in one another's presence. Which meant that our hearts would have shrunk because if you cannot breathe, you cannot speak, you cannot relax, you cannot live. I did not want to become the authority who pressures the life out of other people's hearts. My wondering if I should assert more authority held a fear of my own—of further expanding my heart and further finding myself, of further allowing you to inspire me and me to inspire you. Thank you for your absolutely clear response. Thank you for your faith in my degree of grace, which, without you, could not have shone as luminously this semester, nor which, without you, could have grown in this breathing space that we have created together. You are my amazing grace.

The found soul, whatever its degree of grace, begins to create a revolution. From what you have said in class and written, I perceive the revolutionary's responsiveness—of open-heartedness—mostly to Al Lingis, Norman O. Brown, and each of the artists whose words we have read. A revolution of the heart does not go around and around in circles, recycling heartaches, the same old and constipated shit of Denis de Rougemont's "passion myth," the dim perspective of "woe is me" and "woe is the world." That would cause a tenuous and perhaps even burgeoning revolution of the heart to asphyxiate itself.

The cover and the title of Wendy Langford's *Revolutions of the Heart* caught my eye at a scholarly conference last fall: red heart, one golden cupid, and a couple putti playing violins. I was looking for enlightenment, as always, about love, and since I was planning to focus on the subject of love in the coming semester's BFA seminar, I thought that this book, grounded in sociology, could be a helpful variation to the list of more philosophical studies that I was planning for the class to read, because Langford is a feminist dealing with contemporary heterosexual relationships. Her bleak analysis and outlook—we women and men succumb to idealistic projections of one another and are pretty much doomed—drown in the delusions that beset us as descendants of the absurdly tragic romance between Tristan and Iseult. *Gender, Power and the Delusions of Love,* the subtitle of Langford's book, gives away the secret of love as a crappy status quo. Gender: a righteous femininity and masculinity, respectively locked into women's and men's psyches, grossly inhibit the continuation of the playful, trusting love that initiates amorous relationships. Power: this psychic inhibition disempowers us. Delusions of love: they bind us so tightly that we are cripples whom love has actually disabled. So our hearts emotionally resemble the scorched and battered icon at the center of Langford's cover, the heart, half of which is black, floating like an unanchored wound against a background that suggests a blood-stained wall.

You are the revolution, and you are not a delusion. Love is not a delusion and delusion is not revolutionary. Revolution is not the gory, ashen heart on the cover of Langford's scholarly woe. Love does not have to be up against the wall—interrogated until it dies from the barrage of scholars' arrows or the batterings from lovers' arguments.

Mired in Langford's bleakness, I would define love as an exile into a virtual emotion. But I refuse the stagnancy of a definition that deters what it defines. I breathe the reality of fresh air and pull away from the grief caused by her performance of an autopsy on the heart. I take my heart to the wide-open spaces described by Brown with "there is only poetry." The revolution that is real is the love that conquers all. Revolution is not the archaic and archetypal spectacle conceived by Daddy Knows Best because he invented, built, and aimed the weaponry that disrupts and sickens, humiliates and ultimately deadens the heart. From arsenals of often dizzying and useless information, dumped by the news and entertainment media into brains that have already seized up from the lusterless streams and snags of data that clutter our every day; to the artillery of ideologies that have overwhelmed us because we abandon skeptical intelligence in the need to simply get our day's tasks done; to the emotional as well as physical slaps and beatings in intimate relationships, the incongruency of "I love you" poured into hearts that long ago recoiled from the needling, needy, and just plain sick perpetrators, recoiled into a toxic shock of protest driven into some tiny vault of hope: the shadows and stalkers, the slick and surly and seductive range of a cold patriarchy create exile. (All patriarchs are not cold. I refer to my father as a gentle patriarch.)

Revolution takes us out of exile and brings us home. Revolution is resolutely homegrown; it grows from the heart, from yours and mine. You are the revolution, because you are the poetry. You are the Om, the drone of Love that generates all things. Love has the power to conquer all because, like poetry, it is everywhere to begin with.

Hearing the word *conquer,* you may think of subjugation and destruction, of the vanquished and an arrogant winner. Love conquers all: the winner occupies the loser's heart, like an imperialist or colonizing force. Hearing the word *conquer,* I go to my dictionary. *Conquer,* from the Latin word *conquirere,* to search for, procure. *Procure,* from the Latin word *procurare,* to take care of, attend to, its root being *cura,* which means care and from which the English word *cure* derives. Love conquers all because the lover takes care of the heart, restores it to a sound condition.

Many people would call naïve an individual whose faith in love the healer is absolute. To them, I say, Martin Luther King was a realist. To them I say, I would rather be a realist than a cynic. To them I say, I would rather be a bridge—providing connection and security—than a charred or blistered heart that denies its pain with bluster.

. . . .

*Frueh sings a chorus of Simon and Garfunkel's
"Bridge over Troubled Water."*

"You're loose," she said. At the reception for the student exhibition a student whom I know very little walked up to me and said, "We were saying you look kittenish." I *was* wearing my black leather bustier, but . . . Wow! I am honored to be perceived as loose and kittenish by the people to whom I profess. Loose and kittenish. How rich and simple can you get?

Many of you have asked me what I'll be doing on sabbatical. I'll be writing my book, a memoir, much of which I have already written. I'll be presenting my performance *The Aesthetics of Orgasm,* the one I delivered here this past autumn during the faculty show. I don't know right now what the venues will be. I'll go to Brisbane in July to present a piece I'm calling *The Performance of Pink* at a conference, Making an Appearance: Fashion, Dress and Consumption. I'll be at the Banff Centre in Alberta, right up against the Canadian Rockies, from mid-September to mid-October, in a critical and curatorial studies residency. I'll be enjoying myself. With disciplines I love, like bodybuilding and yoga. With friends and rest and gardening. I'll go on vacations: in Brisbane I'm treating myself to a luxury hotel—at special conference rates!—and spending time poolside, in massages, and at the botanical garden that is next door to the hotel. I'm going to Tucson in May to visit my friend Peggy, and I'll visit my sister Ren in the Missouri Ozarks. I've been wanting to go to Delphi for a number of years, and I'm sure I'll do it on sabbatical. I've accepted an invitation from Al to visit him in his new place, which he describes as "a funky rustic house on a sort of mountain" outside Baltimore. I wonder what I'll dream in his home.

I'm feeling open and excited about my time away from teaching. Which I will miss. As I will miss all of you.

Think of me in pink. A big pink heart that's radiant.

. . . .

Frueh offers chocolates to everyone as she says, "I love you."

MAC's Dubonnet colors Frueh's mouth, and her hairstyle, in a ponytail at the nape of her neck, shows off ornate, bronze-toned earrings from which dangle sparkly pink glass beads. Two vases of mid-range pink flowers, one stage right—roses—and one stage left—variable depending on what is available at a florist—complement the pinks in Frueh's costume: a knee-length leather skirt with a ruffle at the bottom; short brocade boots with organza laces; the laces in the front of her off-white satin brocade bustier. A plate of heart-shaped cookies decorated with pink sugar sprinkles sits on a pedestal near the roses. Frueh eats the cookies throughout the performance, whenever she feels like it.

I am pink flamingo, I am strawberry-milkshake pink. I am the pinks of shells left by our seas and oceans on the planet's sands, I am the pinks of more flowers than you can name. I am all the floral pinks, which means I am more pinks than many people can imagine words to differentiate them. I am the pinks that warm your heart when you are giving and you are given love. I am the pinks that heat your passion to the point of apparently no return, the pinks that seem to compromise you. I am the pinks that ask their wearer for her flair and courage. I am the pinks that temper pain, the pinks that nurture tenderness. I am pro-peace pink. I am the pinks grown so at home with their own beauty that they are not impatient for your love. Pink, I am bountiful and not complacent. In pink I am a warrior, I am a revolution.

Pink is a family of colors that can be designated by two kinship lines: soft and hard. *Soft* means light pink and pale pink. *Hard* means hot pink and shocking pink.

Whether hard or soft, pink doesn't carry the threat of red. It is red's cognate, but we think of it as a faint version and therefore easier to take. Red is bold and pink is demure, and this formulation of difference between red and pink reveals the trivializing association of pink with femininity, especially with the culturally sweetened notions of little girls' femininity. In its hardness and its softness, pink is frothy, piquant, fierce, and delicious, and we are delinquent hearts when we remain unconscious of pink's complexity and dynamism.

Our trifling treatment of pink defends against its potency. I've read that when someone wears pink, she attracts love, or at the least, generates happiness in those who are looking at her. Pink unblocks the heart and releases good feelings. How well fashion designer Betsey Johnson understands this. The walls of her boutiques are painted fuchsia, and it's easy to find pink clothes in them. Pink sells clothes because pink lifts spirits. Buddhists consider attentiveness to right-here right-now a warrior practice, and they know that such attentiveness is at the center of love and enables its release. The performance of pink is the performance of love. Not as an act, a game of surface behaviors, but rather as a lifting of one's own and others' spirits in continuing acts of kindness, lightness, openness, and freedom.

As Andrew Lang writes in his preface to *The Pink Fairy Book*, originally published in 1897, "nothing prevents us from being kind, and no kind man, woman, or beast or bird, ever comes to anything but good in these oldest fables of the world." Fairy tales are simple lessons that help us to be kind. In a contemporary fairy tale of sorts, a group calling itself Code Pink: Women for Peace was staging protest rallies prior to the recent United States–initiated war against Iraq. Longtime social activists Medea Benjamin, Jodie Evans, and Starhawk founded Code Pink, and one reason that they chose the color pink is precisely because it represents the female and the feminine. Not only is Code Pink women-led; primarily women have participated in its acute and humorous performances, such as giving pink slips—actual lingerie—to Senators Hillary Rodham Clinton and Dianne

Feinstein in early March 2003 for not doing enough to prevent the war. Receiving a "pink slip" is, of course, a euphemism for getting fired from a job.

In an idealistic sense, promoting peace is an ultimate kindness. In Lang's words to the child readers of *The Pink Fairy Book*, kindness begets good. Peace is a good, as is the freedom that, ideally, results from kindness. Code Pink "performers," both women and men, wear pink. CNN correspondent Maria Hinojosa, covering a Code Pink demonstration in Washington, D.C., on March 8, International Women's Day, reported that all of the demonstrators were "wearing lots of pink. And not just regular pink, but pink flamingo." Pink flamingo: a hard pink, a strong pink. Flamingo pink: a gay and flaming pink for freedom.

How free I feel when I watch director Todd Haynes's *Velvet Goldmine*, a 1998 film whose fictional story is based in the glam rock period of the early 1970s. My eyes widen with Haynes's vision of camp fashion's splendor and fragility, so that I feel as silly and deliriously gorgeous as the crew of beautiful men who love and fuck one another and sometimes women: rock stars Brian Slade and Curt Wild, and Jack Fairy, apocryphal descendant of Oscar Wilde. Decked in high pink blush, Slade sings to a lily the color of peppermint ice cream. The petals expand as his breath caresses them. I am breathless and I breathe more fully than usual, for I am blossoming, like a flower, like a fairy, like a freedom lover.

Several summers ago, as I dwelled within temperatures near one hundred degrees, in Reno, Nevada, where I live, and within flushes characteristic of menopause, I often wore a hot pink camisole decorated with even hotter pink flowers. Camisole by Betsey Johnson. Flushes, that's what I called my heat, because it felt pink rather than hot flashing red. Pink is a tart's delight. Young tarts, if they're lucky, become fairies.

On a salmon-pink carpet filled with girls' paraphernalia, Slade and Wild, played by Ken dolls, consummate their love. Pink *is* the color of love; and the other day, after I told my friend Mike, a former student, about several male students' reactions this past spring semester to a pair of bright pink suede high heels that I wore to class, he exclaimed, "Orgasm!" So pink is the color of sexual pleasure as well as being the color of love. Seth had surprised me with "I could get into those." I was wearing sheer black stay-ups, and Gabe had grinned, "Great shoes! Great color combination!" And after Patrick noted that he liked my shoes, he bent down to touch one, which astounded me. The shoe's style is at once elegant and playful with its decorative straps and its rosette ornamenting the pointy toe. "I like this, the line," he remarked as he stroked a strap. "I like the rosette," I offered. I thanked each of the students, all in their twenties and all art students, as is Mike, and to each compliment I also laughed, "It must be the pink!" For I must have known that the color pink permitted the young men's comments. I'm sure that the ease and the elation that my body conveyed as I enjoyed my pink shoes gave my students permission to enjoy them too. My comment and my body freed the young men's courage to respond aloud to pink's allure.

Valentines lure some of us because of their abundant pinks. Valentines feature pink because it is the color of happy love and sex. "Nothing says [I love you] like pink," asserts Stanislas de Quercize, president and CEO of Cartier in New York. Cartier introduced a rose gold jewelry collection in time for Valentine's Day 2003. (In a March 17 article in *The Seattle Post-Intelligencer*, de Quercize reveals that the pink collection was conceived two years ago.) Valentines also feature red, like pink, a color associated with romantic passion. Red may proclaim love's fiery pangs and burning defeats. Unlike red, pink refreshes us with the many delicacies and pleasures of romance. Consequently, it embarrasses us— because we read delicate passions as feminine.

Stereotypically, femininity belongs in pink's *soft* lineage. There, it can be a weak and easy color—neither strong nor difficult as pinks in the hard lineage can be. *Soft* derives from an Indo-European base whose basic sense is "fitting, friendly, suited to." Mild and gentle pinks connote innocence, so they are *fitting* for little girls and so-called old ladies, both of whom have been deemed *suited to* not-sex by cultural conventions. The restraints of gender and age conventions domesticate pink into a safe and comfortable color: it conveys the culturally domesticated sexuality of old and young females. Domesticated pinks give their *observers* the comfort of believing that at least some classes of human females are sexually off-limits or pure or undemanding or boring. In its softest tones and connota- tions, pink is not just pale; it is pallid and bland. Pink can be *friendly* to those who wish to relax into the notion that femininity is non-threatening.

Moving up the scale from the softest soft, pink conveys a femininity that is not entirely innocent. Pink is a lingerie color and a lipstick. Meg Cohen Ragas and Karen Kozlowski note in their *Read My Lips: A Cultural History of Lipstick* that "husbands . . . prefer their wives in pink lipstick (or none at all)—and their mistresses in red." Which makes pink a comfortable, everyday sensuousness. Pink is a perfect boudoir color. It *was* a color of

Rococo boudoirs. In lingerie, lipstick, and boudoirs, pink performs a sensuality whose characteristics represent fleshiness, most likely female or feminine fleshiness.

Pink panties and slips with a little lace suited my taste. Light pinks were a girl's choice, or a likely color for a gift. At one of my girlhood birthday parties, I opened a box containing a pair of panties. Following my suburb's custom, which was to show each present to your celebrants as soon as you handled it yourself, I held up the gift—which, I hope, was pink. I heard sometime later that day or the next day that I'd done a tasteless thing by displaying underwear. I don't recall that this was Mom's opinion, and I'd like to believe that it belonged to one of my friend's mothers. I'd like to believe that my mother didn't find garments that touched little girls' sexual parts to be nasty or too sexy to show to other little girls, or inappropriate articles of a little girl's excitement.

The not-quite softest pinks, besides being "little-girl" and "old-lady" pink, are also "sissy" pink. I've loved pink since I was a little girl. I don't remember any pink clothes, other than panties and slips, that I wore as a girl, except a tutu for ballet class, but I remember a humiliating grade school incident whose visual source was the pink knee socks I wore with a dress that showed the whole sock. Vivian, a girl in my class, teased me about them in a very nasty way, the way that people mock fairy men, calling them sissies. Her language attempted to dishearten me—and I mean dishearten like disembowel, to remove my heart. Pink's use in valentines associates it with the heart. I didn't retort with words, I held back tears, and I've defended pink ever since—a warrior for pink and in pink—by wearing it and by telling people it's my favorite color (which it often has been), a *primary* color for me.

Worn with a warrior's passion, pink is an attribute, not an accessory, and it creates an aura, not an outfit. Pink is a state of mind. This is clear not only from my assertion of *attribute* and *aura* but also in the phrase "Think pink," which often appears in news media fashion stories that tout the color as a must-have—this was the case a lot this past winter and spring—and in the phrase "pink think," used by Lynn Peril in her book *Pink Think: Becoming a Woman in Many Uneasy Lessons*. Peril discusses the enforced femininity for women that pervaded the United States from the 1940s to the 1970s and that endures into the current century. Despite the dis-ease that achieving a properly pink femininity may cause some women, a bevy of mid-range pinks can create, for both the woman in pink clothes and cosmetics and a person who experiences her, variously easy states of mind and emotion. In the February 11, 2003 *Edmonton Journal*, Los Angeles stylist Brooke Dulien believes that "a hint of pink" in the midst of other winter clothing colors creates an "approachable, flirtatious" look. Pink think common sense knows that pink does wonders for the complexion, so we should not be surprised that in a *Today* show interview last April 15, when anchor Katie Couric interviewed cosmetics queen Bobbi Brown about spring makeup trends, Couric called pink a "flattering" color. Both women's use of *pretty* a couple times reinforces the idea that pink is a comforting color.

As Brown affirms, "pink is always big in spring, but now, in times of stress, pink makes you feel pretty, and right now, we just need to feel good." Brown is referring to post-9/11 stress, a date that appears, explicitly and implicitly, in other winter and spring '03 fashion stories about pink. Dr. Leatrice Eiseman, a color psychologist, asserts in the March 17 edition of *The Seattle Post-Intelligencer*, "I think a lot of the pink is emanating from this need to wrap ourselves in something that's nurturing. . . . It's a baby blanket color that wants us to wrap up and suck our thumbs. It's a feel good color." Being held by Mommy next to her pink nipples. On March 3, the Sharon Mosley Copley News Service was exuberant about pink, which will "put a smile on your face." The headline is "Pink Pick-Me-Ups," and Erica Archambault, public relations manager for the Gap, posits, "With a winter that seems never-ending and all the uncertainty in the world, we're ready for the bright cheeriness of pink." Mid-range pinks—the feminine—mitigate terrorist threats and impending war—the masculine. Venus pacifies Mars.

Gender convention associates femininity and woman with display, just as it associates them with comfort. And, as pink moves from soft to hard, it also moves from the cozy caress of comfort into the dangers of display. Pink has the capacity to comfort us because, as Dr. Eiseman asserts, it's "fun." Party fun, playful fun. Yet, as pinks grow hotter, floral becomes florid, frail becomes flashy, and no-sex becomes sex-charged. No wonder the cover of David Batchelor's *Chromophobia* is heat-stroke fuchsia; and the endpapers of Bill Dobbins's *The Women: Photographs of the Top Female Bodybuilders* are a voluptuously warm and tangy pink, like petals that I'd like to taste. Flagrant, pyrotechnic, and paroxysmal pinks; shocking pinks that exult, "Orgasm!" Being grasped in the pink embrace of your lover's cunt. Being penetrated by the pink of your lover's cock. *Shock* probably derives from the Middle Dutch *schokken*, to collide, and from the Indo-European base *skeub(h)-*, shove. Our wearing of pink is the display of our animal and erotic fevers and radiance, so the hard pinks we wear, which represent our most intimate skin, collide with propriety and shove us into embarrassment, as much as softer pinks embarrass us because they suggest delicate, feminine passions.

When I was a little girl, I explored my genitals, my beautiful dark pinkness, while looking in the big mirror that faced my parents' bed. In that bedroom where I surprised them fucking one time and where I celebrated myself in my mother's clothes and makeup, I looked attentively at my genitals, my fingers slid into my vagina, and they practiced pressures on my clitoris. My hands embraced my labia and mons veneris and lingered over the various and variable intensities of pleasures that were and are my body. I enjoyed myself visually and sensually.

    I played with pink and I loved myself. The looking and the masturbation weren't a *trying* to love myself or a *learning* to love myself. I simply loved myself.

Pink shocks us out of complacency. It *queers* our complacency. As the gay film director Derek Jarman understood in his *Chroma: A Book of Colour,* "Colour seems to have a Queer bent." And pink has one of the queerest.

Fairy song:

> Thinking pinking we are stinking
> With substances from our pink linking
> With Eros and with Aphrodite
> We are rooted we are flighty
> In the very best of ways
> Flying happy flying gay
> Flying in our pink array

Flying fairies, in our high spirits we are in the pink together. High-flying fairies, in the haute pink of our warrior armor, which is attention to right-here, right-now, we are making revolution, making love.

Frueh enters stage right sparkling in a dress of white moiré velvet. Its skintight fit through the thighs, its bit of a flare to mid-calf, and its luminosity display shape—from nipples to muscles—and movement—of spinal twisting, of rising, walking, and sitting, of bending and stretching. Frueh's arms, legs, and feet are bare and she wears no jewelry. Pearly pink polish decorates her fingernails and toenails. A deep and subtle winey-red colors her lips. Her hair is loose. She walks gracefully and casually to center stage where a standing microphone and a black music stand, holding the text, await her. A folding chair sits to their left, next to a simple table that holds the following items: a large white sheet cake decorated with white icing and white rosebuds and small blossoms; a box of white plastic forks, white paper plates, a cake server, a clear glass of drinking water; a muff of white rabbit fur; and a wreath of white roses.

Some words work miracles. How innocent I am!

With that exclamation, my shoulders, arms, and spine relax, my anus and vagina, my intestines are at ease, my forehead feels the smile that curves my lips and plumps my cheeks, I let my being sing simply, like white roses.

Frueh picks up the wreath and places it on her head.

How innocent I am! I hear Alphonso Lingis celebrating himself with those words of wonder, which serve as a mantra, a verbal formulation of truth, a mantra, an incantation of self-care, a mantra—flowing like a lyric from Al's throat, in my imagination, and full of joy, like one of the value terms that he praises in his book *Dangerous Emotions*. Although Al does not include *innocent* in his discussion of value terms, such as *beautiful, happy,* and *healthy,* I hear it in the chapter "Violations," where he focuses on value terms, and *innocent* resonates throughout the book, in which he titles one chapter "Innocence."

I hear innocence everywhere in *Dangerous Emotions* because that book is a dancing prayer for innocence, whose existence and whose practice by human beings closes their "respectful" and "respectable" distance from one another—people's chosen containment within their individual boundaries of body and ego. I put quotation marks around *respectful* and *respectable,* because in "Violations" Al critiques respect. He asserts, "Respect is respect for the limits, the boundaries, the space of others, and thus for their natures." Within that framework, violations are the welcome and pleasurable actions, events, and unpredictable responses, such as sex and laughter, that create "the dissolution of boundaries." Dissolve those boundaries, and the nature of people—which is their innocence— appears. Distance closed with a caress, a trill of delight, a rollicking good time. In Al's thinking, emotions are dangerous because they violate our discontent, which manifests as complacency.

Essence and innocence are inseparable. So innocence is an innate and always releasable human quality. Human beings obscure their own and others' innocence—they defile it, they veil it, they fear it, they disown it; they lose faith in it—yet innocence is our core and courage. Innocence is both ever-present and in need of our assistance. As both essence and practice, innocence protests our beauty, happiness, and health. It protests our value.

Protesting war, protesting terrorism: our society misunderstands the word *protest* to mean against. *Protest* derives from the Latin *pro,* for, and *testis,* witness, so the protester is actually a witness *for* peace, a witness *for* love. The protester implicitly invokes value terms: How peaceful I am! How loving I am!

How innocent I am! This celebratory declaration is Al's implicit prayer to his readers—for their celebration of themselves.

Let us eat ambrosia.

. . . .

Frueh slices a square of cake, slides it onto a plate, takes a fork from the box, and sits down to eat. Enjoyment and leisure characterize her actions and eating, as they do each time she invites her audience to witness their own innocence with "Let us eat ambrosia."

Al asserts the power of value terms. When we affirm, "How gorgeous I am!" we increase our beauty, and every living thing with which we come in contact rejoices with us in the expansion of our loveliness. Indeed, they expand too. If we exclaim, "How miserable I am!" an equally powerful resonance of effect removes the life from living things. Whether value terms of wonder or woe are resounding within and from us, *I* includes *you.* Using value terms, we make ourselves immeasurable, beyond the range of numbers that age us, that declare us fat, prone to heart attacks, or sexually promiscuous. When I say, "How innocent I am!" I return us to our natures.

Let us eat ambrosia. We who are delicious love to revel in our appetite.

. . . .

Frueh eats cake.

Sweet and white, I am the rose that has always lived in sun and rain, enough to soak and warm my earth. Like all us roses, I have heard that we bud, then bloom, then wither. As if we fit into human beings' notion of woman's beauty, which they diminish into years of budding, blooming, withering, a sequence of loss. That notion sees in seasons—one, two, three, four; now you see it—my corolla—now you don't.

I see this: one, which is the erotic number. One, like Eros, is the connection of everything.

Gaze into my erotic eyes; my vision has no measure. How infinitely beautiful I am! Like the White Rose of Dante's Paradise.

Innocence seems self-explanatory. The innocent are definitely pure and good, perhaps naïve, even foolish. Most people take those meanings for granted; but AI does not. AI knows the connection between innocence and heroes, an erotic connection in which neither term exists in isolation from the other.

The term *innocent victim* shapes people's current misunderstanding of innocence, most likely without their awareness. The innocent victim is abused, not responsible, whereas the hero rises to the occasion and has a job to do; he assumes ultimate responsibility. Those notions designate divergent capacities and values, in which innocence means passivity and heroism means action. Contrast that formulation, which fashions a common model of innocence and heroism, to a phrase of AI's, "the innocence of action," in which innocent and hero are one and the same—our core and courage.

In the common model of innocence, narratives of death connect innocents and heroes. For example, reckonings of the 9/11 attacks on the World Trade Center towers perceive the buildings' workers and visitors who died as innocent victims. The responders are construed as heroes who worked to save their fellow human beings. In those stories, the particulars of physical proximity ironically maintain the separation of innocent and hero.

Accounting and recounting: in narratives related to the previous ones, all the 9/11 dead, whether innocents or heroes, are counted as dead, and as such they are used, by politicians and news media, to give purpose to the living.

When I read AI on innocence, I see the living giving purpose to the living. I am talking about big-hearted people, for shrinking and shrunken hearts are killing and have killed the human beings whom they inhabit. Decrease of spirit is the antithesis of innocence. AI admires big hearts, big core and courage: "a retired person living by the sea where the sea birds are engulfed in an oil spill"; a dancer who "heads for the studio for the day's work . . . [because] dance must exist and her body is made for dancing"; "a guard in the Himalayan forest during the dry season"; a woman who "finds in her heart a song that is hers alone to sing."

Frueh sings some of Bob Dylan's "Love Minus Zero/No Limit."
She changes Dylan's "she" to "it."

> *White roses sing attuned to angels. How clearly they are joining in the sweet and divine textures of our canticles, sung here on earth.*
>
> *Let us eat ambrosia.*

Frueh eats cake.

The singer, the dancer, the guard, and the retired person all do what they have to do, because, as Al observes, "the heroic is obligatory." It is *what I have to do*, a phrase that he emphasizes by italicizing it and by repeating it five times beginning halfway through his essay on innocence. *What I have to do* is not what I am forced to do or what someone asks or demands that I do. Those are standard ways that people think about having to do something: what they have to do is a drag, so it is neither loving nor ethical action.

I see Al's understanding that innocent action is both loving and ethical in the following statement and question, which respectively open and close a paragraph in "Innocence": he asserts, "When I decide to do what I want, I discover what I have to do," and he asks, "Is it not that I discover what I want to do only when I discover what I have to do?" Innocence impels self-discovery through satisfaction of desire. Discovery and desire are reciprocal. When we offer to the universe our desire, we receive discovery. When we offer to the universe our willingness to discover, we satisfy our desire. Innocence instigates us to act in behalf of others, and in so doing, we act in behalf of ourselves. Innocence, unlike an imprisoning purity, built of abnegation, shame, or moral superiority, is instinctual, and we would do well to trust the heart that frees itself from the isolation of self-denial. In our union of discovery and desire we pay attention: we are clear observers of our surroundings and our circumstances, and in that state we are extraordinary, which simply means that we are clean of overthinking and underdoing, of the muck into which we all have sunk sometimes, convinced of our ineptness and incompetence.

Is it wise to trust the inattentive?

Here we are together, singing billows of white roses, attentive to every color all at once. White: it transmits, reflects, and radiates all visible rays of the spectrum. White: ambrosially inclusive.

Innocent, instinctual, unfettered hearts, we are like divemasters who move Al to write: "We entrust ourselves to divemasters in whom clairvoyant attentiveness and courage are instinctual." Innocence is an obligation, innocence obliges a person to act creatively, generously, lovingly, and ethically; in other words, heroically. Innocence compels right action.

In-, not, plus *nocens*, present participle of *nocere*, to do wrong to. The Latin roots of *innocent* suggest that the innocent is one to whom no wrong has been done and it also suggests that the innocent does no wrong to anyone.

In our misunderstanding of innocence, where "innocent victims" thrive, they are wronged. Attacked, by a particularity of molester, abuser, or terrorist, innocents are defenseless and therefore they lose their lives or their innocence itself. So someone else defends innocents, whether they are dead or living, and loss defines *innocent*.

Looking over a list of books, in the University of Nevada, Reno, library, that include *innocent* or *innocence* in the title of the book itself or of a chapter, I see that loss and its correlate, damage, overwhelm descriptions and implications of innocence in a state of health or freedom. (I am interested neither in subtitles nor in the content of the books.) The only titles that indicate health or freedom are *Innocence Found* and *Innocence Re-gained*, and they suggest two intertwined motifs: innocence *may* be essence, and we return to innocence after our corruption. Loss and damage figure in the following titles: *Innocence Betrayed; Innocence Destroyed; Innocence Lost*—six titles; *Innocence Punished; Innocent Bystander; Innocent Bystanders*—two titles; *Innocent Casualties; Innocent Civilians; Innocent Sufferer; Innocent Victim; Innocent Victims.*

Embedded in Al's model of innocence is the reality of freedom—the acts, inspirations, and pleasures contained in the union of discovery and desire. In contrast, embedded in the conventions of misunderstood innocence is the *notion* of innocence as a touchstone of freedom. We assume the reality of loss of innocence and we fear that loss, because we conceive it to be a loss of freedom. Consequently, innocence activates fear.

"Freedom's just another word for nothin' left to lose"—as Kris Kristofferson wrote in the lyrics of "Me and Bobby McGee." In those famous words, freedom is a result of loss. And that's a mild interpretation. More severely, freedom is a state of bereftness. And harsher yet, it is desolation. While we superficially think that innocence is benign, at a deeper level it scares us. We think that the loss of innocence is true and we perform that "truth" in the way that we believe in and act out the many narratives of loss with which our culture burdens us: we anticipate loss of beauty, loss of health, loss of mind—all of which have their roots in loss of faith—and our anticipation creates materialization.

I find myself in white. I am like the girl in Joshua Reynolds's The Age of Innocence, *which he painted c. 1788—simply styled white dress, bare feet, dark hair in waves, touches of pink. Her pinks are the accessories of a sash at the waist and a ribbon tied in a bow that decorates the top of her head. I am not wearing whitest white—a delusion used to sterilize humanity, to bleach the heart of soil.*

Whiter than white: that is the myth of childhood innocence; an ideal created in fine art by *The Age of Innocence*, according to art historian Anne Higonnet in her *Pictures of Innocence: The History and Crisis of Ideal Childhood*, as part of an emerging view of children as ultimate innocents. The sitter for Reynolds's little girl, his great-niece, was about six years old when she modeled for the picture, and in Higonnet's words, the child in the painting represents the "image of the Romantic child [that] replaces what we have lost or what we fear to lose." Innocence *à la* the Romantic child gained popular consensus in the nineteenth century, although depictions, from Charles Dodgson's photos of Alice Liddell in the last quarter of that century to Sally Mann's photos of her children in the late 1980s and early 1990s, have disrupted the ideal. Higonnet elucidates the late-twentieth-century crisis of disruption, beginning in 1980 with the notorious Calvin Klein jeans ads featuring Brooke Shields, who was born in 1965.

Whiter than white: it is not only an impossibility, but a horror. Poet and artist Henri Michaux, writing "With Mescaline," captures that creepiness in his descriptions of "absolute white" and "white whiter than all whiteness": "White without compromise, by exclusion, by the total eradication of non-white . . . mad, exasperated, shrieking with whiteness. Fanatical, furious, . . . implacable, murderous." Whiter than white is a warlord that crushes sanity and joy. Whiter than white is a state of war—*against* innocence expressed and enacted as *What I have to do*. Whiter than white kills innocence, which loses every battle.

The qualities of childhood innocence analyzed by Higonnet alert us to the values that the warlord simultaneously defends and attacks. Immaculateness and blandness overarch the rest. As she tells us, "no class, no gender, and no thoughts" characterize the Romantic child, who is a perfect void, "born innocent of adult faults, social evils, and sexuality," a tabula rasa of "blank" mind.

O this white rose was full of sex and laughter, happily inscribed with primal joy and wonder! O I was a miracle of spirit, mind, and body! How innocent I was when masturbating, looking at my genitals, and dressing up in Mom's nail polish, lipstick, Persian lamb, and mink! O this white rose is all that ease and passion!

One could die trying to be whiter than white. Al, white rose, helps us to live, which is why he writes over and over about kisses and caresses, beauty, seduction, and hilarity. He helps us see that we are born innocent, like the Romantic child; but unlike that paragon, we do grow up, to be reborn as innocents again and again. Al begins "Innocence" by thinking about birth—the amazing reality that each of us exquisitely individual persons is here!

Born to be alive!

His essay elucidates that fact, which expands throughout *Dangerous Emotions*, because we know as we read his book that in each act of our own heroism we are reborn in innocence.

While Higonnet describes the child-innocent in terms of a neutered and neutral purity, she also discusses details of that ideal's middle-class and feminine aspects—"affluent cleanliness and absence of want," "immaculately white fragile dresses on . . . well-fed little bodies"—and the psychic, sexual, and social seductiveness and desirability of innocence are a constant subtext in her book. Powerful in its psychosexual charge even in the late eighteenth century, the ideal innocent, when very young, is also trivialized through what Higonnet sees as miniaturization by clothing that looks too big.

White roses are just the right size for pleasures, full-scale. Fulfilled by our desirability, our affluence of ambrosial, sparkling white, we stroll barefoot into heaven.

The Romantic ideal of childhood innocence informs today's common—and nostalgic— model of innocence itself. The child, the innocent: one can shelter her or ravage her, because vulnerability is her virtue. Being vulnerable and passive, rather than receptive, she is never free. Whereas Al's hero-innocent is beautifully and mightily receptive. Receptivity enables *What I have to do*. Receptivity to desire, to calling, to mission. Receptivity as attentiveness to appetite.

Let us eat ambrosia.

I wondered what a student meant, not long ago, when, as we were talking, he named me an alpha female. I took it as a compliment . . . but soon I was not sure about that, for I, among others I know, have joked about alpha males of the human species: not only are they dominant in an aggressive way, they exhibit overweening aggressiveness along with other unattractive excesses of conventional masculinity. Then I realized that an alpha female would not display the qualities of an alpha male. Of course not! She would be an epitome of conventional female and feminine qualities, and so . . . in my desire to align my thinking with beauty and expansion, I discovered a path that I had previously feared: receptivity. The union of desire and discovery gave me poetic license. Or perhaps I should say they gave me bravado. As Al reminds us in "Innocence," "Bravado swells in feeling seduced by your heroic existence." Ahhh, receptive to the swells of innocence in heart and mind that materialize in gracious undulations that shape my gown.

If we were to confuse right action with self-righteousness, we would be succumbing to a myth of innocence that uses innocence as a symbol of loss. "Innocent victim" is a reductive term, a term of decrease, and in the symbology of "innocent victim," revenge and retribution serve as false increase of the spirit. Near September 11, 2004, I heard something close to the following on National Public Radio's *Morning Edition*: "He's revenging us." I was not listening closely. However, I think that the praise may have come from a New York firefighter about President Bush's conflated war on terror and war in Iraq. *Revenging* rather than *avenging* struck me, not only because the latter is syntactically correct but also because an avenger carries out just punishment whereas revenge implies malice and retaliation. (Even so, *avenge* risks the self-righteousness of *revenge*.)

I think that the speaker may have said, "He's revenging us for our loss." It is possible that my mind added "our loss," because the connection between innocence and loss was in my thoughts. If "our loss" is indeed my addition, it makes sense, because 9/11 as a huge memory of huge loss saturated the NPR story. Many Americans interpret 9/11 as a loss of their country's innocence: the only attacks on the United States mainland, the defenseless civilians who were innocent bystanders.

When people act out the symbology of "innocent victims," in which *attack* and *defend* are foundational, attack serves as cause for revenge. Insidiously, innocence becomes the cause for revenge.

Al does not make innocence into any cause to be fought for, as if it were a political or social program. Rather, innocence causes the effect of heroism. "Revengers" make of innocence a lost cause, and fighting for that cause demands sacrifice. Al does not attach sacrifice or renunciation to innocence. Both equate with loss, giving *up* an element of self—giving up even life itself—in order to prove the existence of whiter than white. Al's right action is *giving*, which is an equivalent of loving and expanding.

When one fights for whiter than white, he fights for his own innocence, even if the mistreatment or death of an innocent victim other than himself is his conscious impetus. Fighting for one's own innocence is a war whose ideology resides in these beliefs: it is good to return to one's innocence but it is impossible. Because the Romantic child is insecure, warlords try to enforce the ideal, ever-failing to safeguard it.

In the 1990s, photographer Inez van Lamsweerde and sculptors Jake and Dinos Chapman taxed cultural security in childhood innocence with an aesthetics of dark humor. Using computer manipulation to add adult features to her little-girl subjects, van Lamsweerde produced the "innocent" as seductive spectacle. The brothers Chapman collaborated on life-size, life-like figures of nude girls sporting misplaced male genitals, designating "innocence" as erogenously available and grotesque.

The white rose reveals an aesthetics of orgasm, innocent of distortion and bizarre delusions. White roses, touched by pink—polish on fingernails and toenails—here we come, reborn, and we don't count the times; here we come, newborn, in act after act, each decided for us by desire and discovery, like orgasm, which no one can plan, because it happens, just like What I have to do.

Frueh strokes the muff, takes it from the table, and puts her hands in it.

My muff—my warmth, my animal enthusiasms and invigoration; my soft seductiveness. Little girls dressing for winter in Chicago, my sister Renee and I each dressed up in muffs. Innocents dress up in white because it's simple, like the snow.

Simple things make my head spin.

I've seen Al's innocence. In his writings, he is traveling the world, which is a traveling within, seeking innocence. I've seen him in the National Aquarium, located in Baltimore, sitting in front of the leafy seadragons, gazing with the wonder of a child, being reborn.

Renée! Which means reborn in French.

O my sister innocent.

O my brother innocent.

Simple things make our heads spin. Like this: you are my ambrosia.

I used to say in some of my art history classes, "There is no innocent eye or I—e-y-e or capital I." How glad I am to wear this white-rose wreath! Tiaraed in flowers, I relish what in Zen is called beginner's mind, and I am ready to act as Lao Tzu counsels in his *Tao Teh Ching*: "Do the Non-Ado." For then, your innocence finds *you*; you are doing *What I have to do.*

I read *Dangerous Emotions* the way I read a mystic text, like the *Tao Teh Ching*. The author of each enjoys the truth of paradox, weaves innocence and experience into a song of softness, does not structure them as sadly polar, the way that William Blake, another mystic, does in *Songs of Innocence and of Experience*. In mystic writings, desire is commonly a negative feeling: desire means greed, grasping, striving, and it indicates the desirer's lack of equanimity, her inability to let things be. However, desire in "Innocence" operates as a kind of humility, which I see this way: being in balance, being in the quiet center that gives birth to the discovery of doing.

Let us sing to the very center of ourselves. Let us crown each other in white roses! And let us eat ambrosia!

❧ SHAKING OUT THE DEAD
An Afterword by Joanna Frueh

In the desert I am always shaking out the dead.

Desert spans about ten million square miles of Earth. And human beings have done their best to build the desert into monasteries, convents, and some resorts and spas—the desert as a place of solitude, where a person's heart can blossom; the desert as an empty place which the human mind can fill with freedom. Desert thoughts: they come when I am empty of worry. Desert clarity: it is divine. Men have called me Desert Rose.

I've lived in two of the four major North American deserts, the Sonoran and the Great Basin. (The others are the Chihuahuan and the Mojave.) In 1990, Reno, located in the northeast of the Great Basin, became my home. The Great Basin is the northernmost of the four deserts, and the coldest one, with the highest elevation. From 1983–85, and in part of 1988 and 1989, Tucson took me—not merely as its inhabitant but, succulently, as its lover. Now, since my moving there in May 2006, it has taken me again. Tucson spreads its funky, sexy toes and fingers into the saguaro and palo verde forests of the Sonoran Desert. There, in Arizona Upland, in the south-central part of the state, is *the* desert for me.

When I refer to Tucson in this essay, I am referring to an environment that includes a city whose pre-mid-twentieth-century stucco homes, directly west of the University of Arizona, house friends of mine in a district of historic preservation, where I too lived

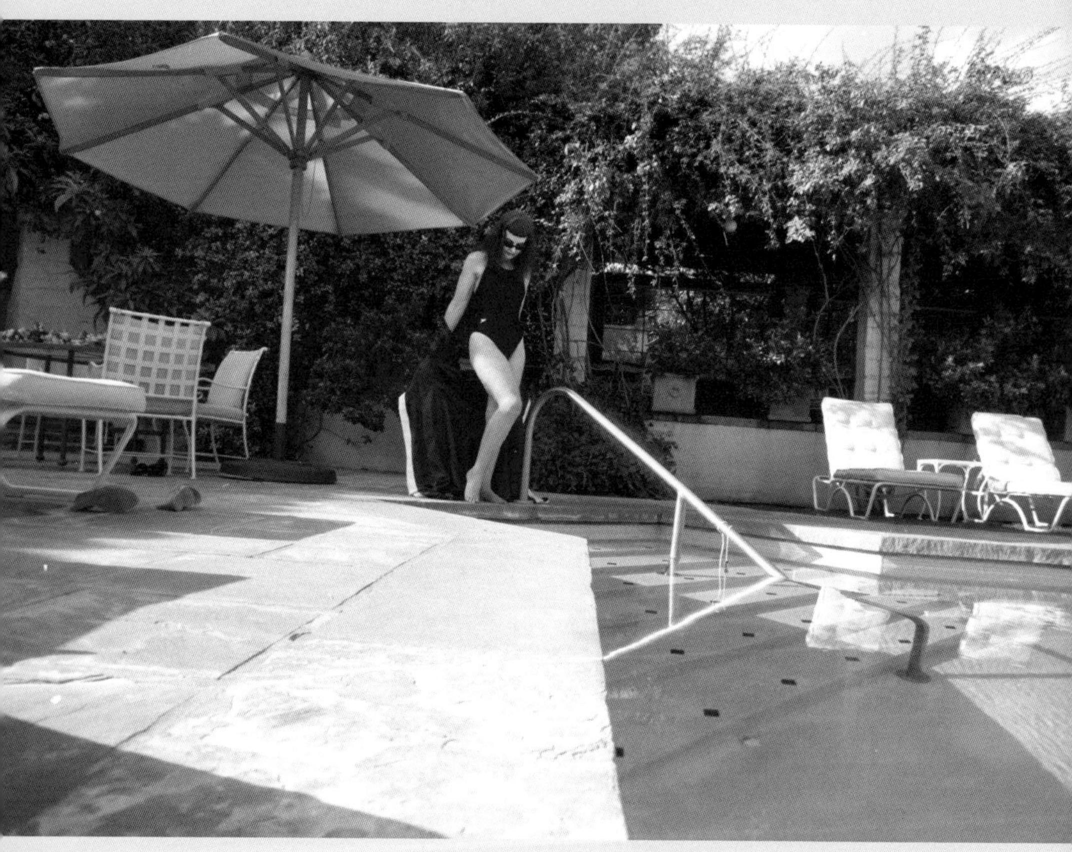

Jill O'Bryan and Joanna Frueh, *rebirthing Aphrodite.*

From the series *Joanna in the Desert,* 2006.

during my first two times as a desert dweller; the Tucson Mountains (to the west of town), the Santa Catalinas (to the north-northeast), the Santa Ritas (to the south-southeast), and the Rincons (to the east); the Shanty, a bar on still-hippie Fourth Avenue, where I drank beer with friends; Mi Nidito, an old-time Mexican restaurant, whose flautas I especially love, located in the barrio; Terra Cotta, where my parents and I would often eat when they visited me and where Russell Dudley, who became my second (and then ex-) husband, lingered for hours on our first date; the former dude ranch, turned into rundown apartments, no longer extant, where Russell and I lived together; the performances that Tom Kochheiser, my first husband, and I composed and rehearsed in our cozy home on Third Avenue; How Sweet It Was, where my friend Peggy and I shopped for vintage clothing finds; the Blue Willow, with its delicious pancakes and chorizo omelettes; the Arizona Inn, built in the 1930s in a hybrid Moorish and Hispanic style—I call it the Pink Fairy Palace—the hotel where my parents stayed and which now welcomes me for in-town vacations; a sky so blue, so high, so wide that it sings me lullabies, and also chorales of awakening.

Tucson, belle of my heart, gives me clairvoyance—simply, clear sight. Some call Tucson's climate and terrain severe. I call them lucid. Some call its summer sun blazing. I call it dazzling, and the air truly shimmers. (Light passing through bubbles of rising hot air refracts in randomly altering directions, and the effect, called shimmer or atmospheric boil, appears as the rippling of distant objects.)

> Desert Rose, she shimmers when you look at her
>
> Glimmers like a star, in unwavering glamour

When I first moved to Tucson, in the heat of June, these words came to me: I've reached paradise at a young age. There, in paradise, twenty-four years ago, every time since, and, to the best of my ability, every day now, I shake out the dead—the fear in a defended heart.

> O Desert, remove obstructions, obstacles, and hindrances
>
> Unknife me so that I am easy in my skin
>
> O Desert that has befriended me
>
> Mend me tenderly

Deserts differ greatly from one another. In fact, different parts of the Sonoran Desert differ from one another. According to climatologists' aridity ratings, the interior Sahara is around 140 times more arid than Tucson, and Yuma, in southwest Arizona—and part of the Sonoran—is around seven times more arid than Tucson. Climatologists consider Tucson to be semi-arid. In the summer monsoon season, mid-July through early September, humidity combines with temperatures over one hundred degrees, and the sultry heat envelops me in sensuousness, brings out the sensuousness in me. Tucson then feels tropically wet, and its biota is partly tropical in origin. Palms are native to some of the Sonoran, not to Tucson, though they have been planted there. Saguaros, one species of the columnar cacti that are a defining feature not only of the Sonoran Desert but also of Tucson, grow abundantly outside the city. While cacti are indigenous to arid tropical habitats, saguaros flourish in Arizona Upland, and they live all but exclusively in southern Arizona and the western Sonoran.

Like all cacti, saguaros are succulents, plants that store water in thick, fleshy tissues. Saguaros are their own reservoirs; 90 percent of their eight tons is water weight. We human beings are also reservoirs, of emotions that eddy up all by themselves or which we dredge up from our past. Those emotions can feel as though they weigh eight tons. They can operate as a gravity most unlike the effects of the earth's gravitation, as a gravity that we don't need. When the gravity of emotions weighs us down on a regular basis, we are likely dragging around dead weight from the past, in our head, our belly, our heart, our forehead; some anger, prick, or misery that we have kept all to ourselves to sink to the bottom of our emotional reservoir. (You done me wrong, and I am housing that believed injury in a liquid eternity.)

For Tom's and my 1987 performance, *Clairvoyance (For Those In The Desert)*, I wrote a song called "Scarlet Women." I saw it then as a celebration of strong women. I see it now as a lyric of reservoir suffering. The song is characteristic of my early performance writing, which is full of emotional and psychic turbulence. I am looking for grace and happiness, looking for a self-transformation. I do find them at times, yet am unable to hold steady in that state of peace, that faith in love. I gave this book the title *Clairvoyance (For Those In The Desert)* because it conveys the ability to see clearly, to have vision, even in what appears to be one's own psychic and emotional wasteland.

"Scarlet Women" is a desert revelry and ecstasy: women's "perfumes . . . mixing with flowers," women who "walk the streets at high noon" and "have no need to run / From heat that makes our heads swim / And makes our bodies shake." I, of course, am one of the scarlet women, and, apparently, ready to shake out the dead. Yet the passion of pain and difference characterizes us scarlet women: burning up, being hotter than anyone else. I speak of my camaraderie with "other scarlet hearts of steel," and that phrase joins with the final words in the song to create for me today a poignant image of reservoir suffering:

> And even though I ache
> I am a scarlet woman
> The bottomless blue lake

As I write, I see steel in that old reservoir of mine, a heart like a knife, sinking, sinking, the dead-weight gravity in the soothing blue of infinite healing. What a tank of turbulence I used to be: *tank* as in reservoir and *tank* as in armored vehicle, defending myself with fear and with passions that depleted me like heat exhaustion. We fear our own deadness, yet we defend it . . . even though we ache.

On a recent night when I was lying on my back in bed, ready to fall asleep, I suddenly saw my body full of knives—my body under the layers of cotton and down on my bed, and my body hovering just a bit above my body in bed (though they also seemed to be the same body). Under my breath (maybe silently) I exclaimed, "Get those knives out of me!" And out they flew, all of them, from everywhere. And they were gone.

Gone, the scarlet heart of steel. Into thin air.

I breathe deeply in the air of the Sonoran Desert. Desert dwellers live in pure, thin air. Heat expands air so that it becomes lighter and less dense than cooler air. Mark A. Dimmitt, the director of natural history at the Arizona–Sonora Desert Museum in Tucson, refers to the "clear atmosphere" of the desert.[1]

Thin air—that is where fear vanishes, fear of being oneself, which is fear of spontaneity and receptivity, fear of living.

Desert Rose, delivered from her own thick skull.

Around seven o'clock on a late July morning in 2005, I was sitting on a bench near the parking lot of Rancho San Rafael, close to my home in Reno, waiting for a friend. An s u v pulled in and "Bad to the Bone" rumbled from the vehicle while birdsong continued to fill my ears. I know the beauty of loud rock 'n roll, and I love the silence that brings the birds inside my body.

My friend didn't show up for our walk, so I enjoyed the Great Basin vegetation and wildlife by myself, and as I was heading away from a pond plied by ducks, having shared a mutual greeting with one of them on a bridge as we moved past one another, I looked up to see a goose, honking, and the following desert thoughts came into my mind. I've heard and read left-leaning journalists and scholars critique the political actions taken by the Christian right: the Clean Air Act destroys the environment, No Child Left Behind devitalizes education, the war on terror is a crusade for oil, fought so that Americans can continue to guzzle not only gasoline but also all the goods derived from Earth. (The word *crusade* is fraught with painful history for Muslims, because the history of the Crusades haunts relations between Christianity and Islam and between the United States and Middle Eastern countries, as Karen Armstrong makes clear in her book *Holy War: The Crusades and Their Impact on Today's World*.) Christ became Christianity, an invention neither of Jesus's desiring nor of his making. Jesus, simply a human being, like Siddhartha Gautama, who became a buddha, like Jesus became a christ. Christ: the Messiah, whose coming is prophesied in the Old Testament. Messiah: a savior to all souls. Buddha: a name given by Buddhists to an awakened human being. Like Jesus, Siddhartha did not intend to establish a religion—an institutional structure with demands for obedience, a hierarchy whose high-ranking administration shapes its flock, whose flock is given words and images with which to shape their souls. Rather, Jesus and Siddhartha were during their lifetimes and are today models of a way of being: compassionate, loving, peaceful. With them as models, we shape *ourselves*.

Any human being can choose to be compassionate, loving, and peaceful.

Jesus, simply a man, who spent forty days and forty nights in the desert. A combination of legend and history tells us that Gautama Buddha spent six years under a bo tree, seeking enlightenment. His desert—solitude—transformed him. By himself, inside himself, he found what he was looking for. In their deserts, Jesus and Buddha were clairvoyants, seeing clearly, shaking out the dead.

Like Jesus, and like some of the Old Testament prophets and St. John the Baptist, early Christians withdrew into the desert from their towns and villages. Beyond the edge of civilization's settlements, full of strife and striving, some early Christians chose to resurrect themselves on this very earth. In "Ocean Boulevard (or Shake out the Dead)," performed by Tom and me in *Solar Shores*, I sang about that kind of resurrection:

> Well, I finally made it
> Take me to the edge
> Anemone, Anemone
> We'll shake out the dead

Anemone: the word had flown into me as I was writing the lyrics. Today I see, as I look up *anemone* in the fourth edition of *Webster's New World College Dictionary*, that the English word for that flower, which belongs to the buttercup family, comes from the Greek *anemone*, altered. Shaking out the dead, we ask to enter an altered state. O Anemone, your red and purple cups fill me with sunlight! Anemone: how did I know the perfect word? Anemone! How sunlight fills the mind when we simply let it.

Retreating from society and following one's heart, not the crowd, is a tradition in many spiritual practices. Unsurprisingly, it is also the practice of some modern artists. Georgia O'Keeffe left New York City and her husband for New Mexico, and Agnes Martin likewise left New York City and lived in New Mexico. In the beguiling honesty of Martin's writings, she advises artists to seek solitude: "To discover the conscious mind . . . requires solitude—quite a lot of solitude. We have been strenuously conditioned against solitude. To be alone is considered to be a grievous and dangerous condition. . . . I suggest to artists that you take every opportunity of being alone. . . . I suggest that people who like to be alone, who walk alone will perhaps be serious workers in the art field."[2] Now and again in her books on the history of religion, Karen Armstrong equates the artistic and mystic consciousness. Martin did not like to be called a mystic. She knew that being a mystic is nothing special, because the conscious mind is available to all human beings. However, a mystic state requires disciplines practiced in solitude, and Martin's words indicate that choosing that situation may not be easy because of societal expectations.

In the desert (and its caves and mountains), Christian monasticism began, and in the desert, both women and men became hermits. In the desert, a person pays attention to what he feels, so easily that naming feelings is beside the point. Slowing down to stillness opens Desert Mind, where any human being can bloom into a buddha. Siddhartha Gautama did not think that he was special.

Desert Rose, she is adapting to the desert every day

In homegrown succulence

In honest sunlight

See her bloom

Outside the hothouse

In dry conditions

In the heat

She grows in rosiness

Adorned aloud adept at desert gardening

Her voice is raising her crowned head

The spoken word—primal engineering of the spirit

The spoken word—feeling free to float in thin air

The spoken word—Rosita Grande, you speak for me

Rising, risen, lightening—the mind alive:

Cabeza de Rosa

Although I suggest above that in Desert Mind a person needn't name her feelings, I will let a monk voice the essence of that state of being. In his preface to Peter F. Anson's *The Call of the Desert: The Solitary Life in the Christian Church,* the Reverend Paul Ziegler, OSB, monk of Quarr Abbey, affirms "there is the solitary for whom the call of the desert is the call of love."[6] People generally consider love to be a feeling. A person can put that feeling into action—I love you. People can feel love *for* someone, or they can feel love *from* someone. But feelings come and go, and according to the Reverend Ziegler, "love is not something one does but something one is."[7] The state of being love may seem transient, but it is human beings' fears—their dead weight—that make love flee, that take away people from closeness to themselves. I connect the reality of *being love* with Agnes Martin's words about happiness, because being love is being happiness:

Happiness is our real condition.

It is reality.

It is life.[8]

How does a person live that reality? "Real life," Martin declares, "is lived by Self Discovery."[9] Self-transformation through self-discovery occurs in Desert Mind. We can transform ourselves into love.

She also attests, "In this life, life is represented by beauty and happiness."[10] Unsurprisingly, those who are dead to life are also dead to beauty and happiness: "*The times when you are not aware of beauty and happiness you are not alive*"[11] (Martin's italics). Those who are dead to life are dead to love. Agnes Martin, modern hermit: a "lover-solitary," as the Reverend Ziegler calls those who find love—find themselves—in the desert.

My first time living in Tucson, I began to call myself "hermit scholar." I did it jokingly and unconsciously. My small study, which I'd painted a soothing, smoky amethyst and whose one very narrow window faced a brick wall, reminded me of a convent or monastery cell, simply because of its privacy and intimacy. The room was not ascetic, as it was filled with books and a scholar and writer's necessary furniture, and I was not a recluse: I lived in that Third Avenue house with a lover and later with Tom, before and after we married, and he and I enjoyed our friends, both in our home and in the rich and profound charms of Tucson. Nor was I an ascetic. My sensualist sex and eating were far removed from the mortification of some desert hermits. Some were truly eccentric: the men who ingested only freshly cut grass and were known as "shepherds"; the pillar-hermits—the *stylites*—such as St. Simeon Stylites, who spent more than thirty years alone on a pillar about sixty feet high and three feet in diameter at the top. Others simply fasted or ate stale bread. Maybe when I began calling myself a hermit scholar is also when I coined the term *hermitude*, in reference to the pleasures of solitude.

The word *hermit*—and, of course, *eremite*—derives from the Greek *eremites*, rooted in *erēmos,* a desert.

> O Desert, I am your hermit lover
> Desert Rose, she is an eremite who laughs because she sits within the
>> seasons of Sonoran subtlety
> Waiting for nothing
>> Orange blossoms scenting the March air
>> Oleander flushing against pink exhilarated walls in May
>> Creosote, whose resin embeds the monsoon air
>> Cholla spines that seem to fly into your skin, like the darts of Eros
> Unexpectedly
> *Erēmos!* How I fly into your arms

Erēmos and Eros! How your embrace is softening the fibers that twisted, hardening, in a distant spell of opacity around my joints and organs like a tangled, tragic romance.

In the pure, thin air of Tucson, a hermit might sense spirits more readily than elsewhere. I have read contemporary pagans who tell us that on Halloween the veil between the human world and the spirit world thins. So, if human beings are attuned to thin air, then contact between the worlds occurs. Maybe the Tucson spirits are happy when a person notices them. Maybe the phrase "The spirits were with us," spoken when a project, a relationship—our life itself!—goes well, acknowledges connections made in thin air. Maybe the spirits themselves cavort in cactus gardens in the city and in cactus fastnesses full of mountain vistas.

In the sixth sense that is Desert Mind, Cabeza de Rosa is cavorting with the spirits.

I am full of levity and gravity in the richest and most complex desert in the Americas, the Sonoran. When I walk here, my feet feel broad, and I am firmly on the ground, because I am aware of gravitation, I am aware that I live on a planet, that it is earth, that plants grow from it. (As we drove into the Saguaro forest, Jill, astounded by its unique beauty, commented, "You know you live on a planet.") I am aware, as I walk either that earth or the pavement that covers it, of my mobility and stability, and I am aware that, as my friend Beth plainly states, "You go where you look." Walking in Tucson one July morning in 2005, I seemed to levitate, twin to the pure, thin air.

Feeling levitation and gravitation, I belong to an expanse—light, silence, space—and I myself expand. John Cowper Powys's *A Philosophy of Solitude* abounds in reservoir suffering: he rails against the modern (Freudian) focus on sex, the enforced gregariousness of social life, and the distressed, uneasy consciousness of industrially civilized human beings. An antidote is awareness of "a few simple elements belonging to that mystery"[12] which is Nature, such as "glimpses of sky, motions of leaves, flickerings of sunlight and shadow, voyagings of clouds, roof-edges against infinite space,"[13] because from them "there suddenly comes over you this reversion, this conversion, this transmutation of spirit."[14] Suddenly we wake up. We look and go into Desert Mind. We are taken aback, in a state of revelation.

Tucson, neither sere nor dune-like, takes me aback. Which means that it takes me back from the surface—of the visible world, of my body itself. It takes me into me. In her book, *Desert: The American Southwest,* Ruth Kirk loves the "halcyon heat" of Death Valley, which she considers to be an extension of the Sonoran Desert.[15] As it slows me, the halcyon heat of Tucson softens me. It transforms me because it melts my heart.

My first summer in Tucson, I was flabbergasted by the heat. I'd never felt anything like it. Maybe I'd been in hundred-degree weather before—certainly stretches over ninety and humid, too—but the dry intensity of the air and the brilliance of the sun—its straightforward and allover touching of my hair and naked skin—drew me simultaneously into Tucson and into myself. The sun excited me right through my clothes, and I kept the car windows rolled down so that I could bask and laugh in the heat and light. Dimmitt helps me to understand the heat: "The aridity allows the sun to shine unfiltered through the clear atmosphere continuously from sunrise to sunset. This intense solar radiation produces very high summer temperatures."[16] Peggy still comments on how, unlike most people, I enjoy the windows down.

In the rush of heat, I am revealed.

My first summer in Tucson, I was amazed by people's bodies. The many bodies (as my memory sees them) stripped of all but necessary clothing struck me as freer and more naked than summer bodies that didn't live in the desert. I loved the revealed bodies, as I loved the revealed land—the jagged mountains; delicately varied browns that can look pink or purple, between the plants, which do not crowd each other. Dimmitt describes a body's sense impressions in the desert: "You'd feel the arid atmosphere pulling moisture out of your body and experience a sensation of pressure on your skin from the intense sunlight. On really hot, dry days you could smell pungent, aromatic terpenes and oils exuded by the parched vegetation."[17] The revealed religions Judaism, Christianity, and Islam originated in desert environments. In Tucson I am happy to reveal myself in single layers of fabric that are small and lightweight. At my Third Avenue house I was happy to lie on a towel in my front yard in my flowered bikini, which I still own. I was glad to feel uncovered in Self Discovery.

I like to float on my back in the pool at the Arizona Inn. Arms like oars, feet propelling me a bit. Gliding, I gaze at the sky, which is so hugely blue that I know why it is called the heavens. Every second is a surprise, nuanced, like the timing of two birds appearing one, then another, overhead, far high and away above the pool in Tucson. I am an angel in their clear sight.

Jill O'Bryan and Joanna Frueh,
the sun comes down and picks me up and carries me away, title (lyric)
by Joanna Frueh from *Clairvoyance (For Those In The Desert).*
From the series *Joanna in the Desert,* 2006.

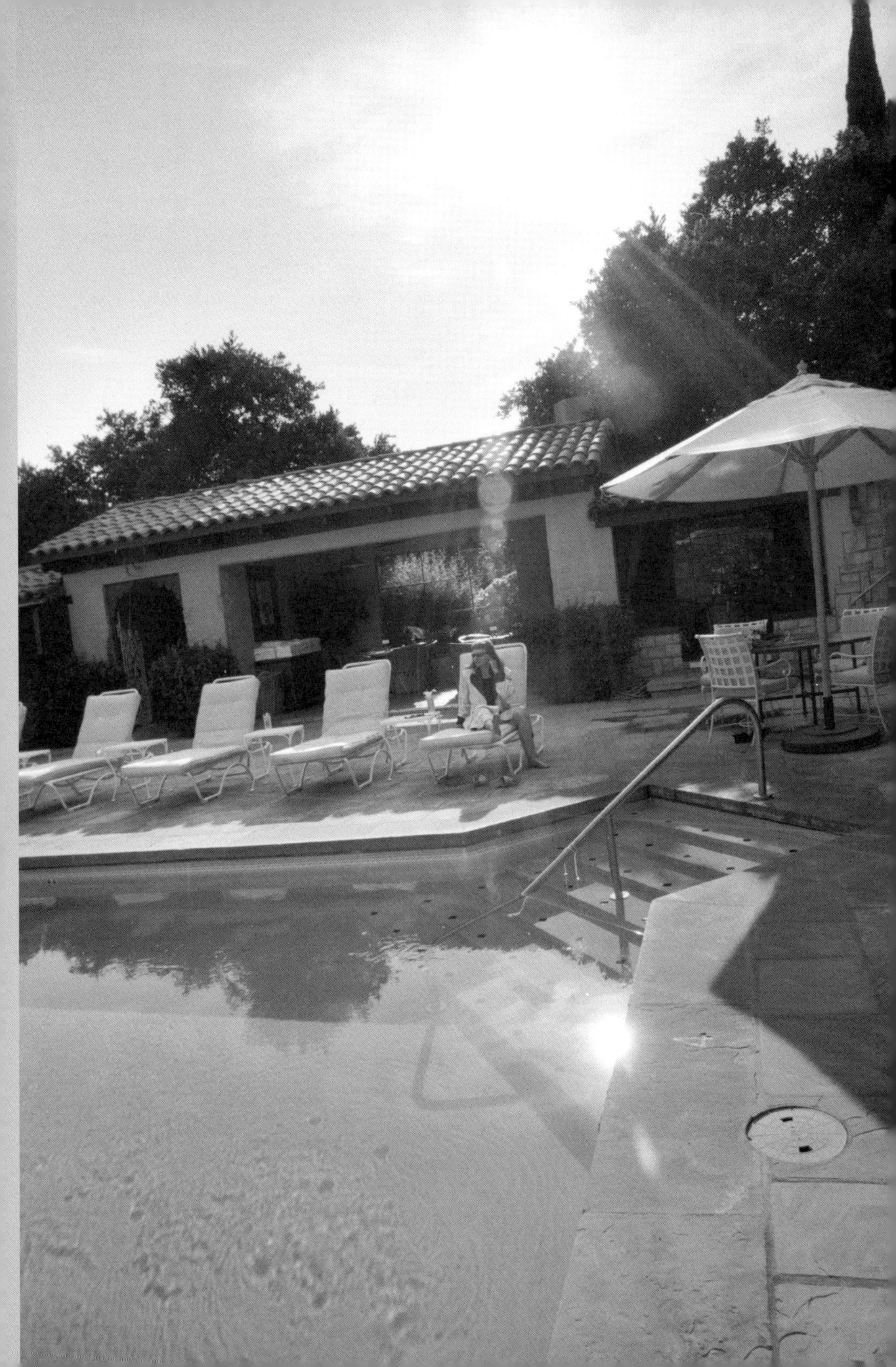

1 Mark A. Dimmitt, "Plant Ecology of the Sonoran Desert Region," in *A Natural History of the Sonoran Desert*, ed. Steven J. Phillips and Patricia Wentworth Comus (Tucson: Arizona–Sonora Desert Museum Press; Berkeley: University of California Press, 2000), 143.

2 Agnes Martin, *Writings*, ed. Dieter Schwarz, 6th ed. (Ostfildern-Ruit: Hatje Cantz, 2005), 117.

3 Francis Scarfe, ed. and trans., *Baudelaire* (Harmondsworth: Penguin, 1961), 190.

4 Mark A. Dimmitt, "Biomes and Communities of the Sonoran Desert Region," in *A Natural History of the Sonoran Desert*, ed. Steven J. Phillips and Patricia Wentworth Comus (Tucson: Arizona-Sonora Desert Museum Press; Berkeley: University of California Press, 2000), 9.

5 Ibid., 10.

6 Reverend Paul Ziegler, "Preface," in Peter F. Anson, *The Call of the Desert: The Solitary Life in the Christian Church* (London: S.P.C.K., 1964), xi.

7 Ibid., xii.

8 Martin, 135.

9 Ibid., 118.

10 Ibid., 135.

11 Ibid.

12 John Cowper Powys, *A Philosophy of Solitude* (New York: Simon and Schuster, 1933), 163.

13 Ibid., 159.

14 Ibid., 163.

15 Ruth Kirk, *Desert: The American Southwest* (Boston: Houghton Mifflin, 1973), 21.

16 Dimmitt, "Plant Ecology," 143.

17 Ibid., 129.

1979

The Concupiscent Critic
Deson Gallery, Chicago, Ill.

1980

Shadows in the Dark Chamber
Nancy Lurie Gallery, Chicago, Ill.

1982

BRUMAS
With Thomas Kochheiser
Oberlin College, Oberlin, Ohio
Randolph Street Gallery, Chicago, Ill.

1984

Justifiable Anger
With Thomas Kochheiser
Cochise Fine Arts, Bisbee, Ariz.
Dinnerware Artists Cooperative Gallery, Tucson, Ariz.

(now known as Dinnerware Fine Art Gallery)
Randolph Street Gallery, Chicago, Ill.

1985
Solar Shores
With Thomas Kochheiser
University of Arizona Museum of Art, Tucson

1986
A Few Erotic Faculties
Dinnerware Artists Cooperative Gallery, Tucson, Ariz.
Washington University, St. Louis, Mo.

Poses of Power: The Female Artist as Hero(ine)
Columbia College, Chicago, Ill.
Women, Art, and Power panel, Rutgers University. Performed at three
campuses: Camden, Newark, and New Brunswick, N.J.
University of Arizona, Tucson

There Is a Myth
Angry: A Speakout forum, College Art Association conference, New York,
N.Y.

1987
Clairvoyance (For Those In The Desert)
With Thomas Kochheiser
Sheldon Memorial Theater, St. Louis, Mo.

Poses of Power: The Female Artist as Hero(ine)
Art panel, Midwest Women's Studies Association conference, St. Louis, Mo.

Words of Love
The Women's Movement as Source for Work panel, Passages: Impact of Four
Decades symposium, Fresno, Calif.
Rutgers University, New Brunswick, N.J.

1988

Has the Body Lost Its Mind?
Theory panel, The Way We Look, The Way We See: Art Criticism for
Women in the '90s conference, Los Angeles, Calif.

Jeez Louise
ARC Gallery, Chicago, Ill.
Washington University, St. Louis, Mo.

Poses of Power: The Female Artist as Hero(ine)
St. Louis Art Museum, St. Louis, Mo.

1989

Duel/Duet
With Christine Tamblyn
NAME Gallery, Chicago, Ill.

Holocaust of Hearts or I Believe
University of Wyoming, Laramie

Jeez Louise
Centenary College, Shreveport, La.

Mouth Piece
Columbia College Dance Center, Chicago, Ill.

Vermilion
Terry Etherton Gallery, Tucson, Ariz.

1990

Amazing Grace
With Russell Dudley
Site-specific outdoor location, Rochester, N.Y.

Duel/Duet
With Christine Tamblyn
Southern Exposure Gallery, San Francisco, Calif.

(Yolanda Lopez participated in this performance.)
Women's Caucus for Art conference, New York, N.Y.

Jeez Louise
Brigham Young University, Provo, Utah

Mouth Piece
Pennsylvania State University, State College

Vampiric Strategies
N A M E Gallery, Chicago, Ill.

1991
Faculties of Love
University of Illinois at Chicago, Chicago, Ill.

The Language of War and the Language of Miracles
Centenary College, Shreveport, La.
Columbia College, Chicago, Ill.

Rhetoric as Canon
Open Session panel, College Art Association conference, Washington, D.C.

1992
Faculties of Love
Rhode Island School of Design, Providence
Weber State University, Ogden, Utah

Fuck Theory
Postmodernism in the Classroom: What Are We Talking About? panel,
Society for Photographic Education conference, Washington, D.C.

Language of Love
Ideas, Words, and Images panel, Women's Caucus for Art conference,
Chicago, Ill.

Mouth Piece
Massachusetts College of Art, Boston

Silver Tongues Untie the (K)-n-o-t-s
Empowerment/Quality/Action: Issues of the '90s panel, International
Association of Art Critics, USA (AICA) at College Art Association
conference, Chicago, Ill.

Speech-O-My-Heart
Beacon Street Theater, Chicago, Ill.

Visible Difference: Women Artists and Aging
Society for Photographic Education western regional conference, Santa
Barbara, Calif.

1993
Mouth Piece
The LAB, San Francisco, Calif.

Oracular Voice
Artists Voices panel, Montage International Student Festival, Brockport, N.Y.

Polymorphous Perversities: Female Pleasures and the Postmenopausal Artist
Artemisia Gallery, Chicago, Ill.
University of Arizona, Tucson
Works Gallery, San Jose, Calif.

1994
Egon Schiele's Monster/Beauty
Perspectives on Schiele symposium, Indianapolis Museum of Art,
Indianapolis

Erotic Faculties
Keynote speaker, Lighting Out: Women and Creative Process conference,
University of Arizona, Tucson

Fuck Theory
Rencontres panel, Women's Caucus for Art conference, New York, N.Y.

Mouth Piece
Syracuse University, Syracuse, N.Y.

Polymorphous Perversities: Female Pleasures and the Postmenopausal Artist
School of the Art Institute of Chicago, Chicago, Ill.
Women and Photography conference, Houston, Tex.

Pythia
International Center of Photography, New York, N.Y. (presented as a
reading, not in costume)
Pioneer Center for the Performing Arts, Reno, Nev.
Keynote speaker, Society for Photographic Education southwestern regional
conference, Tucson, Ariz.

1995

Always Aphrodite
Performed in *Evolution F: The Female Body Electric; A Celebration of Muscle*,
Manhattan Center, New York, N.Y.

1996

Erotic Faculties (Red)
University of Illinois, Chicago
University of Vermont, Burlington

Erotic Faculties (White)
Ronald Feldman Fine Arts, New York, N.Y.
Santa Monica Museum, Santa Monica, Calif.
University of Nevada, Reno

Midlife Bodybuilding as Aesthetic Discipline
Performative Activisms: Alternative Playgrounds panel, Politics and
Languages of Contemporary Marxism conference, University of
Massachusetts, Amherst

Monster/Beauty: Midlife Bodybuilding as Aesthetic Discipline
Southern Illinois University at Carbondale, Carbondale
Women and Aging: Bodies, Cultures, Generations conference, Center for
Twentieth Century Studies, University of Wisconsin, Milwaukee

Pleasure and Pedagogy: The Professor's Body
Sexuality and Pedagogy panel, College Art Association conference, Boston,
Mass.

1997

Dressing Aphrodite
The Style Conference, Bowling Green State University, Bowling Green, Ohio
Nevada Museum of Art, Reno, Nev.
University of Arizona, Tucson
Keynote speaker, Subject to Desire: Refiguring the Body conference, State
University of New York, New Paltz

Erotic Faculties (White)
University of Maine, Augusta

1998

Collecting Myself
Museum of Fine Arts, Santa Fe, N.M.

Giving a Fuck
Censorship: For Shame session, College Art Association conference,
Toronto, Ontario

The Real Nude
Artemisia Gallery, Chicago, Ill.
State University of New York, Stony Brook

1999

Giving a Fuck
University of Nevada, Reno

Vaginal Aesthetics
Dinnerware Fine Art Gallery, Tucson, Ariz.
University of Nevada, Reno (double bill with *Giving a Fuck.*)

2000

The Amorous Stepmother
Learning in Mind and Body session, College Art Association conference,
New York, N.Y.

Monster/Beauty
Plenary session, American Society for Aesthetics annual meeting, Reno, Nev.

The Passionate Wife, the Passionate Daughter
University of Nevada, Reno

Vaginal Aesthetics
Plenary session, Uncommon Senses Conference, Montreal, Quebec

2001

Bloodred Beauty: A Meditation on Mel Gibson's Midlife Allure
Loughborough University, Loughborough, England
School of the Art Institute of Chicago, Chicago, Ill.
University of Kansas, Lawrence
University of Nevada, Reno

2002

The Aesthetics of Orgasm
The Banff Centre, Banff, Alberta
Plenary session, Beyond Sex and Gender: The Future of Women's Studies?
conference, organized by the Women's Studies Network, UK, Belfast,
Northern Ireland
The Palm Beach Institute of Contemporary Art, Lake Worth, Fla.

2003

The Aesthetics of Orgasm
Ohio University, Athens, Ohio (presented as a reading, not in costume)
University of Nevada, Las Vegas

Epiphany without End
In-class performance, BFA seminar, University of Nevada, Reno

The Performance of Pink
Making an Appearance: Fashion, Dress and Consumption conference, Brisbane, Australia

The Sake of Angels
In-class performance, BFA seminar, University of Nevada, Reno

To Carolee: In Apologia; Give Something to Someone
In-class performance, Contemporary Art, University of Nevada, Reno

Voyaging to Cythera
In-class performance, BFA Seminar, University of Nevada, Reno

2004
Ambrosia
The Alphonso Lingis Conference on A Postmodern Ethics of Joy and Coronation Glory, Brock University, St. Catharine's, Ontario

The Performance of Pink
Keynote speaker, Point of View 2004: Sexuality in a Diverse Society conference, Boise State University, Boise, Idaho

2005
Ambrosia
Nevada Museum of Art, Reno

Beauty Loves Company
Hannah Wilke: The Rhetoric of the Pose session, Bodies in the Making: Transgressions and Transformations conference, University of California, Santa Cruz

The Performance of Pink
Collision: A Symposium on Interarts and Interdisciplinary Practices, University of Victoria, Victoria, British Columbia

❧ KEY READINGS

From Joanna Frueh's Childhood to the Present

This bibliography emerges from passion, affection, and influence.

I write about many of these mesmerizing sources as pretty distant memories, which I've sometimes updated with a current look at the material, so I'm mostly writing from my initial experiences of them and my love for them. Since I am not annotating this list primarily as a scholar, I have not searched for the first edition that I read or that was read to me. When I own the book that I'm writing about, in the version in which I first read it, I say so.

Some artists feel that talking about influences on their work spoils its originality. I feel my originality growing from my perception of these origins: my perception that has fascinatingly renewed and skewed this beloved material by inserting my individuality into its midst—learning by heart what mattered to me and what still guides my vision of making art and living life.

I present this collection in the order in which I remember finding the items—or their finding me.

Robert Louis Stevenson, *Treasure Island*, and A. A. Milne,
Winnie the Pooh and *The House at Pooh Corner*

My father read these books to my sister, Ren, and me in the big bedroom that she and I shared at 145 Oak Knoll Terrace in Highland Park, Illinois. Dad read to us little girls when we were in our beds, before we went to sleep at night. He read each book to us more than once because we loved his reading—we laughed and listened and wandered in our imaginations to the places that Dad's voice opened up for us—and we loved the stories and characters. Dad's voice was tucking us in, just as his hands and kisses did.

In Ren's and my early years, Dad invented his own stories, too, and told them to us with gusto. We'd giggle as he related the continuing exploits of the Lima Bean Kid and Chief Ookapoochee—over and over, because we asked him to. Also, Dad taught us the hysterically funny "wrestling" hold, "The Ookapoochee," which we'd all perform on one another by surprise during Ren's and my growing up and even into our adulthood. Dad didn't write down any of his tales, but they are as vividly memorable to me as are *Treasure Island* and the Pooh books.

Visual images animated by language impressed me, as did pictorial accompaniments to writings; I see in my remembered response to *Treasure Island* and the Pooh books my early attraction to the relation between texts and images. Humanity and animals: the classic Pooh book pictures drawn by E. H. Shepard in a playful, tender hand showed, as did the words, the close and humorous connection among Pooh, his cohorts, and the world they inhabited. Pirates and a male world, illustrated by Milo Winter in mushroomy and vegetal colors and reds like maple leaves in autumn. Did I wear a pirate costume one Halloween? Or was it Ren?

Lovable bear: I especially remember honey. "Yo-ho-ho, and a bottle of rum!": adventures far away from home; a world as big as a fairy tale, as potent as the sea, and as breathtaking as the actions of a boy-child hero with whom I identified. "Pieces of eight!"—O I am taken with all of you on the tongue of my father; and enriched as I am flung into the sea of literary possibility—what a girl can imagine, create, and be.

In my bed, close to Ren and Dad, everything felt safe—books, comments, laughter, questions (because we asked them and Dad answered generously), and intimate correlations between the mind and the emotions.

After I learned to read, I habitually did so in bed before going to sleep during my childhood and my teens. What a precious solitude that was from eleven to eighteen, when I had my own bedroom in our 90 Riparian Road house (also in Highland Park). Reading as a treasured and a treasure island.

Fairy tales by the Grimm Brothers and by Hans Christian Andersen

I own the Brothers Grimm, *Grimms' [sic] Fairy Tales,* trans. Mrs. E. V. Lucas, Lucy Crane, and Marian Edwards (New York: Grosset and Dunlap, 1945). This is the Illustrated Junior Library edition with illustrations by Fritz Kredel.

Faerie probably has been a determining factor in my engagement with transformation, as miraculous and amazing events shape fairyland and its inhabitants. The most ordinary of the everyday connects with the most astounding changes in people, from their appearance to their souls: change is of the essence. Images more than narratives stay with me: swans, red shoes, thick forests, castles, princesses, and creatures such as a mermaid and a snow queen. Great costumes and architecture! The foreground of the front and back covers of the book is a medieval scene, a continuous landscape in which a king and queen receive a knight who is about to present them with a dead, green dragon carried by two young men. In the background rise the walls and turrets of a home fit for a dreaming girl like me. I daydreamed about Andersen's Snow Queen, a shimmering glamourpuss, even in faerie, all whiteness and beauty, all wisdom and strangeness, like the icy heat of a femme fatale. Hmmm . . . barefoot, dressed in clinging white, and crowned with a white-rose wreath, I transform the Snow Queen in my performance *Ambrosia,* and her wintry fierceness becomes innocence.

Louisa May Alcott, *Little Women*

This was the first nineteenth-century novel that I remember reading by myself. I lie on the living room couch in our modern house, designed by Dad's friend, Chicago architect Bob Tague; picture windows looking onto the terrace and a happy garden at my right, a sitting area with a Noguchi table when I looked up, straight ahead, from my book; Mom's grand piano, a blond Aalto dining table, a kitchen bar, and the kitchen windows beyond them. The spaciousness of the open floor plan gave my heart and mind room to move, in general and within the lives of Jo, Meg, Beth, and Amy. Jo, of course, was my hero. She is the writer of the four sisters. She publishes her work, she thinks and speaks frankly, and she becomes a giving adult.

The *Little Women* that I read was a hardcover and measured about nine by seven inches It felt good resting on my belly as I read. I responded to the physicality of books, their weight and their scale in relation to my body; those I read, the volumes that lined the Frueh family's bookshelves along a large wall at 145 Oak Knoll Terrace, and the ones that Dad read to Ren and me.

Katy Keene comic books

Katy Keene was a comic-book Bettie Page who kept her clothes on. The comics icon sometimes appeared in a bathing suit, but, unlike Page, the sweet-tart pin-up whose star rose in the mid-1950s, Keene's profession was high-fashion model. She wore fabulous clothes, and she was smart and sexy besides being a superheroine of glamour. Keene first appeared in 1945 in *Wilbur Comics #5*, and her creator, Bill Woggon, styled her with the long brunette hair and thick bangs that played a role in Page's allure, as it did in Keene's. I was born in 1948, and Mom styled my hair in that same fashionable fifties look. I wish I had the drawings of clothing that I created for Katy Keene (as did many of her fans): evening gowns, long gloves, perhaps an elegant and sexy suit or a pair of vampy high heels. In my fifties girlhood, I did not know of Page, but today, as a woman who loves sex and fashion, I'm amused and delighted that the beauties of Katy Keene and Bettie Page resonate in my own aesthetic and erotic self-creation.

Great Tales of Terror and the Supernatural

I own Herbert A. Wise and Phyllis Fraser, ed., *Great Tales of Terror and the Supernatural* (New York: The Modern Library, 1947).

Memory tells me that I read this—the first time—around when I read Freud and Maupassant: eleven years old, give or take. One of the pleasures of this collection is its length—over one thousand pages. I spent many bedtime hours and most of some weekends lying on the library couch, saturated in a continuation of the world of faerie: the startling and visionary states, experiences, and locales that the editors concentrated into this scripture of its genre with stories by Edgar Allan Poe, Wilkie Collins, Saki, Nathaniel Hawthorne, Guy de Maupassant, Rudyard Kipling, H. P. Lovecraft, and numerous other famous and fascinating literary figures. Poe's writings very likely brought me to *Great Tales*, and *Great Tales* very likely brought me to Maupassant. Like *Great Tales*, I found Poe's and Maupassant's work on the shelves in the library at our 90 Riparian Road house, where we had moved when I was eleven.

I reveled in a sensuous mysticism, like when I costumed myself as a gypsy for Halloween, kicked through piles of leaves in the late October afternoons walking home from school, or watched snowstorms from my bedroom window. I learned what runes are, I read about addiction, insomnia, and paranoia, and I met up with the Great God Pan, the Dunwich Horror, and witches on their Sabbath. Gaiety and bittersweet romance combined. Think of the songs "Autumn Leaves" and "Frosty the Snowman," tunes and lyrics combining to thrill a highly imaginative girl through the veils between the material and spirit worlds that are said by pagans to lift on All Hallow's Eve.

Sigmund Freud, *Selected Writings*

I roamed here and there in this book, another huge one, like *Great Tales of Terror and the Supernatural*. (I think that our Freud, like *Great Tales*, was a Modern Library edition.) The case histories intrigued me, and I looked for myself and my family in them. I skipped over parts that didn't interest me and that, presumably, I didn't grasp, though sex, bodies, and gender surely made a strong impression, as did Freud's theoretical concepts, which I must have absorbed.

Freud has occupied very little of my published or conscious thinking about sex and gender—essential subjects that I weave into the erotic focus and fabric of my work. However, the unconscious—Freud's "discovery"—captivates me, and in my book *Swooning Beauty: A Memoir of Pleasure,* it plays a vital and clearly articulated role. Shall I attribute that to my early reading of Freud? Or shall I attribute it to the unconscious itself?

At any rate, I learned, unconsciously, from Freud's presentation of his ideas and his analysands' lives that the details of both intellectual preciseness and personal stories enhance one another.

Guy de Maupassant, *"Boule de Suif"*

Sex is a foundation of this story, one of Maupassant's most famous. Hypocritically virtuous people of various classes and walks of life treat cruelly a courtesan, whose nickname is Boule de Suif. She is young, generous, and lovely to look at, and her morals outshine her fellow characters' cynicism. In my puberty I certainly didn't read this story as a prostitute-with-a-heart-of-gold narrative. I still don't, because his precision with social and emotional details draws me now, as it did on my first reading, to the fact that women whose sexual activity is publicly known, as their profession or as the pleasure of individuals who are as free as they can be within their culture, often disturb people across the social demarcations of age, class, and anatomical sex.

Charles Baudelaire, *Flowers of Evil*

I own *Baudelaire: Selected Verse,* ed. and trans. Francis Scarfe (Middlesex and Baltimore: Penguin, 1961).

The sheer gorgeousness of Baudelaire's language set me awhirl late in my teens. Writing could be very smart and very sexy. Heady rhythms and juxtapositions of words told me about the luxuriousness of the female body (of mine!) and of dark hair in long waves (like mine!). When I read *Flowers of Evil* I was luxuriating in the sex and jewels, the perfumes and the city he described. There I was in Paris on a bleak November day. There I was in someone's scent or arms, in someone's scorn or scorning them. There I was in a mess of eros.

I own Norman O. Brown, *Love's Body* (New York: Vintage, 1966).

Love's Body led me to be myself. As a student in my early twenties, I saw that scholarship, philosophy, and poetry can all be one, that passion and mysticism can fearlessly drive the expression of ideas, that love and action are one and the same, that life can expand erotically—through connection—and that such connection is the reality of One. Brown has always made clear to me that we create the world and that to do so erotically is to create health. As Brown gently assured me, "To heal is to make whole, as in wholesome; to make one again; to unify or reunify: this is Eros in action. Eros is the instinct that makes for union, or unification."

My underlinings and comments in the Vintage paperback tell me that I didn't always agree with Brown, but I paused a great deal as I read the book, letting it do its healing.

My term *soul-and-mind-inseparable-from-body*, which I've used in many performance texts and critical essays, is indebted to Brown, and I realized only recently that the last three words in the subtitle of my book *Monster/Beauty: Building the Body of Love* are indebted to the lucidly mystical title of Brown's book, which uplifts me whenever I read it.

Herbert Marcuse, *Eros and Civilization: A Philosophical Inquiry into Freud*

Like *Love's Body*, *Eros and Civilization* affirmed in my early twenties that Eros can be a way of living—in pleasure, wholeness, and freedom.

Dante Gabriel Rossetti, *The House of Life*

I own Jerome H. Buckley, ed., *The Pre-Raphaelites* (New York: Modern Library, 1968), in which *The House of Life* appears.

I don't know when I fell in love with Rossetti's paintings, particularly the bust-length heads of women surrounded by flowers, though I remember drawing the angel from his *Girlhood of Mary Virgin* when I was a little girl in Ren's and my bedroom at 145 Oak Knoll Terrace. I became enamored with Rossetti's life and poetry when I was a graduate student at the University of Chicago, and I wrote my PhD dissertation, titled "The Rossetti Woman," on both his poems and paintings. *The House of Life* is the heart of the former. It is his magnum opus: one hundred and one poems about love and death, about the death of love, about the extraordinary vivacity that love brings to the one who knows it by feeling it. Rich—for some readers, confusing—syntax; divine language, including *Love* and *Beauty* used as one uses the word *Truth*; natural phenomena intertwining with Eros and philosophical melancholy and ecstasy: they won my romantic devotion by permeating my soul-and-mind-inseparable-from-body. Indeed, that phrase conveys what I most love about Rossetti's poems and paintings.

Elaine Marks and Isabelle de Courtivron, ed., *New French Feminisms: An Anthology*

I own Elaine Marks and Isabelle de Courtivron, ed., *New French Feminisms: An Anthology* (New York: Schocken, 1981).

I read this the year it was published. I was an assistant professor of art history at Oberlin College, in Oberlin, Ohio, and I bought the book at the college bookstore. *Devour* applies to my reading of *New French Feminisms.* Here were kindred spirits, especially Luce Irigaray and Hélène Cixous, who wrote about embodied female writing and whose writing actually exemplified their ideas.

Marks and Courtivron included Simone de Beauvoir and Monique Wittig in their anthology. I'd read Beauvoir's *The Second Sex* in my late teens and Wittig's *The Lesbian Body* and *Les guérrillères* in the years between my MA and PhD. *The Second Sex* was part of my early self-training as a feminist, and Wittig's absolutely frank and absolutely poetic expression—her artistic and intellectual daring—set an example, as Brown's had in *Love's Body,* for simultaneously beautiful thinking and writing. How happy I was to find a feminist cohort into which Beauvoir and Wittig could fit. Into which I could fit myself, for many of the writings in *New French Feminisms* encouraged the erotic freedom I sought, as a woman, a thinker, and a writer.

I own Lao Tzu, *Tao Teh Ching,* trans. John C. H. Wu (Boston and London: Shambhala, 2003).

I'd heard and read about the *Tao Teh Ching* for decades. I read it in 2003.

In this short, sweet book, I read about softness overcoming hardness and about humility. I learn that everything is within me and that all journeys begin where I stand. I learn that peace and quiet is the way of the world. "Do the Non-Ado," I read at the beginning of the sixty-third of the eighty-one verses that comprise the *Tao Teh Ching.* I am learning.

A Course in Miracles

I own *A Course in Miracles* (Mill Valley: Foundation for Inner Peace, 1975).

Here is another book about freedom, love, and health, like *Love's Body* and *Eros and Civilization,* and it is another very thick book, like *Great Tales of Terror and the Supernatural.* I mention the size because I'm always unconsciously looking for a big book in which I can indulge day after day.

At first *A Course in Miracles* was indeed a project! *Father, Son, God's Will,* and *Holy Spirit,* the book's Christian language, bothered me, even though I greatly appreciated the many sensible ideas that, like those in the *Tao Teh Ching,* enlarge my perception of life in its minuteness and magnitude. For example, *A Course in Miracles* transforms the usual (mis)understandings of sin and sacrifice, ideas that have never made sense to me, by showing their "reality" to proceed from the belief that people must suffer.

My friend who recommended the book, a Buddhist of warm, embracing intellect, warned me about the words that he knew would have me rolling my eyes. I read the book very slowly, sometimes only a couple sentences a day. Then I noticed that I was reading through or past the language that had bothered me.

"Love has no limits, being everywhere" is the foundation of *A Course in Miracles,* written as a "dictation" to Helen Schucman from "the Voice." Love, limitless, is *the* transformer.

JOANNA FRUEH

is a performance artist, teacher, and writer.
She is Professor of Practice in the School of Art at
the University of Arizona and Professor of Art History
Emerita at the University of Nevada, Reno. She lives
in Tucson, Arizona.

Library of Congress Cataloging-in-Publication Data

Frueh, Joanna.

*Clairvoyance (for those in the desert) : performance
pieces, 1979–2004 / Joanna Frueh.*

p. cm.

Includes bibliographical references.

ISBN-13: 978-0-8223-4021-8 (cloth : alk. paper)

ISBN-13: 978-0-8223-4040-9 (pbk. : alk. paper)

1. Performance art—Texts. 2. Feminism—Drama.

3. Women—Drama. I. Title.

PS3556.R78C55 2007

812'.057089287—dc22

2007021175